State College

at

Framingham

10-68-948217

AMERICAN PHILOSOPHY
AND
THE FUTURE

AMERICAN PHILOSOPHY
AND
THE FUTURE

Essays for a New Generation

Edited by

MICHAEL NOVAK

Charles Scribner's Sons · New York

for Ben
who was bitten by the Socratic gnat
long years ago
and has turned to biting others

EDITOR'S NOTE

The good advice and warm enthusiasm of John J. McDermott were indispensable for the growth of this volume. The patience of Will Davison of Scribners was discreet, gentle and calming. Miss Kathleen McHale helped with timely forays of research; Miss Charlotte Ackerley assisted with the proofs; and Miss Kathleen Kennedy bore the burden of the typing.

MICHAEL NOVAK

Contents

AMERICAN PHILOSOPHY
AND
THE FUTURE

INTRODUCTION:

Philosophy for the New Generation

BY MICHAEL NOVAK

We seem to be in need, again, of a revolution in philosophy. The much heralded "revolution in philosophy" of the early 1930's is rather tired now: many things in the world around us, and we ourselves, have changed in the interim. "Who are we? What should we hope for? What ought we to do?" Kant's famous questions torment philosophers, at least many younger ones. If the employment of atomic weapons and worldwide guerrilla warfare overtake us, we shall not be able to do philosophy. And surely lovers of wisdom cannot, in sheltered lairs, leave the hard tasks of imagining a new way of life to some slave class, of technicians for example. Restlessness is everywhere stirring among younger people in philosophy. There is a hesitation, as if before a fruitful, cleansing rain.

Where, then, shall we go? What shall we imagine the task of philosophy to be? It is the argument of this book that one of the most overlooked, and yet most fruitful, traditions in our philosophical history is that of the "golden age" of American philosophy—the age of Royce and Peirce, of Mead, Dewey, James, Santayana, and Whitehead. In this American tradition, philosophy was ever to be renewed at the springs of experience, always to be open to the future, designed to be at the service of man's humanity. Experimental, imaginative, open, constructive, critical—the model provided by American philosophy is at once humanistic and revolutionary.

Emerson once said that to be a man is to be a nonconformist,

1

and to be human is to be revolutionary.[1] In an age when the selective service system guides young men into slots predetermined by national priorities, and when our industrial system railroads the future of other young people along the iron tracks of technical specialization, a philosophy of openness and revolution is desperately needed. Such need prompts invention. For even an undirected technological system is inherently open: fresh alternatives arise at every stage of development and rapid change, with swift obsolescence, is built into the system. It remains that technology must be directed. A great cry rises all around us for the defense and exaltation of humanity. "Do not let the future be inhuman!"

That philosophers should analyze verbal puzzles, unpack the meaning of obscure sentences, and play rewarding language games is surely a good not to be contemned. Technical skills are to be esteemed. Clarity is to be prized. But there are also other tasks which other philosophers would like to undertake, and they find sustenance in philosophical traditions just beyond the expanding horizon of the schools of linguistic analysis. It is no doubt true that almost all philosophers in Western history have been, at least in part, analysts of language. But they have been other things as well. And it is those "other things" that now seem to be so much more instructive. Yet what are those "other things"?

Perhaps the best way to make plain some of the new demands laid upon the present generation of philosophers is to describe the new world that technology has created since 1932.

I

In the last forty years, many features in the life of students of philosophy have been dramatically altered. Wittgenstein taught them that every language makes sense only within a framework, and that that framework itself cannot be *stated*, but may only be *shown*. The exigent mind naturally wonders, then, what is *our* framework? How does it differ from that of others? Have we any control over it? It is possible that we are simply stuck with the language we happen to have; that we are able to renew it only plank by plank as the ship of Theseus was renewed. On the contrary, it may also be that swift breakthroughs and slow creative movements are possible.

2

MICHAEL NOVAK

Young people majoring in philosophy today are frequently aware that gradual shifts have occurred in their orientation toward themselves, their world, and their professors—shifts too fundamental to put easily into words. To try to describe the difference they sense, they must proceed by indirection; they do not have words or conceptual techniques for grabbing hold directly. The directions in which to point appear to be these: (1) the ethical neutrality of science and technology; (2) the problem of human values vis-à-vis technological power; (3) the unsettling penetration of other cultures and other traditions into American consciousness; (4) renewed contact with poor and "underdeveloped" peoples; (5) the lack of community; (6) the new relativism, with its insistent questions: "Who am I? Who do I wish to be?" We may take up each of these points in turn.

1. One has the impression, listening to many older philosophers, that they accepted the presuppositions and the standpoint of their historical era much more easily than students now can. Older men seem quite comfortable both in their humanism and in their allegiance to scientific method; some of them speak easily of "scientific humanism." It is more difficult for the young, who have no memories of peace and who know only what it is like to be in a state of war, to see any necessary connection between science and humanism. Hitler favored science and employed technology. Scientists and technicians did not scruple to invent and to make operational atomic bombs, hydrogen bombs, missiles, napalm, and yet unannounced species of technological weaponry. Why then is it good to favor "value-free discourse," as students are still encouraged to do?

An anthropologist who visits a remote town in Latin America may return with slides showing children deformed by malnutrition. The young recognize that it is merely a pretense for that anthropologist to claim that he went as "a disinterested observer." If he so much as used pencil and paper in front of those people,[2] he altered their consciousness of human possibility. The money he spent for pencil and paper might, spent in that village, have prevented one of those children from dying.

The sociologist who devotes funds from a foundation to studying the attitudes of citizens of Oakland toward certain forms of city

3

planning is not, during the years he spends on such a study, devoting his energies and resources to other matters—which may (or may not) have vastly different social consequences, and may (or may not) assist the aspirations of a different segment of the community.

There is no vacuum, many of the young wish to point out, in which "value-free discourse," or "scientific neutrality," or "objectivity" may be kept free from moral considerations. Moreover, precisely in proportion as there is such a neutral method or attitude, that method or attitude is merely instrumental; and its employment may (or may not) be humanistic. Given the structure of our present society, its employment is likely to be subordinated to the interests of a quite small segment of the population: to the military-industrial complex and its guardians. For it is this complex that governs most of the wealth and resources of our nation. The university itself is beholden to it.

Consequently, the much heralded achievement of scientific objectivity seems to the young much less impressive than it seemed to their elders. For many of their elders it seems to have marked an end to discussion; for them, a beginning. Once a scientist has spoken, the young no longer bow down. "What shall we do about it?" they wish to ask. And that question, they notice, is as messy and difficult for the scientist as it is for them. Moreover, it is not enough to divide the problem into two: first, scientific method and, second, its application. The question goes much more deeply—into the very structure of scientific method itself. If science is a set of questions which men put to the universe, it is in a radical way anthropomorphic and subjective. *Which* questions, then, shall we ask, or *ought* we to ask?

2. A related change in consciousness is the one brought about by the immense explosion of technique, information, and new materials since the Second World War. While technology was still in its infancy, every step forward seemed unambiguously good. "Knowledge is power." "Progress is our most important product." Now, however, it does not seem evident that the advancement of power and progress is automatically beneficial to human beings. Discrimination is increasingly required. Technological development

4

has reached a new phase, in which the primary questions are no longer those of technique and power: *"Can we do x?"* For it is obvious that, given enough time and resources, we can do *x*. The primary question is, *"Should we do x?"* For there are a great many other things we could do with the time and resources at our disposal. The technological age has become, therefore, primarily a moral age: the search for criteria for evaluative and decision-making procedures has become paramount.

Soon 85 per cent of the population of the United States, we are told, will be living in cities. Moreover, we have the power, and are already feeling the urgency, to rebuild our cities. On what model, then, shall we rebuild them? What sorts of arrangements best serve the needs of men? The radical issue is to settle upon our image of man. What do we think man is like, this man for whom we wish to build the city? What things best serve his needs, interests, and aspirations? What sorts of things inhibit, diminish, or destroy him?

The answer to these questions is far from plain. Choices will have to be made and risks will have to be run. For the power to make sweeping environmental changes is already operative. Technology *forces* us to confront the question. We have come full circle to the starting point of Aristotle in the *Nicomachean Ethics:* ethics is a function of politics; it requires a vision of the whole human city. Technology depends upon, and works toward, a fundamental unity; it presupposes an "architectonic"—a guiding scale of priorities, a set of criteria. What does it mean to be a human being? Which human capacities ought to be favored, which discouraged? The alternative to making choices about this matter is to let the industrial-military complex make these choices. Sixty per cent of the budget of the United States now goes for military purposes, and most of the country's other resources seem directed toward the mere accumulation of goods by an ever diminishing proportion of the earth's population. Is this the image of man that philosophers, by choice or by acquiescence, support? Philosophical consciousness does not operate in a vacuum. What lovers of wisdom do, or fail to do, affects the entire life of the city. But, of course, the life of the city affects philosophers too: their reflective leisure is paid for, their

5

social status and their sense of their own role is granted and confirmed by the reigning architectonic, the received conventional wisdom. Unless, of course, they are ready for hemlock.

3. The rapid expansion of technology since 1945 has altered the philosophical situation in another way: travel and instant communication have brought other cultures, other linguistic frameworks, other models of wisdom into the imaginative experience of the young. The young are free vis-à-vis Western culture in a stimulating and refreshing way. Those who have served in the Peace Corps and elsewhere are not so certain, now, that the criteria of relevance and evidence accepted by the tradition of the Western enlightenment are sufficient for understanding the human phenomenon. Many young people are aware of belonging to a very various but single human race. They are not quite ready to agree that what is counted as wisdom in the West is in every important respect more "developed" than what they have encountered elsewhere. They may be inclined to treasure the discoveries and achievements of the Western enlightenment; but their own experience forbids them to arrest philosophic progress at its present Western boundaries. They are driven to reflect upon other modes of experiencing and perceiving the self, the relation of body and mind, the relation of ego and world, and the relation of the individual and the community. Western traditions, many are inclined to suspect, have badly construed some of these relations. A creative reconstruction, fed by fresh experience through contact with other cultures, appears to lie ahead.

4. Most young Americans have been taught to view history as a story of human progress, culminating in the United States. The United States represents the most advanced sector of the human race. Other nations are considered "underdeveloped" by comparison. Moreover, in the United States the cutting edge of progress is located in the universities. (Depending on which academic department students serve, they have been taught a more specific location for the cutting edge.) However, a broader experience of the world, gained in travel, in radical social action, or vicariously through modern communications, has disillusioned a growing number of students. Through their service in "underdeveloped" countries,

from India to parts of the United States, many young people have encountered among poor and technically unsophisticated peoples human qualities that they do not find in their parents, their national leaders, or their professors. Often they have discovered an emotional richness and maturity, powers of compassion, sensitivity, and endurance that exceed anything they had met in their academic department. More surprising still, they have often found in "underdeveloped" peoples qualities of intelligence, perception, sagacity, and subtlety which, if they once existed among "developed" peoples, appear to have atrophied. The poor seem to have modes of perception, analysis, and expression that the Western intellectual tradition knows not of.

Consequently, many young people are pressing urgently for a profound revision of "the humanities." For the humanities as they are presently known and taught in the West are largely aristocratic, or at best bourgeois, in inspiration. They represent modes of perception, analysis, and expression proper to only a segment of the human race. They are not sufficiently representative of humanity. And it is not *a priori* certain or immediately obvious that the humanity of professors of the humanities is superior to that of many poor and "underdeveloped" persons. From a theoretical point of view, the emergence since 1945 of an increasingly international culture gives promise of a new conception of the humanities. The new conception will be less culturally restricted, less tied to certain economic and social classes, and less wedded to merely a few among the many historical employments of human intelligence and sensitivity.

Moreover, this new conception of the humanities will draw sustenance from the requirements of the second phase of technological development mentioned above (§2). In recent generations, students of the humanities (certainly including philosophy) appear to have been so impressed by the successes of scientific method that, increasingly, methods of procedure in the various disciplines of the humanities have become "scientific" or "para-scientific." Meanwhile, the literary traditions on which the older conception of the humanities was based have receded both from actuality and from memory; they no longer seem adequate to the complexity of life.

7

Just at this moment, however, the expansion of technological power brought about by the success of scientific method is provoking once more the questions fundamental to the humanities: What is a man? What may he hope for? What ought he to do? In a paradoxical fashion, the success of scientific method is bringing about the displacement of scientific method from the center of human consciousness. The genuinely important and prior questions—questions which science cannot itself resolve but which must be answered if science is to continue to advance—once again press upon us in a living, vital, urgent way. Science is our instrument; it is not a complete image of ourselves. In order to decide what directions future research should take, in order to decide upon priorities for the allocation of our time, energies, and resources, we must make some decisions about what we think it is to be a man.

In this paradoxical way, a confluence occurs between the exigencies of technological living and the discoveries of international living. From both sources arise pressures for a new constitution of the humanities, a more fulsome, more real, more daring vision of human values.

5. By and large, young people in America grow up isolated from other human beings like solitary egos imprisoned in a bag of skin—competitive, impermeable, as windowless as Leibniz's monads. A cocktail party is the liturgical dramatization of our culture: discrete and separate particles flow freely around a room, attracted by sources of amusement external to themselves, liberated from boring companions by the right to excuse themselves and drift elsewhere. A cocktail party is not a community; it is a collection of atomic individuals. "She's leaving home," the Beatles sing, "after living alone for so many years." Solitariness is the birthright and plague of Anglo-American culture. In a mobile, technological society, it is unmitigated by lengthy and unbreakable friendships; the average friendship among Americans is said to last two and a half years. Many friends live at opposite ends of the country and exchange letters (sometimes mimeographed) no more than once a year.

It is not loneliness, however, that is the dominant feature. It is, rather, the inability to see other persons as persons, the propensity

8

to understand them as objects to be manipulated, wooed, made to serve one's own needs. Wherever knowledge is understood to be the power of prediction and control, there even friendship tends to be construed as a function of interests and needs: atomic particles in some mutually self-serving relation. "Adjustment" tends to become the rule of human collectivities. Pleasantness becomes the rule of life. Powerful but errant feelings, unsocialized or unsocializable ideas, controversy, and other rough edges of personal life are suppressed. One does not even try to share deep feelings with others, to touch or to be touched; one tries, instead, to maintain smooth relationships.

Under such conditions, it is improbable that genuine community will often be attained. For community is participation in one another's life; it is a sharing in which persons, respecting one another's ultimate impenetrability, draw out from one another heretofore unknown resources, a sharing in which persons mutually confer upon one another, and thus create, one another's identity.[3] If one has been taught not to allow others to tamper with one's inner life, and to shy away from slipping through the defenses of others, such mutual self-creation is hardly likely. For entering into community is a risky and dangerous enterprise; it is sometimes shattering. A great many features of American life, particularly in the middle and upper classes, steer young people away from such risks. Anglo-American philosophy, with its emphasis upon the analysis of language—"out there," public, unthreatening, tame—is a reflection of a widespread way of life. The overriding myth of American society appears to be the myth of the machine—the mechanical model of human relationships, of human identity, of human interchange. Where this myth is absorbed into the processes of conscious life, men become alienated from themselves: mere objects subject to prediction and control, whether by themselves (each man now divided into controller and controlled) or by others. But life as an object is intolerable. Alienation grows until the credibility of the myth has collapsed. Then liberation and a new sense of life become possible.

Philosophers, especially in ethics, do not attend sufficiently to the power which myths and basic models exercise over conscience

9

and action. Men do not, it seems, act chiefly, or even frequently, according to "principles," to sets of abstract propositions. A creed is not, primarily, a set of words. The ancient word for creeds was better: *symbola*. As the novelist well knows, men act chiefly under the psychic pressure of symbols, of images, of models; words, principles, and rationalizations come much later. Yet symbols, images, and models are not in the domain of the "irrational" or of the "merely emotive." For even rationality itself (or more exactly, the various forms of rationality which various philosophers define) appears to be based upon "a sentiment"[4]—upon various predilections for clarity, elegance,[5] predictive power, simplicity, paradox, complexity, subtlety, inclusiveness, dialectical power, a sense of fitness or appropriateness or conscientiousness,[6] etc. The favorite symbols, images, and models of many Anglo-American philosophers, for example, come out in their choice of metaphors: "unpacking sentences," "solving verbal puzzles," "clarity," "rigor," "therapeutic," "simplicity," "the plain man," "we."[7] One sees, vaguely, the expert in the laboratory, white-coated, authoritative, banishing confusion, extending the realm of purity against the encroachments of messiness. Anglo-American philosophers *abhor,* and are *pleased* by, certain kinds of philosophic performance: those that contradict, or flatter, the image of themselves they cherish. In this they are not different from other men: all operate under the sway of basic symbols.

Among the young, the cocktail party seems to be yielding to the pleasure of folk songs sung together. The jazzband, as Robert Pollock points out below (p. 82), is a native image of the American experience: a community in which the individual finds the inspiration to "do his thing," a crossroads of social discipline and free-soaring individual fantasy. Perhaps because so many features of American life since 1945 tend to isolate the individual from his fellows, and thus to alienate him even from himself, Americans seem to have to relearn community as they once learned to walk. Hardly anything could be more reflexive to man, and yet once the simpler, rural ways had broken down the skill has had to be re-acquired. Americans tend, in fact, to be self-conscious about the establishment of community, about "sensitivity seminars," about learning how to "relate" to one another. They are slowly outgrowing assumptions embedded, unquestioned, in the imagination of Bentham, Mill, Hume, and a long cultural tradition.

In any case, philosophy done under the symbols of eighteenth- and nineteenth-century individualism now misses the mark. The language-frame has changed; the basic experience of life has changed. When John Stuart Mill wrote his famous essay on liberty, he had never watched a president of his nation on television, or been dependent day by day on newspapers and radios for crucial information about distant persons and events he could not possibly know at first hand. His defense of free speech, accordingly, fails to account for the power of mass communications to abuse the public forum by entering into the imaginations, passions, and minds of individuals even against their will. The institutions of free speech no longer have the immunity or power that they used to have. The conventional wisdom is now so heavily reinforced that to think against the stream, without succumbing to bitterness, calls for daily acts of heroism. Philosophers neglect the new phenomena of community life—both admirable and regrettable—at the peril of irrelevance.

6. Finally, the new way of life in America involves a relativism of standpoints so thorough that fundamental moral questions have been reopened. It sometimes seems that Dewey, James, Peirce, and other American philosophers were such decent humanists, men of such integrity, that they never peered into the abyss of nihilism. What if it is not true that human intelligence is a life-serving force; what if the more we employ it, the more rapidly we bring on our destruction? What if a man feels no imperative to make a contribution to society but, on the contrary, to destroy it? Why, after all, is it wrong to murder? (Storms kill men; microbes kill men; men kill men, prodigally.) What if it is true, as his jailer told the hero of *Darkness at Noon,* that Anglo-American ideas of justice and fair play are merely myths by which Americans and Englishmen disguise from themselves the emptiness and terror of life, the absurdity that Joseph Heller chronicled in *Catch 22?* From a scientific point of view, a human being is of no special value; the person is insignificant. From the point of view of recent history, the same conclu-

11

sions would appear to emerge. Yet human beings resist those conclusions; they protest. But why? And on what grounds?

Young people who wish to give their lives to public service, and who often risk beatings, death, or simply failure in doing so, need to earn their way out of a nihilism they inherit with the air they breathe. It is not apparent, in our culture, why a human being has any special value beyond that of sentiment, like that bestowed on keepsakes and souvenirs. But if one is to act on behalf of other men, and in the name of one's own humanity, one has to throw up reasons against nihilism, symbols against emptiness, hope against acedia. Without passionate vision, action is rendered inert.

There is, to be sure, no available common vision; there are no available absolutes. Many sink into the slough of relativity: "Anything goes. What's the difference?" Indifference and apathy characterize a great many of the young. To have been awakened to the life of inquiry and decisiveness, to have been led to the resources of one's own human spirit, is in our day no mean gift. Eastern philosophers attend to such matters—deliberately lead the young out into those inner deserts of abandonment and emptiness, paradox and confusion, until the young become their own teachers and learn the limits of their own capacities. Herman Hesse's *Siddhartha* awakens many Americans from their pragmatic slumbers.

Who am I? What am I capable of? What may I hope for? What should I do? Relativity does not, of itself, put such questions to rest. Relativity is simply a fact of life, a beginning and not an end to inquiry. Granted that there are no absolutes, I am already well launched into life: what am I to make of it? Relativity is not an absolute; it is merely descriptive of our situation; it is not normative; it has no special value. I am conscious and alert, capable of at least some honesty, a member of several communities: how, now, shall I make use of the one life given me?

The young are led by many developments in contemporary America to raise such questions. The traditions of philosophical inquiry include dialectical skills, methods, and the accumulation of reflection on the experiences of other men in other times, to help us deal with them. We will have to find our own way; no other time was quite like ours. Yet it will not encumber us; rather, it will

12

liberate us to learn how men in other generations coped with perplexities as troublesome as ours. One does not study philosophy merely for edification. But if the study of philosophy does not at least include reflection upon various ways in which a man might lead his life, it neglects the disciplines of self-knowledge, of wisdom, and of humanity; and it joins the chorus of the general irrelevance.

II

In correspondence with the contributors to this volume, I took pains to encourage them to concentrate upon the moral dimensions of American philosophy: upon the discoveries and methods that enhance human living. For it seems to be a mistake to construct philosophy upon the model of physics, or as if it were an "objective" and purely technical discipline, whose concern is the analysis of language. The choice of a fundamental model for philosophy *also* needs to be justified. *Why* should philosophy be construed as the analysis of language? The answer to that question requires more than the analysis of language; to meet it, the philosopher must go beyond language analysis. To be sure, the philosopher is required to act as a therapist of language when philosophical concepts are driven into misleading channels by "the grammatical habit"[8] and follow predetermined conceptual lines "owing to the unconscious domination and guidance by similar grammatical functions."[9] But to become wholly *preoccupied* with language— why would a philosopher choose to do that? What could be the reasons for such a choice? "Gradually it has become clear to me," Nietzsche writes, "what every great philosophy so far has been: namely, the personal confession of its author and a kind of involuntary and unconscious memoir; also that the moral (or immoral) intentions in every philosophy constituted the real germ of life from which the whole plant had grown."[10] The moral intention is present even when philosophers try to disguise it, and claim that their interests are "objective" and "purely technical."

> They all pose as if they had discovered and reached their real opinions through the self-development of a cold, pure, divinely unconcerned dialectic (as opposed to the mystics of

13

every rank, who are more honest and doltish—and talk of "inspiration"); while at bottom it is an assumption, a hunch, indeed a kind of "inspiration"—most often a desire of the heart that has been filtered and made abstract—that they defend with reasons they have sought after the fact. They are all advocates who resent that name, and for the most part even wily spokesmen for their prejudices which they baptize "truths"—and *very* far from having the courage of the conscience that admits this, precisely this, to itself; very far from having the good taste or the courage which also lets this be known, whether to warn an enemy or friend, or, from exuberance, to mock itself.[11]

A philosopher is a human being first, a philosopher second. He reflects, it is true, in a disciplined and professional way. But his profession is not like that of other scholars. More than others, he is free of the bonds of one sole method. He is called to *wisdom*—to test and to plumb the full range of man's capacities, to imagine fresh ways in which man might relate himself to his world. With every new human achievement, philosophers must reconsider. Philosophers guard the image of man. They nourish the seeds of the future. (Thus it is that so many other disciplines had their roots in philosophy.) Such a view of philosophy, to be sure, is not popular today; but popularity proves nothing about truth—one has only one life to live as a philosopher and one must choose. What suggests that the present philosophical establishment has too narrow a view of philosophy is the image of the world that goes with it: the sight, the feel, the favorite metaphors, the character, the attitude toward life, of the average department of philosophy, of the usual technical periodicals, of the regular stream of philosophical books. Formidable, one says—as one says of Scholasticism—but relevant? How many sentences can dance on the head of a pin? When it begins to believe in itself, Nietzsche correctly writes, a philosophical school "always creates the world in its own image; it cannot do otherwise. Philosophy is this tyrannical drive itself, the most spiritual will to power. . . ."[12]

One would be blind not to admire many of the philosophers of the present establishment; one would be purblind not to recognize the solid achievements and the therapeutic value of their methods.

14

Yet philosophy advances when a new generation raises new questions. In this case, the question is: What image of man is communicated by linguistic analysis? Is it an image to which a philosopher should give his total allegiance?

> I do not believe that a "drive to knowledge" is the father of philosophy; but rather that another drive has, here as elsewhere, employed understanding (and misunderstanding) as a mere instrument. But anyone who considers the basic drives of man to see to what extent they may have been at play just here *as inspiring* spirits (or demons and kobolds) will find that all of them have done philosophy at some time—and that every single one of them would like only too well to represent just *itself* as the ultimate purpose of existence and the legitimate *master* of all the other drives.[13]

What, then, of "objective" and "technical" philosophy? Nietzsche again gives a description that seems accurate enough:

> To be sure: among scholars who are really scientific men, things may be different—"better," if you like—there you may really find something like a drive for knowledge, some small, independent clockwork that, once well wound, works on vigorously *without* any essential participation from all the other drives of the scholar. The real "interests" of the scholar therefore lie usually somewhere else—say, in his family, or in making money, or in politics. Indeed, it is almost a matter of total indifference whether his little machine is placed at this or that spot in science, and whether the "promising" young worker turns himself into a good philologist or an expert on fungi or a chemist: it does not *characterize* him that he becomes this or that.[14]

Nietzsche then points to the location of presently unexamined questions. "In the [genuine] philosopher, conversely, there is nothing whatever that is impersonal; and above all, his morality bears decided and decisive witness to *who* he is—that is, in what order of rank the innermost drives of his nature stand in relation to each other."[15]

Philosophy as it is presently exercised, moreover, appears to be a tool of the *status quo*. The language it analyzes is the language already employed. Its prejudice, that the chief ill of man which the philosopher must address is lack of clarity, does not in practice appear to be either particularly helpful or even minimally creative in addressing the intellectual problems of our time. Analysis is a handmaiden, yes, handmaiden of the conventional wisdom. So long as philosophers merely take their place as technicians alongside other technicians, who will consider the vast interdisciplinary problems that are arising? Who will reflect upon the whole range of methods open to men, the whole range of images from which they might choose what to make of themselves? Sociologists have been struggling for some time to develop a concept of human action that is sensitive to the impact of social roles and social institutions upon the inner life of the individual. They reject philosophical notions of action as naïve. Psychologists wrestle with concepts of personality, group dynamics, memory, dreams, the unconscious, the nervous system, inquiry, intention. Anthropologists attend to the basic metaphors and rituals of groups—including philosophical societies. Possibly no other age in history offers philosophy so many vistas for creative achievement. Have philosophers suffered a failure of nerve?

Furthermore, the problem remains that individual persons must decide how to *appropriate* the findings of anthropology, sociology, psychology, and other contemporary disciplines in their own lives. (For a story of how confused—and absurd—these efforts at appropriation can become, one might consult "Weekend Confrontation with the Soc. Rels.," *The New Yorker*.[16]) If professional philosophers are afraid to address such problems, what hope have young students of making enlightened decisions? Such decisions must be made. Life must proceed. New theories will inevitably be appropriated. But how badly or how well, that is the question. It is ridiculous to suppose that life can be lived in compartments, like academic departments. Someone must address the interdisciplinary problems. The philosopher, of course, can no longer accomplish the task alone. Yet, by historical tradition and by choice he lives at the crossroads of the human spirit.

The philosopher is a professional question-asker, a shaker of

16

foundations. He is a true believer in no single method of inquiry; he is obliged to accept no single perspective. To those technically proficient in this or that method, discipline, perspective, the philosopher will ever seem uncommitted, skeptical, amateurish, and dangerous. It is at least *one* role of the philosopher to be a danger to specialists: to point out when the expert is naked. Such amateurishness as his requires the greatest professional skill. Hardest of anything is to get free of the conventional wisdom and to ask the questions that are not being asked, to bring together concepts that are growing up in isolation, to force disparate disciplines to clash together so that the discharge of their conflict might light up new possibilities for our becoming human. Philosophy today seems timidly ingrown and inward-turning, just at the moment when the excitement of an exploding world of knowledge cries out for immense efforts of appropriation.

III

I asked the contributors, then, to focus on questions of human living, and explicitly suggested that they might want to turn in the direction of religion rather than of science as a way of bringing crucial but overlooked questions about human values to light. The younger generation will understand this suggestion better than some over thirty. Theology in the university setting no longer means denominational theology; theology is critical concern with alternative images of human identity, human community, and the relation of man to his world. (When philosophers, like anthropologists and sociologists, begin to concern themselves with the role of symbol, ritual, and liturgy in even a supposedly rationalistic life; and when theologians finally appropriate relativism and become able to stand outside "the theological circle"—on that blessed day, the operative distinction between theology and philosophy will be attenuated to the vanishing point. Both are technical, professional disciplines concerned with—among other tasks—fundamental choices concerning human identity and activity.) Each philosopher chooses his own criteria for what he will count as evidence and what he will count as relevant. Either that, or he merely accepts what is in the air. But how does one go about choosing such

17

criteria? How does one choose a way of life? What effect have temperament and style (or what Hare calls "blik"[17]) on one's philosophy? What sort of evidence counts for or against the choice of a way of life? How free is a man "to do his own thing"—or is he, despite himself, trapped by the conditioning he has received?

There are many other questions that philosophers might learn to raise, were they to listen humbly, yet with their most professional instincts, to the music of the young: to the Beatles, to Bob Dylan. What in our culture makes young people as they are? Why are there so many lonely people? Loneliness, a theme for a philosophical investigation of the first importance. It seems, now, as if the young are groping for a new humanism with more urgency than academic philosophers. The Beatles, in any case, speak ordinary language better than Oxford dons.

Tough-minded analysts, of course, will not be persuaded to abandon their own "objective" criteria, methods, and sense of confidence; for many, the system is as impregnable as Scholasticism ever was: analytic, logical, ahistorical, its doors firmly bolted against the sociology of knowledge. Still, fresh experience will in the end rupture even the most accomplished schools. Consequently, the present volume has in the main avoided polemics. The various authors, each in his way, have simply tried to extend the range of discussion. Commonly they begin with themes first articulated by a classical American philosopher and then suggest the fruitfulness of such a line of reflection in our present perplexities. The papers dealing more or less directly with fundamental beliefs—and almost all do —open up the question of "a way of life" and the evidence that might count in making a reasonable preference. Such a question for many persons may, quite properly, have nothing to do with theism or atheism; but the problem of religion seems a good way, in our society, to open the problem up. Moreover, the problem of religion has become an increasingly neutral one, and may be discussed dispassionately, without the harsh polemics and the utter lack of mutual sympathy of even a generation ago.

There is not much point in summing up all the papers that follow. Perhaps a word about their order will help. That word is negative: there is no grand design, no necessary sequence. The

18

unity of the volume lies in its turning to the American past for enrichment and to the future with creative expectation. The unity, then, is like that of a jazzband, which is perhaps the best symbol of the American tradition. There is a community of purpose, in which the individual is not lost, a fundamental motif around which each of the performers, according to his skill, weaves his own way. The fundamental category of the aesthetic; the American vision of the inner life; the American conception of experience; the liberating relativism of William James, and the links between James and Continental phenomenology; reflective judgment as a crucial operation in inquiry and in action; an investigation into the meaning of community; the reflections of a sociologist upon the influence of Chicago on George Herbert Mead; a look at personalist philosophy—these are among the topics of the chapters below. If even a few chapters spark one young philosopher to venture in a direction he might not otherwise have gained the boldness to try, the work will have served its purpose. It does not take many to start a revolution in philosophy. First comes the longing. In time, good performance will follow and lesser performances will be driven to the wings. The task ahead is so vast that we are, no doubt, only at the stage of longing. We hunger. We wonder. At the very least, we are free.

Finally, to establish yet another context, I must admit that a secondary purpose lay remotely behind this book. It has long seemed to me that one of the greatest handicaps of American theology, both Christian and Jewish, has been too great a reliance upon the models of philosophical inquiry established by European traditions. It has been my conviction that American philosophy offers a better perspective—more liberating, more empirical, less Platonic, more down-to-earth, more faithful to their original genius—for the elucidation of Christianity and Judaism than any of the European traditions. The study of American philosophy, in short, could usher in a new and creative age in theology. It is my hope and that of the contributors that both American philosophers and American theologians will turn increasingly to this new world, this rich paradox, this America—and that this volume will be a stimulus in that direction.

NOTES

1. See Robert Pollock, *infra,* p. 80.

2. John Gerassi, *The Great Fear in Latin America* (New York: The Macmillan Co., 1965), pp. 98-99.

3. See Erik Erikson, *Insight and Responsibility* (New York: W.W. Norton and Co., 1964), pp. 221, 228-29, 231-38; see also Novak, "Moral Society and Immoral Man," *A Time to Build* (New York: The Macmillan Co., 1967), pp. 358-59.

4. William James, "The Sentiment of Rationality," in *The Will to Believe* (New York: Dover Books, 1959), pp. 63-110.

5. Willard Van Orman Quine, *From a Logical Point of View* (Cambridge: Harvard University Press, 1953), pp. 78-79.

6. Morton V. White, *Toward Reunion in Philosophy* (Cambridge: Harvard University Press, 1956), pp. 278-88, 299.

7. M. B. Foster, " 'We' in Modern Philosophy," *Faith and Logic,* ed. by Basil Mitchell (Boston: Beacon Press, 1957), pp. 194-220.

8. Friedrich Nietzsche, *Beyond Good and Evil,* tr., Walter Kaufmann (New York: Vintage Book, 1966), p. 24.

9. *Ibid.,* p. 27.

10. *Ibid.,* p. 13.

11. *Ibid.,* p. 12.

12. *Ibid.,* p. 16.

13. *Ibid.,* p. 13

14. *Ibid.,* p. 14.

15. *Ibid.*

16. December 2, 1967.

17. See R. M. Hare, "Theology and Falsification," *New Essays in Philosophical Theology,* ed. by Antony Flew and Alasdair MacIntyre (London: SCM Press, 1955), pp. 100-1.

1

TO BE HUMAN IS TO HUMANIZE:
A Radically Empirical Aesthetic*

BY JOHN J. MCDERMOTT

It is not common to begin a discussion of a philosophical tradition with a first chapter on aesthetics. But, then, the American tradition is an extraordinary tradition. Perhaps more than those of any other culture, America's major philosophers saw the relativity of all human systems and seized the corollary bravely: the final "ground" of human reflection is a kind of aesthetic sense. But what exactly is "an aesthetic sense"? In this introductory essay, John J. McDermott of Queens College comes to grips with the new conception of aesthetics achieved by John Dewey (1859–1952) and William James (1842–1910). Both Dewey and James stressed the participation of the human subject, the superabundance of human experience beyond our limited systems of concepts, and the ongoing flux of time. A theory for understanding the artistic spirit of our time emerges from such emphases; but so does a theory for understanding the science and technology of our time.

"It is . . . the reinstatement of the vague and inarticulate to its proper place in our mental life which I am so anxious to press on the attention." William James[1]

* Aspects of this essay have been offered as lectures to philosophical colloquia at Boston University, the University of New Hampshire, and Pennsylvania State University. Helpful criticism received on those occasions has been incorporated, as well as incisive suggestions from my students in Aesthetics, especially Mr. William Gavin. The entire essay was given an extremely helpful critical reading by my colleague Professor Eugene Fontinell. Some small sections are a reworking of my earlier illustrated brochure, "The Experience of Form as Process" (New York: Paul Klapper Art Center, 1962). J. J. McD.

Two themes occupy us in the present chapter. First, we contend that modern art[2] works a revolution in man's view of himself; it broadens the ways in which he relates to the world and the ways by which he is informed. Second, we hold that the most fruitful philosophical statement of the meaning of modern art is to be found in the thought of William James and John Dewey, interpreted as a radically empirical philosophy of experience. From the time of the nineteenth-century impressionists to the Second World War, these two themes were historically and imaginatively interwoven. We want to make up for the recent neglect of these two themes, in order to show the unusual significance of radical empiricism for contemporary art. We make no effort to develop a complete aesthetic.

The problems we face focus on the relationship of impressionism to the nature of inquiry;[3] the role of philosophy relative to modern art; and the pre-eminence of a doctrine of relations in a contemporary aesthetic. We shall see that the thought of James and Dewey, so long trapped in the narrow epistemological problems of a pragmatic theory of truth, has extraordinary resiliency when looked at from the viewpoint of a generalized aesthetic. Further, if we are to take seriously the title of this volume, then the possibility of an aesthetic in our technological world poses a challenge of considerable importance for the future.

I. MODERN ART AS AN ATTITUDE
"Technique is the very being of all creation." Ronald Barthes[4]

It is now a truism to affirm the decisive importance of modern science for the development of philosophical method and philosophical language. The methodology of contemporary science has been especially effective in forcing philosophy to abandon many of its presuppositions and working categories. Less well known is the fact that no corresponding transformation of philosophical language has taken place in response to the drastic changes effected by the artistic activity of the last seventy-five years. The revolution in art is as embracing as that in science, and relative to the life of the person, a more immediate one. We should not underestimate the extension of modern art as a general cultural attitude. Permeating our advertising, decorating our living space, reconstructing our sense of sound, making hybrids of all the classical art forms, modern art is so pervasive an influence that even the most radical departure from the commonplace fails to cause any consternation.[5] Has any culture heretofore found itself nostalgic for objects and experiences a decade or so removed in time but totally obliterated in experienced form? The revolution in primal shapes, colors, and textures wrought by the influence of modern art on industrial design is now so complete an aspect of our living that it would be difficult to single out a set of visual experiences which has not undergone considerable transformation within a single generation. In his essay on "The Man-Made Object," Gillo Dorfles refers to this characteristic as "formal instability."[6] Coupled with the acknowledgment of such restless formal identity is the effort of man to create forms. Surrounded by what he has "made" and aware of his ability to change its character at rapid intervals, modern man takes seriously his role as constitutor of reality. The shift from a denotative to a constitutive response to the world is rooted not only in modern technology but in modern aesthetics as well.

Moreover, the ingrained dependence on the visual and auditory senses is now experienced as inseparable from the sense of touch. The new art forms struggle against the conceptual domination of our traditional patterns of response. The arts of assemblage, kinetic sculpture, and mixed media make the tactile experience central. Modern in theme, these art activities reinvoke the primitive affection for the hands and symbolically restate the case for *Homo faber*.

No longer separated from his world like a spectator from a picture, modern man has slowly acknowledged the presence of an irreducible factor; how he formulates the environment becomes the environment itself.[7] Recently this insight has been stated in cryptic form by Marshall McLuhan as "the medium is the message."[8] We should not, however, be so surprised at this claim, for early in our century the traditional stranglehold on the meaning of nature, exercised through rigid conceptual models, was dramatically broken

23

by the artistic revolution in the use of "media." Subsequently spurred on by the influence of the generic attitude known as "Dada," modern art assaulted the established aesthetic values. In art as in science, the obviousness of common sense was rejected as a resource for creative work. "Nouns," "things," and the consensus of meaning rooted in an "objective" framework were now taken to be but abstractions from a distinctively personalized aesthetic. While the acceptance of this inconoclastic attitude varied widely, the critical and nonconforming edge of Dada as an attitude is still residual in the activity of modern art to this day. Further, in response to these experiences of negation, modern art sets out to formulate new contexts for the articulation of aesthetic values. The most important factor in this development is the new understanding of technique. For the most part located in the very choice of media to be used, technique often becomes the primary locus for the generating of artistic insight. As the medium is shifted, the nature of aesthetic experience and the attendant questions of meaning, participation, and enhancement undergo a like transformation.[9] In these preliminary remarks we insist only that the notion of reality which emerges from this activity is one which affirms a reality whose very being is its process.

With these factors in mind let us return to our initial question. Those sympathetic to the metaphors of process philosophy usually trace the roots of their awareness to the revolution in speculative science and to certain perspectives in recent philosophy, particularly the thought of Bergson and Whitehead. Modern art, on the other hand, despite its being a more directly experienceable phenomenon and despite its having extensive implications for the meaning of inquiry, has not been brought to bear on the basic philosophical issues of our time. The philosophical discipline known as aesthetics continues to deal largely with antique problems, seemingly innocent of the fact that the art-experience of the last half-century has rendered the questions of beauty, truth in the arts, and the search for objective criteria as simply not to the point.[10] If we survey contemporary American philosophical works on aesthetics, it is astonishing to see how little they have to do with our experience of contemporary art—a situation made clear if we

were to think of the philosophy of science as still dominated by the
problems of classical mechanics. Likewise, in any number of
broadly based attempts to deal with the aesthetic dimensions of
modern culture, the participation of the contemporary philosopher
is at a minimum.[11] Can we offer an analysis of this situation or
must we admit to the contention that philosophical discourse and
modern art are separated by a linguistic and even experiential gulf
too immense to allow for mutual inquiry?

From one side, certain critics and the more articulate artists
have become increasingly concerned with a reflective statement of
their activities; in a word, have become increasingly philosophical
about art.[12] For the most part, however, critics and artists rarely
turn to philosophy itself when conducting such inquiries, and seem
to boycott even those philosophers who have made an attempt to
address themselves to aesthetic concerns. Should we agree with
Herbert Read, in his commentary on Naum Gabo?

> He is virtually creating a new language, a symbolic lan-
> guage of concrete visual images. This language is necessary
> because our philosophical inquiries have brought us to a
> point where the old symbols no longer suffice. Philosophy
> itself has reached an impasse—an impasse of verbal expres-
> sion—at which it hands over its task to the poets and paint-
> ers, the sculptors and other creators of concrete images.[13]

We would argue that Read takes philosophy too literally and con-
demns us to an unreflective participation in the experience of art
and to discourse which signifies sterility of experience. To the contrary, if one is located in a wider philosophical tradition, discourse
can have philosophical intention and yet be continuous with the
basic attitude and creative direction of contemporary art. Although
at times a noble goal, clarity is not the only objective of philosophical discourse. In some instances, particularly those referring to the
plastic arts, philosophical discussion of the experiences in question
may be illuminating in its *inability* to provide adequate linguistic
corollaries as well as in its effort to create new metaphors of articulation. These latter would refer, not to ingrained philosophical lan-

guage, but to the aesthetic qualities of the artistic experiences. The crucial question has to do with one's expectations of inquiry. To the extent that we seek a final statement, or a methodology able to put the vagaries of experience in fixed categories, the tendency is to push the philosophical enterprise beyond the limits of experience. For some, this is precisely the task of philosophy, namely, to transcend experience. But to those for whom the qualities of our experience are inseparable from their peculiarities in the concrete, such a method is fruitless.

A glance at the ambiguity in the basic attitude toward modern art in philosophical circles will give us some perspective. It will also serve as an introduction to the American philosophy of experience begun by William James and crystallized in the essays on the "live creature" by John Dewey.

It can be said that modern art needs no justification beyond its very presence. Yet when philosophers reflect upon the phenomenon of artistic creation, two distinct viewpoints emerge. The first and more generally accepted perspective sees modern art as a distortion of the "real world." This evaluation arises from a base extrinsic to the creative process itself; it has at its core the claim that the new forms which characterize contemporary art are a function of the widespread dehumanization afflicting our century. For support of this position, not only are we directed to the obvious "distortion" in canvases of Rouault, the surrealists, and expressionist protest art, but we are also asked to respond to the over-all presence of dadaistic elements as if they were statements of content rather than an attempt to relocate the aesthetic experience. Recent examples of collage, combine-paintings, pop art, and especially the mysterious versions of assemblage found in the "boxes" of Joseph Cornell seem to sustain the charge that modern art violates our conceptual order and has only a topical significance, of a negative cast.

The major obstacle in the way of this interpretation is its notion of form. Dehumanization in art is taken to be the aberration or distortion of finalized forms, recognized as such by a centuries-old tradition of philosophical and aesthetic sanction. We must acknowledge the depressing truth that twentieth-century man has turned on his brother as never before. And there is no doubt that these circumstances have directly influenced the art of our time,

26

which is said to represent the dark shadow hovering over the human face and the human place. Dehumanization, however, proceeds from still another source. Modern man is also a victim of clarity. Much of our difficulty proceeds from the demand for certitude and an inability to recognize and live with the irreducibility of shadows. Who among us knows the human face, or the nature of man? Have the myriad forms through which man humanizes his environment been approached, let alone exhausted? The departure from the moorings once so clearly recognized and accepted by Western man does not seem to be a fall from grace; it may be a liberation of creative human activity. Dehumanization, then, is often due to the blind defense of traditional versions of human life, now vestigial and no longer able to sustain human needs. Modern art accuses Western culture of sterility and narrow defensiveness. The accusation, often couched as a "manifesto," is at once a rejection of tired forms and a call for a new statement about human creative possibility. The extremes expressed in modern art occur in proportion to the lack of flexibility and imagination characteristic of the cultural attitudes under attack.

If it is folly to think that the old aesthetic values shall return as they were, it is equally true that the new artistic movements are so radical that they preclude any stable, final order. What is at stake seems to be nothing less than a reconstruction of the modes and expectations of inquiry, in which we are constantly obligated to fuse the critique of previous forms with an attempt to create new forms.[14] Thomas Hess, writing on the painter Willem de Kooning, supports this interpretation. "The crisis of modern art presupposes that each shape, even a plain oval, be reinvented—or rather, given an autochthonous existence in paint. Nothing could be accepted or received on faith as a welcome heritage."[15]

Here then is the second way to view modern art, as an articulation of modern man's most distinctive activity, the creation of forms. Whether it be due to simple shifting of context, as in the "creation" of the haunted forms of objet trouvé or in the more aggressive structuring of totally new environments as brought off by the ever changing styles of assemblage, modern art has made innovation a central theme.[16] It is not difficult to find an acknowledgment of this dimension in the assessment of modern art; in-

27

deed, it has become almost a commonplace. The full implications, however, of such an attitude, have not been developed thus far. For the most part, the understanding of innovation has been along the lines of "replacement," an echo of the old metaphysics of objects. The key to the meaning of originality in modern art is not found in a doctrine of the "wholly new" but, rather, in a metaphysics of relations.

Fundamental to this new perspective are two contentions, both of direct philosophical importance: First, the recognition of the inability of nature to act any longer as the objective referent for the creative affairs of men. Rooted in the impressionistic attitude, this development owes much to the modern meaning of symbolism and the acceptance of ambiguity as a persistent dimension in human inquiry. Second, the affirmation that no entity can be experienced in isolation but has to be encountered as a field of relations.[17] Better, the term "entity" should be replaced by "event," that is, a network of relations, historically understood, with a past, present, and future. Furthermore, no matter how these "events" come into being and however diverse their lineage,[18] whenever they become subject to our awareness and touch us in a human way, they become realities of the most direct and intense kind. Citing Thomas Hess once more: "Life as we live it, obviously, is a matter of endless ambiguities and proliferating meanings; transparencies upon transparencies make an image that, while it blurs in superimpositions, takes on the actuality of rocks."[19] Concretion need not be associated with the meaning of "thing," for if we are willing to live with ambiguity, the flow of relations is also concrete and real.

In order to grasp the import of these contentions about nature and relations, we should examine two traditions. One is obvious: the plastic arts from Monet to the present. The other is not so obvious: the metaphysics of relations as rooted in the philosophy of William James. The remainder of this chapter will have as its task to show that these traditions, however different in expression and parallel in historical development, proceed from a single vision and can be allied to each other as philosophical metaphor to artistic creation.

28

II. IMPRESSIONISM AS BREAKTHROUGH:
WILLIAM JAMES AND CLAUDE MONET
"L'exactitude n'est pas la verité." Matisse[20]

The presence of nuance and shading as a function of the gigantic manifests itself in the impressionistic attitude. Unity is achieved not by a decisive appeal to an objective referent but, rather, by a gentle fading into continuous but ever more obscure edges. It is an attitude whereby all insight is fringed, as if we were reaching for a horizon with what William James calls an " 'ever not quite' to all our formulas, and novelty and possibility for ever leaking in."[21] Writing in the *American Journal of Psychology* in 1891, G. Stanley Hall evaluates James's *Principles of Psychology:*

> Passing now to *the work as a whole,* the author might be described as an *impressionist* in psychology. His portfolio contains sketches old and new, ethical, literary, scientific and metaphysical, some exquisite and charming in detail and even color, others rough charcoal outlines, but all together stimulating and suggestive, and showing great industry and versatility. . . .[22]

James's *Principles* is, like an Impressionist canvas, a virtuoso performance, technically proficient and characterized by extraordinary detail. Yet it has an elusive center and its major theme is the fluidity of consciousness. Further, its concluding chapter, "Necessary Effects and the Truths of Experience," renders the entire effort subject to doubt or at best, in James's judgment at least, renders it a bare hint of the desired statement. James shares, then, in the nineteenth-century breakthrough in sensibility. In an essay on James's aesthetics, Jacques Barzun writes:

> One can begin abstractly by saying that through this book [*The Principles*] James struck a deathblow at Realism. The then prevailing views of the mind were that it copied reality like a photographic plate, that it received and assembled the elements of experience like a machine, that it combined ideas

29

like a chemist. For this "scientist" mind, James substituted one that was a born artist—a wayward, creative mind, impelled by inner wants, fringed with mystery, and capable of infinitely subtle, unrecordable nuances. Dethroning the sophistical Realist, in short, James revealed Impressionism native and dominant.[23]

In but a line, too infrequently noted by commentators, James responds to the call of experience: "It is, in short, the reinstatement of the vague to its proper place in our mental life which I am so anxious to press on the attention."[24] Apparently not satisfied with this phrasing, James is bolder in his *Psychology—Briefer Course:* "It is, the reader will see, the reinstatement of the vague and inarticulate to its proper place in our mental life which I am so anxious to press on the attention."[25] This affection for the "penumbra" of experience is no isolated insight in James. It everywhere sustains his contention that conceptual statements are but truncations of the flow of concrete life. Such insulating cuts in the flow are merely functional and should not prevent us from maintaining a reflective confrontation with those areas of our conscious experience not given to systematic definition.

In a more advanced statement of his views, James tells us: "Our fields of experience have no more definite boundaries than have our fields of view. Both are fringed forever by a *more* that continuously develops and that continuously supersedes them as life proceeds.[26] The experiencing of this fringe yields awareness while defying any conceptual formulation. For James, the crucial area of human activity is found precisely where the conceptual order breaks down, for it is in those conscious but inarticulable environs, wherein we experience religiously, aesthetically, psychedelically, that we are open to demons.[27] Although most often not subject to explanation, the meanings of these situations are intensely personal and, in a way proper to their own modalities, crystal clear.

In 1890, the year of the publication of James's *Principles,* Monet tells us of the struggle he has in painting the "haystack" series.

> I am working terribly hard, struggling with a series of different effects (haystacks), but . . . the sun sets so fast that I cannot follow it. . . . I am beginning to work so slowly that I am desperate, but the more I continue the more I see that a great deal of work is necessary in order to succeed in rendering that which I seek: "Instantaneity," especially the "enveloppe," the same light spreading everywhere, and more than ever I am dissatisfied with the easy things that come in one stroke.[28]

Ambiguity bathes our experience and the one-to-one correspondence between the perceptual act and the objective order is challenged. For Monet, the shift in light was decisive, but there can be a multiplicity of other activities (in James's phrase, "the halo of felt relations"[29]) which challenge the finality of our conceptual view of the universe. The important thrust of the impressionist attitude is to see the object as a locus from which to allow the full range of shades and meanings to show. The vagueness is relative; it depends on how prematurely one cuts off inquiry and attempts to answer the question, What is that? The painter Kandinsky understood this revolution better than most, for it was a decisive factor in transforming his own artistic activity. In 1895, Kandinsky stood before a Monet "haystack" exhibited in Moscow. Of this experience, he writes:

> Previously I knew only realistic art. . . . Suddenly, for the first time, I saw a "picture." That it was a haystack a catalogue informed me. I could not recognize it. This lack of recognition was distressing to me. I also felt that the painter had no right to paint so indistinctly. I had a muffled sense that the object was lacking in this picture, and was overcome with astonishment and perplexity that not only seized but engraved itself indelibly on the memory and quite unexpectedly, again and again hovered before the eyes down to the smallest detail. All of this was unclear to me, and I could not draw the simple consequences from this experience.
> But what was absolutely clear to me was the unsuspected power previously hidden from me, of the palette

31

which surpassed all my dreams. Painting took on a fabulous strength and splendor. And at the same time, unconsciously, the object was discredited as an indispensable element of the picture.[30]

The discrediting of the object is no small event in the history of human consciousness. All too often this development is analyzed as the other side of the growth of subjectivism. Such an interpretation is narrow and misguided, for the dispersal of objects does not necessarily throw us back on an introverted self-consciousness, although it does enhance the role of the self in the creative process. By far, the more significant implication has to do with the emergence of relational activity as the focus for meaning. The subject-object duality is no longer to the point, for at both ends these terms are but abstract statements of actually dynamic processes. Pushing further, inquiry moves steadily to an analysis of the interaction between the relational qualities of self-consciousness and the relational qualities of constructed environments. In effect, analysis focuses on "fields" of relationships, rather than on subjects and objects in isolation.[31] From such a viewpoint, the role of "names" undergoes a serious shift. They stand for loci or gathering places of ongoing relational activities, and thereby merely focus attention. In modern art, names of art objects are not to be taken as descriptions of the work. Rather, they merely announce the presence of activity and are bypassed as soon as we tie into the peculiar qualities of such activity. More often than not, such nominal delineations of works of modern art become increasingly less relevant as we broaden our participation. Thus, to speak consistently, there is no single canvas in modern painting; for experienced as an event, the physical environment of such a canvas, the psychic thrust of one's own personal activity at that time, and the myriad historical and cultural factors involved in such aesthetic participation are all irreducible dimensions of the painting. If we can apply such criteria, retrospectively, to traditional works of art, this does not gainsay the fact that such a possibility emerges primarily from the method of modern painting. Among artists, Kandinsky, for one, was aware of the nature of this shift away from the object to the relational event as the real source of meaning. He offers a metaphorical statement of this new philosophical insight.

> This isolated line and the isolated fish alike are living beings with forces peculiar to them, though latent. . . . But the voice of these latent forces is faint and limited. It is the environment of the line and the fish that brings about a miracle: the latent forces awaken, the expression becomes radiant, the impression profound. Instead of a low voice, one hears a choir. The latent forces have become dynamic. The environment is the composition.[32]

Kandinsky's statement is inseparable from the fact that the plastic arts since Monet have set a dizzying pace in the creation of new environments. At first limited to radical shifts within the context of the "painting" or the "sculpture," their activities soon spilled out into "assembled" environments, often creating the need for entirely new evaluative criteria. The task of a modern aesthetic is to achieve discursive continuity with such constructs. Just as single "things" gave way to "environments," so too, the single arts of painting and sculpture have become antique, giving way first to hybridizations with other aesthetic forms and now to new aesthetic creations, *sui generis,* often with no recognizable tie to what was only recently known as art. What is most needed, therefore, is a philosophical outlook which does not ask dead questions, that is, questions which focus simply on content. Whether we say with Kandinsky "the environment is the composition" or with McLuhan "the medium is the message," the problem is clear from the philosophical side—the need for a doctrine of relational activity phrased in aesthetic metaphors.

At this juncture William James again offers a point of departure. James has an original approach to relations: they are rooted in a psychology of experience. His view of self-consciousness is characterized by process and function rather than by entity and faculty. And finally, his anthropology, which is Promethean in outlook, is fully aware of chance, novelty, and the centrality of human creativity. Rather than a structured aesthetic theory, it is his life[33] and his philosophical approach to the problem of inquiry which gives us the basis for a modern aesthetic. Using the assumptions of James, let us make an effort to consider the problems of modern art in a way which shows philosophical concern but maintains fidelity to the quality of modern experience.

III. A RELATIONAL AESTHETIC

"Monumentality is an affair of relativity." Hans Hofmann[34]

William James took his stand over against the associationist psychology of the nineteenth century. Although he shared the empirical temper of that tradition, he could not accept its view that experience is composed of atomistic elements. The reigning opposition was idealism which, in James's understanding, provided an overarching principle of unity, without any experiential sustenance. Rejecting both views, he countered with his doctrine of radical empiricism.[35] The clearest statement of this position was made by James in the "Preface" to *The Meaning of Truth,* written in 1909.

> Radical empiricism consists first of a postulate, next of a statement of fact, and finally of a generalized conclusion.
>
> The postulate is that the only things that shall be debatable among philosophers shall be things definable in terms drawn from experience. (Things of an unexperienceable nature may exist *ad libitum,* but they form no part of the material for philosophic debate.)
>
> The statement of fact is that the relations between things, conjunctive as well as disjunctive, are just as much matters of direct particular experience, neither more so nor less so, than the things themselves.
>
> The generalized conclusion is that therefore the parts of experience hold together from next to next by relations that are themselves parts of experience. The directly apprehended universe needs, in short, no extraneous trans-empirical connective support, but possesses in its own right a concatenated or continuous structure.[36]

34

The crucial aspect of this position is unquestionably found in his claim for the "statement of fact." Central to James's radical empiricism, this affirmation has its roots in a phenomenology of the processes of consciousness. He tells us in his essay on "The Stream of Thought" that "If there be such things as feelings at all, *then so surely as relations between objects exist* in rerum natura, *so surely and more surely, do feelings exist to which these relations are known.*"[37] Quite concretely, we should say a "feeling of *and,* a feeling of *if,* a feeling of *but,* and a feeling of *by,* quite as readily as we say a feeling of *blue* or a feeling of *cold.*"[38] And to the extent that we do not, we accept the empiricist prejudice "of supposing that where there is *no* name no entity can exist."[39] In this way, "all dumb or anonymous psychic states have, owing to this error, been cooly suppressed. . . ."[40]

The search for "what" inevitably ends with a "noun" for a response. The epistemology of common sense seeks names, definitions, and categories. From its critical side, modern art, particularly in its dadaistic overtone, has led an assault on such an approach. In refusing to name its artifacts, or in naming them abstractly, as "#1," or again, in naming them specifically but with no visual correspondence to the work, this art denies to itself and to the participant any substantive identity. Such a denial does not, however, imply an absence of meaning or of intelligibility. Rather, meaning is located in the ongoing fabric of relations, by which we mean it is found neither in an isolated self nor in an isolated thing but, rather, in the environment constituted by shared participation. Any attempts to extrapolate a fixed meaning for other than functional purposes are denials of this process. James had warned of the dangers involved when connections were thought to be but logical bridges instead of experienced continuities.

> Continuous transition is one sort of a conjunctive relation; and to be a radical empiricist means to hold fast to this conjunctive relation of all others, for this is the strategic point, the position through which, if a hole be made, all the corruptions of dialectics and all the metaphysical fictions pour into our philosophy.[41]

35

If we wish to understand the meaning of modern art, we have to place ourselves in continuity with the interiorized structuring of each creation. At all costs, we must avoid the temptation to evaluate this art by virtue of criteria derived from a source extrinsic to the qualities of the creative process. Support for such a contention is offered to us in the following text of James: "Knowledge of sensible realities thus comes to life inside the tissue of experience. It is *made;* and made by relations which unroll themselves in time."[42]

In order to sustain this claim, James takes a position which is bold relative to philosophy but obvious from the side of modern painting and sculpture. "Life is in the transitions as much as in the terms connected; often, indeed, it seems to be there more emphatically. . . . These relations of continuous transition experienced are what makes our experiences cognitive. In the simplest and completest cases the experiences are cognitive of one another."[43] The crucial problem, therefore, in the search for the "form" of a modern painting is the inability to relate it to a reality already given.

In the concrete, to seek a morphology of a modern painting, say, of the abstract expressionist school, turns up the following. We do not confront an object but an event;[44] or, in a name used recently for one kind of modern art but more widely applicable, a "happening." The origins of such an event are obscure, unless we accept a psychoanalytic or sociological reductionism. Should we do so, the experiencing of such an event would likewise be conditioned and we would still be faced with the problem of ever varying qualities in such influence.[45] Despite the absence of an inherited identity, we are able to enter into meaningful relationship to modern art. We enjoy, undergo, and are carried along by it. Its form seems to be its process although with no fixed goal. This does not imply looseness of endeavor or of craft. In the paintings of Mark Rothko, for example, one is fascinated by the intense effort to deal with relationship as such, under the specifics of shading, dripping and ever so subtle internal shifts of color and canvas size. This concern becomes almost obsessive in the work of the late Ad Reinhardt, known as minimal art. The point at issue here is that this galaxy of interiorized relations cannot be rendered meaningful by any appeal to a known object. This does not mean that such paintings are locked up within themselves, but any opening out of their meaning must follow the same nonliteral processes[46] which were central to their creation originally. That the human self can enter into such a process, we shall discuss further on.

Expressions such as "ongoing," "process," "reconstruction," "event," "interaction," so central to a metaphysics of experience, and so often criticized by philosophers as vague, show up again and again in writings by painters and critics.[47] Perhaps the most explicit statement of the position that an ongoing fabric of relations is the source of meaning and intelligibility in a work of modern art was offered by Hans Hofmann. A painter of the first rank, Hofmann was also a teacher and made a serious effort to render in discursive terms his view of modern painting. Holding that a color interval is "analogous to a thought-fragment in the creative process," Hofmann sees such intervals or fragments taking their meaning from their "aesthetic extension," for "any isolated thing can never surpass its own meaning."[48] Actually, he goes beyond James, for according to William Seitz, Hofmann will hold that "the relation between elements, whatever they may be, is always more significant than the elements themselves."[49] Should we not take seriously Hofmann's belief that "relations" rather than isolated "actualities" account for the quality of our response? Seitz clarifies our attitude toward these matters in the following text.

> Traditionally, a painting used to begin as a rough sketch of the main lines or areas of a preconceived image, and this is still often the case; but with Hofmann, painting is from the first stroke a continuing establishment and re-establishment of life relationships. As it progresses, the work moves toward a more perfect integration of all its parts—toward a relational unity.[50]

We need not remain within the rhetoric of painting in order to establish the significance of relations for the modern theme. Perhaps if we were to look at a more aggressive art form, like modern jazz, our meaning would become clearer. Outside of a relational setting, jazz is meaningless, for it proceeds by a series of interwoven tensions. A jazz group is especially revealing, as single members create their music in line with their respective insight but over against other members of the group. We have tension between personal mastery of the instrument and the demand for improvisation; between the developing structure of each contribution and, over-all, an open system. The entire performance is carried on with a sense for group responsibility.[51] The viability of these tensions is manifested only as experienced. It cannot be predicted or planned, as there are no formal or abstract correlations. The qualities of a jazz performance cannot be extrapolated and taught as such. The jazz master is one whose distinctive originality enables the fledgling to create in his own vein; thus, each to his own vision but as a shared experience. Such indirect communication is necessary, for we do not have duplication of experiences or the performance of others' versions. Yet, in a jazz group, the participant senses when the group is not sharing the same experience, articulated by each in his own manner. And, in turn, the experiencing public sense when it "comes off." As in the plastic arts, intelligibility is manifest when one is carried along by the possibilities and relations of the medium in question. This is a cardinal instance of Dewey's contention that *"connections* exist in the most immediate non-cognitive experience, and when the experienced situation becomes problematic, the connections are developed into distinctive objects of common sense or of science."[52]

In jazz the experienced situation becomes meaningful because of the technique. More than any other single factor, as for example the instruments used or the melody as point of departure, it is technique which is decisive in bringing about a creative advance. In the plastic arts, correspondingly, every shift in material used creates a new locus of relations, new problems and, lately, entirely new art forms. In his essay on "The Structuralist Activity," Ronald Barthes states: "It is not the nature of the copied object which defines art (though this is a tenacious prejudice in all realism), it is the fact that man adds to it in reconstructing it: technique is the very being of all creation."[53]

At this point, it should be obvious that modern art sustains an important shift in the meaning of person. No mere copier of forms

38

or even a discoverer[54] of forms hidden, man becomes the creator of forms. The rhetoric of the artist and the critic, on this issue, has often been extreme. Apollinaire, for example, in his work on *The Cubist Painters,* traces the existence of the "world" to the creative work of the artist.

> It is the social function of great poets and artists to renew continually the appearance nature has for the eyes of men.
>
> Without poets, without artists, men would soon weary of nature's monotony. The sublime idea men have of the universe would collapse with dizzying speed. The order which we find in nature, and which is only an effect of art, would vanish. Everything would break up in chaos. There would be no seasons, no civilization, no thought, no humanity; even life would give way, and the impotent void would reign everywhere.[55]

In an exchange of views between the critic Herbert Read and the founder of constructivism, Naum Gabo, a similar position is taken, although more modestly stated. Gabo puts it this way.

> I maintain that knowledge is nothing else but a construction of ours and that what we discover with our knowledge is not something outside us or a part of a constant and higher reality, in the absolute sense of the word; but that we discover exactly that which we put into the place where we make the discoveries. . . .[56]

In his essay on "Human Art and Inhuman Nature," Read simply maintains that some modern artists set out "to invent an entirely new reality."[57] But these contentions, and they are representative of the many manifesto-declarations of novelty that abound in modern art, are too pat; they protest too much. They have meaning in that they clearly delineate the opponent, a mimetic or spectator view of the world. The problem, however, is more complex and surely the creative capacity attributed to the modern artist is more subtle than the replacing of one total view by another.

39

A "new reality" is only one kind of novelty and it is rarely achieved. Further, in time, it too shall be replaced and rendered obsolete. The revolution of modern art is better found in the attitude it takes to all reality, whether obvious to common sense, surreal, or invented.[58] What is novel is not simply new creations, but a way of approaching all art.

The genuine sense of novelty is achieved by virtue of our focusing on processes rather than on products; and by our energizing of relationships, both given and created. If we wish, this approach can be applied retrospectively to classical art, for although it may violate the original intention, the implications of such art would then be considerably widened. No doubt this is why so many modern artists claim profoundly personal relationships with individual classical artists, while creating, in their own vein, a radically different style. From the outside, the well-known fact of the influence of classical drawing on abstract expressionism is difficult to absorb and seems to demand a massive reconstruction of the notion of continuity. Yet, in morphological terms, the internal struggles to achieve the dynamics of line are quite continuous. They key is to dwell within and capture the rhythm, the ongoing dialectic. The identity or nonidentity of extrapolated forms is peripheral to real aesthetic insight, and is not necessary for purposes of understanding or comparison. Gardner Murphy describes a wider sense of creative activity that parallels our description of artistic creation.

> . . . creative activity is the very nature of the primitive life-process itself. The concept of the open system really means that living things are not only intent on their own growth and development, but that they are directing evolutionary processes in accordance with a dynamic which is organismic, rather than mechanical.[59]

That such an inner dynamic, with its own logic, is characteristic of the processes of experience and amenable to human interaction is a distinctive position of William James. In a series of texts, written at different times, he lays the problem bare.

James, in a morbid state and on the edge of suicide, entered this liberating text in his "Diary": "Life shall [be built in] doing and suffering and creating."[60] The full meaning of his commitment at that point is made clear in his subsequent essay on "The Sentiment of Rationality."

> If we survey the field of history and ask what feature all great periods of revival, of expansion of the human mind, display in common, we shall find, I think, simply this: that each and all of them have said to the human being, "The inmost nature of the reality is congenial to *powers* which you possess."[61]

The confidence in the capacity of man to transform his environment proceeds from James's view that the human self and the flow of experience share the same basic relational patterns. The human self, in James's view, has no inherited identity. Gordon Allport writes of James:

> There is, he thinks, no such thing as a substantive self distinguishable from the sum total, or stream, of experiences. Each moment of consciousness, he says, appropriates each previous moment, and the knower is thus somehow embedded in what is known.[62]

The interaction between the human self and the environment is the decisive factor in engendering the experience of identity. The fabric of man's life is a relational schema; it not only deals with the exigencies for human identity but, within conditioned structure, yields the imaginative construction of the meaning of the world. In his *Principles,* James had held to the natively formulating character of conscious activity. The selective work of the mind follows interest, practical or aesthetic.[63]

> Out of what is in itself an undistinguishable, swarming *continuum* devoid of distinction or emphasis, our senses make for us by attending to this motion, and ignoring that, a world full of contrasts, of sharp accents, of abrupt changes, of picturesque light and shade.[64]

41

By the time of *Pragmatism,* published in 1907, James sees the activity of man as even more aggressively constructive.

> In our cognitive as well as in our active life, we are creative. We add, both to the subject and to the predicate part of reality. The world stands really malleable, waiting to receive its final touches at our hand. Like the kingdom of heaven, it suffers violence willingly. Man engenders truth upon it.[65]

As with the modern artist, James's world does not give itself to any conceptually extrapolated or finalized version. "Whatever separateness is actually experienced is not overcome, it stays and counts as separateness to the end."[66] The world cannot be had whole, from any single perspective. Indeed, two minds cannot know one thing, except by a pragmatic verification of a shared experience.[67] Unity is a process achieved only *durcheinander* and not *all einheit.* He rails against the "block universe," holding rather to a "multiverse," unfinished, tychastic, and shot through with novelty.[68] In the search for meaning in a processive world, James gives to man the decisive role; man is the creator of forms.

Notwithstanding all these positions of James and the strength of their supporting texts, rendered almost stereotypical by the commentaries on his thought, we should focus on another perspective too often overlooked. First, we should not forget the full text, cited above (n. 61) of James's remark in "The Sentiment of Rationality." While it is true that he emphasizes the "powers which you possess," he describes man's relationship to his environment as one of "congeniality" and not one of dominance. Further, he stresses the presence of the "inmost nature of the reality," to which such "congeniality" is directed. It can be said that James did not stress adequately his insight into the relational fabric of the affairs of nature, concentrating, rather, on the "energies of men" and the fluid quality of the human self. Yet he was aware of such dynamics and came to hold that only by acknowledging this texture in the activities of nature as experienced can we do justice to the creative thrust of human activity. Rather than the oversimplified emphasis on novelty, as proceeding wholly from the self (a caricature of the modern artist), James presents a taut relationship between a constructing and manipulating consciousness, and the activity of a continually related flow of experience.

A second balancing factor in James's view was found in our earlier discussion, when we indicated James's contention that "life is in the transitions." A text in *Pragmatism* spells out this belief and gives meaning to his affirmation of that "inmost nature of the reality" which challenges the creative activity of man. "Our experience meanwhile is all shot through with regularities. One bit of it can warn us to get ready for another bit, can 'intend' or be 'significant' of that remoter object."[69] Relative to man's needs, including his desire to enhance, experience is malleable. But it is no dummy, for "Experience itself, taken at large, can grow by its edges. That one moment of it proliferates into the next by transitions which, whether conjunctive or disjunctive, continue the experiential tissue, can not, I contend, be denied."[70]

Man, therefore, is called upon to create meaning, to engender truth. This activity places man at the center of the flow of experience. The modern artist has shown that the resources of human imagination are virtually limitless and that man has only begun to articulate the possible dimensions of the human self. Nevertheless, we must maintain that it is a "world" which we wish to create. We seek more than a dazzling array of self-preening evocations of the human psyche. Relations must be forged between the processes of the human self and the affairs of our living space, our topography, our cities, and our artifacts. Modern art, in the last decade, has become aware of this need and, as we shall attempt to indicate, has begun to offer a viable aesthetic for contemporary man. So that modern art on behalf of modern man, in carrying on this endeavor, may avoid the temptation to become overly impressed with the novelty of the effort, at the expense of the task, let us close this section with a stern and incisive warning by William James.

> Woe to him whose beliefs play fast and loose with the order which realities follow in his experience; they will lead him nowhere or else make false connexions.[71]

IV. EXPERIENCE OF THE ORDINARY AS AESTHETIC

"Works of art are . . . celebrations, recognized as such, of the things of ordinary experience." John Dewey[72]

The philosophy of radical empiricism, with which John Dewey[73] was fundamentally in accord, is thematically rearticulated in his *Art as Experience*. Published in 1934, the book was a development of Dewey's remarks as the first William James Lecturer at Harvard University. Dewey's range of concerns and the incisiveness of his judgments make this one of his outstanding contributions and deserving of ever more analysis.[74] Quite aside from these significant general considerations, recent artistic events press us to evaluate the book, especially the first three chapters, from a perspective quite unknown to Dewey. In a word, his sections on the "live creature," "etherial things" and "having an experience" are profound philosophical delineations of the art of the last decade. Dewey's views provide a point of departure for a contemporary aesthetic, rooted in the very fabric of the human condition and capable of transforming our cultural attitudes. Taking James's sense for relations and his processive anthropology, Dewey deals with the interaction of man with his environment. He goes beyond James, by virtue of his insight into the sociological dimension of all inquiry, his ever present sensitivity to the struggle for values and his acute awareness of man's effort and need to control his social environment. It is not excessive to say that Dewey has initiated an inquiry into experiences of which the contemporary art of the ordinary, collage, assemblage, found-objects, mixed media, environmental sculptures, ready-mades, junk-art, pop art, kinetic art, and happenings are intensifications and symbolizations. His view of the aesthetic situation as a phenomenology of the live creature, rhythmically tied to his environment, was anticipatory of today's artistic structurings of such interactions. And, in line with the contention of the present essay, Dewey's book offers sustenance for our belief in the viability of the American philosophy of experience, for purposes of enlightened analysis of the contemporary cultural situation.

44

At the very outset of his book, Dewey tells us that our "task" is to "restore continuity between the refined and intensified forms of experience that are works of art and everyday events, doings and sufferings that are universally recognized to constitute experience."[75] Given the full implication of Dewey's subsequent analysis, the term "restore" is to be read as "build," that is, to achieve relational continuity between the intrinsic rhythms of the human self as a live creature and the attempts to structure enhanced versions of his environment. Two obstacles prevent successful rendering of this continuity. First, our approach to art has been dominated by theoretical statements of its meaning and, more serious, has failed to maintain the relationship between aesthetic refinement and experiential bedding from which such art proceeds.

> *Theories* which isolate art and its appreciation by placing them in a realm of their own, disconnected from other modes of experiencing, are not inherent in the subject-matter but arise because of specifiable extraneous conditions. [This approach] deeply affects the practice of living, driving away esthetic perceptions that are necessary ingredients of happiness, or reducing them to the level of compensating transient pleasurable excitations.[76]

Aesthetic enhancements are too often things apart, and when sought out, are approached for reasons extraneous to the very mode of experiencing which generated them in the first place. The second obstacle then becomes clear, for having systematically separated aesthetic delight from reflective awareness, we become correspondingly anaesthetized to the aesthetic qualities inherent in the live creature. The establishing of continuities between the life of the person and artistic creation cannot take place by the acknowledgment of this art as "great," but only by the intensification and qualitative reconstruction of patterns of feeling already deeply felt.

> Theory can start with and from acknowledged works of art only when the esthetic is already compartmentalized, or only when works of art are set in a niche apart instead of being celebrations, recognized as such, of the things of ordi-

nary experience. Even a crude experience, if authentically an experience, is more fit to give a clue to the intrinsic nature of esthetic experience than is an object already set apart from any other mode of experience.[77]

Dewey then devotes an entire chapter to an examination of the rhythms of ordinary experience. He speaks of the "humdrum," "slackness," "dissipation," and "rigidity" as factors in preventing the integration of personal anticipations[78] and affections with the larger patterns of the human situation.[79] In this aesthetic ecology, Dewey stresses the need to be continuous with animal life and to have one's senses on the *qui vive*.[80] All should be turned to living tissue; suffering and celebration become related aspects of maturation. "The live creature adopts its past; it can make friends with even its stupidities, using them as warnings that increase present wariness."[81] He repeats, in a number of different ways, the significance of having sensitivity to relations. Order is a becoming, a transactional relationship between "doing" and "undergoing." Consistent with our viewpoint on modern art, Dewey insists that "order is not imposed from without but is made out of the relations of harmonious interactions that energies bear to one another."[82] Said another way, form in modern art is the theme of continuity which wends its way through the creation of the work of art, acting not as a constant element but as a living function, holding in tension that narrow otherness of vision and technique. Entering into this process, the live creature must do more than witness. "For to perceive, a beholder must *create* his own experience."[83] And, finally, the person must create the continuities between the rhythm of his own life lived and the experienced participation with those refinements and enhancements present in the world of art.

The recent explosion of that art generally referred to as "art of the ordinary," is created out of the very texture of the continuities sought by Dewey. It takes seriously his claim that "art is thus prefigured in the very processes of living."[84] As early as the Futurist Manifesto of 1912, Boccioni tells us that we can use "furry spherical forms for hair, semicircles of glass for a vase, wire and screen for an atmospheric plane" and in our artistic work over-all, we can

46

incorporate "glass, wood, cardboard, iron, cement, horsehair, leather, cloth, mirrors, electric light, and so on."[85]

Taking assemblage as a cardinal instance of art of the ordinary,[86] we isolate two attitudes, each of which have importance for a contemporary aesthetic. First, any material, found or constructed, can be aesthetically meaningful. What is most important, and here the plastic arts have broken far more ground than other art forms, is the willingness to abandon a hierarchy of material, of composition, and to deny the delineation of acceptable aesthetic forms. The most dramatic instance of this is to be found in the "Watts Towers" of Simon Rodia.[87] Built singlehandedly and under construction for thirty-two years, Rodia abandoned the "Towers" as forever unfinished. They are found in his yard, hard by a railroad siding, in the now well-known depressed area of Watts, Los Angeles. Soaring some one hundred feet high, they are built of steel webbing, concrete, broken dishes, cups, 7up bottles, tiles, and scrap of every kind. Enclosed by a high wall, they are multicolored and shaped as rising spirals or simulations of crowns and grottoes. Crossing and recrossing the lines of sculpture, architecture, and industrial design, they threaten always to be sentimental or grotesque. But they are not. As assemblage, they press upon us a renewed experience of the regenerative powers of the human hands,[88] and bring to the surface how deeply affectionate we are toward our entire setting and all that touches us as human. It would be good to admit to this natively aesthetic quality in our ordinary experience.

A second attitude emerging from the art of the ordinary is the narrowing of the gap between nostalgia and immediacy. Following the criteria of Marshall McLuhan, we render environments aesthetic when they are no longer experienced. Thus, romantic poetry is written in the machine age.[89] Our age is one in which the gap between differently experienced environments has shrunk almost to an imperceptible level. The metaphor of our times is "instantaneity;" the transistor replaces the wire. One experience is "had" differently, at different times and for different purposes. Aspects of our present environment have many aesthetic qualities, heretofore unacknowledged. If we widen the scope of the meaning of aesthetic quality, immediate experience yields new riches. Junk art, found objects and ready-mades, all aspects of our immediate experience, are offered to us for purposes of aesthetic participation. Lawrence Alloway draws the following implications from these activities.

> Junk culture is city art. Its source is obsolescence, the throw away material of cities, as it collects in drawers, cupboards, attics, dustbins, gutters, waste lots and city dumps. Objects have a history: first they are brand new goods; then they are possessions accessible to few, subjected often to intimate and repeated use; then as waste they are scarred by use but available again. . . . Assemblages of such material come at the spectator as bits of life, bits of environment. The urban environment is present then, as the source of objects, whether transfigured or left alone.[90]

This art tends to draw us in from the side of creation rather than observation. The artist, himself, makes of us a more intimate aspect of his art. "By actively participating in the aesthetic transaction the spectator becomes himself a part of the artist's total material."[91] Correspondingly, the extraordinary range of what is offered as aesthetic and the variant number of ways in which this can take place, encourages all of us to render aesthetically our immediate environment. Collage alone has revolutionized the experience of art for young children. Liberated from dealing with formal design perspective and encouraged to utilize all materials, especially those at hand, the child can now forge experienced continuity between what he feels deeply and what he creates as artifact. The end of the Euclidean values of proportion, symmetry, and total accountability has opened the way for each of us to work at a new kind of structuring; one that is continuous with our experience rather than irrelevant to it or even a violation of our actual sensibilities.

The decisive insight of contemporary art is that it does not claim hold of an eccentric, albeit exciting, aspect of human life but, rather, creates out of a sense of the most properly human dimensions. Its credo is, in effect, that to be human is to humanize. The art process is the human process brought to a specific angle of vision, with a claim about man's activity which throws light on the

48

entire range of human affairs. We stand then with Dewey who, in a paraphase of Keats, held that the truly etherial things are made by man.[92]

V. A PSYCHEDELIC/CYBERNETIC AESTHETIC

We have stressed the lag between philosophical articulation and the activities of the contemporary art scene. Even if we were able to generate some energy devoted to closing this gap, we may still find ourselves badly dated. For as we write, two movements of great vitality appear upon the cultural scene. Each has an unusual potentiality for reworking the human situation: the effort to expand human awareness psychedelically[93] and the attempt to extend the human perimeter by means of electronic technology. Both of these revolutions are continuous with the concerns stated above and both share, with modern art, the critique of man's confinement within the geometric or linear view of human experience. Positively these efforts are directed to the massive and crucial problem of how to structure affectivity in a technological society.

The relationship of personal life to the need and experience of community is characterized in our time by a major tension. On the one hand, the scope of our experience has been broadened in a shattering way. Paradoxically this has also increased the intensity of our experiences. "As electrically contracted, the globe is no more than a village. Electric speed in bringing all social and political functions together in a sudden implosion has heightened human awareness of responsibility to an intense degree."[94] Politics enjoins astral physics. We domesticate the heavens and cut distances in a savage onslaught on the limitations of time and space. From another side and at the same time we have an equally profound effort to probe the inner man, from both a behavioral and speculative point of view. Perhaps we can say that the poles of contemporary experience are nothing less than the astral and the nuclear.[95]

For some, in order to develop a sense of community in our present environment, it is necessary to shift the focus of concern from the biological and even the sociological to the activities of cybernetic technology, as a resource for metaphors used to articulate the human endeavor. In a quite different direction, we find those thinkers who hold that we should reconstitute human experience and thereby human feelings and language by virtue of psychedelic activity. Both of these commitments, whether to have us "tuned in" or "turned on," stress total involvement. Institutions such as the school, the church, and our political bureaucracy have shown themselves largely bankrupt in providing nutrition for the human person. Sensibility, affectivity, and a relevant liturgy of celebration are hard to come by. Still we must admit that the psychedelically inspired "trip out" has major difficulties, since the landscape for such a trip often (though not always) remains painfully introverted. The total resource for the lived experience becomes heightened but correspondingly narrowed. The psychedelic community has exclusivity at its core. On the other hand, the revolution in electronic technology extends the hegemony of man and even, some contend, renders our planet but a probe. Yet, here too, we face divisiveness. Few of us can participate directly in planetary experience and many of us find ourselves hopelessly cut off from a world so distant from common experience, from the use of our hands, and even from the use of our machines.

Modern art has moved steadily in the direction of liberating the human person to enjoy his immediate experience. As Martin Buber says, "all is hallowed" and the ordinary sings a distinctive song of its own. Is the psychedelic-cybernetic revolution continuous with this attitude or is it to be another catastrophic break in our experience? Perhaps we are once again faced with the paradoxical situation wherein the dazzling quality of our insights moves us forward at one level only, but generates a feeling of anomie and loneliness for the larger community. The question confronting us can be asked in simple terms. Given the increased extension of man and his growing hegemony over nature, can he achieve a response, in concert, equal to those startling intensifications of personal experience brought on by psychedelics? In a cybernetic technology can we achieve affectivity and personal sensibility, in all aspects of the human situation on a communitywide basis? If philosophy has a contribution to make, it could urge that the last half of this century

50

JOHN J. McDERMOTT

would do well to view the economic and political questions as, at bottom, aesthetic.

NOTES

1. William James, *Psychology—Briefer Course* (New York: Henry Holt and Co., 1892), p. 165.

2. Although we use the term modern art as a functional canopy for all of the major art activities of our century, in this essay the plastic arts are mainly in focus. The references to contemporary art stand for recent events in the modern art tradition.

3. "Inquiry" as used throughout this discussion refers to man's trans- actional quest. He is informed by the world at every turn, literally through his skin and in his dreams, as well as by virtue of more conventional means. Man also informs the world; again literally by creating the contexts in which his awareness takes place. Rooted in Kant, this tension between man getting and begetting the world, is of irreducible importance in modern art.

4. Ronald Barthes, "The Structuralist Activity," *Partisan Review* (Winter, 1967), p. 84.

5. Has any major cultural prognostication turned out to be so wide of the mark as the judgment of Ortega y Gasset on the viability of the new art? Cf. *The Dehumanization of Art* (Garden City: Doubleday Anchor Books, 1956), p. 5: "Modern art, on the other hand, will always have the masses against it. It is essentially un- popular; moreover, it is antipopular."

6. Gillo Dorfles, "The Man-Made Object," *The Man-Made Object,* ed. Gyorgy Kepes (New York: George Braziller, 1966), p. 2.

7. The driftwood sculpture of Louise Nevelson is a notable contem- porary effort to create "environments" or, better, "worlds," out of apparently relationless materials. In an interview in the New York Times, April 28, 1967, she said: "I am asking for an environment to suit me. Look darling, there is no world. We objectify the world in form. That is the world." The combine-paintings of Robert Rauschenberg and the mixed media of Edward Keinholz are other imaginative examples of the limitless array of new human con- structs.

51

8. Marshall McLuhan, *Understanding Media—The Extensions of Man* (New York: McGraw-Hill Book Company, 1964), pp. 7-21. The same point is made from the side of a theory of criticism as found in Barthes, *op. cit.*, pp. 82-88.

9. An interesting comment on the machine, that is, a typewriter, as a shift in poetic media is found in an analysis of the poetry of Charles Olson by M. L. Rosenthal, *The New Poets* (New York: Oxford University Press, 1967), p. 146.

10. There are exceptions to this charge, although rarely found within the context of philosophy itself. One effort to construct a modern aesthetic is reaching its zenith with the publication of the first volume in Susanne Langer's *Mind: An Essay on Human Feeling* (Baltimore: Johns Hopkins Press, 1967).

11. An outstanding example of this problem is found in the six-volume study edited by Gyorgy Kepes under the general title of *Vision and Value* (New York: George Braziller, 1965-66). With multi-contributors to each volume ranging over the cultural and aesthetic problems which challenge us, philosophical perspective can be garnered only indirectly. The issues in question, however, have philosophical significance at almost every turn.

12. Cf. Allen S. Weller, "Art: U.S.A.: Now," *Art: U.S.A.: Now* ed. by Lee Nordness (New York: Viking Press, 1962), pp. 249-52, for a commentary on the increased importance of the reflective statement by the contemporary artist.

13. Herbert Read, "Realism and Abstraction in Modern Art," *The Philosophy of Modern Art* (New York: Meridian Books, 1957), p. 99. Cf. also Herbert Read, "The Limitations of a Scientific Philosophy," *The Forms of Things Unknown* (New York: Meridian Books, 1963), pp. 15-32.

14. Cf. Dore Ashton, "From Achilles Shield to Junk," in Kepes, *The Man-Made Object,* p. 194. In speaking of the Dadaists, he comments that "when they incorporated shreds of daily life in their work they did so with a dual and often equivocal purpose—both to deride and explore."

15. Thomas B. Hess, *Willem de Kooning* (New York: George Braziller, 1959), pp. 15-16.

16. For a significant comparison, cf. "Innovation in Science," *Scientific American*, Vol. 199, No. 3 (September, 1958), *passim.*

JOHN J. McDERMOTT

17. An illustration of our meaning of "field" is found in the analysis of "field composition" by Charles Olson in his essay on "Projective Verse," *The New American Poetry, 1945-1960,* ed. Donald M. Allen (New York: Grove Press, 1960), pp. 386-97.

18. An important but separate endeavor would take on the interrelated origins of the artistic event. Sociological, historical, and psycho-analytical matrices of interpretation, no one of them wholly reductionistic, are themselves irreducible conditioners of the aesthetic quality in each of our experiences. For a preliminary statement, cf. Arnold Hauser, *The Philosophy of Art History* (New York: Alfred A. Knopf, 1958), pp. 21-116.

19. Hess, *op. cit.,* p. 15.

20. Herbert Read, "The Modern Epoch in Art," *The Philosophy of Modern Art,* p. 29.

21. William James, "Notebook," cited in Ralph Barton Perry, *The Thought and Character of William James,* Vol. II (Boston: Little, Brown and Co., 1935), p. 700.

22. Perry, *op. cit.,* Vol. I, pp. 108-9.

23. Jacques Barzun, "William James and the Clue to Art" (New York: Harper & Row, 1956), p. 325.

24. William James, "The Stream of Thought," *The Writings of William James—A Comprehensive Edition,* ed. with an "Introduction" and "Annotated Bibliography" by John J. McDermott (New York: Random House, 1967), p. 45. Referred to hereafter as *Writings*.

25. James, *Psychology—Briefer Course,* p. 165.

26. William James, "A World of Pure Experience," *Writings,* p. 207. Cf. also "Pragmatism and Common Sense," *Writings,* p. 442: "Everything that happens to us brings its own duration and extension, and both are vaguely surrounded by a marginal 'more' that runs into the duration and extension of the next thing that comes."

27. Only by an acknowledgment of man's dwelling on the fringe can we understand the risk-oriented, strenuous ethic of James as well as his much maligned doctrine of "the will to believe."

28. William C. Seitz, *Claude Monet—Seasons and Moments* (New York: The Museum of Modern Art, 1960), p. 24.

29. William James, "The Stream of Thought," *Writings,* p. 46.

30. Wassily Kandinsky, "Reminiscences" (1913), in Robert L. Herbert, *Modern Artists on Art* (Englewood Cliffs: Prentice-Hall, 1964), p. 26.

31. We draw here from the tradition of American social psychology, especially the work of Charles Horton Cooley, George Herbert Mead, and Gardner Murphy. See, e.g., Murphy, "The Human Natures of the Future," *Human Potentialities* (New York: Basic Books, 1958), pp. 302-29.

32. Robert Goldwater and Marco Treves, eds., *Artists on Art* (New York: Pantheon Books, 1947), p. 451. Cf. also, Weller, *op. cit.,* p. 12: "In a sense, the physical facts of nature become less and less important to us in themselves; we have gone beyond a stage in which recognition and identification of material forms is of primary significance. It is the tension between forms, the effects of movements on shapes and qualities, the active spaces which surround solid masses, which seem to be the most tangible things with which many artists need to work. There are of course striking parallels to the social and economic situation of our times. The great problems of our period are not material ones; they are problems of basic relationships."

33. The contemporaneity of James's questions and attitudes becomes obvious to the reader of the recent biography by Gay Wilson Allen, *William James* (New York: Viking Press, 1967).

34. Cited in William Seitz, *Hans Hofmann* (New York: The Museum of Modern Art, 1963), p. 50.

35. The historical and philosophical factors in the development of James's radical empiricism are extensively presented by Perry, *The Thought and Character of William James,* Vol. II, *passim.* The relevant texts are found in *Writings,* especially pp. 134-317.

36. James, *Writings,* p. 314. This mature view is consistent with James's essay of 1884, "On Some Omissions of Introspective Psychology" (*Mind,* 9, pp. 1-26), which became the basis for his chapter in the *Principles of Psychology* entitled "The Stream of Thought." Further, this position maintains the fundamental viewpoint of "The Function of Cognition" (*Writings,* pp. 136-52), written in 1885, and rephrased throughout James's writings, particularly in the group of essays published in 1904 and 1905 under the generic theme of radical empiricism. Of significance for our subsequent remarks in Section IV, these essays of James play a decisive role in the maturation of John Dewey's metaphysics. Cf.

John Dewey, "Experience, Knowledge and Value—A Rejoinder," *The Philosophy of John Dewey,* ed. by Paul Arthur Schilpp (New York: Tudor Publishing Co., 1951), p. 533, n. 16: "Long ago I learned from William James that there are immediate experiences of the connections linguistically expressed by conjunctions and propositions. My doctrinal position is but a generalization of what is involved in this fact."

37. James, "The Stream of Thought," *Writings,* p. 38.

38. *Ibid.*

39. *Ibid.*

40. *Ibid.*

41. James, "A World of Pure Experience," *Writings,* p. 198.

42. *Ibid.,* p. 201.

43. *Ibid.,* pp. 212-13. Cf. John Dewey, "The Experimental Theory of Knowledge," *The Influence of Darwin on Philosophy* (1910), (New York: Peter Smith, 1951), p. 90: "An experience is a knowledge, if in its quale there is an experienced distinction and connection of two elements of the following sort: *one means or intends the presence of the other in the same fashion in which itself is already present, while the other is that which, while not present in the same fashion, must become so present if the meaning or intention of its companion or yoke-fellow is to be fulfilled through the operation it sets up."* A later statement on relational continuities, notably in the realm of aesthetics, is found in Christopher Alexander, "From a Set of Forces to a Form," in Kepes, *The Man-Made Object,* pp. 96-107.

44. Cf. Daniel Abramson, in Nordness, *Art: U.S.A.: Now,* p. 134. "De Kooning's painting is never a situation but rather, an entire event."

45. The problem of reductionism in aesthetic interpretation deserves far more analysis than it has received. For strong statements, cf. Norman Brown, "Art and Neurosis," *Life Against Death* (New York: Random House, 1959) pp. 55-67; Erich Neumann, *Art and the Creative Unconscious* (New York: Harper & Row, 1966); and Arnold Hauser, *op. cit.,* pp. 43-116.

46. Cf. Robert Goldwater, *Primitivism on Modern Art* (rev. ed.; New York: Vintage Books, 1967), p. 98. Without objects, we have "implications far beyond the canvas itself." He cites a remark of

55

Georges Duthuit that "the painter remains in intimate contact not alone with a motif, but also with the infinite nebulousness. . . ." Goldwater then states that "Emotionally as well as in its formal structure, the picture becomes a symbol whose very generality increases its possible meaning." We can crystallize this in Jamesian terms by holding that the lines of meaning stretch out beyond the finished work and are picked up by any number of responses, be they primitive rejoinders to sheer color and shape, aesthetic in the formal sense, or historical and sociological evaluations. Each work of art has a future as well as a past, in that it extends and proliferates its connections out beyond the field in which it was brought to fruition.

47. Cf. for example, Herbert, *op. cit.;* Hans Hofmann, *The Search for the Real and Other Essays,* ed. by Sara T. Weeks and Bartlett H. Hayes, Jr. (Cambridge: The M.I.T. Press, 1967); and Hans Hofmann, "The Color Problem in Pure Painting—Its Creative Origin," in Frederick Wight, *Hans Hofmann* (Berkeley: University of California Press, 1957).

48. Seitz, *Hans Hofmann,* p. 50.

49. *Ibid.*

50. *Ibid.*

51. Cf. André Hodeir, "On Group Relations," *Toward Jazz* (New York: Grove Press, 1962), pp. 73-93.

52. John Dewey, in Schilpp, *op. cit.,* pp. 532-33.

53. Barthes, *loc. cit.*

54. The reigning confusion involved in our notions of creativity, innovation, and discovery is given incisive analysis from the side of a philosophy of science, by Norwood Russell Hanson, "The Anatomy of Discovery," *Journal of Philosophy,* Vol. LXIV, (June 3, 1967), No. 11, pp. 321-52. An interdisciplinary approach to discovery and innovation, especially with regard to the problem of form, is found in Lancelot Law Whyte, ed., *Aspects of Form* (Bloomington: Indiana University Press, 1961).

55. Guillaume Apollinaire, *The Cubist Painters* (New York: George Wittenborn, 1962), pp. 14-15.

56. Naum Gabo, cited in Herbert Read, "Realism and Abstraction in Modern Art," *The Philosophy of Modern Art,* p. 97.

57. Herbert Read, "Human Art and Inhuman Nature," *The Philosophy of Modern Art,* p. 76.

58. Cf. André Malraux, cited in *The Modern Tradition,* ed. by Richard Ellmann and Charles Feidelson, Jr. (New York: Oxford University Press, 1965), p. 517: "I name that man an artist who *creates* forms, be he an ambassador like Rubens, an image-maker like Gislebert of Autun, an *ignotus* like the Master of Chartres, an illuminator like Limbourg, a king's friend and court official like Velazquez, a *rentier* like Cezanne, a man possessed like Van Gogh or a vagabond like Gauguin; and I call that man an artisan who *reproduces* forms, however great may be the charm or sophistication of his craftsmanship."

59. Gardner Murphy, "The Enigma of Human Nature," *Main Currents* (September, 1956), no pagination.

60. James, "Personal Depression and Recovery," *Writings,* p. 8.

61. James, "The Sentiment of Rationality," *Writings,* p. 331.

62. Gordon Allport, *Becoming* (New Haven: Yale University Press, 1955), p. 51.

63. James, "The Stream of Thought," *Writings,* p. 71.

64. *Ibid.,* p. 70. Texts like this abound in the *Principles.* Cf. McDermott, "Introduction," *Writings,* XXXI-XXXV. James makes a specific reference to the artistic activity as "notoriously" selective and, therefore, having "superiority over works of nature" (*Writings,* p. 72). Compare these texts to that of the American painter, Robert Motherwell, in William C. Seitz, *The Art of Assemblage* (New York: The Museum of Modern Art, 1961), p. 97: "One cuts and chooses and shifts and pastes, and sometimes tears off and begins again. In any case, shaping and arranging such a relational structure obliterates the need, and often the awareness of representation. Without reference to likeness, it possesses feeling because all the decisions in regard to it are ultimately made on the grounds of feeling."

65. James, "Pragmatism and Humanism," *Writings,* p. 456. And with Lawrence Durrell, "Does not everything depend on our interpretation of the silence around us?" Cf. *Justine* (New York: Pocket Books, 1961), p. 250.

66. James, "A World of Pure Experience," *Writings,* p. 212.

67. James, "How Two Minds Can Know One Thing," *Writings*, pp. 227-32.

68. Cf. William James, *A Pluralistic Universe* (New York: Longmans, Green and Co., 1909); or *Writings*, pp. 277-304, 482-581.

69. James, "Pragmatism's Conception of Truth," *Writings*, p. 432.

70. James, "A World of Pure Experience," *Writings*, p. 212.

71. James, "Pragmatism's Conception of Truth," *Writings*, p. 432.

72. John Dewey, *Art as Experience* (New York: Capricorn Books, 1958), p. 11.

73. In addition to material in Schilpp, *op. cit.*, a recent statement of Dewey's aesthetics is found in Monroe Beardsley, *Aesthetics— From Classical Greece to the Present* (New York: The Macmillan Co., 1966), pp. 332-42. For a relevant collection of Dewey texts, cf. Richard J. Bernstein, *Experience, Nature and Freedom* (New York: Liberal Arts Press, 1960). Creative reinterpretations of Dewey's thought are found in Robert C. Pollock, "Process and Experience," *John Dewey, His Thought and Influence*, ed. by John Blewett (New York: Fordham University Press, 1960) and John Herman Randall, *Nature and Historical Experience* (New York: Columbia University Press, 1958).

74. For the scattered work on Dewey's aesthetics, cf. references in Beardsley, *op. cit.*, pp. 391-92.

75. Dewey, *Art as Experience*, p. 1.

76. *Ibid.*, p. 10.

77. *Ibid.*, p. 11.

78. Speaking of anticipation of what is to come, Dewey gives depth of meaning to James's contention that "life is in the transitions." Cf. *ibid.*, p. 50: "This anticipation is the connecting link between the next doing and its outcome for sense. What is done and what is undergone are thus reciprocally, cumulatively, and continuously instrumental to each other."

79. Dewey, *Art as Experience*, p. 40.

80. *Ibid.*, p. 19.

81. *Ibid.*, p. 18.

82. *Ibid.*, p. 14.

83. *Ibid.*, p. 54.

84. *Ibid.*, p. 24.

85. Seitz, *The Art of Assemblage,* p. 25.

86. We acknowledge the complexity of the contemporary art scene. From the side of the artist, for example, differences between assemblage and pop art are considerable. In addition to Seitz, *The Art of Assemblage,* one can find these distinctions in Lucy R. Lippard, *et al., Pop Art* (New York: Frederick A. Praeger, 1966) and Gregory Battcock, *The New Art* (New York: E. P. Dutton, 1966).

87. It is extraordinary and depressing that the pathos of the "Watts Towers," relative to our time, has not, to my knowledge, been discussed. The "Towers" were constructed by Simon Rodia, an Italian immigrant and tilesetter, as a monument to opportunity for the disfranchised. Just recently, they looked down upon a new group of deprived, who at the time were destroying Watts as a monument to the hopelessness of their plight. The setting was the same, but some continuities are not as fruitful as others.

88. Cf. Henri Focillon, "In Praise of Hands," *The Life of Forms in Art* (New York: George Wittenborn, 1948), pp. 65-78.

89. Cf. Marshall McLuhan, "Address at Vision 65," *The American Scholar,* Vol. 35 (Spring, 1966), pp. 196-205.

90. Seitz, *The Art of Assemblage,* p. 73.

91. Weller, *op. cit.,* p. 462.

92. Cf. Dewey, "The Live Creature and 'Etherial Things,' " *Art as Experience,* pp. 20-34.

93. Cf. R. E. L. Masters and Jean Houston, *The Varieties of Psychedelic Experience* (New York: Holt, Rinehart and Winston, 1966).

94. McLuhan, *Understanding Media,* p. 5.

95. Cf. R. Buckminster Fuller, "Conceptuality of Fundamental Structures," *Structure in Art and Science,* ed. by Gyorgy Kepes (New York: George Braziller, 1965), pp. 66-88.

59

2

DREAM AND NIGHTMARE:

The Future as Revolution

BY ROBERT C. POLLOCK

For years Robert C. Pollock, then at Fordham University, was a major influence upon a number of younger philosophers because of his lively responsiveness to the American experience and the American philosophical tradition. In this essay, intended to be familiar and introductory, Professor Pollock describes some elements in the life of the American people which have most tantalized and stimulated our philosophers. To be sure, the words "spirituality" and "inner life" came to have a hollow ring in America. The traditional models for such matters, Professor Pollock points out, were European and came to be perceived in America as artificial, irrelevant, and even harmful. Yet the explicit resistance to such words in American theorizing has served to mask the quite different but moving and powerful inner life of Americans. For want of an explicit theory, such matters have often been left unsaid—with the result that many in the present generation, desiring interiority, turn away from pragmatism and look to existentialism or (increasingly) to Buddhism. Professor Pollock asks us to examine our identity as Americans.

We are coming to see that philosophy cannot profitably be studied apart from the socio-cultural history of a people. Happily, so far as America is concerned, such a separation does not come easily, since philosophy in this country is obviously woven into the life-processes of a new world in the making. Accordingly, it is of prime

60

importance to seek out those forces which have formed the American world, and which in turn have been liberated within it. Otherwise we shall be condemned to an aimless wandering in a limbo outside the living stream of events, powerless to shape the future.

In viewing American history we cannot fail to observe the stresses and strains, the tensions and conflicts that mark its course. No nation, it is true, is free of them. Indeed, it would hardly be alive if it were. In this country, conflicts are of a most crucial sort; so much so, in fact, that we may speak of two distinct and antagonistic trends, discernible not only in our society taken as a whole but perhaps in the soul of everyone of us. Henry James observed, "It is a complex fate to be an American."

I. THE DREAM

There is present, on the one hand, a life orientation, not easily described and generally expressed in the term "the American Dream." But there is also present in American life an equally durable state of affairs which can well be designated as "the American Nightmare," which down through the years has evoked in sensitive minds a feeling of profound disenchantment and moral outrage. For while "the American Dream" has motivated countless individuals to transform what was once a wilderness into a new and higher civilization, "the American Nightmare" appears to constitute a quite different process, that of turning something great and wonderful into a moral and cultural wasteland.

In *The Power of Blackness,* Harry Levin raises the question of what constitutes the true America. Gathering together what he says in diverse places in his volume, we find him singling out what he calls "the obvious American thesis, the cheerful trend of a practical and prosperous culture," materialistic in orientation. But against this he offers, as broad assumption, "the symbolic character of our greatest fiction and the dark wisdom of our deeper minds." Together these two constitute an antithesis, "since they act in opposition to more publicized influences, blandly materialistic." In short, we are presented here with a striking study in contrasts, for besides

61

those features of American culture which have become fixations in the minds of critics, there is a current of life which tells a far different story. Levin describes this current as composed of "visionaries rather than materialists, symbolists rather than realists." Moreover, "the vision they impart is not rose-colored but somber, and the symbols through which they impart it are charged with significations that profoundly justify the most searching analysis."[1]

"Which is the true voice of America?" Levin asks. "Tolstoy's opinion," he continues, "may pertinently be cited in this regard. In a letter to an American correspondent he speaks of Emerson, Thoreau, Whitman, and others among our compatriots who have inspired him. Why, he asks, do we Americans pay so little heed to our poets and moralists, and so much to our millionaires and generals?"[2]

While Levin's presentation admirably highlights contrasting directions of American life, it should, I believe, be placed in a far wider framework, one in which thesis and antithesis stand in closer conformity to the complexity and originality of our country. As a cover-all term, "materialism" obscures something highly original in America, namely, the extreme reluctance of Americans to function in a dichotomized fashion. From the beginning, hard exigencies of living have fostered a sense of the organic interconnectedness of things, thereby making it impossible to set God and everyday experiences apart from each other or to tolerate an irreducible dualism of spirit and matter. Against such a background of feeling, it came easy for Americans to accept the physical fact as having an organic place in the scheme of things, and even to grant it a certain primacy with regard to the totality of human development.

Both our literary and philosophical traditions give ample evidence of this profound feeling for the organic structure of existence. With regard to the literary tradition, the very persistence of symbolic consciousness is an impressive indication of an attitude far removed from dualism. As for philosophy, from its early formative stage through to the pragmatist movement there is an unmistakable trend toward a clearer grasp of the nondualistic character of experience.

John Dewey, who had himself in his early years suffered "a

painful oppression," "an inward laceration," brought on by the "sense of divisions and separations," found it necessary to raise his voice against European critics who viewed the American preoccupation with matter as "fatal to any culture." As Dewey saw it, their misgivings stemmed precisely from their failure to see the absolute relevance of matter to the development of ideas and art. With equal cogency he could have shown that the recognition of the primacy of the material fact was intrinsically associated with the rejection of a dichotomized world, and that an integral attitude, so far from favoring a decline in interior life, was, rather, a new stage in its expansion.

Nothing, of course, could be more painfully obvious than the rankly materialistic orientation within American life. But this is not to say that the opposite orientation consists in a turning away from matter in the quest for the "spiritual." Fortunately, in America, the true opposite of crass materialism was seen to lie, rather, in a deeper and more human relation to matter. Whatever the orientation, then, a certain preoccupation with material things is for us the universal fact. Accordingly, the difference of standpoints has its ultimate basis in radically diverse ways of relating to physical realities and the whole of material nature. Hence, the contrast has never been between a this-worldly and an otherworldly direction of life, but between, on the one hand, a vast concern with material success and creaturely comforts and, on the other, a vision of things which finds expression in deeply humanistic and symbolic terms.

Already in the early stages of our history we have in Jonathan Edwards an outstanding example of the superior way of relating to matter—at once humanistic, symbolic, and mystical. Edwards is a man of the frontier, eminently practical, who is moreover blessed with a scientific turn of mind and who shows himself incapable of dealing with the world save on the basis of an organic interrelatedness. Again, there is in Edwards a profound sense of the need for a total confrontation with things, in which a "sense of the heart" is the dominant motif. Integrally related to the world, Edwards finds himself immersed in a wholeness of experience which defies artificial demarcations. Of him, therefore, can be said what has been said of his Puritan forebears: "physical life was simultaneously spiritual,"³ since there exists no line of division between material reality and God, nor between the inward life of the spirit and the whole outer world.

Emerson likewise views material nature as deeply interior to spirit and as radically conditioning immense and awesome experiences. As for William James and John Dewey, both were entirely at home in experiential categories and could resist the dichotomizations that so abundantly flourish out of abstract "ontological" thinking. Accordingly they could clearly perceive that, in the living, complex unity of experience, nature is no merely "external" fact, nor is man himself a mere bystander on the outskirts of the universal process.

Unquestionably, in the crucial matter of man's attitude toward the physical fact, ambivalence reigns supreme in American life, and it is within this framework of ambivalence that we must sort out the dominant trends that activate our culture. Meanwhile, it becomes clear that the stereotypical appraisals of America as a business civilization, a merely technological paradise, a consumer-driven society miss the essential drama of the American world. So too does the view proffered by Bertrand Russell when he declares: "The Power that humbled Job out of the whirlwind no longer finds an echo in American mentality."⁴

Here in all justice it must be said that even the intensive drive toward material gain and the cult of the "bitch-goddess success" have played an enormously positive role in the building of America. Nonetheless, they have set up a pattern of tendencies which stand in violent contrast to the other America, an America which, while fully accepting the world around it and delighting in it, has at the same time expanded human subjectivity itself in arriving at a keener appreciation of its inherence in the world scheme and of its complexity and dynamics.

Henry Adams describes the contrasting orientations as they made themselves manifest in the early stages of our history. Thus he points out how the Puritans aimed at creating a government of saints and the Quakers a government of love and peace. But Adams also shows how the colonization of 1800 exhibits a far different character. "From Lake Erie to Florida," he writes, "in a long unbroken line, pioneers were at work, cutting into the forests with the energy of so many beavers, and with no more express moral purpose than the beavers they drove away."[5] Still, as a profoundly interior fact, the ideality that motivated the Pilgrims of Plymouth, the Puritans of Massachusetts Bay Colony, and the Quakers of Pennsylvania has remained a powerful factor in American life. And what is so particularly revealing is that immersion in a vast creative enterprise and in the events of a real world gave new inward depth to the beliefs of those colonists and those who stemmed from them.

The Shaker communities constitute a case in point. For in them we can see how a remarkably intensive manifestation of the religious spirit easily aligned itself with the deeper exigencies of American life. Indeed, as Constance Rourke writes, they "reflected major movements within the country. . . . Sometimes in major preoccupations they seemed an advance guard."[6] This response to the American experience already found expression in the Shaker assertion that Mother Ann Lee (leader of the original band that came from England in 1774) had flown "into the wilderness of America on the wings of Liberty and Independence,"[7] and when they pictured George Washington as God's servant:

Who with wisdom was endow'd
By an angel, through the cloud,
And led forth, in wisdom's plan,
To secure the rights of man.[8]

The all-important fact is that in America ideality exploded into a mighty historical force, producing an eruption of the human spirit whose repercussions were felt in the world at large. Ideals that in Europe had been rigorously inhibited or locked away in idle dreams were now set loose as an irresistible onrushing force. A virgin continent became a powerful inducement to turn dreams into flesh-and-blood realities. Ideas, likewise, assumed a new status, in becoming linked to a preferred form of life, and in establishing themselves as the source of overflowing energies.

Even the human imagination underwent a far-reaching change with respect to the outer world, inasmuch as men now felt impelled to picture themselves within an unfolding historical drama of divine import. We already see this process taking place among the Puritans. "Under the aspect of the Holy Commonwealth, the crude huts and muddly streets were transmogrified into a focal symbol of God's emerging idea. . . ."⁹

Ideality as a historical force was very much present in the numerous communitarian experiments from the seventeenth century well into the nineteenth. Frederick Jackson Turner in *The Frontier in American History* also offers impressive evidence of the persistence of ideality as a force, in showing how one or another western state was the Mecca of social reformers, seeking to put into practice their ideals. "In spite of his rude, gross nature," he writes, "this early Western man was an idealist withal. He dreamed dreams and beheld visions."¹⁰

It is this linkage of ideality to historical activity which has given our culture a distinctly moral tone and direction. This moral aspect has been too obvious an ingredient of American life to escape the attention of observers. Henry James, for one, was well aware of it, having observed moral consciousness in our nation as "something distinctive and homogeneous," and as an "unprecedented spiritual lightness and vigour." It is also this very need to assign a moral value to all that one thinks and does that has led Americans to justify all their acts, even those that are questionable, on moral grounds and to raise the banner of a crusade against evil.

II. THE NIGHTMARE

What a sharp contrast of trends forms the substance of our national life! On one side, we find a volcanic explosion of moral force in the service of dreams, an explosive force that finds its source in the linkage of a spiritual inwardness with historical creativity and, on the other side, the perennial presence of unlovely elements, among them an obsession with material success and a misdirected moralism with all its neurotic and quasi-psychotic manifestations.

66

"The American Nightmare," as we can see, is much broader in scope than the term "materialism" would indicate, and it may be well at this point to become a little more specific. Thus, along with an almost total preoccupation with creaturely well-being and the symbols of material success, there is the characteristic Know-nothingism which cuts a broad swathe throughout our history. Add to this a chauvinism of a distinctly tribal sort, and we have more than enough to lend substance to Emerson's assertion that our country has a bad name for superficialness, because of its "boasters and buffoons."

Along with all this is the tendency to brutal violence, a hangover, no doubt, from frontier times and drawing new strength from the fluid conditions of a great sprawling society in the throes of a convulsive and rapidly accelerating industrial development. To darken the picture still further, America has become a citadel of what Peter Drucker calls "superpower," which in his view is "a threat to everyone alive today, any place,"[11] and which cannot but exert a far-reaching and malign influence upon our lives, whether "superpower" be economic or political.

Yet despite the omnipresence of nightmare, the America of prophets, seers, poets, and philosophers cannot be overlooked. To those, therefore, who are, like many Americans before them, in the grip of disenchantment, we must reaffirm the reality of "the American Dream." Indeed, it could be argued that what is great in our culture forms a deeper stratum of our national life, despite appearances to the contrary. At any rate, it is this America which has kindled in many hearts a desire to give body and substance to "the American Dream" and to make ideality prevail in a life of endless warfare, through which in the Emersonian phrase, the "idea is forced into act." Moreover, the American temper cherishes not just old ideas but ideas emerging within the ongoing processes of life, those referred to by William James as "ideal novelty."

If we take into account the moral forces that have entered into the making of our country, it is not surprising that the philosophy of nonviolence found fertile soil here. In *Nonviolence in America,*[12] we see how America has played more often the role of teacher than student with regard to nonviolence, because of individuals like Penn and Woolman, Garrison and Thoreau, William James and Jane Addams and Martin Luther King, Jr.

Again, there is the America which, in the face of chauvinism with its dreadful tribal incantations, has yet raised itself to exalted heights of universalism. Wyndham Lewis in *America and Cosmic Man* looks to America for the eventual emergence of a new type of man in which universalism will find its embodiment. But he evidently senses the presence of a countertrend, for while he believes that in America "we should expect the nearest approach to an international outlook it is possible to find . . . ,"[13] he nevertheless realizes that most Americans do not look at the matter in this way. He remains optimistic, however, although apparently aware of the strange contradictions that plague American life. Henry James himself reminds us that the spirit of universalism is alive in the American world, when he writes of the American that he is " 'intrinsically and actively ample, . . . reaching westward, southward, anywhere, everywhere,' with a mind 'incapable of the shut door in any direction.' "[14]

III. THE VOICE OF AMERICA?

The burning question is indeed "which is the true voice of America?" Meanwhile, in taking stock of what is great and authentic in our land we shall be assessing, at the same time, the enormous spiritual resources that lie immediately beneath the surface of American life, waiting to be tapped.

The quest for the true voice of America is fraught with difficulties owing to the fact that we make use of categories that are not relevant to our culture. America defies any attempt to comprehend her in terms of a dualism of spirit and matter which found its true habitat in Europe. And the confusions engendered by the failure to comprehend what is truly original in our culture are legion.

The American warfare against dualisms of every sort can best be understood in the light of something already touched upon, namely, the American involvement in experience as a living, growing reality. Here men found themselves actively occupied with the world around them. The sense of growing experience, involving at once the human subject and the surrounding environment, outweighed the tendency to get bogged down in a world of fixed and static things. The impact of the wilderness and the sheer power of physical America, experienced and re-experienced with the shifting frontier, reinforced this sense of things in process. Faced with the primeval wilderness and with gigantic rivers, lakes and plains and great mountain chains, powers that lay deep within the soul were stirred, and all feeling of an uncrossable chasm between the individual and the outer world vanished. Moreover, experience as something shifting and flowing, and forever taking new shapes, came to the foreground as men built more complex patterns of human existence.

This sense of experience as a process became the dominant fact of American life from its earliest stages. Here again, the Shakers are a case in point. For it is significant that they should have so vividly felt the impact of American life as to bring to fruition insights that were implicit in their doctrine. As Constance Rourke notes, "They were indeed acutely conscious of an identity with American principles."[15] And what is particularly noteworthy is their amazing sense of experience as a growing historical reality. For, as Constance Rourke shows, the Shakers recognized no fixed patterns of experience. "Even in eternity Shakers foresaw no absolutes of experience."[16] In their hymns, too, they were mastered by the idea of change and of experience as something concrete and historical. For, as they saw it, their hymns were devised to induce certain experiences, and were to be discarded when their usefulness came to an end.

William James sought to articulate the essential direction of American life toward unflinching loyalty to experience. And he applied his psychological genius and his gift for observation to an analysis of experience which closed the door on every species of dualism. In his doctrine of pure experience he made it evident that the separation of subject and object takes place in reflective consciousness and that inward experience is radically conjoined to the experience of all that lies without. James had no intention of denying the distinction between subject and object, but he wanted to

69

show how experience itself has an integral character which resists any radical disjunction of what lies on the side of the subject and what lies on the side of the object. What we have, then, is a fertile relationship between experiences within a constant movement of shifting contexts or "concatenations," in which the subject and the object are equally relevant aspects in a process of development. Dewey also builds on the same doctrine. Thus he writes, "experience is double-barrelled in that it recognizes in its primary integrity no division between act and material, subject and object, but contains them both in an unanalyzed totality."[17]

Such a view of experience offers us a valuable key to the historical process in which the developing world of inner experience is intimately bound up with the developing world of outer experience. Hence we have here a basis upon which to translate all of man's activity—religious, philosophical, scientific, aesthetic, economic, social, etc.—into coherent experiential terms and in a way which would enable us to see how trains of experience run together.

Emerson, before James, sought to describe experience in a nondualistic manner. Charles Feidelson, Jr., deals with this in his *Symbolism and American Literature,* bringing out that for Emerson "Reality was neither mental nor material substance but emerging form, and its locus, if we must give it a place, was the act of perception and the act of speech."[18] How natural, then, it was for Emerson to seek an integral experience, one in which experience of outward things, formed also through the development of the sciences, should be intimately fused with the deepest substratum of what is personal. Or, as one writer puts it, Emerson "expanded the notion of experience so that imagination and religious vision go hand in hand with natural science; they are but dimensions of the same integral, dynamic and growing experience."[19]

Once this doctrine of experience was placed in the context of a world seen as radically processive, we can perceive as James and Dewey did, its revolutionary consequences. We can see, too, why, for these men, the drive to new experience became the all-important matter. The thrust toward knowledge and fulfillment became one with the thirst for a larger vision of things, that is, for new and important disclosures within the historical process itself. "Since all experience," says James, "is a process, no point of view can be the last one."[20] Dewey speaks the same language when he views the enrichment of experience as a "gift of the gods." But Emerson had already given beautiful utterance to the American quest for experience when he said, "No man ever came to an experience which was satiating, but his good is tidings of a better. Onward and onward. In liberated moments we know that a new picture of life and duty is already possible."[21]

Within the context of the American orientation to experience, we can clear up confusions engendered by the American emphasis on action. How often Americans have been characterized as activity-prone, and as being so engrossed in action as to bypass themselves. Judging from this sort of criticism it would seem that a full-fledged concern with action precludes deep interiority of life. Yet, once we look at this emphasis on action from the standpoint of an open-ended experience, the change in perspective offers a drastically different view of the matter. True enough, we are always faced in America with ambivalence. Given the circumstances of American life, an overriding preoccupation with action at the expense of self-reflection was inevitable. John Dewey himself was well aware of the tendency to glorify action for its own sake. But he insisted, and here he was speaking for that other America, that pragmatism is "far from being that glorification of action for its own sake which is regarded as the peculiar characteristic of American life."[22] Nonetheless, he had set out to raise action to a new dignity, in view of the fact that experience cannot grow save in and through real relations established between man and man and between man and his world. In order for experience to expand in all directions, bridges must be built, lines of communication established, and real transactions effected. In the face of such irrefutable realism, action takes on a new importance as the indispensable means by which things are brought into more significant patterns of relationship. In short, Dewey saw that men are not passive before their experience but must assume a creative role. Man is at last recognized for what he is, a creator of his own experience, and action is seen to be absolutely indispensable for its liberation and direction.

As for thought, it too assumes a creative function in directing action toward the creation of better and more fruitful experiences. Consequently, the true line of division was seen to lie, not between thought and action but, rather, between action that is intelligent, free and responsible, and action that is none of these things. The intention was not to downgrade thought but, rather, to make it serve in the work of expanding one's vision of reality in an infinite process. Where, in the past, men have reached out beyond the temporal world to a fulfilling experience, viewing it as the goal of the human endeavor, in the American aim, the search has also been for experiential fulfillment, but within the historical process itself. Hence, William James views self-transcendency as taking place within experience, thereby pointing up the fact that the capacity to sense the "more-than" finds its realization only through an enlargement of vision which is a step-by-step affair within the life-process itself.

A dramatic change in the human condition surely took place when men found themselves in an indeterminate situation, where traditions and precedents had lost their hold. Process rather than stasis became the abiding experience, radically transforming the very way in which the individual apprehended himself. Tocqueville had noted that Americans "consider society as a body in a state of improvement, humanity as a changing scene. . . ." But he hardly realized the extent to which Americans were undergoing a profound change of feeling as well as of ideas in their attitude toward things. Indeed, within personality itself the fluid onmoving aspect of inner experience, as a time-dimension embracing past, present, and future, came into the ascendency, inasmuch as it became possible to live a full historical life in an open-ended world. In such a situation it was well-nigh impossible for the individual to put himself in bondage to the seeming fixity of things. For now the mind had discovered in itself a new freedom, that of leaping forward to the future and projecting itself into new forms of human life. The human spirit had become in fact what it was in essence, a traveler, a voyager, an adventurer. Reverting once more to the Shakers, they are also in this respect significant, since the very word "travel" assumed enormous importance in their writings. Mobility and process had come to the foreground of the religious consciousness itself. For example, even though they believed that the millennium had come, they still held that change or "travel" was constantly to be kept in view. Moreover, the very idea of freedom was transformed into freedom to "travel" into new spiritual states.[23]

In America, the drive toward innovation was not something merely external, but a thrust that represented a thoroughgoing transformation in the "within" of personal life. It represented, therefore, nothing less than a new stage in inwardness, an inwardness which in men like Edwards, Emerson, James, Peirce, and Dewey took on cosmic proportions. In our own day this integral conception of human existence is powerfully expressed by Teilhard de Chardin when he speaks of the "upward" and "forward" as "two religious forces . . . now met together in the heart of every man; forces which, as we have seen, weaken and wither away in separation. . . ."[24] While this new integralism is finding its way into the very heart of modern consciousness, it must nevertheless be remembered that it was in America that the old dissociation between inwardness and historical activity was once and for all overcome.

Emerson, as usual, expressed graphically the new way of feeling the world. No one was more concerned than he with the religious component of human experience. Nonetheless, this transcendent orientation served to rivet him to the entire panorama of human existence. As one scholar observes, while Emerson put religion and ethics first, "he made the higher power security for the expansion and ascent of its subordinates."[25] God, as universally energizing spirit, as this same scholar notes, "is a perpetual novelty."[26] Projected against such a view, we can read a deeper meaning into so typically Emersonian a statement as the following: "Nothing is secure, but life, transition, the energizing spirit."[27] The whole movement of things is thus seen to have a transcendent or vertical dimension, while manifesting perpetual novelty in its horizontal direction.

Emerson's outlook was in line with the evangelistic religious movement which forms so substantial a part of American history, and which has played a prominent role in forming the creative dynamic of American life. In this respect H. Richard Niebuhr's work *The Kingdom of God in America* is illuminating. For he shows how "The dynamic liberalism of which Channing and Emerson were the great American protagonists" was closer in spirit to the Evangelical movement than to earlier rationalist liberalism.[28] Niebuhr's seminal book opens new perspectives; it shows how the profound inwardness experienced by Emerson was akin to a perpetual prophetic strain in American life which "demands rebirth rather than conservation" and has its eye fixed on the Kingdom of God, a "kingdom which was prior to America and to which this nation, in its politics and economics, was required to conform."[29] Emerson, therefore, shared with this revolutionary strain "the sense of man's vital relationship to the reality which overarched him, and out of which he came and to which he returned." And with Emerson, as with Evangelism, the relation to the real was "immediate and urgent."[30]

Seen through the eyes of William James, a new kind of interior life begins to emerge, one in which the sense of direction becomes all-important. In this larger interiority every power and capacity takes on new significance. Selectivity and attention, desire and belief come to the center of things in concrete experience, being intrinsically bound up with the entire life of reason. The need to live by risk is seen to form an integral part of a rational life, and, along with risk, the capacity to live one's life with uncertainties. Religious emotion, aesthetic sensibility, and sentiment also come into their own. Nothing, in fact, seemed to escape James's observation, with the result that the transformation wrought in man's experience of himself was nothing less than drastic. And what it added up to was a new confrontation with the entire range of experience, and, since experience is charged with value, with the entire range of value. It meant also an extraordinary sensitivity, not only to present values, but to values that have yet to be born into life.

What so total a reaction upon life involved for James can be seen in his view of a personal biography, which, in its inward transitions and its drive toward new disclosures, feels itself swept up into a larger scheme of things, with immense pressures driving it in one direction rather than in another, and filled with "the dumb willingness to suffer and to serve this universe."

IV. *HOMO AMERICANUS*

Henry Adams surely spoke prophetically when he wrote that from the beginning, "the American stood in the world as a new order of man."[31] Today it is possible to form a clearer picture of that new image of man as it has emerged in and through the strains and stresses of growth that have increased in geometrical progression. *Homo Americanus* is still in formation, still making his own traditions and still pressing on into the future despite a hundred handicaps, many of them self-imposed, like an antiquated educational system and an antiquated economy. Wyndham Lewis writes that Americans "are quite unconscious what a novel kind of people they are."[32] In large measure this is true, yet there is much we Americans can say about *Homo Americanus* and his uniqueness, for the guidelines are forming. This despite what Thornton Wilder appears to hold: "It is difficult to be an American because there is as yet no code, grammar, decalogue by which to orient oneself. Americans are still engaged in inventing what it is to be an American."[33]

In America, the inner world of man was bound to take on the character of an open frontier. Or, as it has been said, regional pioneering gave way to spiritual pioneering. What happened, then, is that the outer frontier experience became interlocked with an inner frontier experience. Living and thinking forward, men were of necessity thrown back on themselves and their own inner resources, but in a way which militated against a dualism of inward and outward.

Henry Adams is pointing up these inward changes when he writes: "Americans seemed to require a system which gave play to their imagination and their hope,"[34] and when he notes further that the American's "dream was his whole existence."[35]

In *The Power of Blackness* Harry Levin recalls that Tocqueville "ventured what was to be one of the major prophecies, when he announced that American literature would deal less with actions and characters, and more with passions and ideas."[36] This was inevitable, considering that the free-ranging force of ideality impelled men to envision goals that went counter to conventional and fixed patterns of life, goals which so far from being merely utopian could affect the processes of history in an open plastic world.

A. N. Kaul in *The American Vision* shows how nineteenth-century novelists were motivated by a social vision which could only be dealt with in a highly imaginative approach. But as Kaul points out, it was not because they were less concerned with the world around them but, rather, because they were more concerned. This may seem a strange thing to say considering that, as Kaul notes, nineteenth-century English novels reflected the radical drives of contemporary society to a degree that makes American writers seem by comparison far removed from social reality. But the difficulty is cleared up once we realize that the American novelist's criticism of society was motivated by attitudes and values that diverged even more radically from the main current of history than was the case with English novelists. As Kaul says, in projecting a vision that could not be brought into connection with the social world in terms of conventional realism, the novelist "had to depart more radically from the imitation of existing reality and rely more heavily instead on the plastic power of his imagination."[37]

Marius Bewley in *The Eccentric Design* notes that the great American novelists are "thinkers and a species of metaphysician: and a passion of intelligence is the virtue we most often find in their work."[38] And in line with what others have said regarding the symbolic direction of American literature, he writes as follows: "Because the American tradition provided its artists with abstractions and ideas rather than with manners, we have no great characters, but great symbolic personifications and mythic embodiments that go under the names of Natty Bumppo, Jay Gatsby, Huckleberry Finn, Ahab, Ishmael. . . ."[39] Doubtless one could go deeper into our intellectual and cultural traditions to find the underlying motivations that account for the fact that, as Bewley says, " 'The new American experience' that Cooper, Hawthorne, Melville, and James had dealt with had been, above all else, an inward thing. . . ."[40] But it is enough here to introduce what I have cited thus far as evidence of the truth of my contention that in America a new kind of interiority came into being, which unfortunately gets lost from sight amid preconceptions imported from an older world.

The very clash between sharply contrasted life-orientations in America has served to deepen personal consciousness and to heighten in Americans a sense of deprivation and evil. Already in the nineteenth century, Emerson caught "the tensions that threaten to turn the dream into a nightmare" in peering into "the abyss of lawless competition, imperialistic expansion, and racial aggression."[41] The struggle between the powers of light and darkness has been too stark a reality to be missed, and it has left its mark on American minds. As one writer puts it: "All the materials for a tragic vision of life, as has been noted, have long been present in America: the classic sin of pride, the inevitable disjunction of ideal and reality, the guilt and shame of failure, the void of disillusionment."[42] Nevertheless, it would seem, according to the writer just cited, that a tragic vision of life has not in fact materialized.

It could very well be that in America a tragic vision of life has never really taken hold but for a good rather than a bad reason. This is to say, in an open-ended situation where the future is paramountly real and men feel the call to change, a tragic vision could never gain the upper hand. No longer did contingency and the terrors of change darken life. Clearly when men can rejoice in process and assume a hopeful attitude in the transitional moments of life when our little islands of stabilization have been swept away, we are in an entirely new situation that cannot be grasped through old categories. New categories are required, and it is precisely the search for new categories that has motivated our thinkers. How, then, can we speak of a tragic sense of life in the new situation without making a total reappraisal of its meaning, and by studiously avoiding outworn categories?

Even the attitude to evil cannot remain the same, for evil does not take on the sort of finality it assumes in a static world. In a world where the future is real and where process fills men with hope rather than with fear, the attitude to evil undergoes a radical change. For now evil can be dealt with in a real movement of things, and there is a resistance to a rationalistic interpretation of evil that would stifle the determination to resist and overcome it step by step in an actual historical process.

In *An End to Innocence* Leslie A. Fiedler affirms that Americans "Of all peoples of the world, . . . hunger most deeply for

77

tragedy."[43] Perhaps what he means is that in America the intensely moral approach to things and the sense of struggle between good and evil has conditioned Americans to tragedy. Whatever his meaning, he declares further that "perhaps in America alone the emergence of a tragic literature is still possible. The masterpieces of our nineteenth-century literature have captured the imagination of readers everywhere, precisely because their tragic sense of life renews vicariously the exhausted spirit. In Western Europe, the tragic sense no longer exists; it is too easy to despair and to fall in love with one's despair."[44]

V. THE FUTURE AS REVOLUTION

In America, as I have tried to show, ideality as a positive force is unfailingly present. And it is always something to be reckoned with. In this country men have felt free to envison ends, even seemingly utopian ends, that can even now determine action. That is, men feel free to live, one might say, eschatologically and prophetically, in a way that endows even distant goals with reality in the present.

In such a situation, ideality as a determining historical force can never accept defeat. Indeed, so far from blunting the creative imagination, defeat merely sharpens it, as well as the volition to rise beyond the limiting situation to a still better vision of human possibilities.

It should also be said here, that in America, where belief in futurity became firmly rooted, that is, belief in "the everlasting coming of concrete novelty into being," to quote James, and where, in Emerson's words, "All has an onward, a prospective look," determinism, which for so long weighed down the human spirit, was finally got rid of. But belief in a genuinely contingent universe and in the perpetual emergence of the new need not beget childish optimism in those actively committed to a creative process. On the contrary, without accepting absolute tragedy, such involvement can make us, in Emerson's phrase, "perceivers of the terror of life," and more poignantly aware of the need for a perpetual con-

78

test with evils that can be eliminated. Emerson, for example, had a sure sense of concrete evils, among them, the failure to achieve an "original relation to the universe," the hankering to destroy individuality, and the difficulty of really experiencing the world. Significantly, the things he would have designated as evil stand out more prominently and more threateningly in a processive open-ended world.

If childish optimism does not normally arise in the minds of those who welcome creative change, neither does pessimism. For pessimism is irrelevant in a processive world. Hope conquered the wilderness, not pessimism. Perhaps it would be more accurate to describe the characteristic American mood as that which James called meliorism. For meliorism is sensitive to the absolute importance of taking the small step forward, or improving an intolerable situation, or in bringing more values into life. Underlying meliorism is a high degree of value-consciousness, and, along with it, a powerful sense of the irreducible character of moral struggle. And moral struggle could not but come to the forefront in a world forever presenting us with new choices, new paths to be taken, new values to be brought into line with old values.

Above all, meliorism is grounded in the awareness that one walks in the dark. As James says, "When very fresh, our minds carry an immense horizon with them."[45] For in an unfinished universe we cannot do otherwise. Yet there is in each one of us something by which we are impelled to venture forth along unaccustomed paths while "advancing," in the Emersonian phrase, "on Chaos and the Dark."[46] Or, as Emerson also says, "The one thing which we seek with insatiable desire is to forget ourselves, to be surprised out of our propriety, to lose our sempiternal memory and to do something without knowing how or why. . . ."[47]

In rounding out this portrait of the new image of man as it took shape in America, it would be profitable to dwell, if only briefly, on the value placed on the individual as an originating center. Henry Adams writes that European travelers passing through America noticed that every American, even the poorest squatter, "seemed to nourish an idea that he was doing what he could to overthrow the tyranny which the past had fastened on the human mind."[48] But such a feeling toward the past carried with it the new sense of the individual's capacity to deal with the future out of the resources of the present. The past no longer held him in bondage, although he was far from disregarding it. On the contrary, the very involvement in history brought with it a new awareness of involvement in all history, an awareness which we find implicit in pragmatism, although still waiting to be brought to fuller articulation. Thus, historically seen, the individual becomes a focal point of innovation and novelty, and can operate with a new range of freedom.

Bound up with the individual's freer relation to both past and future was a more spontaneous and imaginative relation to the community. The American is gregarious with a strong sense of his dependence on the community, but at the same time he is keenly aware of his own self as a testing ground of what he believes. One does not have to go far to find this type of American. Certainly, if we take the whole past in our purview, it is clear that the spirit of innovation and adventure came to the foreground of life, but in a socio-cultural structure which fostered not chaos but dynamic order. Nonconformism was in this way built into an entirely new type of order which found room for it. Where in the past nonconformism was associated with disorder, in America it could be associated, rather, with order, and as the means by which man overcomes chaos brought on by the failure to grow.

"Whoso would be a man," declares Emerson, "must be a nonconformist,"[49] and "Wherever a man comes, there comes revolution."[50] When seen in the context of a new type of order emerging in America, these are important enunciations. And in making them Emerson was transforming religious and political nonconformism into something radically human and in line with the true state of affairs in a growing world.

Emerson had no intention of detaching the individual from society, for his doctrine points in quite a different direction, in showing that a creative commerce with the world finds its point of departure in the singularity and spontaneity of each individual. When, therefore, Emerson declares that "society is in conspiracy against the manhood of every one of its members,"[51] he is not speaking as a European, alienated from institutions regarded as menacing forces but, rather, as an American who knows he can remain true to the community only by upholding the freely developing individual.

Nonconformism is accordingly seen in larger structural terms and not as mere waywardness. It seems clear, then, that Emerson's doctrine is the finest articulation of American pluralism, seen as a type of order which allows for limitless diversification and which indeed produces diversification. Emerson found it altogether repugnant to look at society as something fixed and absolute. Where others saw "the state, institutions, churches, usages, property, 'Rooted like oak-trees to the centre,' Emerson felt that 'society is fluid.' There probably never lived another man on whom the existing frame of society made an impression so vaporous and transitory."[52]

Yet the individual person as Emerson views him does not stand alone, but is intrinsically related to God as energizing force. In fact, man's capacity to draw on the overpowering reality of God establishes the ground of self-reliance, by which the individual person can stand against conventions, customs, and institutions in the name of the spirit. In holding fast to the divine power in his own soul, and in believing, too, that revelation is not something given long ago, "as if God were dead," the individual can undergo what amounts to rebirth. For instead of living the life of a coward in "fleeing before a revolution," he can obey the divinely implanted impulse to reach out to the new and to brave the unknown while finding in himself the power to make a sudden and swift advance beyond the limits which circumscribe us on every hand.

A notable example of the new kind of structural form uniting the individual and society is found in the jazzband, in which individual spontaneity, so far from weakening the cohesiveness and intensity of group life, strengthens it immeasureably. John A. Kouwenhoven, with an eye on Emerson, describes the jazzband this way: "Everybody in a first-class jazz band seems to be—and has all the satisfaction of feeling that he is—going his own way, uninhibited by a prescribed musical pattern, and at the same time all are performing in a dazzlingly precise creative unison."[53] Walter Pres-

81

cott Webb, after citing this text of Kouwenhoven's writes: "American civilization has pursued its theme like a good jazz band in which every player is all the time eagerly watching for his chance to take off on an unannounced solo performance. He who does may strike high and haunting notes of joy or sorrow or violent protest against what is going on, but he cannot tarry long; he must return after his joyous excursion in independence to merge with the group in the common pursuit of the common theme."[54]

It is curious how the jazzband has become a living image of American experience as it relates to a new type of community whose very survival depends on a widening range of individual spontaneity. How felicitously, too, it brings out the creative inwardness which is the life force of our society. For the jazz player is asserting his freedom from all that would hinder him from obeying a higher call; he seeks out a larger vision of life's possibilities and maintains in himself a vivid awareness of something indefinable and beyond his grasp.

Which is the true voice of America? It makes all the difference in the world to know that we have a choice as to where our allegiance lies, and that much depends on our vital commitment to a great national enterprise. Clearly, the true voice of America lies on that side on which we find an extraordinary surging up of the human spirit through which "the American Dream" became a revolutionary force in life. But we cannot appraise the true greatness of our culture unless we grasp the originality of the type of order it brought into existence. For it is a type of order in which dualisms do not easily flourish, and in which, too, experimental categories tend to remain in the ascendancy. Finally, it is a type of order in which old associations give place to more fruitful ones, as in the fusion of inwardness and historical creativity and in the polarization of nonconformism and a growing community.

As to the future of philosophy in America, we cannot overlook the fact that philosophy becomes a historical force only when it succeeds in making contact with what is of universal import and of enduring value in the historical process of a people. If it should show itself incapable of participating in that process, it can have no future worth talking about, nor will it be able to tap the vast potential of energy that has been built up in that process. Whatever future remains to a nonhistorical philosophy will be confined to hollow classroom exercises, a purely academic philosophy which remains powerless to expand consciousness and contribute toward the enrichment of experience.

Santayana writes: "America did not have to wait for its present universities, with their departments of academic philosophy, in order to possess a living philosophy—to have a distinct vision of the universe and definite convictions about human destiny."[55] And in what follows, Santayana shows himself to be fully aware of the opposing aspects of American culture, although by no means along lines which I myself have traced. But he brings out something quite germane, namely, the fact that American life seems divided between the "genteel tradition," apparently associated with university or academic culture, and something more aggressive and revolutionary, and associated with, among others, William James. "His way of thinking and feeling," says Santayana, "represented the true America, and represented in a measure the whole ultra-modern, radical world."[56]

Unhappily, that vision of things which in its entirety has been so ably expressed by literary men and philosophers has more often than not been blurred and even eclipsed by an academic formation that is alien to it, especially in perpetuating a way of looking at things which belongs in the Old World rather than in the New. In short, what is happening is that many Americans are apt to be culturally schizoid, and therefore prevented from sharing fully in their own great traditions and in the creative energies they generate. The end result can only be disastrous, since in being dispossessed of their American heritage, they are particularly vulnerable to all that is meretricious in American life. Possessing neither the Old World nor the New, they become displaced persons. In conclusion, therefore, I would suggest that the future of philosophy in this country does not lie with a merely academic approach, but in an approach which draws sustenence from the America of "the American Dream," with all that it represents in the bursting forth of the human spirit in a great "splurge" of originality.

NOTES

1. Harry Levin, *The Power of Blackness* (New York: Vintage Books, 1960), p. 35.

2. *Ibid.,* preface, p. xii.

3. Charles Feidelson, Jr., *Symbolism and American Literature* (Chicago: University of Chicago Press, 1953), p. 79.

4. Bertrand Russell, *et al.,* "The Political and Cultural Influence," *The Impact of America on European Culture* (Boston: Beacon Press, 1951), p. 10.

5. Henry Adams, *History of the United States: During the First Administration of Thomas Jefferson* (New York: Antiquarian Press, 1962), p. 177.

6. Constance Rourke, *The Roots of American Culture: And Other Essays,* ed. by Van Wyck Brooks (Port Washington, N.Y.: Kennikat Press, 1965), p. 198.

7. *Ibid.,* p. 214.

8. *Ibid.*

9. Feidelson, *op. cit.,* pp. 79-80.

10. Frederick Jackson Turner, *The Frontier in American History* (New York: Henry Holt and Company, 1920), p. 214.

11. Peter Drucker, *et al.,* "Individual Freedom and Effective Government in a Society of Super-Powers," *Power and Democracy in America* (Notre Dame: University of Notre Dame Press, 1961), pp. 3-23.

12. *Nonviolence in America: A Documentary History,* ed. by Staughton Lynd (New York: The Bobbs-Merrill Company, 1966).

13. Wyndham Lewis, *America and Cosmic Man* (London: Nicholson & Watson, 1948), p. 155.

14. *A Marianne Moore Reader* (New York: Viking Press, 1961), p. 138.

15. Rourke, *op. cit.,* p. 214.

16. *Ibid.,* p. 209.

17. John Dewey, *Experience and Nature* (LaSalle, Ill.: Open Court Publishing Company, 1925), pp. 8-9.

18. Feidelson, *op. cit.,* p. 129.

19. Ralph W. Sleeper, "John Dewey's Empiricism and the Christian Experience," *Cross Currents,* Vol. IX, No. 3 (Fall, 1959), p. 372.

20. William James, *Selected Papers on Philosophy* (New York: E. P. Dutton, 1917), p. 238.

21. "Experience," *The Complete Essays and Other Writings of Ralph Waldo Emerson,* ed. by Brooks Atkinson (New York: Modern Library, 1940), p. 314.

22. John Dewey, *Philosophy and Civilization* (New York: Capricorn Books, 1963), p. 16.

23. Rourke, *op. cit.,* p. 209.

24. Pierre Teilhard de Chardin, *The Future of Man,* tr. Norman Denny (New York: Harper & Row, 1964), p. 266.

25. O. W. Firkins, *Ralph Waldo Emerson* (New York: Russell & Russell, 1965), p. 361.

26. *Ibid.,* p. 340.

27. Emerson, "Circles," *The Complete Essays . . . ,* p. 289.

28. H. Richard Niebuhr, *The Kingdom of God in America* (New York: Harper Torchbooks, 1959), p. 186.

29. *Ibid.,* p. 10.

30. *Ibid.,* p. 186. For a superlative treatment of this theme see also Alan Heimert, *Religion and the American Mind, From the Great Awakening to the Revolution,* (Cambridge: Harvard University Press, 1966).

31. Adams, *op. cit.,* p. 159.

32. Lewis, *op. cit.,* p. 12.

33. Eric Larrabee, *The Self-Conscious Society* (Garden City: Doubleday & Company, 1960), p. 21.

34. Adams, *op. cit.,* p. 171.

35. *Ibid.,* pp. 173-74.

36. Levin, *op. cit.,* p. 18.

37. A. N. Kaul, *The American Vision* (New Haven: Yale University Press, 1963), p. 313.

38. Marius Bewley, *The Eccentric Design* (New York: Columbia University Press, 1959), p. 293.

39. *Ibid.,* p. 2.

40. *Ibid.,* p. 292.

41. Levin, *op. cit.,* pp. 33-34.

42. Charles L. Sanford, *The Quest for Paradise: Europe and the American Moral Imagination* (Urbana: University of Illinois Press, 1961), p. 127.

43. Leslie A. Fiedler, *An End to Innocence: Essays on Culture and Politics* (Boston: Beacon Press, 1948), p. 127.

44. *Ibid.*

45. *The Writings of William James,* ed. by John J. McDermott (New York: Random House, 1967), p. 46.

46. Emerson, "Self-Reliance," *The Complete Essays . . . ,* p. 147.

47. Emerson, "Circles," *op. cit.,* p. 290.

48. Adams, *op. cit.,* p. 175.

49. Emerson, "Self-Reliance," *op. cit.,* p. 148.

50. Emerson, "Divinity School Address," *op. cit.,* p. 80.

51. Emerson, "Self-Reliance," *op. cit.,* p. 148.

52. Firkins, *op. cit.,* p. 328.

53. Walter Prescott Webb, *The Great Frontier* (Austin: University of Texas Press, 1952), p. 389.

54. *Ibid.,* p. 390.

55. G. Santayana, *Winds of Doctrine: Studies in Contemporary Opinion* (New York: Charles Scribner's Sons, 1926), pp. 186-87.

56. *Ibid.,* p. 204.

3

WILLIAM JAMES AND
METAPHYSICAL RISK

BY PAUL M. VAN BUREN

Dream and nightmare, an open frontier, risk—Americans have always been afraid that their project (their errand into the wilderness, their imagination of "a new order of the world" as it says, in Latin, on the dollar bill) might turn out badly. On this at first dark and unknown continent, and now in the dark and unknown reaches of technological power, Americans have always sensed that there may not be any rules made up in advance, no finished and a priori *world "out there" to operate as an absolute, secure standard by which to measure themselves. They have had to make the rules as they go along, have had to change their image of themselves and of human possibility over and over again, and have lived—except for periods of delay and stability like that from 1945 until recently—in a state of continual intellectual and social revolution. In an essay of unusual felicity and grace, Paul M. van Buren of Temple University notes how easily William James thus came to a position reached only with anguish and fear by certain European thinkers. Faced with relativity, finitude, risk, Americans tend to hang loose; this is the air they have breathed since birth. Theologians unfortunately— as Professor van Buren hints—have missed the basic note of American philosophy, perhaps because of its very casualness and implicitness. Besides, it is not expressed in those marvelous, harsh, and abstract German words so beloved of theologians—only in everyday down-to-earth words, secular words, accustomed words.*

87

William James is reported by his sister to have said of a summer rental: "It's the most delightful house you ever saw; it has fourteen doors, all opening outwards." That house was as if designed for its summer occupant, and for those who want their universe and their ideas complete, neatly arranged and secure, James's philosophy will ever seem too loose and open. It was not intellectual laziness or lack of care that made for this looseness. On the contrary, the character of James's thought and language reflects faithfully the world about which he thought and wrote, the loose, changing, surprising world of our experience, not without order and connections, but not without disorder and disjunction as well. James had a lifelong love affair with creation; if he saw this experienced world to be a messy one, he gloried in wearing her scarf of muchness and eachness with a lover's faithfulness. To have accepted the world of the rationalist, the neat closed universe of the absolute, to have agreed that "the first morning of creation" wrote "what the last dawn of reckoning shall read,"[1] would have been for James an act of betrayal to the world of radical empiricism. "In this real world of sweat and dirt," he wrote, "it seems to me that when a view of things is 'noble,' that ought to count as a presumption against its truth, and as a philosophic disqualification. The prince of darkness may be a gentleman, as we are told he is, but whatever the God of earth and heaven is, he can surely be no gentleman. His menial services are needed in the dust of our human trails, even more than his dignity is needed in the empyrean."[2]

James was accused by others and by himself of being a popular lecturer, unskilled in and unsympathetic to the careful work of logicians and mathematicians. Although a professor of philosophy for most of his working life, his degree was in medicine, not philosophy, and he began his career at Harvard teaching physiology and anatomy. So described, James hardly sounds worth serious consideration in a volume on the future of American philosophy. American he certainly was,[3] but was he not a popularizer, a public speaker, a teacher of an era now past? He was all this without question, but I should like in this essay to show from several sides that James was ahead of his critics and warrants a place, not in our history books, but in our contemporary conversation, as one from whom we have something to learn. I intend to do this by discussing five features of James's work: his style, his much criticized case for "the will to believe," his pluralism, his "humanism," and his view of language. In each of these I want to draw out a recurring theme that is important in any further development of a contemporary metaphysics: the place of risk, in the hope of suggesting one possible way through a difficulty that seems to block understanding between English-speaking and Continental philosophy today. I point out that as a theologian, not a philosopher, I see the problems of contemporary philosophy from a certain angle and in connection with particular problems. Whatever limitations this particular approach may have, it is part of what I wish to argue on James's behalf that its particularity is not only no disqualification, but simply the only way to proceed, frankly accepting one position in the context of many.

I

It is proper and helpful, I believe, to reflect on the style of James's writing if one wishes to understand his thought. Most of his philosophical work was written to be given as lectures. At times James expressed regret that this form was inadequate to the intricacies of the subject, but this complaint seems to have expressed his sensitivity to his critics more than his own view of philosophy. A man's philosophy was the articulation of his style of mind, his form of life, James argued, and this was surely true of James himself. His close friend Charles Peirce called his writing "racy" and tried to persuade him that this was no way to write philosophy, a field in which it is proper to employ terms designed to put off the ordinary reader and to be available only to those skilled in philosophic argument.[4] The terms, Peirce argued, should be as precise and therefore as far removed from our ordinary discourse as possible. In an interesting anticipation of much later developments in philosophy, James refused his friend's advice, holding for what we have come to call "ordinary language." Rough and ready, popular and down to earth as is our ordinary language, there and for that reason is where James wanted to do his work, using just those concrete, robust tools with which in practice we do get about "from next to next" in our ordinary experienced world. The images, examples and terms of James's arguments were those of a man who wanted above all else to keep his thinking close to "this actual world of finite human lives" and in "the richest intimacy with facts." The ideal of an absolutely precise logical language was no ideal for one who wanted to speak of this world of flux, the plurality of our experienced world. James took the alternative, and the result is a style marked by charm, even a touch of elegance, no small wit, and a robustness that calls the reader to share James's far from uncritical love affair with the whole of our experienced world.[5] No naïve cultural or naturalistic optimism followed from this choice. Leibniz's *Théodocée,* defending this world and all its evils as the best of all possible worlds, led James to remark that the author's "feeble grasp of reality is too obvious to need comment from me. It is evident that no realistic image of the experience of a damned soul had ever approached the portals of his mind."[6]

To resort to "ordinary language" is to run a risk which can be expressed by saying that our philosophy will be no more airtight, no more logical, than our lives. Precisely, thought William James, and smiled. That was exactly where he wanted to be and the style in which he wanted to do his philosophizing. The advantages of accepting this risk were more subtly expressed later in the way in which Wittgenstein worked his way free of the *Tractatus,* but I think that even Wittgenstein did not learn as well as James how to smile on this "rough ground" without absolutes. The charm of James's style is the mark of the success with which he was able to free himself from any vestigial longing for a world secured by an absolute or a guarantee of truth or perfection.

II

Time and again over the years, James apologized for having chosen the title "The Will to Believe" for an early essay. What he meant and said clearly enough in the essay itself was that we have a *right* to believe, that there is a justification for beliefs in certain sorts of matters, although we have only partial evidence for any definite conclusion. There are cases, James argued, when we must choose one belief or another, and in such cases not to choose is only to make another choice. Critics of this essay and its central thesis, including Bertrand Russell, have justified James's frequent complaint that critics objected to the title, apparently, without having read the essay itself. James did not claim that our beliefs about the world were simply a matter of will. "Just try and see if you can make yourself believe that Abraham Lincoln never existed," was James's response in anticipation of that absurd idea. Nor did he recommend jumping to conclusions where further evidence was available for the looking. But James did mean that our jump to a conclusion in some important matters was itself a piece of the picture we wanted to understand, itself part of the state of affairs about which a conclusion had to be made. In such questions as whether life is worth living, whether novelty is possible in this world, whether we have free will, and whether our actions add something to the make-up of the future, or not, we must decide without knowing "for sure," and the way in which we choose will itself contribute to the making of a world in which our belief works and thus prove itself to be true. These sorts of jumps create in part the conditions of their own realization, making for the truth of the position which we choose.[7]

The aspect of this thesis to which I wish to draw attention is the nature of one sort of question to which James felt it applied. In the essay in which he first propounded the thesis, James focused on two sorts of questions, the moral and the religious, or, lest we construe these more narrowly than James, the questions, "What do you think of yourself? What do you think of the world?" Neither logical demonstration nor empirical verification will be able to settle these questions. How we take things to be, the frame of reference within which we establish what we are going to take into account in any proof, is not itself capable of proof in the same ways.

Long before the issue was posed in the thirties, James was aware that we deal with many more sorts of problems than those which can be settled by logical demonstration or empirical verification. He urged the use of empirical verification wherever it was applicable and thought we should always try to ask the pragmatic question, demanding what he called "the cash value" of a proposition.[8] But James realized that we are concerned for other matters, that we have questions which such procedures will not settle, and among these are questions of religion and metaphysics.[9] These questions, which he frequently posed as questions about how we are to use words (the question concerning the good or the truth he usually dealt with as a question of how we use the words "good" and "true"), are those which have to do with the way in which we see the world and our place in it.

During the course of his life, James came to view the serious work of philosophy more and more as the study of metaphysics, and as James applied himself to this study, his way of working bears interesting anticipations of the "revolution in philosophy" of a generation later. He would have been comfortable with a later understanding of metaphysics as a clarification of the ways in which we say how things are, as one or another proposal to see in a particular way what we have been looking at all along. The question about facts, for James, had to do with how we are to use the word "fact," and his conclusion was that a fact was what we carved the world up into, our way of coming to terms with our experienced world, ever in part a product of our own view of things.

To carve out facts in some particular way, to detect patterns in the world, to see the world in a certain way, was a matter of belief, a venture involving risk. As James saw it, there was no getting around this. Metaphysics meant one choice or another, one belief or another, and therefore risk no matter which way one moved. He saw this and he did not recoil. He took life and this world to be really open-ended, dangerous, and venturesome, and he liked it that way. "I am willing that there should be real losses and real losers. . . . When the cup is poured off, the dregs are left behind for ever, but the possibility of what is poured off is sweet enough to accept."[10] What distinguishes the thought of James from so many philosophers before and since his time is not so much that he saw the element of risk in all human thought and action, but that he felt that this risk gave life a high flavor.

III

Nowhere does this character of James's thought become more evident than in his championing of one side of what he repeatedly called "the most pregnant issue in metaphysics," the issue of the one and the many and his devotion to the choice of pluralism. The title of his Hibbert Lectures, *A Pluralistic Universe,* but more especially the way in which he introduced the subject in his Lowell Lectures, lead us to what James meant by pluralism. The world is one, James argued, in some important ways. It is one as a "universe of discourse," one by our way of speaking of it as a universe, a totality. It is one insofar as we can pass from here to there and from then to now by means of the continuities of space and time. The universe is also one as it is connected by lines of influence and by causal connections which we detect; it is one insofar as we create lines of connection by our human efforts. The world is one, that is, in more ways than one. The form of the presentation has already made the point: the "universe" is not one thing but a number of things, a number of ways of slicing up what experience runs into, and in each case, it is one "in so far forth." " 'The world is One,' therefore, just so far as we experience it to be concatenated, One by as many definite conjunctions as appear. But then also *not* One by just as many definite *dis*-junctions as we find. The oneness and the manyness of it thus obtain in respects which can be separately named. It is neither a universe pure and simple nor a multiverse pure and simple."[11]

The form and style of the argument is an important part of what James was driving at. The metaphysics of pluralism must itself be open to the plurality of experience, the plurality, we should say today, of language-games. Each of these may have its own justification in its own usefulness for our getting along with some aspects of our experienced world. Insofar as each language-game can actually be played, insofar is it to be allowed its place. But there are other games to play as well, and the pluralist asks only that we allow that thus far we have not learned how to do justice to each by subsuming them all under one set of rules.

Resting as it does on what we find to obtain, it is evident that such a metaphysics cannot be dogmatic. An absolute pluralism would be a contradiction in terms. It would close off the future, excluding in advance the possibility of greater or higher degrees of unity yet to be detected or constructed. That would be, not James's pluralism, but atomism. In doing battle with any and every sort of monism with the weapon of "ever not quite," James never defended an atomism of any sort. It was in this connection that he criticized the empiricism of Locke and Hume, which he distinguished from his own radical empiricism. By radical empiricism James meant that we must take seriously and start always from a position open to all of our experience. We do not experience the world as so many discrete sense-data, so many distinct billiard balls. On the contrary, we experience the world as a world, albeit a world in more ways than one, with no one way serving all purposes. Causal, aesthetic, political, economic, and linguistic connections are as much a part of the "what" of our experience as any "this" or "that." Logically, perhaps, atomism is the opposite of monism, but for a radical empiricist, the alternative fashioned by "ever not quite" had to be pluralism.

"Ever not quite" was not only a weapon with which James fought Royce and the rest of his philosophic foes; it was also the standard for his own metaphysical camp. The metaphysics of pluralism as James presented it is—one might almost say, in principle (a precursor of Gödel's theorem, as it were)—unfinished, subject to genuine novelty. The editor of *Some Problems of Philosophy,* on which James was working when he died, not misleadingly used the word "novelty" in each of the chapter headings for the last third of this work. Novelty, risk, reorganization are built into this view of things by the same factors which exclude any monistic metaphysics. The world may *yet* be one, James insisted, only we don't see how this can be, and a great deal counts against this being the case *at present*. It may yet be one, in the sense not only that it may be one in some way which our experience of it does not let us see, but it may be one in the sense that its unity may lie ahead of us. The universe may be growing into one, in some sense not clear to us. James's metaphysics and all his philosophical work was future-oriented. The theoretical possibility of unity in things was, he felt, a question about the future, and one of his repeated objections to rationalists was that they pointed to a unity already established. James's universe was unfinished, open to the future. It was a world-in-the-making.

This open-ended, future-oriented, unfinished character of the

94

universe of pluralism was connected with James's belief in free will, the conviction that men can and do change the world, actually change it, so that the genuinely new comes into play by human choice.[12] The world being made is being made by us, to some extent. The issue here, James insisted, was not theoretical but practical. The issue was pragmatic, for if belief were not a philosophical belief for living, what interest could it have? The question that matters in life is what we shall make of life, what is to happen to our world. James was, we may say, existentially interested in this question, or, in his terms, pragmatically interested. A metaphysical view of things or a view of the universe as unfinished, still in the making, with ourselves as responsible in some ascertainable ways for what is to become of our world, a metaphysics involving risk, is the consequence of the method of pragmatism built on radical empiricism.[13]

Perhaps at this point we can begin to see one way in which two apparently divergent lines of thought in James's idea of God may be seen to be consistent. On the one hand, James argued that God should be conceived as an ultimate, not an absolute. The absolute, for James, was the great first principle of the rationalist mind which stood at the center of a monistic universe, prior to everything else in every sense of the word. The absolute held all things together and all things were of and from the absolute. Against this idea James set the ultimate, the *telos* that may yet appear, the unity of things that may yet arise. The absolute is from eternity; the ultimate has to be realized, and that means that the ultimate has to be realized in part by us if it is ever to be. God is the end toward which we press, the goal for which we strive, not the creator from which all comes. All this sounds close to Dewey's definition of God as the sum of our ideals, the unification of our ideal ends.

There is, however, another way in which James speaks of God.[14] God is, in other places, a limited, active agent in things, one element within the many forces at work in the universe. God is but one entity within the plurality of this universe, not certain to win, and not assuredly the most powerful, needing our help as much as we need his in order that a better world may have a chance of being realized. In connection with this line of thought, James

95

suggested that the appropriate religion for a pluralist would be polytheism, but he seems to have felt that, as polytheism has been transformed into monotheism, the religious (as distinct from the philosophical) interest in God has retained the original sense of the divine in polytheism: God is but one helper among many.

If we keep in the foreground the element of risk in James's metaphysics, these two strains in his thought may be seen to be less incompatible than they appear when simply set side by side. As a radical empiricist, and on the basis of his studies of religious experience, James seems to have felt that he could not discount the possibility of some higher or other consciousness than that of ordinary men. He had no religious experiences of his own to go on, but even in the later part of his life, in the writings coming from the time after he had finished his Gifford Lectures and had turned his attention centrally to the problems of metaphysics, James seemed to remain open to God as a possible hypothesis. The God that seemed to James possible, however, was a limited God in a pluralistic universe, concerned for men as religion said he was, but surely not omnipotent.[15] Whether or not this God (this idea of God) would turn out to be ultimate, whether he would be the telos of our life and world, was, for James, an open question. There was a risk in this enterprise for God as for man, and the outcome was in important respects in our hands. If we hold these elements in James's thought together, we see that he was not saying the same thing as Dewey, for Dewey seemed to be sure that God was but the name for our human ideals. For James, God was at least this, but perhaps this was not the last word. Here too the open-ended character of his metaphysics is evident. The metaphysical story, if it is truly a story about the universe of our human experience is a story not yet finished. In this way, James, although not what one would call a religious man himself, sought to justify religion, in the sense that he tried to leave a door open for its claim. To a religion that claimed to have the secret of all questions, however, that promised final, inevitable and perfect victory, as to the atheist who cried that all religion was absurd, James would answer quietly, "ever not quite." Pluralism meant for James a profound willingness to reside without regret in an unfinished universe, a world still in the making, avowing the risk involved in human existence and the existence of our world.

IV

Metaphysical risk can be expressed by saying, simply, human metaphysics. Metaphysics as an account of how things are is always a human account, a view of things which is our view. However chastening this thought may be to the metaphysician, it was one of which James never lost sight. In all our ideas, concepts, understandings, and truths, "you can't weed out the human contribution." James seems to have held by this before he ever borrowed Schiller's name of "humanism" for it. He was trained and began teaching as a natural scientist, but he was no believer in scientism or in any form of scientific naturalism. He was a verificationist, but one who knew that any verification held only in the terms that we set up for the process of verification.[16] The result was that James was constantly concerned for truths, not Truth, and ever argued that "Truth" was as changing and living and growing as the ones who pursued it.

Although every truth is someone's truth, all thought and language being in this sense relative to the thinker and speaker, still there are strong checks against solipsism and the total devaluation and leveling of all ideas which James's relativistic theory might at first suggest. As we saw, that opposition to monism led James by no means to atomism, it being for him only a theoretical not a practical alternative, so in this case opposition to the rationalist belief in Truth did not lead to the total relativity of all ideas. James argued that "truth" is a word we use for our ideas, for what we *say* about our experienced world. Our experienced world is not true or false, it just is; but when we come to speak of it, to hold certain ideas about it, then the question of truth is important. Not any idea goes. Some ideas are more true, some are false. The issue is settled, again pluralistically, in more than one way. An idea is true if it leads me on from next to next in my experience, if I find that with it I can make useful and helpful connections in my experienced world. There is a further control on our ideas, however, which James called "common sense," the "funded truths" of our own past experience and the experience of those who have gone before us. A new idea has to fit in with the old ideas somehow. There may have to be changes, corrections, of the new idea or of some of the old ones before this fitting in can take place, but if the idea is to be true for me, it has to come to terms with all the other truths, all the other beliefs which I have. That rules out capriciousness. A new scientific theory, for example, in order to work, "must derange common sense and previous belief as little as possible, and it must lead to some sensible terminus or other that can be verified exactly. To 'work' means both these things; and the squeeze is so tight that there is little loose play for any hypothesis."[17] The "squeeze" from the side of "common sense," however, means that the question of any truth is a human, social enterprise. Some "Truth" which was not someone's truth was no truth for James.

This view of the human risk in all thought enabled James to see the human element in everything we say about the world. The picture of pure facts "out there" as over against our possibly distorted view of them "in here" was precisely what James objected to in the rationalist metaphysics of his day. It is important to see that James did not have to fight against this in his own mind; he wasn't in the least tempted by such a view of reality. "The notion of a reality calling us to 'agree' with it, and that for no reasons, but simply because its claim is 'unconditional' or 'transcendent,' is one that I can make neither head nor tail of. I try to imagine myself as the sole reality in the world. . . . What good it would do me to be copied [by a human mind], or what good it would do that mind to copy me, if further consequences are expressly and in principle ruled out as motives for the claim (as they are by our rationalist authorities) I cannot fathom. When the Irishman's admirers ran him along to the place of banquet in a sedan chair with no bottom, he said, 'Faith, if it wasn't for the honor of the thing, I might as well have come on foot.' "[18]

In an important and unavoidable way, facts are man-made. We carve out groups of stars and call them constellations, "and the stars suffer us patiently to do so." Our scientific theories are our human reports of nature, and facts are what we carve our world into. But if facts are what we carve the world into, it is terribly important to us that we do do this and that we do it in some ways and not in others. In no way did James mean to denigrate facts or theories or constellations. In no sense did he think it made no difference how we carved up our experienced world. But he did insist that however we went about this, the human element was always part of it and that our metaphysics ought to be honest about this.

James put his point graphically by saying "we are not the readers but the very personages of the world-drama." Some supposed world of pure facts, or of things-in-themselves, or of absolute Truth untouched by the human element, any way of speaking of reality as though it lay "back there" somewhere beyond, behind, or other than the world of our experience, was for James nonsensical and even repellent and he used all his skill to try to wean us away from such a view of things.

V

The last and, for our present situation, the most important aspect of James's thought has to do with the risk involved in language. Wittgenstein once formulated the gnawing question which can lead us astray in this matter in these words: "Is there some reality lying behind the notation which shapes its grammar?"[19] Wittgenstein's whole aim was *not* to answer "No," but to lead us away from trying to answer this question at all, from so construing philosophy that we allow the slim edge of the old philosophical wedge to slip in between "reality" and our language. In contrast to those who would say that there is a reality behind our language to which it points or which it reflects, and also to those who would say there is no such reality, or not one we can know, he wanted us to learn to look at language in such a way that this question would not even arise. The only world I can talk about is the world I can talk about, Wittgenstein seems desperately to have wanted to say, and that he wanted to say this desperately is perhaps the problem. James did not seem to be desperate but took this important tautology as his starting point in its basic form: the world we experience (speak of) is the world we experience (speak of). Our talk about the world may prove with further experience and talking to need emendation. That risk, the fact that we have to do our talking and understanding as it were from within our words and our understanding, the self-referential character of all speaking and thinking, was what Wittgenstein saw, and his later philosophy was a struggle to get over feeling that this was an unfortunate limitation to our language. James, on the other hand, saw this and seemed to have no feeling that it might have been otherwise. He was, if I may put it that way, comfortable with the element of risk, of insecurity, that characterizes all language and thought. Wittgenstein was haunted by the ghost of an older philosophy that whispered about a reality (of course ineffable, of course beyond my experience, yet surely the foundation of my experience, for if I experience something, there must be that something which I experience) which hovered behind our words, with which our words ought to correspond. He tried to lay that ghost, to still forever the suggestion of a real behind our talk about the real. How easily we are seduced by our language itself into listening to this whisper! I think it can be said that James was not haunted by this ghost, however simple the problem seemed to him. Had Wittgenstein met James, I believe he would have gone away muttering to himself, "It's all so much more complex than he is aware of, so much more subtle." But he would also have gone away filled with envy! He would surely have been right about the problem being more complex than the way in which James saw it, but that James saw it in such a way that it really was not a problem for him, that he knew the risk in metaphysics and was at peace, that he was aware of the self-referential character of all language and did not want or try to evade it, is a feature of his thought that commends him to our attention in the present situation in philosophy.

The point which I am making may be clearer if we see it more directly in James's work. Wittgenstein detected more than one problem in James due to his not having consistently seen the linguistic form of philosophical problems.[20] That Wittgenstein made a remarkable advance over James in this matter cannot be denied. But James was quite consciously interested in the problem of language and this is evident enough from any of his later works. His pragmatism was a rough anticipation of the use theory of words: find the cash value of a word, see how the word is used, its "particular go," and many a problem can be dissolved, James argued. This approach is evident even in some of his earlier essays. The words "change" and "gift," for example, he saw as two importantly different sides of the same coin, "the one being simply a disparaging, and the other a eulogistic, name for anything on which we have no effective claim."[21] Language is how we come to terms with the world, for without "adjectives and adverbs and predicates and heads of classification and conceptions" we would not be able to handle "the real world" at all.[22] Language is a rough tool, perhaps, and nothing we say in words is ever all that is to be said; something is always left over. But this was not for James an invitation to chase the will-o'-the-wisp of some reality beyond our words, some supposed real world abstracted from or posited behind our experienced world.

In an important essay with a typically Jamesian title, "The Sentiment of Rationality," James said: "In every proposition whose bearing is universal (and such are all the propositions of philosophy), the acts of the subject and their consequences throughout eternity should be included in the formula. If M represent the entire world *minus* the reaction of the thinker upon it, and if $M + x$ represent the absolutely total matter of philosophic propositions (x standing for the thinker's reaction and its results), what would be a universal truth if the term x were of one complexion, might become egregious error if x altered its character."[23] All propositions of philosophy, and not least those of metaphysics, are of the $M + x$ sort. The question about the world is always the question of what we say about the world, how we are to speak, and it is solely of our speaking that the question of truth is in order. To ask if our speaking of the world is true is to ask not about the past, however, not about some conformity of our words with an eternally settled "that," but about the future, about how we can move ahead with these words. "Fact," as we have mentioned, is for James our word for moving ahead with our experienced world. James no more than Wittgenstein doubted that there was an experienced world which we run up against with our word "fact," and woe to us if we misuse the word. The word whose leading we cannot follow, the use of a word which blocks our movement from next to next may exact a high price.

What Wittgenstein was trying to make clear was already clear to William James. It was clear in his radical empiricism, which freed him to see that the only world we can talk of is the world we do talk of, and it was clear in his pragmatism, which rested its case and tested every other case by asking that we follow the leading of our language and see where it would take us. James in his own way had said, "Don't think, but look!"

If the metaphysician stands unavoidably within the picture he is trying to get clear about, if he is an actor, a *dramatis persona* in the drama of the universe, his description of that universe, his proposal for how it shall be seen and spoken of is itself a part of that universe and his proposal or description must be taken into account as one factor in deciding whether that description will turn out to have been helpful, "true" in James's sense of the word. Life and language are one, for James as for Wittgenstein, and to speak of life is to take a step into life's future, following the leading of our language.

How can we know that the leading will prove satisfactory? Much can be brought to bear on this which can help us from mistakes, but in the last analysis, we cannot know for sure in advance. Here we must decide, for to wait until all the evidence is in is to wait for evidence that will include the fact that we sat and waited. Therefore the safest course, paradoxically, is to take the risk. I have found only one reference that indicates directly that James may have read Kierkegaard ("We must live forwards, a Danish thinker has said, but we understand backwards"[24]), but their agreement in this important area is clear. To live is risk, to speak is risk, and to seek some other security at this point is to turn one's back on life. If we are to use language (and how else shall we be human?), then we must use our human language with its self-referential character. No appeal to a pure logic, to any supposed *a priori* that is prior to our mastery of the technique which is language, no assertion of an absolute Truth or any other M without an x can change this character of the language we use.

The objections to this were not wanting. " 'In other words,' an opponent might say, 'resolve your intellect into a kind of slush.' 'Even so,' I make reply,—'if you will consent to use no politer word.' For humanism, conceiving the more 'true' as the more 'satisfactory' (Dewey's term), has sincerely to renounce rectilinear arguments and ancient ideals of rigor and finality. It is in just this temper of renunciation, so different from that of pyrrhonistic scepticism, that the spirit of humanism essentially consists. Satisfactoriness has to be measured by a multitude of standards, of which some, for aught we know, may fail in any given case; and what is more satisfactory than any alternative in sight, may to the end be a sum of *pluses* and *minuses,* concerning which we can only trust that by ulterior corrections and improvements a maximum of the one and a minimum of the other may some day be approached. It means a real change of heart, a break with absolutistic hopes, when one takes up this inductive view of the conditions of belief."[25]

James has been mostly known by students of theology and religion through his *Varieties of Religious Experience.* This is too bad. That book marks a turning point in James's work, the last fruits of the experimental psychologist, only in the last chapter pointing to what had already become his chief interest and was to occupy the rest of his years, and a subject far more important for the present problems of religious thought: metaphysics. James could have lived happily with a later conception of metaphysics already mentioned: a proposal to view things in a particular way. James would have wanted to underscore that it is always our view, *our* way of saying how things are, that is at stake, and that how we come out on this matter is as important for our life and our world as anything else about us. A crucial feature of James's metaphysics, I have tried to show, is the avowal of risk, and it is at this point that James had something to say to our present religio-philosophical situation. Theology today is bogged down in gross misunderstandings between those who look to certain "existentialist" philosophers, sure that the rest of us have turned our back on the real issue of language's involvement in life, and those who walk with analytic philosophy and find certain French or German thinkers hopelessly entangled in category blunders. Perhaps James could help both sides, and American religious thought could do worse than follow some of the leads provided by William James in seeing that metaphysical risk and recognizing the self-referential character of language, being two sides of the same coin, have the same "cash value."

103

NOTES

1. William James, *Some Problems of Philosophy* (New York, 1911), p. 189.

2. William James, *Pragmatism,* (Cleveland, 1963), p. 57.

3. That is not a parochial judgment: *Il a pu passer en Amérique pour le plus cosmoplite et en Europe pour le plus américain des philosophes* (M. Le Breton, *La Personalité de William James,* 1925, p. 35).

4. Review of James's *Principles of Psychology, The Nation,* in Peirce's *Collected Papers,* ed. Arthur Burks (Cambridge, Mass., 1931-35, 1958), 8.57.

5. Cf. James's correspondence, especially with his brother, and commentary, in Perry, *The Thought and Character of William James* (New York, 1935), Vol. 1, *passim.*

6. *Pragmatism,* p. 30. Cf. the discussion following, pp. 30-33.

7. *The Will to Believe.* Cf. "The Sentiment of Rationality"; also Lecture 8 of *A Pluralistic Universe* (New York, 1909), pp. 317 f.

8. *Pragmatism.* The second lecture is as clear a presentation of this as can be found in James's writings.

9. James's growing interest in philosophy and especially in metaphysics is evident in his published work and well presented in Perry, *op. cit.* Some examples of his use of the "verification principle," his recognition of its limits, its metaphysical character, and also of his analysis of language, can be found in his *Pragmatism,* especially the second, sixth, and seventh lectures.

10. *Pragmatism,* pp. 190 f.; cf. pp. 187 f.; *Some Problems of Philosophy,* Ch. IX ff.

11. *Pragmatism,* pp. 100 f.

12. "Free-will pragmatically means *novelties in the world,* the right to expect that in its deepest elements as well as in its surface phenomena, the future may not identically repeat and imitate the past" (*Pragmatism,* p. 84).

13. *Ibid.,* pp. 187 f.

14. This second way of speaking of God, as a higher consciousness, but limited, characterizes the conclusion of his Gifford Lectures. It needs to be balanced by his treatment of religious belief and God in his later Lowell and Hibbert Lectures, as well as in some of his other essays. A letter to Thomas Davison, quoted by Perry, *op. cit.,* Vol. I, pp. 737 f., is to be noted. Of the early essays, "Reflex Action and Theism" is especially worth attention.

15. "When John Mill said that the notion of God's omnipotence must be given up, if God is to be kept as a religious object, he was surely accurately right; yet so prevalent is the lazy monism that idly haunts the region of God's name, that so simple and truthful a saying was generally treated as a paradox: God, it was said, *could* not be finite. I believe that the only God worthy of the name *must* be finite" (James, *A Pluralistic Universe,* pp. 124-25).

16. Cf. William James, "The Sentiment of Rationality," *Essays on Faith and Morals* (Cleveland, 1962), especially p. 94 and note.

17. *Pragmatism,* p. 142.

18. *Ibid.,* p. 152.

19. Wittgenstein, *Philosophical Investigations* (Oxford, 1958), § 562.

20. *Ibid.,* § 342. Cf. § § 610, 342, and in Part II, p. 219.

21. William James, "The Dilemma of Determinism," *Essays on Faith and Morals,* p. 159.

22. William James, *The Varieties of Religious Experience* (New York, 1902), p. 56. That James would not be totally lost in contemporary analytic discussion may be indicated by the following, from *Some Problems in Philosophy,* pp. 199 f.: "The conceptualist rule is to suppose that where there is a separate name there ought to be a fact as separate; and Hume, following this rule, and finding no such fact corresponding to the word 'power,' concludes that the word is meaningless. By this rule every conjunction and preposition in human speech is meaningless—*in, on, of, with, but, and, if* are as meaningless as *for,* and *because.* The truth is that neither the elements of fact nor the meanings of our words are separable as the words are. The original form in which fact comes is the perceptual *durcheinander,* holding terms as well as relations in solution, or interfused and cemented. Our reflective mind abstracts divers aspects in the muchness, as a man looking through a tube may limit his attention to one part after another of a landscape. But abstraction is not insulation; and it no more breaks reality than the

tube breaks the landscape. Concepts are notes, views taken on reality, not pieces of it, as bricks are of a house."

23. "Sentiment of Rationality," *op. cit.,* pp. 97 f.

24. *Pragmatism,* p. 146. The fact that just this same remark occurs in *A Pluralistic Universe,* p. 244, suggests that this may have been picked up somewhere and was all of S.K. that James knew.

25. "Humanism and Truth," from *The Meaning of Truth,* in *Pragmatism,* p. 232.

4

KNOWING AS A PASSIONATE AND PERSONAL QUEST:
C. S. Peirce

BY DAVID B. BURRELL

Charles Sanders Peirce (1839–1914), we have learned, accused William James of being too "racy" and writing in too popular a vein; and Wittgenstein, we are told, would have accepted James's sense of relativity and risk but accused James of getting to that point too easily. No one has ever accused Peirce of such faults (if faults they be). Peirce, too long neglected, is an American Wittgenstein: tough, terse, sinewy. In a long, concerted, painful investigation Peirce tried to track down what it is that leads men—in a position of relativism and risk—to accept some propositions, however tentatively, as true and to reject others as false. Such an act of assertion, he felt, goes beyond the mere act of getting clear about the meaning of the propositions. Such an act requires an additional energy; it commits the integrity and intellectual standing of the agent; and such acts follow one another in passionate, progressive sequence. Professor David B. Burrell of the University of Notre Dame has reconstructed Peirce's trail down the labyrinth of such a difficult problem. It is astonishing—and yet it can no longer surprise us—that in the end the trail comes back to "a kind of aesthetic sense." What is this last redoubt of human inquiry and responsibility, this last sense for the "satisfactory," the "simple," the "clear," the "useful," the "elegant," the "fitting," the "appropriate," or whatever it is that leads us to say with peace in our hearts and minds, "P is true"? It cannot yet be said that philosophers have fully explored this territory. Peirce ventured into it, cautiously, as empirically as any man has.

Pragmatism likes to set itself off from earlier philosophies by firmly rejecting the assumption that knowing is taking a look; it avows, instead, that knowing is an activity of a much more complicated sort. Kant, of course, developed systematically the postulate that knowing is primarily an activity and not a passive gaze. And one can trace Kant's revolution to the medieval notion of an agent intellect. Yet however profoundly the roots of the Renaissance may be sunk in the Middle Ages, Kant can be said to be the first to take the agency of intelligence seriously. But the ponderous teutonic form of his thought apparently neutralized his discovery, just as hierarchical thinking diffused many penetrating Scholastic insights. So Kant was typed as an "idealist," and the accent on knowing as a robust activity came to be associated with the pragmatists.

The most conscious and deliberate philosopher among those who transformed pragmatism was certainly Charles Sanders Peirce. Kant's legacy was an enduring reverence for intelligence and its activity. Peirce was not only schooled in this tradition but took Kant as his master, pondering the first *Critique* for two hours each day for more than three years. In the "Transcendental Dialectic," especially, he found the source of an *élan* peculiar to intelligence: inescapable and irrepressible questions for which the fashioning of answers outstrips our capacities. Intelligence is endlessly inquiring intelligence. Ceaselessly active, thoroughly active, inquiring intelligence suggests to Peirce a new paradigm for understanding other activities. But activity is not enough: whoever seeks, finds; inquiry requires resolution. The only resolution for inquiring intelligence, however, is union with—the word must at this point be pardoned —reality. So one who would trace the labyrinthine ways of inquiry cannot be content simply with mapping abstract byways, as logicians do. One must also learn to recognize the exits, and become skilled in discriminating rewarding strategies for dealing with concrete, contingent things. How can we be sure when probing intelligence strikes its mark? If we assume that mind is aimed at reality—

DAVID B. BURRELL

indeed that "reality" as a notion or a question arises only for mind
—what are the marks of the real, of an inquiry consummated?

This question was crucial for Peirce in his endeavor to put
idealism to work. He had to show that idealism's reverence for
intelligence was fully justified—not because mind is more exalted
than what it sets out to know but simply because intelligence alone
can discriminate reality from illusion. The first part of this essay
concerns the activity of intelligence. An explicit and chronological
account of Peirce's attempts at resolution comprises the second
part. The final section probes the philosophic nerve of Peirce's
work: How do we employ criteria for judgment if we cannot formulate them?

I. ACTIVE INTELLIGENCE IN SEARCH OF A MODEL

To say that intelligence is active shifts the epistemological
spotlight from mind to self. Knowing becomes less detached and
more involved with human concerns. The way then lies open to
conceiving intelligence on the model of a passionate quest. This is
not properly speaking a model, of course, for "quest" already suggests cognitive features. But pragmatism shares this weakness with
every epistemology which refuses to reduce knowing to taking a
look. Knowing has no proper analogue outside itself. To compare
knowing to a quest, however, accents certain features more than
others. These features prove interesting because they fly in the face
of many common presuppositions about knowing. To think of
knowing as a quest prompts one to think of its goal. It implies
movement and progression, and it requires lawlike procedures, for
a well-conducted quest systematically touches all bases and over-
looks none. But a more important matter also comes to light. A
quest suggests that there is some affinity between the subject and
the goal sought.

If knowing is a quest, it is far more than a mere mental exercise. It is a demanding way of life with its own asceticism. Peirce
lived such a life. But however consuming the goal may be, one must
learn to survive along the way, so techniques of living are never to

be disdained. One must also be equipped to find one's way; hence, involvement requires discrimination. One has to learn how to read the signs which indicate the next step. One needs a certain emotional distance from one's immediate concerns, canons of interpretation, rules to follow as guidelines while one is still on the way.

It should be clear by now that comparing knowing with a human activity so rich and emotive as "quest" does not provide a model so much as it offers a parable. But this observation simply underlines a feature central to the thought of Peirce: understanding, inquiry, has no adequate model outside itself. His insistence on the singularity and uniqueness of cognitive relations links him more with Kant, Hegel, and the so-called idealist tradition than with the pragmatist movement he inspired. Furthermore, Peirce asserts that the structure of knowing explains the structure of the world. One can find no trace of a reductionist effort in his thought when he links knowing with activity; one finds instead a thoroughgoing attempt to unite the two so that the inner exigencies of each illuminate the other. What action adds to knowing is a point, a focus. What understanding adds to action is discrimination, direction.

Activity is by definition involvement with the real world. The man of action is "in the thick of things." Reality is definable (if at all) by interaction between the subject and his world. Understanding, on the other hand, requires a certain detachment. It seems aloof. By contrast, knowing in the full sense intends to find out what, truthfully, a thing is: how we may best act regarding it. Unlike simple understanding, knowing is not content with meaning. It is not satisfied with a mere detached understanding of possible meanings. The quest for knowledge aims at reality and is not complete until the question of truth supersedes the question of meaning, and is satisfied. So the "real world" is not alien to intellectual inquiry; it quickens and enlivens it as its intended goal. Only someone who has never tasted this quest could regard the intellectual enterprise as detached and unreal, and settle for the brute givens of mere activity.

A host of clichés express a felt opposition between thought and action. To call them into question helps bring out the rule-like features of action, on the one hand, and the goal-directed character

110

of inquiry, on the other. If we accentuate the rule-governed character of action, we can distinguish activity from mere behavior, response from mere reaction. If we accentuate, on the other hand, inquiry and its orientation to a goal, we see that the entire human person is engaged when inquiry is under way.

But to speak of a goal may beg the whole question of the structure of human knowing; and "involvement" is more persuasive than illuminating. Furthermore, the indefinitely progressive character of inquiry is apparently antithetical to one's ever *arriving* at a goal. And finally, if we have no other guide or touchstone than inquiry itself, how are we to recognize the goal should we ever achieve it?

These are some of the questions that Peirce elicits. The last one in the series is the question of the *Meno*. Every inquiry worth the effort aims at knowing what the thing *is* that it is investigating— where "knowing what the thing is" must be taken in the full-blooded sense of knowledge certified as true. Whence the certification? If we professedly do not know what x is—else why inquire about it?—then how are we to recognize the genuine article for what it is? The term "recognize" spontaneously evokes a visual situation, where we identify something encountered by sight as the item described. This is a tacky enough problem in itself, but knowing what something is remains more elusive still than visual identification.[1] To appreciate the problem, take something which we could never encounter by sight, like society or the atomic structure of matter, religious faith or even knowledge itself. To be able to say confidently what these are involves (*a*) understanding much about them, (*b*) discriminating which salient features to fasten upon, and (*c*) deciding that only these features are "essential." It is difficult enough to fasten on criteria for visual identification; yet visual identification need not depend on invariant features. Knowing what something is, however, means singling out certain features as both invariant and revelatory. For to call a feature *essential* implies not only that it is bound to be present but that its presence should tell us something about the object. A judgment like this is never straightforward; it involves reflexive, self-critical moments. A person can come to appreciate what he does understand; he then assesses its relevance to the goal of knowing what it is that he is after. To know

111

what something is in this full-blooded sense is to realize that one is on the way to grasping it.

The tactile metaphor of "grasping" is a natural one and bespeaks a realism on the side both of intelligence and of the object. Moreover, the first of these factors dare not be minimized. Here lies the weakness of precritical realism, common among Scholastic philosophers, for example. Although things known are asserted to be real, that assertion is said to proceed not from intelligence but from some sort of animal faith.[2] In fact the realist did not really *assert* it at all, but only kicked or stamped his foot as a sign of contact with "reality." The two most plausible reasons for this position are actually inverse faces of the same philosophical coin. The reality of things, of the world, is conceived to lie outside the ambit of intelligence. Anything known must then in some fashion remain over against the one knowing it, and this "over againstness" seems most appropriately identified with some sort of independent existence. So from the side of intelligence there is no possible way of *affirming* the independent reality of things, since this aspect is independent of and ever foreign to mind. Furthermore, were objects not over against the knower and in some way external to him, they would never have been *given* in the first place.

The feeling, then, was that one had to step outside intelligence to acknowledge the stubborn unintelligible fact of real existence. But this conviction does not follow from the reflections we have just entertained. For we presupposed an *understanding* of "something being given," of an object "over against" a subject. So there is something to be known here, an understanding attained reflexively and accessible only by metaphor, but no less communicable and hence intelligible for that. Something else must be at work, then, to persuade us that intelligence and reality can never meet on equal terms: a feeling that knowing is an ethereal operation, poles apart from the muscular exertion and earthy interaction which evidences the real. Instead of resting attentive to intelligence and its role in our lives, we allowed our imaginations to be captured by an ontology that neatly divides the world into spirit and matter. Like most ontologies, this one solved no problems, but rather focused our attention on some and made others disappear. And like most categorical divisions, this one could not provide its own principles of discrimination. What makes matter to be matter and spirit, spirit? Is it simply that one is not the other? Do they interact? If so, how? If not, who dreamed up the distinction? Or is it that "simply knowing" is not a form of interaction with matter? If so, this is a statement about spirit and deserves evidence. Instead it turns out to be a prejudice, and the entire world-view shows itself as the dream of a pious realist who divided where he should have tried to understand.

The act of knowing, then, has as much claim to reality as the thing known. Unless, of course, it forfeits that claim by insisting on imagining itself as an alienated spectator. But such a role-conception requires extraneous and subversive influence, for the spontaneous aim of intelligence is to grasp its object. And if the grasp is not opaque and violent but, rather, calm and lucid, it is no less real for that. Indeed the *realization* that we have understood something in such a way as really to know it carries a testimony to reality all its own. This is the activity known in ancient and medieval philosophy as *judgment*. Judgment clinches inquiry—we know that we know, and are ready to stand by our knowing—and so links the inquiring intellect with an object originally given in an independent fashion. Significantly, we are drawn to a term as earthy as "realize" to flesh out the full-bodied sense of "know" which culminates in a judgment.

If Peirce's dedication to exhibiting the reality of inquiring intelligence were to take its place in the philosophical tradition, it would help us elucidate the role of judgment. And on Peirce's own principles, an investigation is more authentic the more it extends an ongoing inquiry. So we should not be surprised if a scrutiny of his papers sheds some light on that singular activity which can serve to draw an inquiry to its conclusion. The remarks are scattered and his position shifts, but the scattered remarks betray a pattern and the shifts in position show a definite progression.

II. STAGES IN A DEVELOPING POSITION[3]

We shall have to take for granted a certain consensus about judgment: that it (1) is not another piece of knowledge, another fact about a thing; and yet (2) is the natural consummation of inquiry. But what it is, exactly how one consummates an inquiry, is much more difficult to say. Peirce endorses (1) by placing judgment beyond the logician's concern and eschewing any hope for a logical diagram of it. He accepts (2) by pointing out that judgment is nothing other than an inquiry's achieving its purpose. This move suggests the analogies of action, volition, and purpose. It also provides an opening to the prime feature of judgment—the one preventing it from being pictured as a kind of sign-relation—its capacity to analyze and correct itself. *Purpose* highlights this feature since we can presumably know the purpose of our inquiry and in the face of new facts or a developing understanding review our past judgments with respect to the purpose as we see it now. Peirce's usual word for judgment is "assertion." Our program will be to examine Peirce's statements about assertion or judgment according to the successive analogies he invokes: action, volition, and purpose, showing at each phase the central role *assertion* plays in his development.

A. Assertion as Action

Peirce tends to speak interchangeably of propositions, judgments, and assertions as conceptual signs. He also has "propositions asserting" (5.569), and even asserting their own truth (5.340, 4.282).[4] This usage seems to deny any division between meaning and assertion, and even suggests an opening to the radically "pragmatic" slogan that "all meaning lies in the consequences."[5] Yet Peirce emphasizes again and again that this is not what the "pragmatic maxim" means to him, that pragmatism entails the reality of general ideas (5.428, 504), and that it is a program for determining meanings, not bestowing them. Hence Peirce maintains the distinction between *meaning* and *assertion* that we pointed to earlier as *understanding* and *knowing*.

When pressed for precision himself, Peirce readily recognizes that assertion is something over and above meaning. He accuses the Germans of confusing the issue by using the one word *Urteil* indiscriminately for assertion and assertible,[6] where "assertible" is the same as "meaning." But the accusation is leveled against logicians,

114

who are supposed to distinguish clearly what ordinary usage blends together. Ordinary usage cannot be accused of "confusing" meaning and assertion (understanding and knowing), because its role is not to be precise but to be vague. By using notions interchangeably, it shows how closely interwoven they are. Meaning and assertion are certainly related in the general sense that we come to know of an ability only through its act, that we come to know an assertible only through assertion. Act is its normal completion, what it is for. "The sole vehicle in which a concept can be conveyed to a person's cognizance" is a judgment (5.547). A proposition asks, as it were, to be asserted. But if this be true, what does assertion add to meaning? Certainly not "more meaning," for we have already suggested that the two are incommensurable, as act and ability. But once it is admitted that assertion is not a "purely representitious event" (5.547), the search for an "assertory element" poses "a difficult question" (4.56). What is it?

Aristotle's notion of act as a generalization of energy gives Peirce a category of *secondness* (4.542).[7] In this sense, "the judgment . . . involves an act, an exertion of energy, and is liable to real consequences and effects" (5.547). This move emphasizes the fact already noticed: assertion is not a further increment of meaning: "neither the predicate, nor both together, can make an assertion. The assertion represents [rathei] a compulsion . . . to attach the predicate to the subjects as a sign of them taken in a particular way" (3.435). Although this activity is reflected back into the structure of an assertible (2.337, 4.56), a well-formed proposition is not yet a judgment—"the logician does not assert anything" (4.79, 352, 397). Rather, "a judgment is an act of consciousness in which we recognize a belief and a belief is an intelligent habit upon which we shall act when occasion presents itself" (2.435). Such *recognition* "may come very near action, . . . but in general [is a] virtual resolve, . . . a peculiar act of the will." What accounts, then, for "assertion seeming so different from other sorts of signification is its volitional character" (2.436), and since "volition involves action and reaction" (2.437), it seems that we have at least located the assertory element as a kind of *second,* an act, an exertion of energy with real consequences and effects.

115

If we were to stop here, however—with a "categorial explanation"—we would be violating Peirce's pragmatic maxim and misusing the categories. But it might be helpful to take stock of what we have said, and incidentally to remark the correct role of phenomenological categories in inquiry.

Peirce had already assumed a firmly anti-Cartesian posture: negatively, by showing that knowledge simply is not the kind of thing that needs unshakable foundations to build upon, nor does it even reductively demand a clear and indubitable basis from which further progress might be explained (5.263). This posture amounted to a rejection of deduction as the paradigm of human knowledge. Peirce was to replace this by "abduction," his label for the pervasive features of scientific method: "studying facts and devising a theory to explain them. Its only justification is that if we are ever to understand things at all, it must be in that way" (5.145). This move allowed him to develop a positive theory of perceptual judgments. Such judgments, often made instantaneously, are the "limiting case of abduction" (5.186). Thus he incorporated the body of Aristotle's *Posterior Analytics* by giving an effective meaning to the metaphor of the routed army making a stand. Aristotle is perfectly clear that what he called "induction" is the "originative source" of all scientific knowing, since it alone can yield the definitions or proper principles. As relatively determinate, these definitions can shape the direction of an inquiry; and as containing much that is yet vague, they still leave room for the process of explication which is science. By giving "induction" a logical status as abduction, Peirce removed it from the role of a genial and inspired preamble to scientific inquiry, and did Aristotle the favor of redistributing the weight of the *Posterior Analytics* in a way that Aristotle's own reflections seem to demand (5.144).

From this new kind of "foundation," then, inquiry was capable of launching hypothetical forays carried by the continuous relation of *thirdness,* which allows each significative moment not only to pass on but to contribute to the initial momentum. The *whole* meaning is the trajectory which relates any single stage to the target. But how is one assured of being "on target"; what is to count as a hit? To extend the metaphor a moment, in a "high-powered"

116

inquiry what is to prevent one from losing control and orbiting about the goal indefinitely? This is of course the question Hegelianism poses for philosophy, and Peirce intended to capture in his sign-relation of *thirdness* the heart of Hegel's dialectic (1.491, 544). Hegel demonstrated in spite of himself that *thirdness* does not consummate inquiry of and by itself. We have seen how Peirce apparently answers this dilemma by invoking *secondness*. If we were to treat this as his reply, we should be able to oppose him neatly to Hegel, and show him as the progenitor of "pragmatism" in one fell swoop: inquiry is consummated in action.

But this is too neat a reply. We have Peirce's testimony: "If pragmatism really made Doing to be the Be-all and the End-all of life, that would be its death. For to say that we live for the mere sake of action, as action, regardless of the thought it carries out, would be to say that there is no such thing as rational purport" (5.429); we also have his warning that a search for the "assertory element" raises a "difficult question." Peirce does not use words lightly, so we ought to be surprised to have arrived so quickly at an answer, even if we did not recognize that coming up with a categorial niche does not answer a question; it merely directs and guides further inquiry. The categories do not provide an explanation but offer a program; they are not terminal, but heuristic. What is needed now is a model which can serve like the diagrams in mathematics to focus our experience, now guided by the category, on the salient features of assertion and suggest fruitful associations (5.148).

B. Responsible Action

Peirce carries on the search for what is peculiar to the act of assertion under the guiding analogy of willing. But while he laid stress on the elements of action/reaction in 1893, ten years later he will focus on the peculiar twist which volition gives to action, in particular its demand that action be responsible. In the Pragmatism Lectures of 1903 he speaks of judgment as "an assertion to oneself" whereby one personally assumes responsibility for the truth of what one says (5.29-30). Such an act is quite clearly above and beyond "apprehending meanings," and is more like adopting a proposition as one's own (5.115).

There are two aspects to the act, which Peirce recognized in 1897: the intention of "the judger . . . [is] to impress upon himself the truth of a proposition," but the paradigm case is "going before a notary and assuming formal responsibility for its truth" (2.252). What at first appeared to be distinct, however, is gradually recognized as closely related: "to assert a proposition is to make oneself responsible for it" (5.543). Responsible to whom? Not merely to oneself, but to oneself as belonging to the community of inquirers: "solitary dialectic is still of the nature of dialogue" (5.546). Judgment, then, will be explicated on the model of intersubjective discourse, but what suggested the model? The fact, perhaps, that "every new concept first comes to the mind in a judgment" (5.546). Thought is essentially a to-be-asserted, and after accurately recognizing that the proposition-sign "retains its full meaning whether it be actually asserted or not" (2.252), one must nevertheless admit that unasserted it remains somewhat emasculated—incomplete and unconsummated. The close relation between assertible and assertion—as reflected in ordinary speech—must be brought to light to counterbalance the realization "that the act of assertion is an act of a totally different nature from [that] of apprehending the meaning of a proposition" (5.30). And both viewpoints must be held firmly to keep an effective balance: "The volitional element is quite extraneous to the substance or 'meaning' of a concept. . . . For it is no pragmaticistic doctrine that responsibility attaches to a concept; but the argument is that the predication of a concept is capable of becoming the subject of responsibility, since it actually does become so in the act of asserting that predication" (5.547).

The example Peirce uses to accentuate the "assertory element" in judgment is a "very formal assertion, the features of which have purposely been rendered very prominent." But the formality only highlights the normal situation:

This ingredient, the assuming of responsibility, which is so prominent in solemn assertion, must be present in every

> genuine assertion. For clearly, every assertion involves an effort to make the intended interpreter believe what is asserted, to which end a reason for believing it must be furnished (5.546).

> When a writer makes an assertion, his principal purpose is to induce the reader to believe in the reality of the fact asserted. He has the subsidiary design of causing the reader to follow along his line of thinking . . . (4.353).

Once one's attention is directed to assertion as the natural completion or fruition of an assertible (meaning), and thence to the intersubjective dimension of thought, observations like the above begin to pour in. Implication ceases to be a purely formal operation and one is sensitized to the "pragmatic implications" woven into the texture of ordinary speech; logic is expanded to make room for statements as well as propositions, to consider use in addition to form.[8] The added dimension is *point* or *purpose*, the end for which a proposition is used. This dimension introduces the most fruitful element in pragmatism, and suggests Peirce's most mature view on the "difficult question" of assertion. But before looking further, let us consolidate the gains made under the guiding principle of responsibility.

The most striking is perhaps the personal element: "The words 'reasonable' and 'perverse' imply that assent is as free as choice ever is, and so proclaim their volitional strain" (1.330). There is something essentially communitarian about thought, and yet the assertions which culminate and initiate it demand that one be willing to step out of the ranks and stand up to the community, personally backing one's thoughts by the act of asserting them. But the two dimensions are only superficially antithetical. As we are finally realizing after the demise of that individualism which so rankled Peirce, genuine community demands self-assertion, and assertion in turn becomes less defiant and more effective the more one acknowledges his own radical need for the community. The analogy of responsibility leads to the further simile: meaning is to assertion as community is to person. This captures the essentially Hegelian insight that the very thing that distinguishes judgment from

119

meaning will also account for their being so closely related in function.

But to admit the personal dimension is to raise the question of ethics—especially when one speaks of "assuming responsibility." So we are given a clue to Peirce's insistence that logic presupposes and is governed by ethics—a strange, even unwelcome notion at first blush, yet one which promises to put us on the "trail of the secret of pragmatism" (5.130). Peirce's scheme presumes the interrelatedness of thought and assertion that we have remarked, specifically the fact that formal analysis is developed to clarify the process of functional argument, to elicit the logical doctrine virtually contained in any act of reasoning. *Logica utens* (language usage) must be the final judge of any *logica docens* (formal system) proposed to explicate it (2.186 ff.). A systematic picture gives a clarity and perspicuity which makes it useful as a ready measure for any actual course of reasoning, but the final measure of reason can be none other than reasoning itself. And reasoning takes place in a community, via judgments, as the "sole vehicle in which a judgment can be conveyed to a person's cognizance or acquaintance" (5.547). Now if judgments are the kind of thing that one personally adopts, so must that reasoning process also be which culminates in adopting them. So Peirce insists that one may not be able precisely to formulate the general habit of thought determining a judgment, but it is essential that he *"approve* it as conducive to true knowledge" (2.773, italics added). "If we did not approve, we should not infer" (5.130). And since "self-approval supposes self-control . . . , *logica utens* (or usage) is a particular species of morality" (5.108; cf. 4.540).

This distinction between *logica utens* and *docens,* as well as the subsequent move from use to responsible use or morality, draws upon the fact that propositions as logic must study them are "incomplete." The very construction of propositions presupposes their actually being used in making judgments for the sake of inquiry (e.g., 2.337). We analyze what we find, and what we find is actual use: form follows function. This aphorism introduces us into Peirce's most mature (and most "pragmatist") treatment of assertion as relative to a purpose. It will also permit us to do justice to his pregnant remark that if logic be regulated by ethics, ethics in its turn is subject to aesthetics. The challenge to the view we have just outlined, of course, is to develop its virtualities further. For fruitful as it is to recognize the role of approval in reasoning—and useful as some contemporaries have found it in re-establishing the relativity (and hence utility) of distinctions like analytic/synthetic—there is something wanting thus far.[9] It is of course the sense of expectancy one always feels at being told that a certain course of action is ethical. Why? And the "why" cannot help but implicitly call the whole procedure into question—since ethics does not, cannot, answer its own threatening questions. Something more is always needed—something which may well not be able to be said but finally only hinted at. In the meantime, however, more must be said, if only to frame and give a perspective to Peirce's startling remark that "he who would not sacrifice his own soul to save the whole world, is, as it seems to me, illogical in all his inferences, collectively. Logic is rooted in the social principle" (2.654).

C. Roots of Responsibility

Judgment may be considered a limit of inquiry. Since there is nothing in the mere sign-relation of meaning to assure its convergence on a limit, however, the preliminary heuristic tack was to assume the "assertory element" of judgment as a kind of *second,* an act, an exertion of energy. The model suggested was volition, which captured the sense of personal responsibility evidenced in the range of postures we assume in proposing our thoughts to the community (i.e., to ourselves and to others). As responsibility invoked ethics, however, the model carried us well beyond *secondness* to show the instability of the pragmatist slogan: "Inquiry is consummated in action." For if action is to be admirable human action, then it had better be responsible; and to request the criteria of responsible action is to initiate a further inquiry. We are back in *thirdness,* then—well inside the cognitive realm of inquiry—when we ask, as we must: When may one approve a course of reasoning, when is one justified in asserting an idea? The classical response was in terms of purpose: whatever fulfills the purpose envisaged for inquiry may be said to be correct or justified. "Good" is closely associated with "aim," "end," and "function," although it cannot be

121

said to be defined by them.[10] Peirce unabashedly adopts this heuristic scheme to temper his insistence that inquiry *per se* is potentially endless, and so must always be kept open; he gives willing permission to halt any particular inquiry when its purpose is served (5.212, *ad fin.*).

Lest the terms in which we have cast the issue suggest that we are dealing with mere systematic difficulty for Peirce, it is worth recalling that we are faced here with the substance of the *Meno* question: "How do we recognize the truth when we find it?" For judgment has been traditionally associated with truth, and to know when to terminate an inquiry is to say that one has satisfactorily answered the question posed, has arrived at the truth. Posed in this way, however, it sounds foreign to Peirce, for we know that he regards truth as a regulative ideal which inquiry (hopefully) approaches as a limit (2.113; 5.407). But nevertheless he speaks of the "main points [of an analysis as] pretty near to the truth" (2.322), of there being "reason to think there is some truth in pragmatism" (5.35); nor does he hesitate to say of a provisional "rude division of triadic relations" that "we need not doubt [it] contains important truth, however imperfectly apprehended" (2.234). Let us take an extended example. Peirce's image seems to be that of a finer and finer approximation to the truth: 0 is contained within the interval $\pm 1/2$, as it is also within $\pm 1/8$, $\pm 1/1000$, and $\pm 1/n$ ($n \pm 0$). Continuity assures both that a continuous function within any of the intervals will take 0 for one of its values, and that a closer approximation will always be possible. But once this has been said the mathematical image shows more by its inadequacy than by what it can say. For the clarity and precision of mathematics stems directly from the fact that the general purpose of the inquiry is severely delimited and hence transparent to the inquirer. One is interested in no more than the formal relations that can be manifested among the distinct objects of an (assumed) collection, once they are subjected to a set of defining properties. Because the purpose of the inquiry is so explicitly contained, judgment in mathematics is reduced to checking whether the operations have been carried out as defined.[11]

The example together with our critique of it suggest two sa-

122

lient features of judgment. The first is that one should be able to say, as one easily can in the example, that while the interval $\pm 1/1000$ contains 0, nevertheless $\pm 1/n$ $(n > 1000)$ approximates it better. One must be able to say, in other words, how well a proposed response corresponds to the question posed—fulfills the purpose of the inquiry. Outside of mathematics, it is doubtful whether this can ever be estimated with exactitude, nor can one hope for a "perfect fit" in anything outside of logic—indeed anything beyond the propositional calculus.[12] What we need is the ability to judge an approximation as approximating—that is, as both approaching and falling short of its goal. Hence Peirce says of his general theory of signs in 1902: "Close examination encourages the student to believe that this is something like the truth, but so far as it has been carried, excites doubt whether this be the whole story . . ." (2.322). Now this doubt requires, of course, that in some way we already know the goal about which we are inquiring. Here we have the *Meno* paradox, and Peirce's answer is substantially the same as Aristotle's (though much more sophisticated in its attention to method): of course we already know the goal, but only vaguely— in such generality that the knowledge can be of no use except to entice us to inquire more about it.

In Peirce's terms, this means that we can survey the purposes of our inquiries, and so know in general what to expect them to turn up. And this implies the second feature of judgment, which was manifested in criticizing the use of a mathematical example to illuminate the process of inquiry. One object or state of affairs may be subjected to many styles of inquiry, and we would want to be able to say that at least some were more revelatory than others. The capacity to survey the purposes of our inquiries, to take stock of the general "points of view" from which we are considering something, may not logically entail the ability to adjudicate among them, yet in fact we do evaluate at least some of them, and feel warranted in doing so. (The relative merits of viewing man as an object of economics, sociology, or psychology may be hard to assess, but one can certainly contrast these viewpoints, as a group, with physiology.) There is no doubt, however, that judgments of this kind are more tenuous than the first, so that one of the practical tenets offered by pragmatism is tolerance and pluralism in admitting forms of inquiry. Even the most unlikely projects can unwittingly witness to the truth—like the "nominalist" campaign to reduce meaning to denoting and so analyze *thirds* into *seconds* (1.344).

Both facets of judgment—appraising an inquiry as approximating its aim, and evaluating the adequacy of diverse approaches to the object—suggest an assessment of sorts, and yet one radically different from ordinary assessing in that we can have no preconceived standards. That the aims of an inquiry can be scanned and so the general outlines of its goal known before inquiry does not entail that the object can as yet properly be conceived. Such conception, in fact, is the first goal of the inquiry. So the vague, general grasp which serves to elicit inquiry can hardly double as a standard with which to measure its success. It simply is not determinate enough to be useful—in this way or in any other. By contrast, in taking Plato's metaphorical "solution" to the *Meno* problem literally, and accepting the assessment model at face value, Neoplatonists like Augustine were compelled to postulate a primordial intuition of truth, against which "imperfect truths" could be measured and their inadequacy read off. Since they tended to treat knowledge on the model of vision, judgment became a unique kind of seeing, or "intuition." Peirce rejected such a simple model.

But how can a man assess without a standard? He can, for example, be constructing one as he moves along, gradually approximating one. And such a solution does not initiate a regress, since it is simply a manner of describing the critical faculty which can assess without a standard because it "tends to correct itself." Peirce cites this feature as

> . . . one of the most wonderful . . . of reasoning and one of the most important philosophemes [sic] in the doctrine of science . . . ; namely that reasoning tends to correct itself, and the more so, the more wisely its plan is laid. Nay, it not only corrects its conclusions, it even corrects its premisses (5.575).[13]

One would look in vain, however, for rules of correct self-correcting. The deductive, consequential role of reasoning may be codified with some success; the reflective, assessing role involving self-correction cannot be, under penalty of regress—who will watch the watchmen? This capacity of the deliberately formed habit by which one is self-analyzing—"self-analyzing because formed by the aid of analysis of the exercises that nourished it—[is] the living definition, the veritable and final logical interpretant" (5.491). Now the "final logical interpretant" is defined three years later in the letters to Lady Welby as the "one Interpretative result to which every Interpreter is destined to come if the sign is sufficiently considered."[14] As "that towards which the actual tends," it is the *normative* factor of inquiry which defines the truth as its ideal consummation. The self-analyzing or reflective dimension of habit, then, would be its psychological correlate. (Traditionally, one would have pointed here to the reflective *nature* of the faculty, but as nature must manifest itself in habits of operation, Peirce is just as accurate in pointing to the dimension of *habit*. Furthermore, Peirce has rhetorical reasons for using one term, "habit," to call attention to the all-pervasive factor of thirdness.)

But some observations are needed at this point to quiet a skeptical query whether Peirce has not invoked a *deus ex machina*. What is this power of self-criticism, that is, how does it operate? One factor stands out; unlike reason's role in drawing consequences, this self-analyzing, reflective role is not rulelike. At least its rules are not perspicuous like those for consequences, nor, if a set of them could be drawn up, would one use them for assessing in the same literal manner in which logicians would have us following their rules in drawing conclusions. If in assessing we follow rules, the rules are more akin to moral guidelines than to procedures for playing a game.[15] We may appeal to simplicity, fruitfulness, elegance, coherence, and like notions, but these cannot be called criteria. They are simply not available in unambiguous form, to be invoked at will. If reason can function more or less procedurally in drawing consequences, in critical assessment it faces quite another matter. By suggesting that the way we follow rules in assessing is more like allowing ourselves to be guided by moral principles than like following a pattern, we have helped reinforce Peirce's analogy of judgment to volition and ethics. And the recent (and profoundly

125

traditional) insistence that neither moral decisions nor evaluations can effectively be made in the abstract illuminates the "contextual" factor of judgment.[16]

Reason cannot correct itself once and for all, but only in inquiring. We look to encyclopedists for information, but for an evaluation we turn to someone who has a working familiarity with a field. Peirce has expressed this by noting that the deliberately formed habit is "self-analyzing because [it is] formed by the aid of analysis of the exercises that nourish it." We ought not be put off by the circularity, because the fact that "control may itself be controlled, criticism itself subjected to criticism" (5.442) is exactly what is at issue. It is noteworthy that only the person expressly engaged in forming a specific habit of inquiry will stop to analyze the exercises designed to develop it. One who is content to "learn about" a field can do so simply by going through the paces; critical analysis will be an incidental by-product of his mental acuteness. But someone who needs both the durability and flexibility of a habit of inquiry cannot afford to leave his position untested as he moves along. And correlatively, a greater ease and familiarity in employing the habit helps him to discern what might count as a test or analysis of its procedures.

Here we have the bite, then, of the pragmatist insistence that judgment is tied up with the purpose of an inquiry, and that the one who can most effectively assess how well an inquiry is serving its purpose is the actual inquirer.[17] Although the "final logical interpretant"—the truth sought for—is an ideal limit, reason's self-corrective power when used by an expert with a feel for his subject gives an assurance of being on course, of being "pretty near to the truth." The familiarity or feel of the expert—Peirce's solution is a human one, not a Godlike, intuitive one. For all that, however, the fact that human knowledge is "a self-correcting enterprise which can put any claim in jeopardy though not all at once," ought not lessen our wonder at this unique power.[18]

D. An Intellectual Sympathy

But what could one possibly mean by the "familiarity or feel of an expert" for a field of inquiry? This phrase invites development by its excessive vagueness, and yet already suggests Peirce's ethics in schematic form. Before examining this phrase in detail, however, let us collate the few remaining statements on assertion. Peirce defined *judgment* in 1893 as "the actual calling to mind of the substance of a belief, not as personal to ourselves, but as holding good, or true" (4.53). *Belief* in this definition is said to be a "habit of which we are conscious," and the negative clause apparently corrects an earlier definition (1880) when he had been content to call judgment a "representation to ourselves that we have a specified habit" (3.160). "Holding good, or true" is explicated (in 1896) as the "conditions [to which] an assertion must conform in order that it may correspond to the 'reality,' that is, in order that the *belief it expresses may be stable*" (3.430, italics added). Peirce goes on to show how one comes to accept a belief as stable, and gives his most lucid account of assertion:

> Neither the predicate, nor the subjects, nor both together, can make an *assertion*. The assertion represents a compulsion which experience, meaning the course of life, brings upon the deliverer to attach the predicate to the subjects as a sign of them in a particular way (3.435).

"This compulsion," he explains, differs from mere *secondness* in that while it "strikes him at a certain instant, he remains under it forever after." Hence the need to embody it in a proposition, to give it the "permanent conditional force [of] law." The sign that the proposition so embodies a judgment "is the copula of the assertion."

In this passage, Peirce manages to incorporate the functional relatedness of proposition and assertion as well as to do justice to their intrinsic difference: the "assertory element" is like a compulsion but one which the "course of life"—not a single staccato event —brings upon the inquirer. What is it like for "the course of life" to "bring something upon one"? It seems very close to Peirce's description of "deliberately—that is to say reasonably—adopting an ultimate end of action." This "must be a state of things that reasonably recommends itself in itself aside from any ulterior consideration." For Peirce, this is enough of a lever to move us into his schematic resolution: "Since the only kind of goodness that such an ideal can have" is that it be admirable—"namely, esthetic goodness . . . , the morally good appears as a particular species of the esthetically good" (5.130).

We have supplied the associations too freely and so moved too quickly, but a little reflection should fill in the gaps. What finally convinces us we are entitled to make an assertion, adopt a course of action? Finally, nothing but the fact that after weighing the arguments and evidence, we feel it is correct to do so—where the use of "feel" rather than "see" conveys at once the intimately personal and the aesthetic elements. But the resolution remains schematic. The best clue Peirce can give us to the nature of this feeling is that

> It is a sort of intellectual sympathy, a sense that here is a Feeling that one can comprehend, a reasonable Feeling. I do not succeed in saying exactly what it is, but it is a consciousness belonging to the category of Representation, though representing something in the Category of Quality or Feeling (5.113).

It is an "intellectual sympathy," very like the feel (or familiarity) of the expert, because while it does license assertion, the latter is put forward with a certain consciousness of its inadequacy.[19] If our judgments are to respect continuity, they will be aware of approaching and yet not touching the truth of the matter. This is manifested by a "habit's being ready to be broken in case reasons should appear for breaking it" (2.315). That is, we can recognize in what respect our judgments are vulnerable, can accept or reject a criticism as relevant or not, a capacity which presupposes an awareness of the extent to which we have committed ourselves. Because this awareness is direct—conscious, but not self-conscious —it is not expressible, but discloses itself only upon further inquiry, in the recognition with which one greets criticism (cf. 5.300). This sense of approximation is corrigible and perfectible, as one is usually unsure in the beginning of an inquiry which objections to count

128

as relevant. The expert hand betrays itself not necessarily in being able to respond to every such challenge, but by knowing which to take seriously and which to discard.

III. JUDGMENT AND CRITERIA

The key to Peirce's studied position on judgment would seem to lie in a "feeling of sufficiency" aware enough of its grounds to discriminate among challenges, recognize genuine threats, and parry the rest. Such a feeling would provide for the conscious appraisal that issues in self-correcting intelligence. But *feelings* are not the sort of conscious states that we ordinarily count on for discrimination. It sounds strange to speak of "a feeling of sufficiency being aware of its grounds," since feelings have no grounds. At least when we want to speak of something in the arena of consciousness *prior* to any question of grounds, feelings seem to be the best candidate.

We do often speak, though, of our own reactions to a proposal in terms of our feelings about it. It seems that both our initial guiding impressions and our final sense of propriety amount to something at least akin to feelings. Though we would not speak of these feelings themselves being "aware" or actually "judging," we might well have recourse *to* them in making an appraisal, and might even like Peirce find no better way of describing judgment. But can we locate any ready candidates for this role of inner barometer? Peirce suggests aesthetic responses, and these seem to offer unusually appropriate examples. One speaks of a "sense of unity," a "feel for simplicity," an "eye for form." It is congenial to speak of these in an aesthetic context, but are descriptions like these confined to aesthetic judgments, or do they direct us to the very stuff of any judgment? It would stand to reason that appraisal would stand out more clearly in artistic discrimination. For since the materials are not conceptual, the reasons one might offer in support of a particular judgment are not available in a ready linguistic way. We are forced to speak metaphorically of texture, body, contrast, harmony, blend, conflict, and the like, as if to underscore what kind of response art,

129

music, and poetry demand. They require a wholeness of attention and sensibility, indeed a wholeness on the part of the person himself, since the entire assessment demands and works an adjustment or attunement of the person with the object. Aesthetic appraisal especially forces us to encounter the object at a level where we allow ourselves to be moved and shaped by it.

But Peirce has suggested that something like this is present in every judgment. It is simply more dramatically the case in aesthetic responses because we are less tempted here to think the reasons we might offer in support of a judgment would prove adequate to the task of appraisal. Yet the same sort of descriptive phrases attend any judgment we make. And the signal feature of their use—namely, that they demand a certain attunement of subject with object—suggests one license for Peirce's speaking of judgment and discrimination without needing to posit extrinsic standards. For to recall that we simply cannot speak of simplicity or directness or candor without somehow sharing in them suggests that the model of judgment is not a comparison between two items alien to one another, but a gradual attunement of self with object. The active, hypothesizing self returns to the reflective, meditative self at the moment of assessment. It is this self and not merely the intellect which allows for self-correction. What makes the judgments can by that same conscious quality of appraisal correct them.

But language like this is suspiciously psychological. It purports to describe yet is replete with terms bearing an extensive cultural heritage. Certainly a judgment is an assessment of sorts. And assessing relies on standards. To speak of regarding evidence in favor of a hypothesis as sufficient is certainly to imply some method of discriminating sufficient from insufficient. If not, how can judgments perform the role intended? How can one ever move from opinion to knowledge?

This is the standard objection to any proposal like the one we have extracted from Peirce. And one must acknowledge its force against the later, doctrinaire pragmatist position which adopted so much of Peirce's spirit and vocabulary yet manifested so little patience with his logical and semantic subtleties. According to this later position, norms and standards evolve with the social and cultural milieu. Hence a judgment amounts to little more than taking up one's position within the prevailing conventional wisdom. Introduced as a radical philosophical venture, this form of pragmatism finished by denying itself the resources with which to criticize the *status quo,* and predictably satisfied itself with the more pedestrian if often insightful task of social commentary.

The differences between Peirce's "pragmaticist" program and the pragmatism it inspired were already marked enough in his own day for him explicitly to disclaim paternity. He seemed particularly provoked by the movement's insouciance for logical and epistemological reflection. The present discussion is a case in point. The popular pastiche known as "pragmatism" uncritically accepts the model for judgment according to which one measures a state of opinion against certain norms or standards. It simply assumes that this is what we do, and then proceeds to examine the status of the purported standards. Finding no warrant to claim them as "absolute," it posits them as "conventional" and presumes the job done. But in fact the job was never undertaken, for this maneuver simply avoids the more substantial philosophical task of explicating judgment by substituting a form of cultural accommodation.

Anyone who purports to explain a characteristic form of activity must account for its intent—its intersubjective intent as embodied in the language we employ to describe that activity. When we assert something to be the case, we do just that. We judge more accurately, certainly, the more conscious we are of our grounds and of their culturally relative facets. But however provisional and conditioned our assertion may be, it remains an assertion. Similarly, the norms we invoke, to the extent that they function in our making the assertion, are regarded as just that: normative for human understanding and discourse. All this Peirce respected and explicitly acknowledged. But the baffling question, the question he dared to ask, is: How do these norms function? We have seen that he was unable to answer this question to his own satisfaction, but in grappling with it he executed some of those astute turns which distinguish large minds from small. The most important of these was to liberate himself from the simple model of judgment as assessment. This opened the way to a style of explanation more consonant with

131

the original intent of judgment: to state what is the case.

The assessment model supposes that we compare our state of opinion with some definite standards, much as the naïve realist desired us to compare our articulations with articulated states of affairs "out there." In both cases, the standard must be clear and definite, otherwise no comparison would be useful. But the language we use to describe the norms for judgment is inherently vague. We speak of *sufficient* evidence, a *simpler* account, a more *fruitful* hypothesis, a *unifying* theory, a *coherent* explanation, and defend or criticize research methods by their ability to reveal *relevant* data. Now each of these terms implies an evaluation and so is expressed in a usage that is recurrent yet variant. Expressions like these form a special class that has been dubbed "systematically ambiguous," since they *will* be invoked but are never required to meet the same set of conditions for their application. Traditionally called "analogous terms," one could summarize their peculiar usage by noting that their meaning, role, or function will normally shift from one context to another, even though we are impelled to employ the same term in many, varied contexts.

This means that no clear-cut and definite characterization of, say, the *simpler* account, will ever be forthcoming. For any such formulation would have to be invariant over any context, and would unduly restrict the term in its proper functioning. So there are no definite canons of simplicity—or fruitfulness or relevance—yet these are characteristically acknowledged as *norms* for judgment. So we cannot meet the most basic requirement for the simple assessment model of judgment, namely, that the standards be unequivocal and available in a definite enough way to act as paradigms for comparison. Hence if a man allowed himself to be guided by the logic of our discourse about judgments, he would begin to distrust the comparison model.

But have we anything to offer him in place of what we have called the simple assessment model? Can we propose an alternative way of conceiving what is clearly an assessing role of the intellect? What we have, and what Peirce had, is not simple but it should prove illuminating. That is the affinity of this kind of usage, this sort of notion, with Kant's *regulative* principles—or, rather, with the shape of the intellectual demands that force one to a consideration of the world, the self, and God. It is always difficult to tell in Kant whether the so-called regulative principles are to be identified with the three classical questions: the world, self, and God; or whether these three become issues because of some more basic demands of inquiring intelligence. If this latter be the case, then these demands themselves have better title to the status of regulative principles. And it seems the latter is the case, for Kant invariably speaks of an imperious demand for complete explanation, or (as he would put it) "totality in the synthesis of conditions" (B380, B391). This demand for totality—or coherence or unity—thrusts us into considerations of the transcendent and does so inevitably, for it is natural to the intellect, as he never tires of repeating (B723, 694, 704). So questions about the world, self, and God will not down, though they can admit of no adequate answer since they know no unambiguous formulations.

Yet this disturbing consequence does not warrant our relegating the *a priori* intellectual demands involved to a "merely subjective" realm, as Kant tried to do (B708, 362). For the same requirements of unity, coherence and sufficient reason are operative in every inquiry, scientific as well as metaphysical. Kant has demonstrated clearly what metaphysics had manifested time and again before him, namely, that an indiscriminate employment of these norms outside of a context already controlled ends in mystification. These norms represent demands internal to inquiry itself, they make reference to the *élan* motivating every inquiry; and for this precise reason cannot alone constitute an inquiry. They are not forms of investigation (as Kant's categories are meant to be), but principles of assessment, of judgment. Yet if the desired term of any investigation is a judgment that one's contentions are in fact true, then (on Kant's own terms) the judgment constituting an object relies as much on the one set of *a priori* principles as on the other. Though their roles be different, regulative principles have every bit as much claim to reality and objectivity as the constitutive do.[20]

This Kantian detour is actually a short cut, for Peirce confesses time and again the extent of his dependence upon Kant, specifically on the *Critique of Pure Reason,* and notably the section

"Transcendental Dialectic" (1.3, 5.382 n. 1). His remarks yield only indirect evidence that he read Kant in the fashion sketched above. But my reading would be consistent with Peirce's insistence that sustained, self-correcting inquiry approaches a true statement of what is in fact the case in the world, and so constitutes the real for us.

And it is significant that many of these same norms—simplicity, coherence, unity, and the like—arise in aesthetic discrimination. Indeed they reappear in Kant's *Critique of Judgment* (esp. Introduction, #5) in a more obvious way, perhaps (as I have suggested) because the non-conceptual status of art clearly blocks attempts to supply an unequivocal formulation for them. However that may be, this inability to provide a context-invariant way of expressing the norms for judgment does suggest a certain kinship with feelings. This kinship, reinforced by other systematizing motives, could also have influenced Kant's tendency to relegate them to the "merely subjective." It certainly lends an initial plausibility to so typing them, for nearly every man of common sense as well as every beginning philosophy student is prone to consider evaluations and judgments as "subjective," meaning a matter of feeling and not of fact.

The task of the philosophy teacher since Socrates has been to undermine the common sense of fact enough to interpose an area between feeling and fact where issues arise for discussion and are established (if at all) by appeal neither to feeling nor to fact but to rational argument. Perhaps a difference between the mere teacher of philosophy and a philosopher like Peirce is that the latter goes the whole way with Socrates and recognizes a final point where argument too shows its inadequacy, and his own personal assent is drawn from something more akin to feeling. A feeling purified by argument and dialectic, no doubt, as aesthetic feeling is sensitized by attention to fine discriminations, but more of an attunement of the whole person with the subject of inquiry than a purely intellectual result. Such at least represents, I feel, the final position of Charles Sanders Peirce on judgment as the consummation of inquiry, and fleshes out the parable of knowing as a passionate and personal quest.

134

NOTES

1. Cf. Kenneth M. Sayre, *Recognition: A Study in the Philosophy of Artificial Intelligence* (Notre Dame, 1965).

2. Cf. Bernard J. F. Lonergan's critique of Etienne Gilson's *Realisme thomiste et critique de la connaissance* (Paris, 1939) in "Metaphysics as Horizon," *Gregorianum* 44 (1963), pp. 307-18; recently reprinted in *Cross Currents* 16 (1966), pp. 481-94 and in Lonergan, *Collection* (New York, 1967).

3. This section represents the substance of an article published in *International Philosophical Quarterly* 5 (1965), pp. 522-37, entitled "C. S. Peirce: Pragmatism as a Theory of Judgment."

4. Peirce will be cited unless otherwise noted from *The Collected Papers of Charles Sanders Peirce,* Vols. I-VI, ed. by Charles Hartshorne and Paul Weiss; Vols. VII-VIII, ed. by Arthur Burks (Cambridge, Mass., 1931-35, 1958), where citation will be given in the standard volume and paragraph number fashion: thus 5.161 is taken as referring to Vol. V, paragraph 161.

5. John Dewey, *Reconstruction in Philosophy* (New York, 1920), ch. 6 (Boston, 1948), pp. 154-56.

6. For the distinction of "assertion" and "meaning," see 2.252, 309, 315, 437; 5.30, 86, 424 n.

7. Peirce's phenomenological categories for intentional activity may sound esoteric at first but a discussion of Peirce can hardly avoid employing them. With characteristic directness and a touch of the pedantic, he calls them *firstness, secondness* and *thirdness.* They are typed as "phenomenological categories" and he means them to be just that: descriptive not explanatory, starting points rather than resolutions. *Firstness* is the most difficult of the three to locate. His remarks about it are confusing (cf. 1.304), but for our purposes we can regard it as consciousness prior to any reflection, the very possibility of anything being present, or as Peirce puts it: "the present in its direct positive presentness" (5.44). The other two categories are more relevant to our discussion and more readily identifiable. *Secondness* betokens the direct confrontation with an object other than me. The paradigm is stumbling over an obstacle or slamming into a barrier. *Thirdness* is backing off to notice that the obstacle was a guy wire or the barrier a glass door.
   Every act of seeing that, knowing that something is the case

135

is an example of *thirdness,* or full-blown intentional activity. The other two categories are seldom if ever directly applicable but only reductively present, for to observe is to observe *that* something is the case. *Thirdness* is synonymous with the sign-relation that constitutes intentional activity, but such activity presupposes *secondness* and *firstness.* With *secondness* Peirce acknowledges a given without granting it a privileged cognitive position—for assuming a position is already well within *thirdness.* And with *firstness* he countenances consciousness as a unique ability without demanding that of itself it yield any information.

8. For "pragmatic implication," see C. K. Grant, "Pragmatic Implication," *Philosophy* 33 (1958), pp. 303-24; Max Black, "Presupposition and Implication," in *Models and Metaphors* (Ithaca, 1962), pp. 48-63; and P. H. Nowell-Smith, "Contextual Implication and Ethical Theory," *Aristotelian Society Supplement,* 36 (1962), pp. 1-18.

9. Cf. Wilfrid Sellars, "Counterfactuals, Dispositions, Causal Modalities," in *Minnesota Studies in the Philosophy of Science II* (Minneapolis, 1958), pp. 225-309, especially pp. 287-88.

10. Nowell-Smith concludes the article cited (note 8) by suggesting that "Aristotle was right, both in commending those who said that 'good' means 'what things aim at' and in refusing to commit himself to this as a definition of 'good' " (p. 18); cf. *Nicomachean Ethics* I, 6.

11. The observation is made by Bernard Lonergan in *Insight* (London, 1957), p. 310.

12. This is the crucial role of continuity: always to leave room for a better approximation, yet assure that each contains the limit, and even that after a certain point it is adequately defined, i.e., further approximation becomes irrelevant (cf. Lonergan, *Insight,* pp. 59-60). The fact that continuity is so important even to mathematics lends a formidable rhetorical force to Peirce's use of it, but one is inclined to agree with Murphey's final judgment that he never succeeds in showing how continuity plays the systematic role he says it does. Murray Murphey, *The Development of Peirce's Philosophy* (Cambridge, Mass., 1961), ch. 18, especially pp. 405-7.

13. Compare Plato: "Then the dialectic method proceeds alone by this way, demolishing the hypotheses as it goes, back to the very beginning itself, in order to find firm ground; the soul's eye, which is

really buried deep in a sort of barbaric bog, it draws out quietly and leads upwards, having the arts we have described [mathematics] as handmaids and helpers" (*Republic* VII, 533b; Rouse trans.)

14. Reprinted in Philip Weiner, ed., *Values in a Universe of Chance* (New York, 1958), p. 414. I am indebted to John J. Fitzgerald for the loan of his Ph.D. thesis: "Peirce's Theory of Signs as the Foundation of his Pragmatism" (Tulane [typewritten], 1962), which contains the interpretation we have adopted here, on pp. 92-93. One might also cite 8.184 "[the final Interpretant is that] which *would finally* be decided to be the true interpretation if consideration of the matter were carried so far that an ultimate opinion were reached."

15. Cf. Burrell, "Obeying Rules and Following Instructions" in K. Sayre and F. Crosson (ed.), *Philosophy and Cybernetics* (Notre Dame, 1967).

16. For instance, R. M. Hare, *Language of Morals* (Oxford, 1952), ch. 4: "Decisions of Principle," pp. 56-78.

17. Cf. W. B. Gallie, *Peirce and Pragmatism* (Harmondsworth, 1952), pp. 130-31.

18. The citation is not from Peirce but from W. Sellars, "Empiricism and the Philosophy of Mind," in *Minnesota Studies in the Philosophy of Science I* (Minneapolis, 1956), p. 300; reprinted in *Science, Perception and Reality* (New York, 1963), p. 170. Peirce's remarks on the "lumen naturale" of Galileo are interesting, however, 1.80-1; 6.477.

19. On judgment as "feel," cf. J. J. C. Smart on "Theory Construction" in A. Flew, ed., *Logic and Language* (2nd series; Oxford, 1953), pp. 238, 241, and of course Michael Polanyi, *Personal Knowledge* (Chicago, 1962).

20. Cf. Burrell, "Kant and Philosophical Knowledge," *New Scholasticism* 38 (1964), pp. 189-206.

5

THE FOX ALONE IS DEATH:
Whitehead and Speculative Philosophy*

BY ANDREW J. RECK

It is an egregious mistake to think that Americans are only auto mechanics and industrial technicians, practical men whose minds are exhausted by the making and employment of constantly improved tools. Practical reason left to itself operates in too narrow a circle of light; thus restricted, it becomes blind, falsely secure and inert. The art of living demands a taste for all of life, a willingness to explore far reaches as shafts of light are sent out into the darkness, a rounded respect for as much of the total world-environment of men as can be imagined. The art of living, in short, requires a view of the world, a hunger for metaphysics. A metaphysics in the service of the art of living, of course, is tentative and open and constantly changing its base; it is not fixed, stable, given in advance, static. Yet a creative and open metaphysics is difficult to articulate and make explicit. To leave it merely implicit and unexamined, however, is hardly to have the courage to face one's assumptions. Some men, at least, must have the stamina to trace out those presuppositions and basic orientations toward ourselves and our world which the rest of us are content merely to take for granted. No American has wrestled so hard to express the implicit assumptions of the American way of life—its dynamism, openness, and sense of relatedness, even its technical and mathematical virtuosity—as

* The preparation of this essay was made possible by a grant from the Tulane University Research Council, which furnished me the leisure in 1967-68 to do research on speculative philosophy. A. J. R.

ANDREW J. RECK

Alfred North Whitehead (1861-1947). Andrew J. Reck of Tulane University presents an admirably clear statement of Whitehead's ambition and achievement: and something of a picture of ourselves, necessarily abstract and yet strangely beckoning.

I. THE ART OF LIFE

"The function of Reason," Whitehead has written, "is to promote the art of life."[1] He added: ". . . the art of life is *first* to be alive, *secondly* to be alive in a satisfactory way, and *thirdly* to acquire an increase in satisfaction."[2] In this conception of the role of reason in life, Whitehead disallowed both transcendentalism and dualism, affirming instead that mind has an organic basis and that it evolves in nature and develops in the individual organism. Hence reason is no supernatural active intellect, nor is it seated in a spiritual ego dwelling apart from the physical body with which it is loosely associated. Like the naturalists and the pragmatists, Whitehead maintained that reason inhabits the living organism and that its work is practical. But he differed with the pragmatists and with some naturalists when he insisted that reason is speculative as well as practical, that it is indeed genuinely practical only so far as it is speculative.

Life, whose function reason is, according to Whitehead, is a process happening in nature. It manifests the cosmic principles which prevail in nature as a whole. Whitehead, like Bergson, detected in life two major tendencies with cosmic import: a descending tendency under the sway of the physical order of efficient causation, and an ascending tendency under the influence of the mental order of final causation. Were life merely repetitive, with the same old appetitions being mechanically satisfied in the same old ways, it would eventually fade away, the monotony of habitual behavior eliminating all the intensities of experience. Mind injects novelty, which saves life from the death caused by unceasing repetition. But novelty, too, has its hazards, the hazards of anarchy. For a life of anarchic appetition, tossed about incessantly by various new and incoherent impulses and satisfactions, faces swift extinction. It is, according to Whitehead, reason which overcomes the two deaths that menace life, the death of repetitive appetition and the death of anarchic appetition. Reason regulates itself, introducing ". . . a higher appetition which discriminates among its own anarchic productions. . . . Reason civilizes the brute force of anarchic appetition."[3]

Reason, then, is practical. Exclusively practical reason is, in Whitehead's phrase, "the Reason of Ulysses"; it is "Reason as one of the many factors within the world," and Ulysses "shares it with the foxes."[4] Practical reason does not suffice for the art of life, however; and when it usurps the total office of reason, the results are disastrous. It is not enough to be alive, or even to be alive in a satisfactory way; to stay alive, to fend off the death of monotony, it is necessary to win novelty, to increase satisfaction. Here the reason of Ulysses fails: it does not enhance the quality of life. Despite its much vaunted practicality, the strategy of Ulysses rarely solves real problems, but pressed by interminable exigencies, it consists almost wholly of evasive tactics. Even when Ulysses, at his best, restricts reason to solving practical problems, one relentlessly following upon the heels of another, he has reduced reason to mere methodology, and finally weighted with fatigue, he loses his wiliness. Preoccupation with methods, with means, blinds the exclusively practical man to the nature of goals, of ends, so that mechanism no longer subserves but rather supplants final causation in the conduct of life. Thus futility and doom are the fate of Ulysses, and as Whitehead has remarked: ". . . the bones of his companions are strewn on many a reef and many an isle."[5]

To live, to live well, to live better—this threefold urge demands that reason be more than practical. It must supply a theoretical understanding of life and of the world. Hence reason must be theoretical. According to Whitehead, theoretical reason seeks to understand ". . . the Universe, or at least factors in it, . . . in their character of exemplifying a theoretical system";[6] it is, in Whitehead's phrase, "the Reason of Plato," who shares it with the gods.[7] The reason of Plato, moreover, is "enthroned above the practical tasks of the world. . . . It seeks with disinterested curiosity an understanding of the world."[8] Liberated from exclusive concern with keeping alive, reason is driven forward by its own appetition from partial to complete understanding. It not only furnishes a vision of what is possible for life; it also infects life with this new dynamism. Thus reason "constitutes itself the urge from the good to the better life."[9]

"Speculative Reason" is Whitehead's term for theoretical reason in its proper sense. By means of the adjective "speculative" Whitehead sought to distinguish this kind of reason not only from practical reason in its usual senses, but also from methodological reason, a species of practical reason operative in the special sciences. Looking beyond means to ends, beyond mechanism to possible goals, beyond efficient causation to final causation, speculative reason is, Whitehead affirmed, "in its essence untrammelled by method. Its function is to pierce into the general reasons beyond limited reasons, to understand all methods as coordinated in a nature of things only to be grasped by transcending all method."[10] Although Whitehead admitted that "the bounded intelligence of mankind" can never attain the "infinite ideal" of speculative reason, he nonetheless held that "what distinguishes men from the animals, some humans from other humans, is the inclusion in their natures, waveringly and dimly, of a disturbing element, which is the flight after the unattainable."[11]

II. A CRITICAL, OPEN VISION

Speculative reason, breaking through the mold of conventional concepts and habits of action, seeks the origin, the causes, and the reasons for life. Although it has far-reaching practical consequences, speculative reason is essentially theoretical. Unfolding in the endless "adventures of ideas" that make human civilization, speculative reason finds its highest and most conspicuous expression in speculative philosophy. What, then, is speculative philosophy?

Whitehead offered his conception of speculative philosophy in Chapter I, Part I, of *Process and Reality,* and again in Chapter XV, Part III, of *Adventures of Ideas.* "Speculative Philosophy," he wrote, "is the endeavour to frame a coherent, logical, necessary system of general ideas in terms of which every element of our experience can be interpreted."[12] This definition ascribes to speculative philosophy the internal criteria of coherence, logic, and necessity as well as the external criterion of adequacy—i.e., interpreting every element of experience. It contains both an empirical and a rational side.

The concession to rationalism consists in the requirement that the system be coherent and logical. The system is deemed logical if it is consistent, it violates no rule of inference, and its basic concepts are logically determinable. The coherence of the system signifies more; it "means that the fundamental ideas, in terms of which the scheme is developed, presuppose each other so that in isolation they are meaningless."[13] Here the requirement is one of strict internal relatedness for the conceptual elements in the system. For Whitehead, it is, in principle, "the business of speculative philosophy to exhibit this truth" that "no entity can be conceived in complete abstraction from the system of the universe. . . ."[14] Further, the necessity of the system pertains to the demand that its fundamental concepts be universal. At this juncture, Whitehead departed from rationalism: the necessity of the system means, he wrote, "that there is an essence to the universe which forbids relationships beyond itself, as a violation of its rationality. Speculative philosophy seeks that essence."[15]

Whitehead departed from rationalism in other respects as well. He explicitly repudiated traditional rationalistic philosophy for mistakenly supposing that the fundamental principles be clear and distinct axioms from which by deductive methods alone the rest of the system could be inferred. Rather, both the test and the origin of philosophical principles, according to Whitehead, point to experience; consequently, his philosophy is empirical.

Whitehead's concession to empiricism is evident, first, in the requirement that the system of general ideas be able to interpret "every element of our experience." By "interpretation" he meant "that everything of which we are conscious, as enjoyed, perceived, willed, or thought, shall have the character of a particular instance of the general scheme."[16] The external criteria of speculative philosophy are here made explicit: the interpretation should be "applicable" and "adequate" to experience. Apparently the empirical side received from Whitehead paramount emphasis. "Our datum," he said, "is the actual world, including ourselves; and this actual world spreads itself for observation in the guise of the topic of our immediate experience. The elucidation of immediate experience is the sole justification for any thought. . . ."[17] But Whitehead is no positivist. True, speculative philosophy must attend to experience; it must at least be descriptive. However, description, while a necessary condition, is not sufficient. As Whitehead stressed, "the primary method of philosophy is descriptive generalization."[18]

Generalization is rooted in experience. It takes observed and analyzed elements of immediate experience as the clues to the nature and structure of remote experience and beyond. Nevertheless, empirical observation cannot suffice for a comprehensive speculative philosophy, since all observation proceeds through awareness of difference, a limitation playfully illustrated by Whitehead: "Sometimes we see an elephant, and sometimes we do not. The result is that an elephant, when present, is noticed."[19] Thus just those elements of experience which are most pervasive and hence most effective for valid generalization are the most difficult, if not impossible, to observe. To supply the requisite difference, "imaginative generalization" must supplement observation. Whitehead has compared this method of discovery with the flight of an airplane. "It starts from the ground of particular observation; it makes a flight in the thin air of imaginative generalization; and it again lands for renewed observation rendered acute by rational interpretation."[20]

The method of generalization, therefore, utilizes "specific notions, applying to a restricted group of facts, for the divination of the generic notions which apply to all facts."[21] This guarantees the empirical requirement that the system at least apply to experience and that the items of experience be interpreted in terms of the general conceptions of the system. After selecting a specific set of notions and generalizing them into the basic conceptions of the system, the method of generalization must proceed, according to Whitehead, in "unflinching pursuit of the two rationalistic ideals, coherence and logical perfection."

Since Whitehead was aware that rationalism has led historically to false systems, he maintained that the coherence of the categorical scheme of generic notions should not take precedence over the interpretation of experience, and that the generic notions, once achieved, should never be held dogmatically as certain. "Metaphysical categories," he insisted, "are not dogmatic statements of the obvious; they are tentative formulations of the utmost generalities."[22] Thus the logician's alternative of true or false cannot readily be applied to the basic categorial scheme, and if applied, "the answer must be that the scheme is false."[23] Whatever truth the scheme possesses is dependent on "unformulated qualifications, exceptions, limitations, and new interpretations in terms of more general notions."[24]

As W. Mays remarked: "The method of philosophical construction put forward by Whitehead resembles the hypothetico-deductive method used by the scientist and the mathematician."[25] In Whitehead's words, speculative philosophy "embodies the method of the 'working hypothesis.' . . . Such an hypothesis directs observation, and decides upon the mutual relevance of various types of evidence."[26] This does not mean, as Mays sometimes suggests, that Whitehead's speculative construction is intended to be the hypothetico-deductive method of the mathematical physicist. If this were Whitehead's intention, then clearly his achievement is a failure. Speculative reason, let us recall, is "untrammelled by method." "In short, it prescribes method."[27] The first step in the construction of a philosophical system, already mentioned as imaginative generalization, involves, according to Whitehead, "philosophic intuitions," so much so that he even described philosophical system "as an attempt to coordinate all such intuitions. . . ."[28]

The differences between speculative philosophy and science are not restricted to the origins of the enterprises; they pertain to purposes, too. One main difference in this respect appears supportive rather than divisive. Speculative philosophy, Whitehead affirmed, "seeks those generalities which characterize the complete reality of fact, and apart from which any fact must sink into abstraction. But science makes the abstraction, and is content to understand the complete fact in respect to only some of its essential aspects. Science and Philosophy mutually criticize each other, and

144

provide imaginative material for each other. A philosophic system should present an elucidation of concrete fact from which the sciences abstract. Also the sciences should find their principles in the concrete facts which a philosophic system presents."[29] Hence, in contrast with the specialized theories of the sciences, speculative philosophy is comprehensive: the purpose of its working-hypothesis is "to coordinate the current expressions of human experience, in common speech, in social institutions, in actions, in the principles of the various special sciences, elucidating harmonies and exposing discrepancies."[30]

Speculative philosophy as conceived by Whitehead resembles science in the "openness" of its systems. Often the charge is raised against speculative philosophy that, despite (or because of) its ambitious and dogmatic claims, it suffers inevitable refutation. After all, the history of Western thought is strewn with the wreckage of philosophical systems. Kant, whose shadow falls over contemporary antimetaphysicians, personified the opposition to philosophical speculation. Kant argued that, while speculative metaphysics is a dejected pseudo-science torn between dogmatism and skepticism, science in the guise of mathematics and physics had attained final perfection in its basic conceptions and in the body of knowledge built upon these conceptions. But as Whitehead has shown, Kant's contrast of certain science with uncertain philosophy is mistaken. As the careers of Euclidean geometry and of Newtonian physics have testified in the nineteenth and twentieth centuries, science, no less than speculative philosophy, undergoes radical revisions of its ultimate categories. This does not mean that there is no hope of attaining truth in science and in philosophy. On the contrary, for Whitehead, the quest for true principles should be unrelenting. However, Whitehead has borrowed a term from mathematics to describe the approach to truth in science and in philosophy as "asymptotic."[31] Under the circumstances, of course, this does mean that the system of philosophy, like that of science, can never be closed; it must remain open for revision, addition, and alteration. In a sentence Whitehead summed the matter up: "The proper test is not that of finality, but of progress."[32]

In the course of defining speculative philosophy, Whitehead

made several remarks concerning related issues which are germane to the contemporary philosophical situation. Let us attend to these.

First in order of consideration are his remarks on language. Today Anglo-American philosophers in large numbers are occupied with the analysis of ordinary language, with the intention of solving or resolving all philosophical problems thereby. The dominance of linguistic analysis is, no doubt, a major factor responsible for the neglect of Whitehead's philosophy in the British Isles, a neglect so total that one British commentator on his thought has even migrated to the United States. For, although Whitehead recognized that language is "the tool required for philosophy,"[33] he nevertheless concluded that in genuine speculation "words and phrases must be stretched towards a generality foreign to their ordinary usage. . . ."[34] Reliance on ordinary language restricting philosophy to an examination of its usages would, according to Whitehead, confine thought to a range of older and antiquated generalities. In particular, the grammar of ordinary language has the subject-predicate form, a logical structure participating in the ancient substance-predicate metaphysics. However useful this structure may have been to formulate conceptions of reality and of relatedness in the past, it is inadequate to experience and to the scientific study of nature. In place of the older logical forms, multirelational logical systems have developed, and in place of the older sciences of substances, each static and unrelated, new sciences of dynamic process have arisen. Because speculative philosophy must adjust to the consequent modifications in basic conceptions, it cannot limit itself to ordinary language or ordinary usage. When it does employ ordinary language, as perforce it must, unless it is to be stated in purely symbolic calculi, speculative philosophy must use words and phrases as "metaphors mutely appealing for an imaginative leap."[35]

Second in order are his remarks on subjectivism. For Whitehead the dominant bias of modern philosophy, originating in Descartes and continuing in the philosophies of the British empiricists and of Kant, has been subjectivistic. This bias, as Ivor Leclerc notes, has made "epistemology . . . basic to the whole philosophical enterprise."[36] It has raised the specter of solipsism: how, from the enclosure of one's own subjective experience, can knowledge of an objective reality be possible? Whitehead repudiated this subjectivism, adopting instead "the 'objectivist' standpoint of Greek and medieval philosophy."[37] Today various kinds of subjectivism flourish in European philosophy; the Danish founder of contemporary existentialism proclaimed that truth is subjectivity. Obviously Whitehead's search for a system of philosophy which would comprehend all experience and reality in its categories and principles is alien to the subjectivistic concerns of the existentialists. While consciousness is initially subjective, it should not, according to Whitehead, remain so. "Philosophy," he affirmed, "is the self-correction by consciousness of its own initial excess of subjectivity. . . . The task of philosophy is to recover the totality obscured by the selection."[38]

Finally, Whitehead clarified the relevance of philosophical speculation to practice. As we have seen, the wisdom of Ulysses and the foxes bears the deficiencies of exclusively practical reason. American pragmatist thought, despite its explicitly theoretical intentions in the work of thinkers like C. S. Peirce, has been used, rightly or wrongly, by those who would denigrate inquiry for its own sake and direct attention solely to the solution of short-run practical problems. Whitehead was outspokenly opposed to this point of view, and to its implied reduction of philosophy to methodology. His position has, however, been misunderstood. On the one hand, A. D. Ritchie has accused Whitehead of undervaluing "the stimulating effect of practical wants."[39] On the other hand, A. E. Murphy has charged that "the effect" of Whitehead's speculative philosophy, "when it is seriously applied to the interpretation of experience, is to 'justify' some human interests by according them a status in 'ultimate reality' which they neither require nor can reasonably maintain."[40] Whitehead's position escapes both charges. "Whatever is found in 'practice,'" he said, "must lie within the scope of the metaphysical description. When the description fails to include the 'practice,' the metaphysics is inadequate and requires revision."[41]

Furthermore, practice is itself affected by the systems of phi-

147

losophy. In seeking to frame the coherent, logical, and necessary systems of general ideas applicable to and adequate for experience, speculative philosophers perform a significant service to civilization. Their systems, Whitehead maintained, "are the way the human spirit cultivates its deeper intuitions. Such systems give life and motion to detached thoughts."[42] Indeed, Whitehead has gone so far as to compare the ideas which dwell in systems of philosophy to "some species of animal, or plant, or microbe, which lurks for ages as an obscure by-product of nature in some lonely jungle, or morass, or island. Then by some trick of circumstance it escapes into the outer world and transforms a civilization, or destroys an empire or the forests of a continent."[43]

III. NATURE ALIVE

"The final problem," Whitehead declared, "is to conceive a complete [παντελής] fact."[44] Such a conception, he continued, can be formed only in terms of "fundamental notions concerning the nature of reality."[45] Commenting on this passage, Ivor Leclerc has remarked that Whitehead, by so conceiving his philosophical task, has placed himself "fully in the great philosophical tradition."[46] In Whitehead's own context, the "fundamental notions concerning the nature of reality" are equated with "the seven main factors interwoven in fact" allegedly divined by Plato: "The Ideas, The Physical Elements, The Psyche, The Eros, The Harmony, The Mathematical Relations, The Receptacle."[47] In spite of the admission that "it is most unscholarly to identify our modern notions with these archaic thoughts of Plato," Whitehead nonetheless pressed his thesis: "All philosophical systems are endeavours to express the interweaving of these components."[48] Although Whitehead considered Plato to be the guide in the construction of philosophical systems, Leclerc cites Aristotle as the classic model with which to compare Whitehead's metaphysical achievement. "Whitehead," Leclerc asserts, "is stating the basic and essential metaphysical problem of which Aristotle has given the classic formulation."[49] Thus Whitehead's problem of conceiving a complete fact is construed to be equivalent with

148

Aristotle's quest for an elucidation of being *qua* being; and Whitehead's actual entities and Aristotle's concrete substances are viewed as playing analogous roles in their otherwise disparate systems of metaphysics.

Whitehead's speculative system, presented in *Process and Reality,* is of course not usually regarded in relation to classic Greek philosophy. Whitehead himself was far more concerned to relate it to modern philosophy, especially to his British predecessors, Locke and Hume. As the title of the work reveals, it is most readily classified as a modern variety of process philosophy. But it would be wrong to infer that Whitehead is a process philosopher only trivially distinguishable from other process thinkers—e.g., Bergson. While the typical process philosopher is so preoccupied with the flux and so disdainful of logic and abstract theory that flux, process, becoming, change, motion are blurred together, Whitehead refused to abandon logic and abstract theory; he was more inclined to draw intellectualist distinctions. True, he was not always exact in his usages. Concerning the term "process," which is synonymous in Whitehead's writings with "flux," there are, as William A. Christian has pointed out, presystematic usages divergent from the systematic ones.[50] Nevertheless, within the system the term "process" has two meanings: (1) concrescence—i.e., in Christian's words, "growth or internal change"; and (2) transition—i.e., again in Christian's words, "change of status in relation to other things."[51] Further, according to Whitehead, change is not identical with becoming. Strictly (systematically) speaking, growth or internal change, concrescence, is not change; it is becoming. The fundamental entities in Whitehead's system do not change; "they merely *become.*"[52] Change denotes the sequence of differences between these fundamental entities constituting an event,[53] or it describes the adventures of universal characteristics in the evolving universe of actual things.[54] Moreover, the process of the fundamental entities in Whitehead's system must not be confused with motion: "An actual entity never moves; it is where it is and what it is."[55] Finally, the becoming of an entity is its perishing. "The ancient doctrine that 'no one crosses the same river twice' is extended. No thinker thinks twice; and, to put the matter more generally, no subject experiences twice."[56] And yet paradoxically for Whitehead the perpetual perishing of the fundamental entities is tantamount to what he has termed their "objective immortality."[57] The entities become data for all subsequent entities.

This introduces another feature marking Whitehead's philosophy off from the typical process philosophy. For Whitehead, process is not the sole theme of metaphysics. To formulate "the complete problem of metaphysics" in *Process and Reality,* Whitehead cited two lines of a famous hymn:

> Abide with me;
> Fast falls the eventide.

He proceeded to comment: "Here the first line expresses the permanences, 'abide,' 'me' and the 'Being' addressed; and the second line sets these permanences amid the inescapable flux. . . . Those philosophers who start with the first line have given us the metaphysics of 'substance'; and those who start with the second line have developed the metaphysics of 'flux.' But, in truth, the two lines cannot be torn apart in this way. . . ."[58] No doubt, according to Whitehead, "the flux of things is one ultimate generalization around which we must weave our philosophical system,"[59] but as Victor Lowe has observed, even italicizing the word "one" when he quoted the line above, the other "ultimate generalization" for Whitehead is the idea of permanence.[60] Resuming the commentary on the lines of the hymn almost two hundred pages later, Whitehead said: "In the inescapable flux, there is something that abides; in the overwhelming permanence, there is an element that escapes into the flux. Permanence can be snatched only out of the flux; and the passing moment can find its adequate intensity only by its submission to permanence. Those who would disjoin the two elements can find no interpretation of patent facts."[61]

Whitehead's metaphysics may also be approached through consideration of his own label, "philosophy of organism."[62] Like other thinkers of his generation—e.g., John Dewey, Whitehead fell under the influence of Darwin and the theory of biological evolution. In this regard perhaps, Victor Lowe esteems Whitehead's

150

philosophy of organism to be "the ultimate intellectual achievement of the nineteenth century,"[63] although as a mathematician sensitive to the formal patterns and structures of process as well as to the process itself, Whitehead conspicuously belongs to the twentieth century. At any rate, his conception of organism is remarkably original. The term "organism" in its systematic usage never signified for Whitehead the full-bodied natural organism encountered in ordinary experience, recognized by common sense, and studied by the sciences in their descriptive and classificatory stages. That full-bodied natural organism is rather a society or organization of more basic organisms. Indeed, Whitehead distinguished two interconnected but intellectually separable meanings of "organism": one microscopic, the other macroscopic. Neither satisfies the ordinary concept. Organism in the microscopic sense is the actual entity, to be considered below, and in the macroscopic sense is "the givenness of the actual world, considered as a stubborn fact. . . ."[64] The microscopic meaning is primary. As Whitehead said: "The philosophy of organism is a cell-theory of actuality. Each ultimate unit of fact is a cell-complex, not analysable into components with equivalent completeness of actuality."[65]

Whitehead's introduction of his system as philosophy of organism is also connected with his conception of philosophy's role in the critique of scientific abstractions. Accordingly, classical Newtonian physics had projected a cosmological scheme which deprived life, mind, and value of their proper place in the world. This cosmological scheme, with its notions of absolute time, absolute space, matter, and exclusively mechanical causation, presented, in Whitehead's terms, "nature lifeless."[66] As Whitehead declared: "The status of life in nature is the modern problem of philosophy and of science. Indeed it is the central meeting point of all the strains of systematic thought, humanistic, naturalistic, philosophic."[67] Hence the basic categories of science and philosophy had to be reconstructed and reinterpreted in a full-scale cosmology which takes account of life, its forms and values. The need was, as Whitehead put it, for a doctrine of "nature alive." To meet this need, he maintained "that neither physical nature nor life can be understood unless we fuse them together as essential factors in the composition of

151

'really real' things whose inter-connections and individual characters constitute the universe."[68]

What, then, are the basic categories of Whitehead's philosophy? In Chapter II, Part I, of *Process and Reality,* Whitehead
sketched his categorial scheme. The remaining five hundred pages
of the book, of course, flesh it out, just as the entire body of his
works illuminates and even revises it. Necessarily condensed, the
sketch contains no fewer than forty-five categories: one category of
the ultimate, eight categories of existence, twenty-seven categories
of explanation, and nine categorial obligations. Add to these what
Whitehead modestly called in the next chapter "some derivative
notions," which include, among other concepts, that of God, and
the performance may well dishearten the most sympathetic student.[69]

Although it is beyond the compass of the present essay to
discuss in detail the categories of Whitehead's metaphysics, it is
useful to consider, in brief, his central notions. Whitehead himself
has lightened the task by singling out four notions for special consideration: "that of an 'actual entity,' that of a 'prehension,' that of
a 'nexus,' and that of the 'ontological principle.' "[70] They underscore, by Whitehead's own assertion, his endeavor "to base philosophical thought upon the most concrete elements in our experience."[71] Let us consider each notion.

The category of actual entity is a category of existence. Whitehead defined "actual entities," also termed "actual occasions," as
"the final real things of which the world is made up."[72] Nothing is
more real than actual entities. They are, he continued, "drops of
experience, complex and interdependent."[73] An actual entity is
conspicuously what Whitehead has called "a complete fact." The
similarity between Whitehead's metaphysical endeavor and Aristotle's, already mentioned, is manifest here, in that the pluralism of
actual entities parallels Aristotle's pluralism of individual substances. But the differences are also remarkable. The actual entity
is no entity recognized by common sense and ordinary observation:
it is microscopic. Nor does the actual entity endure in time: its
existence is atomic; it perishes the moment it becomes. Moreover,
the actual entity is qualitative; it is a drop of experience. Further,

actual entities are not separate, independent entities; they are related and interdependent. Finally, every actual entity is objectively immortal; it is "felt" by all subsequent actual entities.

The ontological principle is a category of explanation. It reinforces Whitehead's pluralism in its demand that only actual entities serve as reasons for what is. As Whitehead said: "According to the ontological principle there is nothing which floats into the world from nowhere. Everything in the actual world is referable to some actual entity."[74] In sum the principle maintains: "no actual entity, then no reason."[75] The demand for a reason is, however, not reducible to a demand for an efficient cause alone, since speculative reason for Whitehead, as previously noted, seeks final causes. Hence Whitehead readily termed the ontological principle the "principle of efficient, and final, causation," adding that this "means that actual entities are the only *reasons;* so that to search for a *reason* is to search for one or more actual entities."[76]

The notion of "prehension," another category of existence, comes into play when the actual entity is analyzed. While various modes of analysis are available, Whitehead chose analysis in terms of prehension as that mode "which exhibits the most concrete elements in the nature of actual entities."[77] Prehensions not only denote the internal qualities of an entity being brought to unity; they are also—indeed, essentially—"concrete facts of relatedness,"[78] involving that entity in a complex of relations to other things. "A prehension," Whitehead amplified, "reproduces in itself the general characteristics of an actual entity: it is referent to an external world, and in this sense will be said to have a 'vector character'; it involves emotion, and purpose, and valuation, and causation."[79] In stressing the role of prehension in constituting the actual entity, Whitehead in effect attributed *feeling* to all actual entities.

Every actual entity prehends all past actual entities, and is in turn prehended by all future ones. The prehension within an actual entity involves at least assimilation of the data furnished it; but it includes as well an internal form which imparts unity to the complexity. This internal, or subjective, form points forward, toward a satisfaction attainable within the entity itself. Having attained its satisfaction, the entity perishes, to be in turn prehended by later actual entities. In this way, prehensions are facts of relatedness, and actual entities are immortal.

Thus the fourth notion central to Whitehead's metaphysics looms into view—the notion of "nexus." A nexus is "a particular fact of togetherness among actual entities."[80] Common words for "nexus" are "society" or "organized group." Since actual entities are for Whitehead microscopic, whether identified as electrically charged particles in physics or as drops of experience in psychology, they are elements component in the objects of common sense and ordinary experience. These latter objects are nexūs of actual entities, societies of occasions.

Whitehead singled out the four notions mentioned above not simply because of their centrality to his system, but also "by reason of the fact that they involve some divergence from antecedent philosophical thought."[81] For a balanced understanding of his system, therefore, it is necessary to consider three additional notions: creativity; eternal objects; and God.

Creativity is "the category of the ultimate."[82] Describing it as "the universal of universals characterizing ultimate matter of fact," Whitehead wrote: "It is that ultimate principle by which the many, which are the universe disjunctively, become the one actual occasion, which is the universe conjunctively."[83] He continued: " 'Creativity' is the principle of *novelty*. An actual occasion is a novel entity diverse from any entity in the 'many' which it unifies."[84] By applying the ultimate category of creativity in the interpretation of the cosmos, Whitehead, like Bergson with the *élan vital,* viewed the world process as a "creative advance."[85]

The notion of "eternal object" is that category of existence which stands out in contrast with the category of actual entities— with, in Whitehead's words, "a certain extreme finality."[86] Eternal objects designate "Pure Potentials for Specific Determination of Fact, or Forms of Definiteness."[87] Their function in Whitehead's system is reminiscent of Plato's Ideas—the forms or universals. In his presystematic writings on nature and modern science, Whitehead had appealed to this type of being when he contended that objects "ingressed" into events.[88] The inclusion of the notion in the

154

mature system has, however, troubled many commentators. Some have objected on the grounds that the category of *eternal* objects does violence to the process character of Whitehead's system; others that it allows too immense a domain of pure possibility.[89] Whatever the outcome of these objections, the doctrine of eternal objects is clearly a major factor in the theme of permanence which Whitehead accepted as the counterpart of the theme of flux. Eternal objects are ideals. Like past actual entities, they are prehended by the present actual entity, although they are timeless. Whereas the prehension of actual entities by a present actual entity is physical prehension, the prehension of eternal objects is conceptual prehension. Every actual entity is di-polar, physically prehending past entities and conceptually prehending timeless ideals. Hence every actual entity intersects lines of efficient and of final causation.

Finally, Whitehead's notion of "God" is worthy of consideration. In *Process and Reality* the notion of "God" is a derivative one, at least by explicit statement. For Whitehead maintained that "God is an actual entity, and so is the most trivial puff of existence in far-off empty space."[90] As creativity is the category of the ultimate, it follows that "God is its primordial, non-temporal accident."[91] Among the commentators on Whitehead, William A. Christian has elaborated most consistently the side of Whitehead's doctrine according to which God is an actual entity and, therefore, *not* a person, since a person is definitionally a nexus of actual entities.[92] On the other hand, Charles Hartshorne, conceiving God to be a central and not a derivative notion, has construed the Whiteheadian God as a unique personal order.[93] Indeed, Hartshorne has reported that once in private conversation Whitehead had described God "as a 'society of occasions' (with personal order)."[94] Victor Lowe, also discussing the problem of God in Whitehead's philosophy, has suggested that it is "impossible to specify the exact logical structure of Whitehead's metaphysical position."[95] Nevertheless, the major outlines of Whitehead's doctrine of God are discernible. God as a cosmological principle has a dual nature: primordial and consequent. In his primordial nature God prehends the eternal objects; in his consequent nature he prehends all actual entities. Thus he determines the relevance of permanent but possible ideals to the

155

flux of actual entities; and further, he assures objective immortality to every actual entity. Whitehead's theory of God, more so perhaps than the other major categories of his metaphysics, has served to baffle and to inspire other philosophers.

IV. VISION RULES THE WORLD

Whitehead's place in American philosophy has yet to be assessed. While his contributions to logic, mathematics, and the philosophy of science antedated his arrival at Harvard, he constructed a major system of speculative metaphysics afterward.[96] Historians and interpreters of American thought, disregarding the fact that Whitehead remained a British subject throughout his life, count him as one of the five or six classic philosophers who have flourished on the American scene since 1880.[97] One commentator has gone so far as to dub Whitehead a "violent convert to America" who put "the crown" on the development of American thought.[98]

Unquestionably, it has been tempting to relate Whitehead to other major American thinkers. James Feibleman has pointed out the similarities between Whitehead's philosophy and Peirce's,[99] similarities which are all the more fascinating because Whitehead apparently knew nothing of Peirce's works, except the logic, prior to the completion of *Process and Reality*.[100] Although Whitehead seems to have known little of Royce's work, his welcome at Harvard in the 1920's, reported by William Ernest Hocking, Royce's most famous disciple, was prepared, in part, by the remaining influences of Royce's speculative idealism.[101] Of Whitehead, Hocking himself has written: "From no man have I received so wide a sense of the dignity of the human calling to think the world; from no man have I learned so much."[102] The affinity idealists felt for Whitehead found perhaps its highest expression when R. F. Alfred Hoernlé hailed Whitehead's philosophy as a sign of the revival of idealism.[103] The connection between James and Whitehead is more direct still. In advance of constructing his own philosophical system Whitehead had apparently read James. The originality of Whitehead's philosophy notwithstanding, the notion of the actual entity as a drop of experience and the doctrine of prehensions reveal, as Victor Lowe has demonstrated,[104] a striking closeness to James's radical empiricism in terminology and conception.

Santayana, Dewey, and Whitehead were contemporaries who read each other's works. The postscript to Santayana's *Realm of Essence* contains reference to Whitehead's notion of eternal objects: Santayana, while citing Whitehead for corroboration of his own theory of essence, criticized him for regarding objects as ingredient in things and events.[105] In turn Whitehead comments in *Process and Reality* on Santayana's doctrines.[106]

The Whitehead-Dewey relations are complex. Whitehead contributed to the volume on Dewey in "The Library of Living Philosophers" edited by Paul Arthur Schilpp; he ranked Dewey with Bacon, Descartes, Locke, and Comte for having "disclosed great ideas relevant to the functioning of the social system," praising Dewey as "the typical effective American thinker; . . . the chief intellectual force providing that environment with coherent purpose."[107] Dewey responded in one sentence by noting that Whitehead had written with "his characteristic generosity of spirit."[108] Similarly, Dewey contributed to the Schilpp volume on Whitehead; his essay is a probing attempt to interpret and evaluate Whitehead's thought from his own point of view.[109] Whereas Dewey commended Whitehead for attending to human experience for the generic traits of existence, he objected to Whitehead's conception of philosophy as a systematic scheme analogous to mathematics. Unfortunately, Whitehead had been too ill to prepare a rejoinder to any of the contributions to the Schilpp volume. However, the thrust of Dewey's criticism had been made plain in a 1936 symposium on Whitehead's philosophy held before the Eastern Division of the American Philosophical Association; he at that time had charged Whitehead with indecisiveness concerning the interpretation of philosophical principles, with vacillating between the genetic-functional method of explanation which stems from the natural sciences and which concentrates on developmental processes, on the one hand, and the formal method of explanation which derives from symbolic logic and mathematics and which focuses on static structures and relations, on the other hand.[110] Whitehead in reply de-

157

clined to choose between these methods, maintaining instead that an adequate philosophy must fuse them.[111]

However laudatory in print Whitehead may have been of Dewey's philosophy, he was somewhat harsh in private conversation, if Lucien Price's record is accurate. On one occasion, Whitehead compared Dewey with Confucius, and condemned both their philosophies for promoting cultural stagnation.[112] On another occasion, while praising Dewey as a person, Whitehead admitted a "coolness" to his thought, because Dewey's "emphasis . . . is on security," whereas "the vitality of man's mind is in adventure."[113] On a third occasion, to Dewey's detriment, Whitehead compared him with William James, accusing him for having "enormously narrowed" James's thought.[114] Calling James "one of the great philosophic minds in history," Whitehead praised James for his "consciousness of the ever-present complexity and possibility in human experience" and for his "awareness of the wide scope and the interrelations of all questions. . . ."[115]

The story of Whitehead's place in American philosophy thickens as thinkers other than the classic ones are reviewed. Whitehead's work in mathematical logic and the philosophy of science reached these shores before he did. C. I. Lewis has related how in 1910-11 as Royce's assistant at Harvard he got from Royce one of the first copies of *Principia Mathematica,* initiating him into the field of symbolic logic.[116] Lewis' appreciation of Whitehead's presystematic writings extended certainly to his works on the philosophy of science, as evident not only in the essay he contributed to the second edition of the Schilpp volume,[117] but also, it should be added, in Lewis' construction of his own philosophy.[118] Similarly, George Herbert Mead was inspired by Whitehead's presystematic writings when he undertook his own forays in constructive philosophy.[119] Today Willard Van Orman Quine, advancing logic and ontology, continues investigations he inaugurated when he was a Harvard student under Whitehead. Indeed, Whitehead "launched" Quine in his career by writing the Foreword to the latter's first book.[120]

In addition to Whitehead's influence on subsequent developments in logic and the philosophy of science, his impact on speculative thought in America has been most profound and pervasive. This is, of course, not to say that his reception here was completely amicable. On the contrary, his thought encountered considerable caustic opposition. On the side of idealism, W. M. Urban articulated an attitude shared by many American philosophers when he attacked Whitehead for unintelligibility and complained that he could not understand Whitehead's language.[121] On the side of naturalism, Stephen Pepper, whose conception of metaphysics as world hypothesis invites comparison with Whitehead's conception of speculative philosophy, initially rejected Whitehead's system as confused eclecticism. Whitehead, he charged, had mixed the root metaphors, and had concocted an illegitimate fusion of mechanism and formism.[122] More recently Pepper has revised this judgment; now he concedes that Whitehead was groping for a new root metaphor, "the actual occasion," upon which he sought to base an original world hypothesis.[123] Pepper translates Whitehead's concept into one of his own, "the purposive act." After showing the limits of Whitehead's success in elaborating this concept into a full-blown metaphysics, Pepper has published a system of his own grounded on the same concept.[124]

So strong is Whitehead's influence among speculative philosophers in America that it is, in fact, possible to discern a school of Whiteheadians on the American philosophical scene. In its midst three thinkers, all of whom knew Whitehead personally and even studied with him, stand out: F. S. C. Northrop, Charles Hartshorne, and Paul Weiss. They now deserve our consideration.

F. S. C. Northrop, as a young graduate student in the years immediately following the First World War, pursued his studies in England, with McTaggart at Cambridge and with Whitehead at London. As Northrop says, Whitehead's influence on him was formative. Northrop credits Whitehead with doing three things: directing Northrop's "philosophical analysis of the theory and method of 20th-century physics," making it unequivocally clear to Northrop that a reconstruction of the fundamental assumptions of the modern world as regards both scientific and humanistic thought is necessary, and impressing upon Northrop the fact that "in either science or philosophy one cannot be too suspicious of ordinary language."[125] Although Northrop eventually "left Whitehead's epistemological philosophy of both common sense and physics for that of Einstein,"[126] his orientation remained Whiteheadian.

Northrop's first book, *Science and First Principles,* projects a new cosmology consonant with recent developments in relativity physics, quantum mechanics, and physiology. Northrop's cosmology is based on one ultimate macroscopic atom. He writes: "This universe must be constituted not only of the moving microscopic atoms of the traditional atomic theory, but also of one large physical macroscopic atom, spherical in shape and hollow in its interior except for its inner field, which surrounds and congests them."[127] Whitehead, who had studied Northrop's theories as they appeared in the technical journals prior to book publication, regarded the doctrine of the macroscopic atom as the only alternative to his own cosmology of microscopic actual entities.[128]

From constructive cosmology Northrop went on to the study of epistemology, culture, anthropology, and law. In *Adventures of Ideas* Whitehead had explored the role of key ideas in the history and formation of Western civilization.[129] Northrop, in a sense, has generalized Whitehead's enterprise. In *The Meeting of East and West*, appearing soon after the Second World War, Northrop explicates the implicit philosophies shaping modern cultures.[130] In particular, he attends to theories of knowledge and of experience, showing the ramifications in institutions and values which a culture undergoes from stressing the theoretical component or the empirical component in knowledge. Despite, or because of, the speculative character of his inquiry, Northrop's intentions are palpably practical. Believing that conflicts between nations are generated by their philosophies, he hoped to disclose those principles which promise to reconcile rival systems. Northrop's investigations extended to anthropology and law: anthropology because it enables the investigator to uncover the philosophical principles operative in a people, constituting its institutions and its laws; law because it is the key to the realization of international peace. Beyond doubt, no living American philosopher matches Northrop in understanding law, its complexity, its limits, and its effectiveness.[131]

In a related series of works, Northrop has also addressed him-

self to the pressing problems of international peace.[132] Always
he has striven to demonstrate how social institutions and movements spring from basic if implicit beliefs about knowledge, reality,
and value. Amidst the struggles and wars that engulf and threaten
to engulf contemporary man, Northrop points to the ideological
factors as causative. Certainly, in a world rent with ideological
differences, the best strategy for peace may be devised, not by the
diplomat or the soldier, but by the philosopher.

Charles Hartshorne, who in 1925 became a colleague and for
a semester an assistant of Whitehead's at Harvard, was, he says,
"never in the usual sense a 'pupil' of Whitehead's."[133] Hartshorne
asserts that he had already formed his basic convictions "that reality consists of feelings, that these are essentially 'social' . . . , that
there must be a supreme, all-inclusive mind, . . . that the future is
open and in process of determination, that there are new facts from
moment to moment, and even new divine cognitions, that process is
all-inclusive."[134] He credits Whitehead with reinforcing and crys-
talizing into technical doctrine these basic beliefs. Further, Hartshorne praises Whitehead as having been "the only living thinker
who seemed to have a grasp of these matters, and also the only one
in whom I could find the sort of systematic clarity and comprehen-
siveness that we admire in Leibniz."[135] These remarks, despite the
high esteem expressed for Whitehead, are unnecessarily defensive
of Hartshorne's own merits as an independent and creatively original thinker.

No philosopher today equals Hartshorne in the adoption,
adaptation, elaboration, and advocacy of Whiteheadian ideas.[136]
He has expounded the metaphysics of process in numerous essays,
several of which have been collected in a book bearing the apt title,
Reality as Social Process.[137] Hartshorne's first book, *The Philosophy and Psychology of Sensation,* is especially germane to an understanding of Whitehead's theory of prehension; it inquires into
the nature of feeling and propounds the theory of the affective
continuum. According to this theory, "the contents of sensation
form an 'affective continuum' of aesthetically meaningful, socially
expressive, organically adaptive and evolving experience function."[138]

Hartshorne's major contributions, however, have been in the area of theology and religion. After two early books in which he argues for a new naturalistic theism based on process cosmology and modern logic,[139] Hartshorne offers, in *Divine Relativity,* an original process theology, with panpsychistic and panentheistic elements. God is presented as a being who is both active and passive, who creates and enjoys his creatures but suffers and sorrows with them as well. While this conception of God is close to the meaning believed and felt in religion, it has received rigorous formulation, perhaps for the first time, in Hartshorne's theology. God, accordingly, contains within himself the contrasting predicates of eternity and omniscience, of temporality and world-inclusiveness. As Hartshorne affirms: "God, as supremely excellent and concrete, must be conceived not as wholly absolute or immutable, but rather as supremely-relative, 'surrelative,' although, or because of this superior relativity, containing an abstract character or essence in respect to which, but only in respect to which, he is indeed strictly absolute and immutable."[140] In recent years Hartshorne has undertaken to demonstrate that the ontological argument, restated in modal symbolic logic, can be employed to prove the existence of the relative, process God.[141] Hartshorne's process theology, which owes so much to Whitehead's notion of God, may well become the dominant expression of natural theology in America in our time.[142]

Paul Weiss, after studying under Morris Cohen at the City College of New York, enrolled in the graduate department of philosophy at Harvard University, where he did his major work in logic under Whitehead and received his Ph.D. in 1929. Weiss moved from logic to metaphysics. His early book, *Reality,* which was dedicated to Mrs. Whitehead, shows the strong influence of Whiteheadian ideas, although it reacts against Whitehead on the issue of substance. Resembling *Process and Reality,* Weiss's book proposes an intricate, descriptive, explanatory system of sixty-six categories to embrace all knowledge and all reality. Since then, Weiss has confessed misgivings about long lists of categories, when in remarks on Whitehead he criticized his mentor for not having reduced dialectically his categorial scheme to a more manageable set.[143] In *Reality,* moreover, Weiss rejects Whitehead's conception of temporally atomic actual occasions. "No reality," Weiss asserts, "is completely confined within the span of a moment and it cannot therefore perish with the passage of that moment. Realities persist while they change. . . ."[144]

Weiss went on from metaphysics to pursue his investigations into ethics.[145] Soon he became aware of the deficiencies of the system in *Reality.* Eventually he grasped that the "reality" of the early system was only one aspect of reality, "actuality," and that it had to be supplemented with other modes of being. To explain the fact that the diverse strivings of actualities converge in a unified cosmos, Weiss came to posit "ideality." However, since ideality imposes so vast an obligation upon actualities that they can realize only part of it, Weiss came to posit God, in order to make possible the realization of ideality. These speculations, so crudely sketched here, culminate in Weiss's mature system, *Modes of Being,* which has been hailed as the most daring and complete system of metaphysics to appear in America since the end of the Second World War. In *Modes of Being* Weiss posits a fourfold universe, a cosmos with four categories or modes of being: actuality, ideality, existence, and God. Actualities, whether simple or compound, are active; they are spatial and temporal beings.[146] Ideality is revealed in the guise of the Good, the Future, and the Principle of Perfection; it is possibility that ought to be realized.[147] Existence is "sheer vitality," "a cosmos of energy."[148] God is a finite, relative, and irreducible mode of being: singular but not contingent, determinate and inward but no mere ideal, existent but simple and eternal.[149]

It is hoped that the foregoing sketch may serve to suggest the novelty of Weiss's metaphysical scheme. Mention should also be made of the fact that since 1963 Weiss's publisher has been bringing out, first in fascicles, later in bound volumes, his day-to-day thoughts as he has formulated his system and worked out its ramifications.[150] In addition, in recent years, Weiss has speculated on law, art, history, religion, and education.[151]

That American philosophy today has been enriched by the speculative system of Whitehead and the active presence of thinkers schooled in his thought should be beyond doubt. Northrop, Hartshorne, Weiss have carried on Whitehead's philosophy as he would have wished—with independent creative originality. They are speculative thinkers who, like Whitehead, have examined the entire range of human experience. They have constructed complex abstract theories, but they have also directed their thoughts to the concrete issues of human life. A record of Whitehead's legacy into the second and third generations—for Whitehead's students have had students, too—cannot now be traced. But it should be clear that Whitehead's achievement as a speculative philosopher set an example which beckoned and continues to beckon many American thinkers.

The future of speculative philosophy in America will in large part be determined by thinkers schooled in Whitehead's thought. And since speculative philosophy is central to civilization, the future of American civilization will reflect their impact. It is impossible to state the case better than Whitehead did in the closing sentences of *Science and the Modern World*. "The great conquerors, from Alexander to Caesar, and from Caesar to Napoleon, influenced profoundly the lives of subsequent generations. But the total effect of this influence shrinks to insignificance, if compared to the entire transformation of human habits and human mentality produced by the long line of men of thought from Thales to the present day, men individually powerless, but ultimately the rulers of the world."[152]

NOTES

1. Alfred North Whitehead, *The Function of Reason* (Princeton: Princeton University Press, 1929; Beacon Press Paperback, 1958), p. 4.

2. *Ibid.,* p. 8.

3. *Ibid.,* p. 34.

4. *Ibid.,* p. 10.

5. *Ibid.,* p. 12.

6. *Ibid.*, p. 9.

7. *Ibid.*, p. 10.

8. *Ibid.*, pp. 37-38.

9. *Ibid.*, p. 38.

10. *Ibid.*, p. 65.

11. *Ibid.*

12. Alfred North Whitehead, *Process and Reality* (New York: The Macmillan Co., 1929; Social Science Bookstore Reprint), p. 4.

13. *Ibid.*, p. 5.

14. *Ibid.*

15. *Ibid.*, p. 6.

16. *Ibid.*, p. 4.

17. *Ibid.*, p. 6.

18. *Ibid.*, pp. 15-16.

19. *Ibid.*, p. 6.

20. *Ibid.*, p. 7.

21. *Ibid.*, p. 8.

22. *Ibid.*, p. 12.

23. *Ibid.*

24. *Ibid.*, p. 13.

25. W. Mays, *The Philosophy of Whitehead* (London: George Allen & Unwin; and New York: The Macmillan Co.; 1959), p. 51.

26. Alfred North Whitehead, *Adventures of Ideas* (New York: The Macmillan Co., 1933), p. 286.

27. *Ibid.*

28. *Ibid.*, p. 184.

29. *Ibid.*, p. 187.

30. *Ibid.*, p. 286.

31. *Process and Reality*, p. 6.

32. *Ibid.*, p. 21.

33. *Ibid.*, p. 16.

34. *Ibid.*, p. 6.

35. *Ibid.*

36. Ivor Leclerc, *Whitehead's Metaphysics* (London: George Allen & Unwin; and New York: The Macmillan Co.; 1958), p. 26.

37. *Ibid.*, p. 28.

38. *Process and Reality,* p. 22.

39. A. D. Ritchie, "Whitehead's Defence of Speculative Reason," *The Philosophy of Alfred North Whitehead,* ed. by Paul Arthur Schilpp ("The Library of Living Philosophers") (Evanston and Chicago: Northwestern University Press, 1941), p. 335.

40. Arthur E. Murphy, "Whitehead and the Method of Speculative Philosophy," Schilpp, *ibid.*, p. 380.

41. *Process and Reality,* p. 19.

42. *Adventures of Ideas,* p. 185.

43. *Ibid.*, pp. 186-87.

44. *Ibid.*, p. 203.

45. *Ibid.*

46. Ivor Leclerc, *op. cit.*, p. 17.

47. *Adventures of Ideas,* p. 203.

48. *Ibid.*

49. Ivor Leclerc, *op. cit.*, p. 17.

50. William A. Christian, *An Interpretation of Whitehead's Metaphysics* (New Haven: Yale University Press, 1959), pp. 28-29.

51. *Process and Reality,* p. 320.

52. *Ibid.*, p. 124.

53. *Ibid.*, p. 114.

54. *Ibid.*, p. 92.

55. *Ibid.*, p. 113.

ANDREW J. RECK

56. *Ibid.*, p. 43.

57. *Ibid.*, p. 94.

58. *Ibid.*, p. 318.

59. *Ibid.*, p. 314.

60. Victor Lowe, *Understanding Whitehead* (Baltimore: Johns Hopkins University Press, paperback edition, 1966), p. 260.

61. *Process and Reality*, p. 513.

62. *Ibid.*, p. v.

63. Victor Lowe, *op. cit.*, p. 295.

64. *Process and Reality*, p. 196.

65. *Ibid.*, p. 334.

66. Alfred North Whitehead, *Nature and Life* (Chicago: University of Chicago Press, 1934). These two lectures were reprinted as Chapters VII and VIII of Whitehead's *Modes of Thought* (New York: The Macmillan Co., 1938), where they bear the titles "Nature Lifeless" and "Nature Alive."

67. *Modes of Thought* (Capricorn Paperback), p. 205.

68. *Ibid.*

69. Fortunately Donald W. Sherburne has prepared a most helpful guide, *A Key to Whitehead's 'Process and Reality'* (New York: The Macmillan Co., 1966).

70. *Process and Reality*, p. 27.

71. *Ibid.*

72. *Ibid.*

73. *Ibid.*, p. 28.

74. *Ibid.*, p. 373.

75. *Ibid.*, p. 28.

76. *Ibid.*, pp. 36-37.

77. *Ibid.*, p. 28.

78. *Ibid.*, p. 32.

79. *Ibid.,* p. 28.

80. *Ibid.,* p. 30.

81. *Ibid.,* p. 27.

82. *Ibid.,* p. 31.

83. *Ibid.*

84. *Ibid.*

85. *Ibid.,* p. 32.

86. *Ibid.,* p. 33.

87. *Ibid.,* p. 32.

88. See Alfred North Whitehead, *An Enquiry Concerning the Principles of Natural Knowledge* (Cambridge: Cambridge University Press, 1919); and *The Concept of Nature* (Cambridge: Cambridge University Press, 1920).

89. Even Whitehead's disciple, Victor Lowe, is troubled by the doctrine of eternal objects. He proposes to assign the role of eternal objects as potentials to Whitehead's category of propositions. See Lowe, *op. cit.,* pp. 317-22.

90. *Process and Reality,* p. 28.

91. *Ibid.,* p. 11.

92. William A. Christian, *op. cit.,* pp. 409 ff.

93. Charles Hartshorne, "Whitehead's Idea of God," *The Philosophy of Alfred North Whitehead, op. cit.,* pp. 515-59.

94. Charles Hartshorne, *Divine Relativity* (New Haven: Yale University Press, 1948), pp. 30-31.

95. Victor Lowe, *op. cit.,* p. 290.

96. In *Understanding Whitehead,* Victor Lowe divides Whitehead's works into three periods: (1) logico-mathematical period (*ca.* 1891-1913); (2) the second period dealing with the philosophy of natural science (*ca.* 1914-23); and (3) the final period of the philosophy of organism (*ca.* 1924-47). See also Nathaniel Lawrence, *Whitehead's Philosophical Development* (Berkeley: University of California Press, 1956).

97. Max H. Fisch, ed., *Classic American Philosophers* (New York: Appleton-Century-Crofts, 1951); and John E. Smith, *The*

ANDREW J. RECK

Spirit of American Philosophy (New York: Oxford University Press, 1963).

98. H. B. Van Wesep, *Seven Sages* (New York: David McKay, 1960), pp. ix, 400.

99. James K. Feibleman, *An Introduction to Peirce's Philosophy* (New York: Harper & Row, 1946), pp. 459-63.

100. Victor Lowe, *op. cit.,* p. 266.

101. W. E. Hocking, "Whitehead as I Knew Him," *Journal of Philosophy* LVIII (1961), 505-16. Reprinted in *Alfred North Whitehead: Essays on His Philosophy,* ed. by George L. Kline (Englewood Cliffs: Prentice-Hall, 1963).

102. W. E. Hocking, "Whitehead on Mind and Nature," *The Philosophy of Alfred North Whitehead, op. cit.,* p. 404.

103. R. F. Alfred Hoernlé, "The Revival of Idealism in the United States," *Contemporary Idealism in America,* ed. by Clifford Barrett (New York: The Macmillan Co., 1932), pp. 301-7.

104. Victor Lowe, *op. cit.,* pp. 340 ff.

105. George Santayana, *Realms of Being, One Volume Edition* (New York: Charles Scribner's Sons, 1942), pp. 169-71. Since *Realm of Essence* had been first published in 1927, Santayana's references are to works which preceded the 1929 publication of *Process and Reality.*

106. *Process and Reality,* pp. 77, 85, 215, 216, 231, 240.

107. Alfred North Whitehead, "John Dewey and His Influence," *The Philosophy of John Dewey,* ed. by Paul Arthur Schilpp ("The Library of Living Philosophers") (Evanston and Chicago: Northwestern University Press, 1939), pp. 477-78.

108. John Dewey, "Experience, Knowledge and Value: A Rejoinder," Schilpp, *ibid.,* p. 519.

109. John Dewey, "The Philosophy of Whitehead," *The Philosophy of Alfred North Whitehead, op. cit.,* pp. 641-61.

110. John Dewey, "Whitehead's Philosophy," *Philosophical Review* XLVI (1937), 170-77.

111. Alfred North Whitehead, "Remarks," *Philosophical Review* XLVI (1937), p. 179.

169

112. Lucien Price, *The Dialogues of Alfred North Whitehead* (Boston: Little, Brown and Co., 1954), p. 176.

113. *Ibid.,* p. 255.

114. *Ibid.,* p. 338.

115. *Ibid.*

116. C. I. Lewis, "Logic and Pragmatism," *Contemporary American Philosophy,* ed. by George P. Adams and William P. Montague (New York: The Macmillan Co., 1930; Russell & Russell, 1962), p. 32.

117. C. I. Lewis, "The Categories of Natural Knowledge," *The Philosophy of Alfred North Whitehead,* ed. by Paul Arthur Schilpp (2nd ed.; New York: Tudor Publishing Co., 1951), pp. 703-41. Of this essay Victor Lowe writes that it is "the best article-length account of the philosophy of the 1920 books that I know of, written by someone other than Whitehead" (Lowe, *op. cit.,* p. 191 n.).

118. C. I. Lewis, *Mind and the World-Order* (New York: Charles Scribner's Sons, 1929), pp. 15, 95, 152, 244, 431.

119. See Andrew J. Reck, "Introduction" to George Herbert Mead, *Selected Writings* (New York and Indianapolis: Bobbs-Merrill Co., 1964), pp. lx-lxi. Consult the index for Mead's numerous comments on Whitehead.

120. Alfred North Whitehead, "Foreword," in Quine, *A System of Logistic* (Cambridge: Harvard University Press, 1934).

121. W. M. Urban, "Whitehead's Philosophy of Language and its Relation to Metaphysics," *The Philosophy of Alfred North head, op. cit.,* pp. 303-27.

122. Stephen Pepper, *World Hypotheses* (Berkeley: University of California Press, 1948), pp. 112-13.

123. Stephen Pepper, "Whitehead's 'Actual Occasion,'" *Tulane Studies in Philosophy* X (1961), 71-88.

124. Stephen Pepper, "A Proposal for a World Hypothesis," *The Monist* 47 (1963), 267-86, and his *Concept and Quality* (La-Salle, Ill.: Open Court Publishing Co., 1967).

125. F. S. C. Northrop, *Man, Nature and God* (New York: Simon and Schuster, 1962), pp. 15-16, 19.

ANDREW J. RECK

126. *Ibid.,* p. 211.

127. F. S. C. Northrop, *Science and First Principles* (New York: The Macmillan Co., 1931), p. 120.

128. *Process and Reality,* p. 508 n.

129. See A. H. Johnson, *Whitehead's Philosophy of Civilization* (Boston: Beacon Press, 1958).

130. F. S. C. Northrop, *The Meeting of East and West* (New York: The Macmillan Co., 1946).

131. F. S. C. Northrop, *The Complexity of Legal and Ethical Experience,* (Boston: Little, Brown and Co., 1959). See also Andrew J. Reck, "The Philosophical Context of F. S. C. Northrop's Legal Theory," *Tulane Law Review* XXXIV (1960), 505-22.

132. F. S. C. Northrop, *The Taming of Nations* (New York: The Macmillan Co., 1954); *European Union and United States Foreign Policy* (New York: The Macmillan Co., 1954); and *Philosophical Anthropology and Practical Politics* (New York: The Macmillan Co., 1960).

133. Charles Hartshorne, "Whitehead and Contemporary Philosophy," *The Relevance of Whitehead,* ed. by Ivor Leclerc (London: Allen and Unwin, 1961), p. 21.

134. *Ibid.,* p. 22.

135. *Ibid.*

136. See Andrew J. Reck, "The Philosophy of Charles Hartshorne," *Tulane Studies in Philosophy* X (1961), 88-108.

137. Charles Hartshorne, *Reality as Social Process* (Glencoe: The Free Press, 1953).

138. Charles Hartshorne, *The Philosophy and Psychology of Sensation* (Chicago: University of Chicago Press, 1934), p. 9.

139. Charles Hartshorne, *Beyond Humanism* (Chicago and New York: Willett, Clark and Co., 1937); and *Man's Vision of God* (New York: Harper & Row, 1941).

140. Charles Hartshorne, *Divine Relativity,* p. vii.

141. Charles Hartshorne, *The Logic of Perfection* (LaSalle, Ill.: Open Court Publishing Co., 1961); and *Anselm's Discovery* (LaSalle, Ill.: Open Court Publishing Co., 1965).

142. Charles Hartshorne, *A Natural Theology for Our Time* (LaSalle, Ill.: Open Court Publishing Co., 1967).

143. Paul Weiss, *The World of Art* (Carbondale: Southern Illinois University Press, 1961), p. 159.

144. Paul Weiss, *Reality* (Princeton: Princeton University Press, 1938), p. 209.

145. Paul Weiss, *Nature and Man* (New York: Henry Holt and Co., 1947); and *Man's Freedom* (New Haven: Yale University Press, 1950).

146. Paul Weiss, *Modes of Being* (Carbondale: Southern Illinois University Press, 1958), pp. 23-26.

147. *Ibid.,* pp. 120 ff.

148. *Ibid.,* pp. 185-186.

149. *Ibid.,* p. 331.

150. Paul Weiss, *Philosophy in Process* (Carbondale: Southern Illinois University Press, 1963-), I, II, ... See Andrew J. Reck, "Open Thinking," *Yale Review* LV (1966), 432-35.

151. Paul Weiss, *Our Public Life* (Bloomington: Indiana University Press, 1959); *The World of Art; Nine Basic Arts* (Carbondale: Southern Illinois University Press, 1961); *History: Written and Lived* (Carbondale: Southern Illinois University Press, 1962); *The God We Seek* (Carbondale: Southern Illinois University Press, 1964); and *The Making of Men* (Carbondale: Southern Illinois University Press, 1967).

152. Alfred North Whitehead, *Science and the Modern World* (New York: The Macmillan Co., 1925), pp. 299-300.

6

A MAN AND A CITY:
George Herbert Mead in Chicago

BY ROBERT M. BARRY

The structure of one's language has a great deal to do with one's train of thought. But language is a social institution and there are many societies and many social groups. The rich speak a different language from that of the poor. The mentality of the city is not that of the farm. Philosophers in England thrive on different emotions from those professionally acceptable on the Continent. American philosophers inherit questions and stimuli that never trouble German philosophers. Even the belief that there is only one truth and one objective technical method for doing philosophy, one way of thinking that is accessible regardless of geography or historical position—even such a belief occurs only at certain places and at certain times, under specifiable conditions. The sociology of philosophy is as fascinating as the philosophy of sociology: the sociologist criticizes philosophical concepts and methods as naïve, and vice versa. Earlier we heard from a theologian; now from a sociologist. In as nonpolemical, clear, and direct a way as possible, Robert M. Barry of Loyola University in Chicago stresses the importance of social forces in shaping a man's image of himself and of society.

George Herbert Mead was an unusual man. Though acclaimed by his colleagues for his sustained and brilliant insights, there is a rather serious problem about placing his thought in a single, proper context. He was employed as a Professor of Philosophy and claimed by the philosophical tradition, yet there has been a

173

continuing attempt to see him as a sociologist and social psychologist, for his thought is more than ordinarily rich with suggestions for social scientists. This duality in his perspective, however, functions to dissipate his thought and its influence. Part of the problem is an uncritical belief that the actual world is adequately represented by the academic departments of the university. Since there is no single academic perspective that is wholly capable of doing justice to his thought, he is relegated to an unimportant place in the academic hinterland.

Mead is partially responsible for the problems of interpretation that surround his thought. Not having published a single volume during his lifetime, he never provided a single context that could act as a touchstone for later interpreters. His posthumous works have been constructions from his manuscripts, articles, and even from student lecture notes. As a consequence he had virtually no control over the way he was presented to the public. He has been represented as a commentator and critic of Watson, Darwin, Bergson, animal psychology, cosmology, social theory, etc.; in short, he has been placed in the perspectives of the academic situation that prevailed during his life. Yet, as Hugh Duncan has recognized, Mead has been edited and interpreted by scholars who are not interested in human action as a dramatic event, but are interested in human action from a narrowly philosophical position.[1] Consequently, Mead has been placed in the theoretical philosophical tradition and understood as a perceptive, though empirically ungrounded, social theorist.

Mead was long aware of the intimate relationship between philosophy and the concrete life of man.[2] He was sensitive to the fundamental role of community as well as to the importance of politics in the life of man.[3] While this was true of Mead before he came to Chicago, it was in Chicago and with Chicago that the creative powers of Mead's mind emerged. The reason for this involves both the unique abilities of Mead as well as the unprecedented development of a city that reflected the convergence of those forms of technology and life that are typical of the twentieth century.

A man and a city: forms of thought are related to forms of life. Though this is prevalent enough a theme in the history of

174

American thought—the continual linking of the New England town meeting and the notion of democratic theory—the situation of the city of Chicago moves this theme to a new level of understanding. For the rapid development of Chicago occurred at the very time that new technological capabilities, new artistic forms, new forms of democratic precedure, and new conceptions of human nature were converging. Man felt capable at least of influencing if not yet of controlling his social world. In brief, new forces had appeared in the world and were reverberating in all areas of human community and consciousness, and George Herbert Mead was on the scene.

One would have to go far to match the fifty years of development that took place in Chicago from 1880 to 1930. The Great Fire, which destroyed almost all of the city, also wiped out many of its archaic limits. The destruction called forth an unreserved commitment to rebuilding the city and permitted all sorts of new possibilities to fill up the creative imagination. The opportunity was comparable to that of the Pilgrims two hundred and fifty years earlier: a cultured people confronted the open possibility of an (almost) unstructured situation.

The 1880's were given over to architecture. And it was a busy time. The architects who led the way in rebuilding the city included such men as Dankmar Adler, Daniel Burnham, William Holabird, William Le Baron Jenny, John Root, and most importantly, Louis Sullivan (who had a young assistant named Frank Lloyd Wright). There was not only a proliferation of new buildings, but an architectural revolution was launched. There were new technical possibilities; the twelve-story Tacoma office building of steel skeleton, by Holabird in 1888, was the first of its kind in the world. But the entire architectural achievement exhibited not merely technical virtuosity; it carried with it the awareness of the "significance of architecture to the quality of human relationship in the city."[4] There was a general cooperation between architects and the business world. Not only was there an awareness that "form follows function," but there was a heightened awareness that both together create a new environment and that the human mind can play a role in this creation.

In 1889 Jane Addams and Ellen Gates Starr moved into an

175

old house on South Halsted Street, formerly belonging to Charles J. Hull but donated by its owner Helen Culver. Here, in the heart of the foreign-born population—the *11th U.S. Census* (1890) lists 70 per cent of the Chicago population as having two foreign-born parents, and an additional 7 per cent as having one—was "the beginning of what was to be one of the great social movements in modern America—the Settlement House movement."[5]

Yet 1889 was also the year that John D. Rockefeller began his financial contributions to the new University of Chicago and this educational giant became the intellectual center of the mid-west. As Commager remarks: "It was no accident that the new University of Chicago . . . came to be the center of sociological study in America."[6] The university established close ties with the community. The faculty continually worked with the resources and needs of the community.

Among those faculty members who were deeply involved in the life of the city was George Mead. Mead was a close friend of Jane Addams and "for many years [he] was an active and successful treasurer for Chicago settlement houses."[7] He was actively involved in the Experimental School at the university—begun by John Dewey—and served in various capacities, including the editorship of *The Elementary School Teacher*. He was a member of the City Club of Chicago for almost twenty years, not only serving for many years as chairman of its Committee on Public Education, but also as author of a report on the importance of vocational training. Additionally, he delivered a report to the City Club on the role of the laboring man in the city, stressing the importance of the laboring man's view in city planning.

Mead was a central figure in Chicago. He took part in the confrontation of American traditions and the new problems of the immigrant. Mead believed that the problems brought about by the appearance of the immigrant could be solved by the development of the unique interests of the foreign born and the creation of channels of communication by which the immigrant could play a significant part in the development of his own community and city. The concern with vocational training, the modification of the educational system, the fostering of the development of a rich sense of community in terms of the new environment—all these are attempts to encourage the appearance of new strengths and untapped resources within the new citizens. For the new citizens had to be shown that their interests were not merely legitimate, but proper and necessary. The continuation and development of a democratic community is dependent upon the exercise of informed, cooperative participation in community life. The sensibilities of the new citizens had to be reflected in the concerns of the community before these citizens could feel at home in the community.

Only in this framework can one appreciate the deep ties that Mead had to the immigrant community, whose children would provide the creative dynamism for future growth. Every group in which Mead had membership involved either the immigrant or those who dealt with the immigrant: the Experimental School, the settlement houses, and the City Club Committee on Public Education, whose three subcommittees studied hygiene, vocational work, and the school as a social center.

To recognize as clearly as possible the posture adopted by Mead, one must understand the role of the City Club in the affairs of Chicago. When he gave the presidential address, Mead defined the goals of the Club as "finding effective means of coming into intimate touch with the problems of the City, and of helping to formulate the ideas and public sentiment by which the problems must be solved."[8] On another occasion he reported: "We have undertaken city planning [which involves] . . . an interest in housing, . . . transportation, sanitation, health. . . ."[9] Much of the planned study of the city of Chicago was undertaken at the initiation of the City Club.[10] Charles Merriam, one of the pioneers of regional study and planning, who was a professor at the University as well as an elected official of the Chicago City Council, points out quite explicitly that the major support for the regional studies of Chicago was derived from the backing of the City Club.[11] Graham Taylor, internationally known for his leadership in social welfare, explained that the City Club was organized by the executive board of the Municipal Voters' League and had as its purpose "to rally, inspire, and train a large group that would be more active in its dealing with city problems."[12] He evaluates its thirty years of activity in the following words:

177

The Club has amply justified the heavy exactions its founding and development have cost its leaders. So intelligently has it studied and understood many issues faced by the municipality that its criticisms and recommendations of public policies have strongly influenced public opinion and have had to be reckoned with, when not heeded, by public officials.[13]

If active participation in the City Club places Mead in the role of affecting, to some degree, the decision-making in the public life of the city,[14] this must be linked to his active participation in the life of the immigrant. For what he was dealing with was not merely the confrontation of diverse nationalities in a single community with democratic aspirations, but also the radical eruption of technological advancement which strained and, at times, distorted the imaginative capabilities of individuals. Some aspects of technology even weakened that supportive relationship the community offers to persons who have to cope with new situations: new occupations had to be learned; with a higher concentration of people new friendship ties had to be established; and new educational forms had to be followed. The problem was not simply the transition from farm to city life, as if a person merely changed the house in which he lived. Rather, it was a transition from a rural life, whose patterns had been developed over the life of mankind, to a city life whose characteristics and qualities involved an ideographic as well as an experiential revolution: totally new patterns of life rhythms, thoughts, and experience.

The individual was disorganized as a consequence of disruptive social and technological innovation. He was isolated from the meaning of his work, unsupported by institutions, and devoid of meaningful community life. Though there may have been different opinions about the precise remedy, it was commonly agreed, if democracy was to work, that the individual had to be put in a more intimate and active contact with the rich community life that democracy seemed to offer. This was, of course, more clearly a promise than an achievement. But part of the promise was the appearance of such institutions as the settlement house. Jane Addams, in a phrase rivaling the past achievements of European Christianity, referred to the settlement houses as "Cathedrals of Humanity" for they were "to include all men in fellowship and mutual responsibility even as the older pinnacles and spires indicated communion with God."[15] Another part of the promise was the new consciousness that men were responsible for the cities in which they lived; though the meaning of the phrase "city planning" was only slowly emerging out of the conservationist policy.

It was left to Mead to provide a theoretical expression of the truths that were functioning as presuppositions in this social thought. He did this initially by calling attention to the existence of a social world that was common to the individuals who shared communication and experience. He saw that "all living organisms are bound up in a general social environment or situation, in a complex of social interrelationships and interactions upon which their continued existence depends" (*M.S.S.*, 228).[16] By calling attention to the relationship between life, social environment, and continued existence, Mead was indicating the minimal prerequisites for all life forms. With the appearance of man, which signals the appearance of "mind," the social dimension grows in complexity and organization. Thus the appearance of man almost necessarily results in the emergence of a whole new series of powers and capabilities which are reflected in the upsurge of science, technology, and the forces of human life.

Not only does Mead give a temporal priority to the existence of a society—each of us is born into a society—but he even recognizes that the individual "derives his human nature from his social interactions and relations with that community as a whole" (*M.S.S.*, 229). The conditions under which the person becomes human are the conditions that are found within the particular configuration of the society that prevails during the person's life. Mead is giving a new type of priority to the social world; a priority, as we shall later see, that sustains personal uniqueness through social action.

The priority that Mead gives to the common social world goes beyond a temporal priority. Mead is calling attention to the actual existence of man rather than to the academic problems that philosophers seem to prefer. He perceives that man exists in a present situation that includes reality and is reality. What is real (and is this not the primary concern of the philosopher?) is located in that area whose boundaries are set by the limits of human experience in the present, common social world. This is the present structuring of the results of previous men's activities; it is the retained contents of what has been tested by previous generations; it involves those realities that exist in the area of man's manipulation or action; it contains delivered, captured, or discovered realities whose fulfillment lies in the future of human actions; it embraces those suspicions, assumptions, conjectures, multiple directions, and various sensibilities that may involve even greater depth, or beauty, or goodness. In brief, the common social world contains the existing totality of conditions under which man can be human.

Packed into this idea of the social world we find a series of notions that permit this model to be used quite creatively. Mead says "the world is a world of events" (*P.P.*, 1).[17] But the event, a "happening," is that "which becomes . . ." (*P.P.*, 21), at least from the perspective of the world. From the perspective of man, the event is the result of human action, or is human action itself, since the results of the action are part of the act. To this extent, that is, insofar as both perspectives result in either the emergent quality or newness, the event contains a variety of patterns. There are those patterns from the past, those which are wholly new and within the present, and also those patterns or general conditions from which the future will arise.

The event, the newness continually emerging within present human experience, is linked to the totality of human life. For with the appearance of new patterns of living there are consequent changes in personal sensibilities. New goals, new social roles, new artistic forms appear. The event contains new understandings of the past and points to a new future. Tied to the individual as well as to the social, the event emerges by itself, yet is contingent upon human action. To understand the linking of the event to the totality of human life, as envisioned by Mead, the concrete situation in Chicago must be kept in mind. The total community of the city was deprived of the creative participation and concern that the new citizens could contribute to the common good. All the groups had their own, divergent interests, which not only tended to keep the different groups apart but also prolonged their "separation by difference." All citizens needed some common social concern which would function to give them communal experiences and provide a foundation for a growing sense of experiential unity.

From Mead's perspective, we are here dealing with this problem: "a lack of adjustment [read: creative action] between the individual and his world" (*P.A.*, 6).[18] Mead had a deep-seated belief in the role of community in perfecting man. Chicago was populated by diverse individuals whose actions did not attain maximum effect owing to their containment within narrow, smaller communities. Thus, for Mead, it is not merely community life, but an over-reaching community life, that functions as an ultimate norm. This over-reaching community life is not merely imposed as an external norm, however, it is continually sustained in experience, at least minimally, by the action of individuals.

The continued and dominant emphasis on the priority of the community is reflected in two allied notions: the emergence of mind and the development of the self. Mind is the ability of the individual to deal with meaning. The mind is anchored in society, for it is here that meaning is preserved and available for the use of individuals. Yet mind is not a thing, it is a process that arises out of the relationship of man to society. The process is specified by the actual appearance of meaningfulness in a social context. Though Mead is most concerned with the appearance of mind and its various stages of development from gesture through communication to consciousness, the significance of his idea of mind lies in his emphasis on the social as its proper area of activity and its place of emergence. Mind, with its appearance in time paralleling the appearance of man, is the key to the individual sharing of common meaning concerning objects of discourse and activity.

The development of self is quite similar to the emergence of mind; both are clearly bound up with society as well as mutually involved. The self develops, appears, if you will, as a consequence of the human organism's relations to the social process and to persons within the process. The dominant characteristic of being a self involves the ability of a human organism, at the stage of develop-

181

ment in which it has achieved a mind which permits it to deal with meaning, to be an object to itself by reflection. This self-reflection develops, in early life, through the mechanism of play and, later, through games. In play activity the child assumes the role of others; he is a policeman, doctor, jet pilot, his own father, mother, etc. In a game the child adopts the role of the others involved in the game. His role-playing becomes general and even universal. Not only does he play checkers by thinking about the game from the position of his opponent and the moves that he is inclined to make, but he is able, and even required, mentally to play all the positions in a baseball game. In this activity the self is progressively understood in its relationship to the roles of others and the reaction of others to the emerging self; for example, the position of a particular player on a ball team is understood in terms of the relationship of the other positions to his. Getting outside oneself by assuming the attitude of others toward oneself is the fundamental characteristic of the self: the self can be both object and subject. But the self becomes subject only through the assuming of many objective roles.

The recognition of both mind and self as dynamically emerging within a social structure is Mead's fundamental insight. It permitted him to set up his method of advancing the social situations he confronted. With a deep sensitivity to the importance of community life, and with the recognition that individuals develop under the conditions of the society in which they live, Mead believed there would be greater social harmony if the various members of the diverse ethnic groups could, through their own action, create a single community. For this larger community would provide the conditions that would be common to the action of all. All men would be unified to some greater degree because now their action would take place with an eye on those goals that would benefit all the people. What was primarily needed was an "intelligent process within ourselves . . . [that] would enable us to take the helm into our own hands and direct the course of our conduct, either in thought or action" (*S.W.*, 377).

While he admits a cognitive power that functions in the directing of human action, Mead relates this power to the activity of man in the world of human affairs. This ought not to be too surprising, however, for the fact that the person develops on the terms of the society is clear indication that human cognition is related to concrete social problems. Mead's vision of the range of the cognitive is much wider than the historical notion of the cognitive, with its emphasis on what Dewey called the "spectator's view of knowledge." This new understanding of knowledge is related to action and imbedded in a whole series of relationships and sensibilities. The range of the cognitive, as Mead understood it, must be seen in the historical situation of Chicago's aesthetic sensibilities, expressed in its architectural and artistic tradition. (This emphasis must be contrasted with the rather common, though unfortunate, linking of action with the scientific tradition rather than with the aesthetic tradition.) A person does not merely know the world, but his knowledge of the world involves a multiplicity of possible alternative actions and their various expected consequences. Even the sense of the future, of long- and short-term expectations that are contained in particular visions of the world, will affect what is known by placing emphasis on particular combinations of characteristics. Human action is dramatic and tied to the whole world of human life.

Human action is the basic dimension to man's life in the world. The role played by the cognitive power takes its place among the various other directions of interest that coexist in human experience. When he speaks of human action, Mead chooses the broader view and places it in a social and dramatic context. Action is linked to event; the former considered from the personal, the latter from the social perspective. From either perspective action is creative; it brings about new worlds. Action produces a "changed situation"; the social world is "reconstructed by the action of the individuals" (*P.A.*, 89). In the continual process of action there are four stages: impulse, perception, manipulation, and consummation. Not only is each of these stages located in both society and the individual; each is also found in temporal sequence. Impulse is generated from the society by the social drawing out of an attitude. It results in a new perception of the world. This perception is tested by the person's active manipulation of

183

the world found in experience. The consummation is not the conclusion of the action, for the act is never bound; the consummation overflows into a new direction of concern, an aesthetic appeal.

To understand Mead in terms of the actual problems of the society in which he lived, the analysis of creative action must be understood in the context of the functioning of Hull House, which had multiple relations to its members as well as to the larger community, the city. Mead's thought operated in this concrete context; it cannot be fully understood in a negative way, merely as a reaction to what he considered the improper academic (i.e., scientific and philosophical) positions of his time.

Mead asks: "Wherein lies the creative activity or the reconstructive activity of an individual in a democratic society?" (*P.A.*, 662). He presupposes a problem, a breakdown, between the individual and the world. In the case at hand the immigrants, as well as the whole city, are not acting in a manner that results in mutual enrichment of their lives. What can be done? The solution involves the creation of "some project which can meet that particular problem, . . . [but it must be one] on which the community as a whole can [possibly] work or act" (*P.A.*, 663). Further, the solution must begin in the existing present, with the interests of the people, and try to establish a "community in such a way that what he [the individual] does can be a natural function in the community" (*P.A.*, 663). What the individual does must be capable of being shared or entered into by other persons with the fullness of their sensitivities.

In the settlement house program, groups were created which initially had as their purpose the fulfillment of the interests of the persons involved;[19] and, eventually, "a reconstruction of the [social] situation [so] that different and enlarged and more adequate personalities may emerge" (*S.W.*, 148). This results in a reconstruction of the social world for all concerned, for all those whose interests are involved.[20] Those who had been members of the created groups would not only have their interests sustained as valuable, but these interests would carry them beyond themselves into the community. The paralleling self-confidence enhances the persons and opens up for them a new social situation that moves beyond the horizons of the settlement house. Those persons in the community who have pejoratively judged the immigrant would then become aware of the contributions of the immigrant in the improvement of the community. The result is a changed social situation which would place the immigrant in that situation of natural concern for the common good of the larger community. Alternately, because of the new accomplishments of the community, the other members of the community would have to enlarge their vision of what the community could achieve. Thus these new possibilities would prompt new activities which would provide new horizons and consequent greater achievement for the whole community.

Three discernible factors were operative in this idea of social development: personal interest, social reconstruction, and a belief in a larger community. Mead was opposed to the idea, prevalent in the Western world, of a "given moral order with which the individual must accord, if he wants to be valued" (*S.W.*, 379). (Because Royce was unable to get out from under this "given moral order" and acknowledge the individual as the creator of the social order, Mead judged him to offer an escape from American life rather than an interpretation of it.) For Mead personal interests were accepted as beneficial. The interests of persons, given their proper realm of social encouragement and culminating in significant action, will result in a created environment. Interests are not to be judged negatively, for whatever they contain by way of valuable direction will be expressed and retained within the community. What is not of value will be eventually by-passed.

Mead realized that the fruition of interest would arise out of the experience of reconstructing one's world in terms of the community of interests. Since many interests will quite naturally conflict, the mind would examine the situation in terms of operative possibilities. By formulating new possibilities the mind would be offered various new worlds. The solution lies in the direction of reconstructing "a new world harmonizing the conflicting interests" (*S.W.*, 149). As T. V. Smith describes it, the mind "transforms through action the discrepant into the accordant."[21] Mead was sensitive to the destructive power of hostile interests which result in the triumph of the self over the enemy. He saw that these interests must be linked to a reconstruction of the community, wherein there will be a useful place for all interests. The conflict of interests must be handled by an active reconstruction of the social world so that enlarged and more adequate persons with ever deepening and broadening interests will emerge in the new social world. In both kinds of reconstruction, personal and social, the same organized social relationship was involved. This is due to the fact that social and personal reconstruction are reciprocal; either one entails the other.

Mead's constant belief in some larger sustaining whole provides the support for his theory of creative action. As personal and social reconstruction advances toward some goal of social progress, the possibility of attaining a universal human society continually appears in human consciousness. What makes the belief in a sustaining whole so important in Mead's thought is that this belief links him with the actualities of the American religious tradition. It supports his concern for social development, and provides the context, along with the theory of social action, for subsequent American social thought. Yet this belief in a sustaining whole is to be found over the whole range of the development of American culture and is not merely part of Mead's vision. The belief in a sustaining whole has been kept alive because it is continually verified in different contexts, yet never exhausted in any one context.

It is rather difficult to spell out precisely the influences that have entered into Mead's belief in a sustaining whole. This is due in part to the fact that little work has been done on the early religious influences on Mead, or, for that matter, on the whole series of problems involved in the relationship between the religious tradition and the philosophical tradition.[22] Yet the major part of the problem is the lack of specific structure in American Christianity which, not completely adapted to an institutional form, remained a "prophetic movement."[23] Because American Christianity involved the antithetical commitments to both freedom and denominationalism, the problems were compounded on all levels. How can there be a "Church" in the face of multiple denominations? Does it make sense to speak of the possibility of denominations when freedom of

186

decision is the basis of religious life? How can there be a successful nation that allows for no religious preferences in the political area, that stresses freedom of religious commitment, yet depends upon religious norms for a general moral tenor among its citizens? How can one have religious people, generally also leaders in their communities, do work in the civic and social realm, when religion is generally unconcerned with the world?

It is not that these problems went unsolved. They were attacked continually, but they have to be solved in each age and in each community. Among the factors involved in the solutions are those that are unique, relevant to the time, place, and sensitivities of the religious community that confront the problems. Even granted the plasticity of unique factors, however, there is a continuity. The unifying framework, the continuity embracing the uniqueness, the "dominant idea in American Christianity," as suggested by H. Richard Niebuhr, was the "idea of the Kingdom of God."[24] This idea, allowing for and even encouraging multiple forms of diversity, was a matrix that gave shape to the active community movements of the Christian churches. It permits the believer to accept the freedom of personal religious decision, with its consequent multiplicity of denominations, by acknowledging the various levels of unity in God's Kingdom with a hope for a future, perfect unity. The idea of the Kingdom of God permits the believer to accept democracy as a means for achieving the unity of a real Kingdom. It permits the believer to recognize that specific action can take on significance because it is a contribution that affects in some way the whole of meaningful spiritual community. In brief, this "superdenominational consciousness"[25] can be found appearing in the corporate concerns of the Puritan Covenant, through Charles Finney's "revivalism" with its excess energy overflowing into social concerns (e.g., Abolitionism), down to the Social Gospel movement of Rauschenbusch. The Kingdom of God has been the image that has unified the dynamic life of the American religious spirit.

Mead draws upon this movement through his undergraduate days at Oberlin College as well as through his father, a professor of theology at Oberlin Seminary. Henry Steele Commager has described Oberlin College in the following terms: "For half a century [it] had triumphantly combined orthodoxy in religion with radicalism in politics and social relationships, and [it was] where a lively social conscience was a prerequisite to graduation."

Yet, in spite of the orthodoxy in religion that was ascribed to Oberlin, Mead was not a religious man in the doctrinal sense of the term. Mead's son, Henry, reports that his father, during his college days, had "succeeded in refuting the dogma of the church to . . . [his] own satisfaction." Henry then calls attention to the fact that his father was the product of "many generations of Puritan theology."[26] Mead's religious position can best be understood in a rejection-continuity pattern. As he himself admits, "we are not likely to exaggerate the critical importance of religion . . . in the building up of the great American community" (*S.W.,* 382-83). Perhaps his religious position can best be described by using his own sketch of the American pioneer as a self-portrayal: "His religious principles and doctrines . . . were put into such shape that he could carry them about with him" (*S.W.,* 383).

Mead, as a student of Royce's at Harvard, was deeply impressed with the notion of the "Blessed Community," Royce's phrase for the Christian Church. He rejected Royce's position, however, because of its emphasis on the extraworldly features of his community. This rejection, paralleling his rejection of church dogma, was highly selective. Mead accepted Royce's idea of a sustaining community, but he rejected the *a priori,* feudal structure associated with it. He accepted his concept of freedom, his idea of the role of thought in the universe, and his belief in spiritual reality. Yet Mead rejected all of the extraworldly features of Royce's system, for these were incapable of dealing with the particular and the specific factors that were operative in daily life.

Mead adopts an empirical view, and what seems to be a secular posture in his concern with the world of human action. His taking the world seriously must be understood as part of that religious tradition, dominant in America, that takes the Incarnation seriously, at least in terms of the importance of the world for the perfection of man. Mead justifies the Church because it has preserved "in the minds of the community . . . the faith in a social

188

order which did not [yet] exist" (*S.W.*, 259). But this "social order," this vision of what might be, this "sense of the larger social whole" (*S.W.*, 169), is the context in which Mead is able to discern the emergence of human action and the continual creation of society.

While at his first teaching position at the University of Michigan, Mead wrote to his wife's parents: "I have learned to see that society advances—men get closer and closer to each other and the kingdom of heaven is established on the earth, as far as man becomes more and more organically connected with nature [through his action]."[27] Though this contains elements of youthful effusion, it was not only written after he had "succeeded in refuting the dogma of the church," but its theme is sustained in his other, later writings. He calls attention to the fact that "Christianity . . . [has contained] certain assumptions in regard to human society and . . . man's place in the universe . . ." (*P.A.*, 466). These assumptions are expressed in a series of values which continue in existence even though "we are forced to redefine them if we are to use . . . [new] means to secure them" (*P.A.*, 474).

Throughout his life, Mead was fascinated by the pervasive social concern that was part of the Christian tradition, for he believed "there can be nothing sacred but the shared."[28] Though this involves a tradition that is working out a new relationship between the world and the Christian heritage, it is hardly less Christian because it is new. In the end it is T. V. Smith's judgment that must prevail: "Mead was more Christian than he intended."[29]

Mead brings together three interweaving factors: a sense of wholeness derived from Christianity,[30] the immediate community, and the action undertaken. None of these is to be taken from a theoretical perspective, for Mead was working in the context of a living tradition that was rooted in the genuine action of man, and he took seriously the quality of human relationships.

His language, however, does not convey that timbre we expect from one who continually deals with the concrete. Yet once his thought is set in its full context—from the aesthetic as an environment, through the development of democratic personalities, and these in contact with an emerging technology—it becomes progressively easier to discover the focus of his thought: the city of Chicago.

At all events, while his language may tend to hide his concern with the concrete, there are elements of his heritage, flowing more deeply through his thought, that reveal themselves in his language. These elements provide his hope of unification as well as his concern with the immediate task of the American venture. He conveys what his whole task is about with sensitive biblical imagery:

> This present is the scene of that emergence which gives always new heavens and a new earth . . . [as we] make our own the values in which we are involved through those undertakings in which the community of all rational beings is engaged (*P.P.,* 90).

NOTES

1. Hugh H. Duncan, *Language and Literature in Society* (Chicago, 1950), p. 227.

2. ". . . I became interested in philosophy, and [the] meaning of American life . . . [and] have been able to follow the connection that has gradually been established between abstract philosophy and daily life." Letter of Mead to his parents-in-law, Mr. and Mrs. Samuel Northrup Castle, June 19, 1892, Ann Arbor, Michigan. (Unpublished. From the Mead Papers at the University of Chicago.)

3. Long before Mead came to Chicago he was aware of the importance of a "foothold in society where we can work out to this end . . . [viz.] the practical application of morals to life. . . . We must get into politics of course—city politics above all things because there we can begin to work at once in whatever city we settle because city politics need men more than any other branch —and chiefly because . . . according to my opinion the immediate application of the principles of corporate life—of socialism in America, must start from the city. . . ." Letter of Mead to Henry Castle, October 21, 1890, Berlin. (Unpublished. From the Mead Papers at the University of Chicago.)

4. Hugh H. Duncan, *Culture and Democracy* (Totowa, New Jersey, 1965), p. 155.

190

5. Henry Steele Commager, "Foreword," to Jane Addams, *Twenty Years at Hull House* (New York, 1961), p. ix.

6. *Ibid.*

7. Helen Swick Perry, "Introduction," to Harry Stack Sullivan, *The Fusion of Psychiatry and Social Science* in *Collected Works,* (2 vols.; New York, 1956), Vol. II, p. xxi.

8. *City Club Bulletin,* XII (April 19, 1920), 95.

9. *Ibid.,* V (1912), 215.

10. Charles Merriam, *et al., The Government of the Metropolitan Region of Chicago* (Chicago, 1933), p. ix.

11. *Ibid.*

12. *Pioneering on Social Frontiers* (Chicago, 1930), p. 71.

13. *Ibid.,* pp. 71-72.

14. Though he recognizes the existence of this realm of Mead's work, Andrew J. Reck in his Introduction to his edited collection, *Selected Writings of George Herbert Mead* (New York, 1964), does not grasp the significance of the practical dimension to Mead's thought; he is aware of Mead's interest in social reform, but does not grasp the fundamental link between thought and its grounding in community life. Cf. pp. xxxiii-xxxvi. Hereafter: *S.W.*

15. Jane Addams *op. cit.,* p. 114.

16. *Mind, Self and Society,* ed. Charles W. Morris (Chicago, 1934). Hereafter: *M.S.S.*

17. *The Philosophy of the Present* (LaSalle, Illinois, 1932). Hereafter: *P.P.*

18. *The Philosophy of the Act,* ed. by Charles W. Morris, *et al.* (Chicago, 1938). Hereafter: *P.A.*

19. Among the groups initiated were boys', men's, women's, and working women's clubs; the interests involved drama, recreation, Shakespeare, oratory, art, and nationality clubs.

20. Omar Khayyam Moore, in his work on the creating of a proper learning situation for a child by the use of such techniques as a "talking typewriter," states that the theory behind his work "builds on the work of George Herbert Mead" ("Autotelic Responsive Environments for Learning," *The Revolution in the Schools,* ed.

by Ronald Gross and Judith Murphy [New York, 1964], p. 195).

21. T. V. Smith, "The Religious Bearing of a Secular Mind," *Journal of Religion,* XII (April, 1932), p. 206.

22. There has long been a feeling of what can be called disaffection between the American philosophers and the American religious tradition, which cannot be identified with the anti-intellectualism found in the culture. It is rooted in the transition from the religious-dominated college of the nineteenth-century to the twentieth-century college in which there were professionally trained philosophers. Quite generally in the nineteenth-century college the president, a clergyman, taught the religion courses as well as the few philosophy courses that were offered. With the appearance of the technically trained philosopher there was a secular alternative to the religious perspective. Cf. C. Wright Mills, *Sociology and Pragmatism,* ed. by Irving Louis Horowitz (New York, 1964), pp. 35-56.

23. Henry F. May, "The Recovery of American Religious History," *American Historical Review,* LXX (October, 1964), p. 85.

24. H. Richard Niebuhr, *The Kingdom of God in America* (New York, 1959), p. xi.

25. *The Lively Experiment* (New York, 1963), p. 116.

26. H. C. A. M., "Biographical Notes," *Philosophy of the Act,* p. xxii.

27. To Mead's parents-in-law, Mr. and Mrs. Samuel Northrup Castle, June 18, 1892, Ann Arbor, Michigan. (Unpublished. From the Mead Papers at the University of Chicago.)

28. T. V. Smith, *op. cit.,* p. 206.

29. *Ibid.,* p. 210.

30. Robert J. Roth recognizes a "sense of wholeness" is operative in the thought of Dewey; but Roth does not offer any suggestions as to the origin of this and believes that Dewey's denial of transcendence is a serious limitation on his religious thought. Cf. *John Dewey and Self-Realization* (Englewood Cliffs, 1962), pp. 100-24.

7

JOSIAH ROYCE:

Analyst of Religion as Community

BY JAMES COLLINS

In Chapter Four, we heard of Peirce's notion of the interpreting community—the final recourse of our judgments about reality. In this chapter, leisurely and steady in its movement, James Collins, the distinguished historian of philosophy from St. Louis University, shows how this concrete notion of community came to the timely assistance of Josiah Royce (1855-1916). In the first decade of our century, Royce was trying to work out a philosophical theory that would, in a neutral and critical way, elucidate the main themes of Christianity—the concrete manifestation of religion most obvious in our society. Royce's interest here was in the philosophy of religion. His problem was how to be concrete without losing a general, independent perspective. Royce belonged, of course, to the idealist rather than to the pragmatist strain in American philosophy. The degree, then, to which he moved in his later years toward positions on religion enunciated by Peirce, James, and Dewey is all the more remarkable. His notion of "the loyal community" provides the beginnings of a model for communities of inquiry and concern: whether of the whole human family, the scientific community, the Church, or the radical political community of which today we hear so much.

Histories of American philosophy are strictly a twentieth-century phenomenon. They are instructive to consult, because of the shifting patterns in the national search for self-identity which they help to mold and also to mirror. Using them as an initial clue about the intellectual resources now at our disposal for the study of religion, we quickly notice that they point toward Josiah Royce (1855-1916) as a major crux in any general interpretation of the American modes of philosophizing.[1]

Prior to the Second World War, it was customary for the historians to emphasize the idealistic motif in American philosophy, taking that motif not only in the ordinary sense of a concern for demanding practical standards and community values but also in the more technical sense of a theory of knowledge and reality dominated by the role of mind and its structures. In this perspective, Royce was naturally hailed as the maturest thinker in our tradition. He was admired for his assimilation and reworking of the grand epistemological and metaphysical themes in German idealism, for his resolute systematic reinterpretation of more recent evolutionary and logical findings, and for his characteristic stress on the practical aim of all philosophizing as a service to the community of men. This high evaluation of his work withstood the discounting practices of the personalist idealists, who were dissatisfied about the function of the individual self within the Roycean absolute thought and will. But Royce's relative position in American philosophy was profoundly modified by two more recent trends: the concentrated research into the origins and growth of American pragmatism, and the efforts made to rewrite the story of American philosophy along naturalistic lines. Although intrinsically independent of each other, these newer approaches tended to locate Royce toward the periphery of a native movement of thought which he could indeed adapt with marvelous dialectical agility, but whose basic process of de-absolutizing the cognitive and practical orders he was unable to withstand. Perhaps the extreme point of recession was reached in a historical study of the "seven sages" of American philosophy, from whose august company Royce was firmly excluded.

At the present time, however, the effort is being made to achieve a more balanced appraisal of his philosophical contributions. A careful look at the documentary basis of the relationship between Royce and William James, for instance, is sufficient to show that the latter did not seriously intend his butcher-shop criterion of tough-minded and tender-minded thinkers to settle the respective issues between his own pragmatism and Royce's idealism. Dramatic characterization of this sort is useful for attracting attention to philosophical differences but not for resolving the argumentation itself. Similarly, Santayana's inclusion of frontiersman Royce within the cultural class of the genteel tradition makes for an arresting paradox in the sociology of philosophers, and yet it does not legitimate any inference about the invalidity of Royce's analysis of human activities. Hence the current attitude is to include Royce among the "classic American philosophers" (in Max Fisch's phrase) and to regard the interplay between Royce and his philosophical contemporaries as constituting what Charles Frankel calls "the golden age of American philosophy." Among those who are sensitive to phenomenological and existentialist evaluations, the many-sided debt which Gabriel Marcel acknowledges to Royce's metaphysics is a further indication of his centrality in our country and his proper initiative in respect to European sources.

Yet there is a danger that Royce will be appreciated for reasons that remain extra-philosophical and unrelated to present issues in philosophy. This happens, for instance, when one reads him primarily as a representative cultural voice of his age, or as a component in the Harvard scene at the turn of the century, or even as a foil for the minds who were engaged in developing pragmatism and its variants. Royce's significance cannot be assigned solely to his stature in the classic age or to his germinal impact upon pilgrims toward existentialism, without at the same time removing him so far from the philosophical discussions of our day that his thought loses all present-tense urgency. To perceive this urgency, we must see Royce as a mind in the act of philosophizing, not as a cultural sample or historical exhibit. And an analogy must be recognized to hold between the problems with which he wrestled and those which provoke our attempts at philosophizing today.

Only one strand in such a complex comparison can be examined here, but it is a lively one. A primary reason for the fluctuation in historical estimates of Royce lies in the prominent position occupied by religious problems in his thought. For those who de-

195

scribe the spirit of American philosophy in terms of its concern for practical values and community relationships, this interest in the meaning of religion manifests the strength and authenticity of Royce's mind. Yet this same interest provokes hesitation in the degree that American philosophy is regarded as coming only recently and painfully into awareness of its distinctive technical nature, which was previously obscured by the *mésalliance* between religious ideals and philosophical procedures. The ambiguity generated by Royce's attention to the religious aspect of life raises a twofold question. Does Royce himself attempt to maintain philosophical rigor in his treatment of religious matters? And can his procedures and findings in this sphere serve us in turn, without corrupting our philosophical aims or weakening their pertinency to man's present religious searching?

Thus the particular strand of Royce's work which I propose to examine is his philosophy of religion. Even here it is necessary to restrict myself to some reflections upon his last major writing in this area: *The Problem of Christianity* (1913). This book brings to a climax Royce's lifelong preoccupation with the human sense of religion. My task is to bring out the general significance of this book both for the Roycean conception of religion and for our contemporary efforts in the philosophy of religion.

I. AN INCOMPLETE PHENOMENOLOGY OF RELIGION

It is important to understand why Royce accepted the invitation to deliver at Oxford in 1913 the Hibbert Lectures, on which *The Problem of Christianity* was based. For at first glance, it would seem that he had crowded all he had to say on religious topics into the stream of books and articles issued between 1885 (*The Religious Aspect of Philosophy*) and 1901 (*The World and the Individual*, a metaphysical contribution to the theme of the Gifford Lectures: natural religion). In all these publications, Royce made it clear that his philosophical inquiries were initially sparked by religious questions, and that these questions continued to sustain his speculative investigation of God and immortality, free selfhood and

196

JAMES COLLINS

individuality. Since his metaphysical, ethical, and logical studies
during this fruitful period had found their common focus in a determination of the human meaning of religion, the project of deliv-
ering the sixteen Hibbert Lectures was apparently doomed to repetition of stale positions. Yet Royce felt impelled by the radical
insufficiency of his previous work on religion to engage the problems again and, in point of fact, achieved here his freshest and most
mature teaching on the nature of religion. A closer look at his work
up to 1901, as well as a weighing of the new factors introduced
after that date, will show why he had to devote still more reflection
to religion and how he was able to supply new oil for his lamp.

In his first phase, Royce attempted to make a phenomenological approach to religion, in the classical or pre-Husserlian sense of
"phenomenological." He suggested that, in outer form, his treatment could be regarded "as a sort of roughly sketched and very
incomplete Phenomenology of the religious consciousness, first on
its moral, and then on its theoretical, side."[2] By this he meant that
the philosopher must impenetrate the religious attitudes of mankind, with the aim of uncovering their common suppositions and
structural aim. For the general plan of probing into the suppositions of religious affirmation and action, he was indebted to Kant.
Royce consciously modeled his analyses of error and doubt and evil
upon the Kantian pattern of asking about the general conditions
which permit man to live through these existential states. But it was
what Royce called "the other Hegel," that is, the author of the
Phenomenology of Spirit rather than of the *Logic,* who led him to
concentrate precisely upon the interplay between religious faith and
human error and doubting, between religiously hopeful action and
the gnawing presence of evil. Royce was far ahead of current
Hegelian scholarship in emphasizing that the phenomenological
aspect of Hegel's philosophy is important for the study of foundations. He also appreciated its sensitivity toward the metaphysical
implications of the shapes of religious consciousness. To uncover
the general conditions in reality which permit the religious man to
develop these modes of experience is to engage in a speculatively
significant enterprise, one which yields some metaphysical knowledge of the structure of beings.

Yet Royce never permitted himself to be classified simply as a Hegelian, whether in philosophy of religion or elsewhere. This reluctance to be so typed rested on several considerations. He drew a sharp distinction between Hegel himself and the later Hegelian school; he found his own affinity to lie more with Hegel than with the schoolmen and, in Hegel, with the phenomenological strain of thought; and he acknowledged a very deep influence stemming from Fichte and Schopenhauer. From these latter thinkers, Royce learned to view the life of selfhood and spirit primarily as one of internal purposing, of a will toward realizing an enduring purpose in the natural matrix of chance and evolutionary process. Out of this unique blending of German sources, he developed the leading conviction that a phenomenology of religious experience must examine will as well as thought, or rather, must plumb the thoughtful aspect of religious experience to the core level where its volitional and striving internal nature is revealed. Religious experience, like every other type of human experience, is never purely receptive and observational, but achieves its meaning through an active and ceaseless striving of the human self toward the divine. The active view of intentionality and experience elaborated by Husserl and Scheler finds a striking analogue in the Roycean notion of the purposive religious attitude.

What accounts, then, for the admittedly incomplete and fragmentary nature of Royce's early phenomenology of religion? This question cannot be answered by making the general remark that human religious experience is concerned precisely with the striving, unfulfilled self in its condition of search and temporal incompletion. For the sense of the question is not that this phenomenology investigates an as yet uncompleted *being* but, rather, that its *analysis* of the human religious condition contains gaps, unexplored regions, and methodological deficiences. It is precisely as a theory about the religious aspect of our life that Royce eventually becomes dissatisfied with his findings up to 1901.

What he had set out to do was to deepen our understanding of the ingrained human custom of having religion. He saw that this custom or general intentional attitude was inherently complex: religion always included the three factors of action, belief, and feeling. Royce was more confident about attaining a theory of religion in terms of the first two factors, which philosophy could directly inspect, than in function of the third element of feeling. Given the necessary co-presence of religious action and belief, he specified two chief methods of analysis: the ethical and the metaphysical. The ethico-religious order of inquiry was to start with man as an agent, and thus to stress the operative work of will in shaping religious meanings. And the metaphysico-religious order of inquiry was to begin with the conviction that religious statements have a reality import, and then to explicate the theory of being implied by such statements. Ideally, Royce hoped that these two methods of the moral and the metaphysical study of religion would converge in an adequate philosophical determination of the meaning, value, and foundation of religion. Presumably, the affective factor in religious existence would then be indirectly subtended within this encircling movement.

As his reflections actually developed, however, they did not lead to the desired convergence. The ethical order followed in *The Religious Aspect* did issue in an idealistic conception of the relationship of human purposes to an organic spiritual totality. But as Royce observed, this result advanced the theory of religion only to the point where it can function as a support for moral convictions. Similarly, the metaphysical order pursued in the essays on God and immortality and in *The World and the Individual* benefited his theory of being much more than his theory of religion. Royce was able to reconcile the religious attitude more satisfactorily with his own idealistic view of the internal meaning of being than with the traditional alternatives of realism, mysticism, and critical verification. But far the greater portion of the analysis was devoted to articulating his metaphysics of the intending idea than to the structure of religious intentionality, in its own peculiar texture.

Thus the two methods led in fact to a bending of the phenomenology of religion to the requirements of ethics and metaphysics, without achieving a distinctive unification in the study of religious thought-action-experience for its own sake. This remorselessly instrumental treatment of religious reality raised a doubt for Royce as to whether or not his moral and metaphysical conception

199

of individuality could indeed respect and take into account the religious formation of the human spirit as a characteristic purposive meaning. Whereas his critics suggested that the danger lay in cutting his moral and metaphysical cloth to fit a preconceived religious pattern, Royce himself made the opposite estimate. His conception of religion was in mortal peril of becoming swamped by his other systematic preoccupations, and even of disappearing from sight as an irreducible human attitude.

As the twentieth century opened, then, Royce came to recognize that the obligations of a phenomenology of religion cannot be fully discharged in the classical idealist manner. It is not enough to work out the implications of a human finitude included in a system of divine life, within which the individual human agents function as related but self-affirming pulsations. A theory of religion based upon this internal relationship to the absolute tends to snatch the human person too rapidly from our temporal order and from the religious acts of believing, groping, and worshiping. It places the emphasis so resolutely upon the function of human selves as constituting the inner life of the absolute that it washes out the distinctive features of the human religious community known in ordinary experience. The clear lesson for Royce was that he must develop a proportionate method for appreciating the religious phenomenon as it actually displays itself in this world.

The need for a humanly adequate methodology of religion was reinforced by the particular course of discussion during the first decade of our century. Hard upon the delivery of Royce's Gifford Lectures came William James's contribution to the same series: *The Varieties of Religious Experience* (1902). This perceptive work spelled out in vivid prose what was lacking in the Roycean approach to religion up to that time. For James plunged into a direct, sympathetic examination of the actual forms of religious faith and activity, taken in all their bewildering diversity and empirical wealth of detail. At the same time, he sought to draw out of the particular given modalities of religious experience some common meaning, centered around the individual's need for salvation and for assurance (from a more than human power) that good efforts will not be permanently frustrated. The confidence which

James had in the method of direct impenetration of religious expressions provided, as it were, a fresh spur to Royce.

Royce was by no means a passive receiver, however, of the Jamesian findings on the meaning of religion. He regarded James as the master of psychological description of the individual believer's feelings and aspirations. From this angle of vision, the quality of religious life depends upon the soul's personal search for a higher power and source of goodness, upon the inner dedication and reaching out of the alone to the Alone. Without revoking this component, however, Royce sought to broaden the religious relationship from individual to social religious experience. "All experience must be *at least* individual experience; but unless it is *also* social experience, and unless the whole religious community which is in question unites to share it, this experience is but as sounding brass, and as a tinkling cymbal."[3] This criticism was not peculiar to the theory of religion but, rather, was a prolongation of the abiding general differences which set off Royce from James. In every discussion of the pragmatic method for determining meaning and the nature of human experience, Royce's strategy was to move from the individual to the communal perspective. Thus his stress upon the social kind of religious experience was in keeping with the rest of his philosophical argumentation.

Royce's religious horizons were also broadened by developments in his own moral philosophy, as expressed in *The Philosophy of Loyalty* (1908). Here he tried to overcome the earlier objection that his concern about the integration of the individual self with the absolute left little room for interpersonal moral relations among men. To accept the motivation of being loyal to the ideal of loyalty itself is not a piece of redundant formalism. In terms of human commitment, it means shaping one's active life by a steady, consuming devotion to the human community. And given Royce's repeated teaching on the contribution of ethics to the theory of religion, he was bound to make the experiment of specifying the loyalty principle as a practical dedication to the welfare of the religious community. This enabled him to make the return movement from a metaphysical dialectic between the human individual and the absolute self to a religious awareness of community in its

201

experiential aspect, a social grouping in human history. And although he referred to the topic of the religious community simply as an "application" of his ethical accentuation of loyal devotion to community life, religion for Royce involved something more than an instance of ethical obligation. The very heart of the Roycean conception of religion lay in the actualization of a divine-and-human sociality, within a temporal network of intentions and expressive actions which cannot be reduced in principle either to metaphysical principles or to ethical ideals.

The great barrier to such a reformulation of the nature of religion still lay in the loose, polemical use which the pragmatists were making of the term "Hegelian," as the characterizing note of Royce's philosophy. Royce soon saw that it was not enough to distinguish between Hegel himself and the Hegelian followers, or even to prefer the phenomenological to the system-building Hegel. These fine points of distinction might be brushed aside with the remark that, whatever its precise historical roots, no idealistic theory of religion can avoid distorting the import of our religious experience; idealism always forces religion into a preconceived mold of abstract principles. A full turn of the historical spiral was thus achieved, since Royce now found himself in a situation analogous to that confronting Hegel. Both men were challenged to show that they could understand and respect the reality of concreteness, without surrendering their respective philosophical methods. Royce accepted this challenge most pointedly in the sphere of the philosophy of religion. It was here that he sought to manifest the concreteness of his thought, by working out the leading idea of the religious community.

II. THE MODERN CONTEXT FOR PHILOSOPHY OF RELIGION

In his masterpiece of religious analysis, *The Problem of Christianity*, Royce completes his phenomenology of religion and establishes his own sort of hold upon religious concreteness. To make this work more accessible to our own uses today, we may first of all ask the question: In what spirit does one do a philosophy of religion? The response furnished by Royce's own example is a complex one and is only gradually conveyed to us.

To do philosophy of religion in the Roycean spirit is to engage in a historically conditioned, rather than a timeless, enterprise. Examining the religous responses and possibilities open for the men in his own age, the philosopher of religion cannot simply repeat former views of the meaning of religion, and should not try to do so. While there will be some continuity among believers from age to age, there will also be some deep-reaching modifications in their entire cultural reality and hence in the human component of the religious relationship. Whatever the permanent truth conveyed by the religious convictions and worship of mankind, it achieves realization and vivifying influence in the human community only through the concrete historical forms operative at a particular time. Otherwise, the salvational message of religion would have a static and insipid note of here-it-all-is, which would dissipate the mystery and the hope for historical development which draw men to this message and its way of life.

Looking at the modern setting for religion from his vantage point of half a century ago, Royce shows remarkable prescience in identifying three significant trends. (1) The first condition for maintaining the relevance of religion is that it actually meet our *human needs* and receive enduring support from them. One can make an archeological trek from the ruined temples of one civilization to those of another, and find in each instance that the original confidence in a divine source and guarantee eventually transformed itself into a detached insensitivity toward new aspirations in a given society. "The goal of religon is something beyond all our transient strivings. But its path lies through the realm of human needs. And so, when a religion loses touch with human needs, it dies."[4] If the fear of the Lord is the initial step toward wisdom, then surely the fear of the mortality of one's treasured religion is a second step along the same highway.

Royce was by no means enamored by the writings of the Modernists* during the opening decade of our century. He felt that

---

* Major religious writers, especially in France, who tried to understand religion in terms of modern progress as it was then conceived. In *Three Modernists* (New York, 1968), John Ratté examines the religious ideas of the men whom Royce read: Loisy, Tyrrell, and Sullivan.—Ed.

they were inclined to dissipate the force of religion by removing all wonder concerning the founders of religions and by disorienting the religious search away from its aim of practical union with an eternal, suprahuman reality. But he was also able to distinguish between these defects and the one sound point the Modernists were making: that Christian religion, in particular, has its foundations in social human nature as well as in divine initiative, and that neglect of the former can only lead to skepticism concerning the latter. Royce saw the possibility of a tragic separation opening up here between the analysts of religion and its relationship to human needs and the official defenders of the divine origin and goal of religion. His forecast was that the relevance of religious belief and practice in our time will depend upon overcoming this dualism and reweaving the pattern of religion as jointly a divine and a human work.

Today, we can specify in more depth and detail than Royce did the needs and values of man which incline him toward religion, and which also define the pertinence of any particular religious expressions. The psychological and psychiatric studies of the religious traits in personality and social structures have greatly increased our understanding of the human footing for religion. But we are still far from having achieved an integration between such findings and the outlook of most believers and religious spokesmen. The therapeutic usefulness of these findings is widely recognized, but the problem of interpreting them and relating them to the divine source and goal of religious strivings remains acute. There is still a real danger that, apart from therapeutic techniques, the psychological and the theological approaches to religion will remain quite disparate. To overcome the split between these two readings of religious life, a distinctive philosophical account of the methodologies involved must be furnished. Otherwise, the fear of a totally naturalistic account of religiousness will alienate the believing mind entirely from its psycho-social context.

(2) As a second distinguishing mark of the modern matrix for religious existence and also for philosophy of religion, Royce lists the vastly accelerated tempo of scientific and cultural changes in our era. Having served his apprenticeship in the analysis of evolution at the cosmic and biological levels (the theme of his popular

204

The Spirit of Modern Philosophy), Royce now concentrates on the religious implications at the third level, namely, that of *cultural evolution*.

> Physical science and the industrial arts are altering the very foundations of our culture, of our social order, and of our opinions regarding nature. This alteration is now taking place at a rate for which no previous age of human history furnishes any parallel. Apart from chance catastrophes, which seem unlikely to happen, these processes of mental and of social change are likely to continue at a constantly increasing rate. In consequence, man's whole spiritual outlook will probably soon become different from any outlook that men have ever before experienced. . . . Nothing in human affairs is so sacred as to be sure of escaping the workings of this law of accelerated change.[5]

With but a single modification, this text can still stand as an accurate statement of our pervasive awareness of the quickening pace in all the sciences and technology, as well as the consolidation between such changes and our entire view of the universe and man's life therein. The one correction which we would have to make is that a catastrophic ending of the entire process is indeed within the order of likelihood, in our age of nuclear fission. The catastrophe would not be purely a matter of natural chance, but is built into the system of human options.

On the premise that we can somehow take the nondestructive path in the use of natural energies, however, Royce's point still remains valid. The radical transformation of our ways of experiencing, valuing, and acting reaches down to our religious commitments and responses. The·latter cannot be segregated from the ever increasing ratio of scientific and cultural changes without withering and dropping away from the vine of human life. But Royce warns that this situation cannot be effectively met by combining a colorful rhetoric of religious dynamism with an actual policy of rearguard action and eroding concessions. If the religious mind takes seriously the truth of the human foundations of religion and the repercussions of cultural change upon our entire outlook, then it will as-

205

similate and orient the accelerating process rather than remain basically suspicious and out of sympathy with it.

From Royce to Teilhard de Chardin, religious thinkers have been trying to foster a positive appreciation of evolution at all levels. Royce himself does not conclude that the cultural changes are simply to be imposed upon a somewhat passive and reluctant religious mind, a mind that would thus prove itself primarily defensive and separatist. Insofar as there is a free religious acceptance of the human condition today, there can also be an active contribution by religious men to the constructing of a scale of values and the ultimate direction taken by the world of constant research and decision. Furthermore, religious conviction and action are never totally confined within a dominant outlook. In the course of passage from one outlook to another, the internally evolving forces themselves have a thrust of intentional meaning which remains as yet unsatisfied. One *outlook* is succeeded by another, but the generative *human tendencies* are steadily operating both to keep some continuity in human history and also to achieve new modalities of meaning and value. The religious component in cultural evolution need not fall victim to the sheer replacement of one cultural formation by the next; reflection on the role of religion in cultural evolution may overcome our temptation to underestimate the rate and pervasiveness of the process.

Yet it is not sufficient to add a layer of religious teleology to the theory of evolution. Such a tactic only provokes the reply that, while a Teilhardian view of the religious finality for cosmic and human evolution is intriguing for the imagination, it is quite dispensable for any rigorous work on the actual factors in change. Such a response is justified, since it is an equivalent way of saying that the theological reading of evolution cannot get very far in this world without a philosophical analysis of the relations between the several kinds of human knowing and interpreting. In the philosophy of religion, a profuse sympathy for the teleological approach to evolution is no adequate substitute for an analysis of the methods of research. That is why Royce's own theory of religion is painfully built upon his comparative methodology and his study of the internal agencies in cultural evolution.

206

(3) For his third trait of modernity relevant for the inquiry into religion, Royce calls attention to the sociological factor in cultural evolution. From an *institutional* standpoint, religion is no longer at the center of power in modern society. Not only have the interests of men fanned out to embrace all the direct aspects of our experience, but these interests are organized and supported by institutions quite distinct in aim from any ecclesial institutions. Men now have the experience of being able to devote their best energies and aspirations to the structured activities within the artistic and scientific worlds, within the industrial and political forms of social life. Institutional forms of religion find themselves at the periphery of an intense and constant focusing of human energies upon the university, the centers for arts and communication, the technological complex and the government establishment.

> If all churches and priesthoods and congregations were temporarily to suspend their public functions and their visible doings, our marketplaces and factories and merchants and armies would continue to go on, for the time, much as usual. . . . Worldly weapons can no longer be used either to propagate or to preserve religion. Religion must find its own way to the hearts of the coming generations. And these hearts will be stirred by countless new cares and hopes. The human problem of religion will grow constantly more complicated.[6]

Realistically, we cannot expect any waning of the complexity and attractiveness of the nonecclesial institutions, which are the fonts of a dynamism that is reshaping our sensibility, our intelligence, and the options for the good use of our energies.

An awareness of the rededication of human thought and emotion to the framework of nonecclesial institutions lies behind both the death-of-God theme and the present religious celebration of the secular. It is noteworthy that Royce is a close reader of Nietzsche, and is hence cognizant of the latter's radical interpretation of the shift of credibility and inspiration from the churches to other institutions. Nietzsche's argument is that once real values are shifted, life is withdrawn from institutional religion and indeed from all

207

acceptance of God. The suspension of both public religious functions and private belief in God is permanent, not just temporary, since nothing worthwhile is lost by their removal.

Nevertheless, Royce refuses to group Nietzsche with Max Stirner and other anarchic individualists; he discerns in Nietzsche an affinity with Roycean social idealism itself. This unexpected judgment is founded on several considerations. One attitude shared by the two men is a distrust of the theistic God, viewed as a separate creator and source of arbitrary power over the world. Both Nietzsche and Royce feel that such an overweening deity would be a threat to the integrity of human values. On another score, Nietzsche's stress on the surpassing of our conventional selfhood strikes a sympathetic chord in the American idealist, who remarks that no community of men is worth saving unless it is leavened by selves who are striving to transcend any present set of limits. Nevertheless, Royce also observes that a genuine sense of the need to be saved permeates the writings of Nietzsche. Nietzsche opens up the human self to the divine presence, but then backs away from any designation of this relationship as a religious search for salvation, because of his image of the absolute as a life-destroying power. One cannot directly sever Nietzsche's distorting image of the absolute from his underlying sense of the divine, however, because the turning of the human spirit away from churches and toward other institutions symbolizes, for Nietzsche, the antivital character of all religious beliefs. Unless a philosophical analysis is made of this sociological issue, the religious potentiality in Nietzsche's attack on God can never be released.

Royce's insistence on a philosophical study of the relation between religion and our institutional modes of existence precipitates a question about the effectiveness of current religious celebrations of the secular. To the degree that theological talk about the holiness of secularity is lacking in a comparative philosophy of human institutions, it fails to persuade men who structure their lives in an institutional framework and yet who do *not* see its religious significance. The theme of sacred secularity must take up the task of showing *believers* the opportunity to make a religious interpretation of all the institutions engaged in transforming this world. But in its present unsupported condition, this theme cannot furnish independent grounds why men so engaged should acknowledge a religious aspect in their corporate lives. In this respect, the appeal to the secular is on the same logical footing as the older appeal to design and the more recent one to the religious teleology of evolution. All these modes of suasion presuppose, for their interpretative force, the presence of religious conviction. It is left for the philosophy of religion to work out the intrinsic relationships leading from our social life to a recognition of its divine source. Royce's major effort at clarifying the logic of community and institutional change has, therefore, a prototypal import for the study of religion in a modern intellectual setting.

III. PHILOSOPHICAL REFLECTION ON CHRISTIANITY

It is customary to read *The Problem of Christianity* primarily for its reworking of Charles Peirce's theory of signs and its application of this theory to the general problem of community, and to regard the explication of the meaning of Christianity as a secondary feature. From the standpoint of metaphysics and ethics, there is good reason for this approach.[7] But for present purposes in philosophy of religion, I would like to reverse the emphasis and consider everything else as functional here to the philosophical elucidation of the Christian reality. Having set himself this latter task, Royce finds it necessary to bring to bear all the intellectual resources which can shed some light upon the concrete form of Christian religious life. The manner in which he meets this challenge is one of the instructive analogues which can guide contemporary thinking on the relationship between philosophy and Christianity.

To grasp what Royce is doing, we must first of all recognize that his entire discussion up to this point is an integral part of his effort to make a philosophically responsible exegesis of Christianity. That task is not an addendum tacked on, as an afterthought, to an already fully constituted theory of religion. Quite the contrary; from the outset of Royce's philosophical researches into the nature of religion, he maintained a steady commitment to the work of making philosophical sense out of the Christian experience. He knew that a long-range preparation is required, both in order to develop a broad basis in general methodology, metaphysics, and ethics, and also to bring out from within a rigorous philosophy of religion the exigency of eventual concrete reflection upon Christianity.

That exigency can now be expressed in terms of the two earlier topics of the phenomenology and the modern context of philosophy of religion; for both topics lead into the philosophical thematizing of Christianity. The phenomenological study of religion remains essentially abstract and incomplete, until it reflectively grapples with the actual modes of religious meaning and action, including the Christian actuality. Royce's philosophical analysis of Christianity has the function of giving ultimate concretization to his theory of religion. The latter does not display its full strength and permit judgment to be made on its weakness, until it makes an attempt to probe the intentionality operative in the Christian attitude. Because the Christian attitude fosters that devotion of the individual to the community in which loyalty essentially consists, Royce finds here an actual concretion of religious experience by which to test and develop his metaphysical and ethical notions on the loyal community. Similarly, his reflections on the modern setting for religion apply with clarifying pertinence to Christian doctrine and social life. For the clash between an immobilist and a thoroughly evolutionary conception of religious reality becomes especially acute and enlightening when the Christian creed and cult, prophetic and institutional offices, are related to the transformation of human society in our time.

What should be the stance of the philosopher of religion vis-à-vis Christianity, so that he may retain full control over his integrity of method and yet make a reflective engagement with this religious reality in its own structure and life? Royce's complex way of meeting this issue does not depend upon a prior resolution of the faith-and-reason relationship, but emerges more directly from his own conception of how a philosopher should conduct himself in studying any concrete actuation of life. In this respect, he sets a pattern for at least one contemporary style in the philosophical treatment of Christianity.

210

From the outset of his philosophical work, he adheres to the maxim that "what is only yours and in you, is not divine at all. . . . Take heed lest your object of worship be only your own little pet infinite, that is sublime to you mainly because it is yours, and that is in truth about as divine and infinite as your hat."[8] In keeping with this wry advice, Royce seeks systematically to avoid any purely idiosyncratic reaction (whether favorable or highly critical) toward religious affirmations. He aims at a precise determination of those aspects of religious life which constitute a common bond among many selves, and hence which can be tested out according to public canons of evidence. No exception can be made in the treatment of Christian belief and action, on penalty of converting a philosophical analysis into a eulogy of one's pet religious hat.

Royce joins this rule of stringent neutrality in philosophical statements on Christianity with a unique blend of other considerations. He serves notice that his personal religious assent does not extend further than the findings reached through his philosophical investigation. And yet he does not imply that his philosophical conclusions are in any way exhaustive of the reality of religion. This openness in principle to further plumbing of our relation with the divine accords with Royce's metaphysical conclusion that "for us, creatures of fragmentary consciousness, and of dissatisfied will, as we here in the temporal order are, the individuality of all things remains a postulate, constitutes for us the central mystery of Being."[9] Since his metaphysics of the absolute self is tempered by this sense of mystery concerning man in his temporal condition, Royce grants to other inquirers the freedom to hold more than the minimal basis set forth in his philosophy of religion. His attitude toward his own religious doctrine is that "a man could hold that and much more too," depending upon the man's ability to perceive and bring to judgmental form the additional evidence which broadens his religious insight.

Without relaxing the rigor of his method, however, Royce is able to strike two new notes in *The Problem of Christianity:* personal testimony and an approach to revelation. There is a noticeable role for *personal testimony* in the proclamation of the Christian message. Must this element be methodically set aside in philosophy

211

of religion, and discounted as a factor of privacy that cannot meet the standards of public evidence? Royce replies in the negative, since the act of giving witness comes *from* the individual and yet, in its intentionally structured purpose, is addressed *to* a community of other men. Testimony places upon them a demand to inspect their own experience for some confirming or disconfirming evidence.

Royce does not hesitate to draw an analogy here between the first-level religious witness and the philosopher of religion. The latter is also speaking out of the depths of his own study of the religious phenomenon and toward the depths of subjectivity in his readers and fellow inquirers. Along with the commonly shared method, then, philosophers of religion must also seek to achieve intersubjective understanding of the realities under discussion. Royce remarks that his interpretation of the Christian ideas on suffering, atonement, and salvation is not a totally impersonal account, "merely telling anybody's old story over again." Instead, it is hammered out through a juncture between his metaphysico-ethical thought and his unique personal travail in this life. Here, at last, Royce finds a distinctive basis for including *religious feeling* in his theory. Not only the methodic factor but also the aim of "addressing at least some few readers who are able to understand, and perhaps sometimes to echo, a cry of genuine feeling when they hear it," keeps his treatment of the Christian religion within the philosophical order.[10] The presence of an intersubjective factor in the work of philosophers of religion, as well as among religious believers themselves, helps to define the practical nature of the theory of religion. It is especially valuable to have this point made by Royce, who very severely segregated his personal sorrows and biographical facts from his philosophical argumentation.

That the philosophy of religion attains its full concreteness through reflective treatment of the claim to *revelation,* as well as through the factor of personal witness, is another affirmation of Royce's maturest years. Ultimately, a thorough study of the religions of mankind cannot avoid the presence of a revelatory claim in many of them, or leave a reference to this claim merely implicit. One advantage of a formal philosophical study of Christianity is that it makes this question of revelationally modified religion quite unavoidable.

212

As a safeguard for his philosophical integrity, Royce devotes a good portion of his Bross Lectures on *The Sources of Religious Insight* (1912) to what he names "the religious paradox" or "the paradox of revelation." Whether the claim is overtly made or not, there is a revelational aspect in every religion. Taken in the broadest sense, revelation concerns the intercourse between the divine and the human, with the emphasis placed upon the initiative taken by the divine reality in somehow manifesting itself to man. Every conception of religion as a product of human desire and activity must be qualified by the further recognition that the religious attitude involves an opening toward the divine and some manifestation of the divine presence in human experience. For this reason, Royce would be unable to agree with Bonhoeffer and those theologians who begin by assigning a purely artifactual meaning to religion, and quite obviously must end by setting up a contrast in principle between religion-as-a-human-product and the revelational union with God. Such a contrast is demanded, not by a direct phenomenological study of human religiousness, but rather by the onesided approach to religion only on its human productive side. To correct this abstraction, one must attend to the general sense of a principle of revelation at work in every religious opening to the divine.

But here a paradox develops, since the conscientious person must have some helping comprehension of the nature and destiny of man in order to discern the fulfilling divine presence.

> The pardox is that a being who is so ignorant of his duty and of his destiny as to need guidance at every point, so weak as to need saving, should still hope, in his fallible experience, to get into touch with anything divine. The question is, how is this possible? . . . Unless there is something in our individual experience which at least begins to bring us into a genuine touch, both with the fact that we need salvation and with the marks whereby we may recognise the way of salvation, and the essentially divine process, if such there be, which alone can save—unless, I say, there is within each of us something of this interior light by which saving divine truth is to be discerned, religious insight is impossible, and then no merely external revelation can help us.[11]

213

Here we find Royce brooding over the problem of how revelation in any mode is possible as a communication of meaning and a participation of life, as between the divine source and the finite, temporal, groping being of man. Revelation should be discriminatingly welcomed as that which brings an *appropriate realization* of man's desire for eternal life. Royce treats this issue philosophically, without becoming entangled in theological questions about the divine freedom in the order of grace. His point is that the revelational relationship is not a one-way street, but includes in its meaning some answering discernment on man's part. Royce uses this theme of the religious paradox to insist that, within the modern context, religion must not only meet the needs of human nature but also satisfy the desire for some sort of divine revelation. Indeed, these are not entirely separate issues, since one of the permanent needs of man is precisely for establishing that sort of religious communion with the divine in which the latter manifests its presence and brings man to a life he seeks. This is not theological immanentism, but simply a stress on the free, humane quality of the acceptance of religion in its revelational character.

We can now see why Royce delays coming to the problem of Christianity, until he is well equipped with Peirce's theory of signs and the community of interpretation among active selves. Not until he is in possession of this supple theory of human knowing and loving does Royce feel confident about mastering the concrete richness of the Christian life. The individual experience upon which a man relies, in order to judge the appropriateness of a divine revelation and to give testimony about its religious worth, is not that of a closed-off solipsist. Since every aspect of our cognitional, affective, and volitional experience exhibits the triadic relationship between the meaning, the interpreter, and the minds being addressed in the process, the individual believer has a social complexity to draw upon for his religious insight. His response is not only socially founded upon the community of interpretation but is also addressed to this entire active community.

Within this perspective, Royce can enliven the themes of the union of believers as a common people of God, the essentially social nature of the redemptive process, and other Christian ideas based on the sociality of religious experience. Our salvation is not an individual affair, but consists in our loyal participation in the beloved community of persons.[12] Since the Christian religious experience is social in its sources and its intended goals, Royce does not regard the church as a perverting or an artificial form imposed from the outside upon private religious life. Philosophy of religion requires a constructive ecclesiology as its culmination, since the social religious experience of the interpreting community is the decisive guide for the theory of religion.

Our several lines of investigation can now be drawn together in the conclusion that Royce's endeavors in philosophy of religion lead, by an essential convergence, to the thematizing of Christianity. Unlike the deists, he does not define a philosophical approach to religion by its exclusion of the Christian religion, since to do so would be to condemn that discipline to perpetual remoteness from the concrete unification of human religious experience. And unlike the reductionists who do consider Christianity, but only in order to view it as a variant of something else, he has the courage and good sense to respect its proper contours. At the same time, Royce's strenuous preparation for the task of making a philosophical reflection upon Christianity is a salutary warning against any facile underestimation of the complexity of the undertaking. That is why we have had to approach the thematization process in gradual stages. Only after the philosopher of religion studies the bearing of his general theory of method and knowledge, metaphysics and ethics upon his conception of religion, can he achieve some control over his statements on the meaning of Christianity. In developing this latter theme, moreover, he has to take into account the religious potencies of man considered precisely in his modern historical condition. The Peircean logic of interpretation recommends itself to Royce, because it can account for the evolving community of scientific research and institutional organization, and at the same time can bring the Christian religious community into meaningful relations with the modern course of evolution as a whole.

There is no short cut known to me whereby the believing mind can participate genuinely in the philosopical study of religion and yet avoid the main *kinds* of issues raised by Royce. This is not to say that one must also follow Royce's purposive idealism in order to do good work in philosophy of religion. In fact, the particular findings about the meaning of Christian religiousness which he made need not be narrowly construed, so as to support only his special account of the absolute and the finite order of selves.[13] But it is a fair test of the philosophical quality of any essays we make today in the theory of religion that they should show their ability to handle the basic sorts of questions propounded in his writings. Royce is there to remind us about what it takes to become a philosopher of religion and to make a thematic development of Christianity in the method, and not just the vocabulary, of philosophy.

NOTES

1. Royce has a prominent place in H. G. Townsend's idealistically oriented *Philosophical Ideas in the United States* (Cincinnati: American Book Company, 1934), but is reduced to a transient shadow in H. B. van Wesep's *Seven Sages: The Story of American Philosophy* (New York: Longmans, Green, 1960). There are balanced chapters on Royce in H. W. Schneider, *A History of American Philosophy* (2nd ed.; New York: Columbia University Press, 1963), and J. L. Blau, *Men and Movements in American Philosophy* (Englewood Cliffs: Prentice-Hall, 1952), from a naturalistic standpoint; and in W. H. Werkmeister, *A History of Philosophical Ideas in America* (New York: Ronald Press, 1949), and J. E. Smith, *The Spirit of American Philosophy* (New York: Oxford University Press, 1963), from an idealistic standpoint. Royce receives full representation in the anthologies edited by M. H. Fisch, *Classic American Philosophers* (New York: Appleton-Century-Crofts, 1951), and by Charles Frankel, *The Golden Age of American Philosophy* (New York: George Braziller, 1960). In *Royce's Metaphysics* (Chicago: Henry Regnery, 1956), Gabriel Marcel devotes two chapters (pp. 121-46) to Royce's later theory of interpretation and the meaning of Christianity.

2. Royce, *The Religious Aspect of Philosophy* (New York: Harper Torchbook, 1958), p. xvi. Royce gives a lengthy analysis of Hegel's *Phenomenology of Spirit,* in his *Lectures on Modern Idealism* (New Haven: Yale University Press, 1964), pp. 136-212.

216

3. Royce, *The Problem of Christianity* (2 vols.; New York: The Macmillan Co., 1913), Vol. I, p. xvi. For a Roycean view of the Royce-James relationship, see J. H. Cotton, *Royce on the Human Self* (Cambridge: Harvard University Press, 1954), pp. 191-204. The current attractiveness of Royce's philosophy of religion is indicated by the republication of *The Problem of Christianity* in three separate editions during 1967-68 (published by Archon Books, University of Chicago Press, and Regnery Gateway).

4. *The Problem of Christianity,* Vol. I, p. 387.

5. *Ibid.,* Vol. I, pp. 388, 390. Royce's voracious interest in the comparative methodology of the sciences and the analogous meanings of evolution is vividly recorded in *Josiah Royce's Seminar, 1913-1914* (New Brunswick: Rutgers University Press, 1963), edited by Grover Smith. It includes an exchange (pp. 72-85) with T. S. Eliot on applying the logic of interpretation to the evolution of religions, and on the phenomenology of creedal expressions. In this seminar, Royce refers several times to distinctions obtained from Husserl's *Logical Investigations.*

6. *The Problem of Christianity,* Vol. I, pp. 391, 393. For Royce's opinion on Nietzsche's teaching concerning truth, self, and religion, cf. *The World and the Individual* (2 vols.; New York: Dover Books, 1959), Vol. II, p. 283, n. 1; *William James and Other Essays on the Philosophy of Life* (New York: The Macmillan Co., 1911), pp. 230-32; *The Sources of Religious Insight* (New York: Charles Scribner's Sons, 1912), pp. 15, 60. Historical analysis of the God-is-dead thinking is made by James Collins, "A Kantian Critique of the God-is-Dead Theme," *The Monist,* 51 (1967), 536-58, and on a grand scale by Cornelio Fabro, *God in Exile: Modern Atheism* (Glen Rock: Paulist-Newman Press, 1968).

7. This approach to Royce's later period has yielded fruitful results, in the metaphysical and ethical areas, in two unpublished St. Louis University doctoral dissertations: by F. M. Oppenheim, *Royce's Mature Idea of General Metaphysics* (1962), and V. C. Punzo, *Royce on the Problem of Individuality* (1963), as well as in Peter Fuss's Harvard dissertation, *The Moral Philosophy of Josiah Royce* (Cambridge: Harvard University Press, 1965).

8. Royce, *The Religious Aspect of Philosophy,* pp. 12-13.

9. *The World and the Individual,* Vol. II, p. 433; the next quotation is from *The Religious Aspect of Philosophy,* p. x. Royce remains closer to Kant than to Hegel in refusing to transcend completely

the human correlation between mystery and postulation, even though he does develop a metaphysics of the absolute and a logic of the divine-human community.

10. *The Problem of Christianity,* Vol. I, pp. xiv-xv.

11. *The Sources of Religious Insight,* pp. 25-26.

12. "We are saved, if at all, by devotion to the Community. . . . We are saved through and in the community. There is the victory which overcomes the world" (*The Problem of Christianity,* Vol. I, p. xvii; Vol. II, p. 390). A thorough exposition of the notion of the beloved religious community is made by J. E. Smith, *Royce's Social Infinite* (New York: Liberal Arts Press, 1950), pp. 126-61. In the moving Berkeley Conferences which Royce delivered at the University of California in 1913, just after having published *The Problem of Christianity* and having received notice of Charles Peirce's death, he expressed gratitude at having earlier been able to send the book (with its strong acknowledgement of indebtedness) to Peirce. Peirce had given the book his careful attention and general approval in the last exchange of correspondence between the two philosophers. Royce declared that he had not fully understood and appreciated Peirce's theory of knowledge until he began to probe the nature of Christian religiousness. Peirce's logic of the interpretive community gave a new concreteness and scientific relevance to the Roycean theme of loyalty and religious dedication to the growing community. See the Harvard collection, HUG 1755.5/ Royce MSS, Vol. 84, lecture 3.

13. Royce's internal analysis of Christianity in terms of the Pauline Epistles leaves three questions unanswered. (1) What effect would more recent biblical studies on the Old Testament and the Gospels have upon his concept of Christianity? (2) What relation exists between the religion of Christian Scriptures and other world religions? (3) What retroactive effect would Royce's theory of the self-interpreting religious community have upon his own earlier conception of the system of life formed by the absolute self and limited selves?

8

HUMAN EXPERIENCE AND GOD:
Brightman's Personalistic Theism

BY DANIEL CALLAHAN

It is a commonplace that science today does not give us an absolute, "objective" picture of a real world "out there" and separate from human experience. The questions men put to "the world" are human questions, and the answers are cut to suit the questions. The verification of a hypothesis tells us what the criteria for verification, which men have invented, allow us to be told. It is only an extension of this commonplace to note that science, then, is a projection of man, a prolongation of anthropomorphic interest. It tells us as much about man as about "reality." Thus modern empirical science comes full circle to a flirtation with idealism, the view that all our talk of "reality" reduces in the end to talk about "mind." Regularly, there has been a strain of idealism in American philosophy disposed to take this tendency seriously and to deal with it in—to empiricists —shocking forthrightness. Daniel Callahan, who has taught at Temple and at Brown universities and is now an editor of The Commonweal, *has a somewhat different orientation toward religion and philosophy from that of James Collins (see Chapter Seven). Edgar S. Brightman (1884-1953), Dr. Callahan notes, recognized that all experience implies relations to the whole of experience, and tried to create a hypothesis about God that would illuminate human experience. Dr. Callahan levels a sharp critique, first of Brightman's own proposals, and then of traditional alternatives to Brightman. Callahan recognizes frankly that all conceptions of God are finite and anthropomorphic; philosophers of religion, he sug-*

219

gests, would do well to begin from that point. The mystery is as much "man" as it is "God," and mysteries are for slowly getting to the bottom of, not for mystification.

Though a prolific writer, and in many respects an original thinker, the impact of Edgar Sheffield Brightman (1884-1953) on American philosophy was not great, even during his lifetime. Since his death in 1953 his small influence has rapidly waned. In part his own historical fate is of a piece with the gradual demise of the personalist movement in America. To be sure, the word "personalism" remains much in vogue in theological circles, especially among Roman Catholics. But this latter "personalism" finds its roots mainly in Martin Buber and Emmanuel Mounier; its orientation is theological rather than philosophical. Brightman's "personalism," by contrast, was directly in the stream of German and American idealism. Indeed, W. H. Werkmeister once wrote: "Of the idealistic systems, personalism seems to be most widely accepted today."[1] That it could once have been so strong is traceable to a handful of American philosophers, now neglected, who among themselves created both a "school" and a tradition at the end of the nineteenth and during the early decades of the twentieth centuries. Among them were Borden Parker Bowne, A. C. Knudson, and Brightman at Boston University, Ralph Tyler Flewelling (founder of *The Personalist*) at the University of Southern California, and George Holmes Howison at the University of California (Berkeley). What life remains in this tradition is very much to the credit of Peter Bertocci of Boston University, a student of Brightman's and the editor of his uncompleted attempt at a systematic metaphysics.[2]

I do not want to suggest here that the time has come for a Brightman "revival," nor do I want to bemoan the fate of American personalism. Instead, I would like to do two things: first, sketch out the main lines of Brightman's theism; second, indicate the attractions and pitfalls in Brightman's attempt to develop a philosophy of God fully consonant with human experience. The pitfalls, as it happens, far outweigh the attractions. They provide fair game both for the linguistic analysts (who like to sharpen their swords on anyone scented with idealism) and those of an existentialist temper (who will find Brightman's way of handling the "self" far too cool, abstract, and detached for their tastes). Nonetheless, Brightman's philosophy of God has many lingering charms, not the least of which was his sustained effort to bridge the traditional gap between the nature of God and the nature of man. It was Brightman's glory that he had the nerve to confront and attempt to overcome two major stumbling blocks in historical theism: that God is "wholly other" than man, beyond man's understanding and beyond any sharing of his problems, and that God is infinite and absolute in his nature and power. Since men have been commended for tackling lesser idols, a word of praise for Brightman is surely in order.

I

A convenient way of approaching Brightman's theism is by grasping his personalism, his theory of value, the role he assigns to experience, his reliance on hypothesis, and his emphasis on empirical coherence as the most reasonable norm of truth. The net result of his philosophical approach was to lead him directly to his most celebrated (if not necessarily most important) thesis: God is finite.

"Personalism," as Brightman defined it, is "that philosophical system which holds that the universe is a society of selves, unified by the will and immanent causality of a Supreme Self, and which, therefore, defines matter and the whole system of physical nature in terms of the active, conscious will of the Supreme Self, while it regards human selves (and whatever other selves there may be) as enjoying an existence of their own, dependent, it is true, upon the will of the Supreme Self, yet no part of it."[3] Brightman does not hesitate to drive his personalism to a radical conclusion: to be real is to be personal, and "to say that the real is personal is to assert that all is consciousness."[4] Two epistemological premises undergird this conclusion. The first is that all knowledge begins with experience, with what Brightman called the "datum-self." Anything posited outside the self must be inferred from what is given in experience; we can know nothing of reality but that which has some relation to personal experience. The second premise is that since

221

personality is the leading characteristic of the experienced self, it is a legitimate extrapolation to posit personality as the main attribute of the entire universe. It is much more reasonable, for instance, to explain all reality in terms of mind than mind in terms of other aspects of reality, particularly matter. "If matter is utterly impersonal," Brightman wrote," then spirit is a delicate and fragile stranger in the world, an immaterial effect of matter. . . . If, on the other hand, personality is the eternal reality in the universe and what we call matter and energy and their laws are simply the functioning of a cosmic personality, then the relation between matter and spirit is a relation between spirit and spirit, and our conscious existence is reasonably connected with the rest of the universe."[5]

I would call attention to the word "simply" in that last passage. For all the elaborateness of Brightman's systematic mind and philosophy, his vision of reality was direct and uncluttered; everything fits together in a relatively simple way. The rationality of the universe, he said, was for him a matter of "animal faith" (borrowing Santayana's phrase). Once we get hold of the key—"personalism" —the rest falls into an orderly place. An important instance of this order is the way he confidently moves from the personal nature of reality to God. Since it is only reasonable to ascribe personality to the nature of reality, it is equally reasonable, he argues, to take the next step and assert the existence of a Supreme Person who performs on a cosmic scale the functions that our consciousness performs on a finite scale: the organization of reality and the conservation of value. Personalism is thus eminently well suited to help interpret the meaning of religion, "for the Supreme Self may be identified with God, the object of religious worship."[6]

Brightman at one point helpfully summarized the main theses of his personalism.[7] (a) Experience is our starting point in all thought and our only omnipresent fact is our self; the self is our whole conscious experience. (b) There is a principle of logical coherence in our self. (c) There are objects independent of our experience of them (but only inferred from experience). (d) The external objects are other selves (and their personal experience), physical objects, universals, and values. (e) The laws of appearance described by the sciences are to be accepted, but it is also necessary to transcend these laws in order to confront problems not touched by science. (f) The external objects inferred from our experience are more rationally explained as an aspect of mind than by any other hypothesis. (g) The community of minds communicates through the objective order of the concretely experienced will of the Supreme Self. (h) The nature of the Supreme Self is known and defined through the facts of self-experience. (i) The experience of value points to the existence of a Supreme Value worthy of worship. (j) The fact of evil in the universe indicates that the Supreme Self is achieving values by conscious effort under difficult circumstances. (k) Finally, human immortality is guaranteed by the goodness of God.

The idealistic roots of Brightman's personalism are immediately evident. In particular, the influence of George Berkeley is pronounced (though modified to Brightman's purposes). "Personalism," he explained, "certainly does not hold that only human persons are real; nor does it hold that trees and gold and skies are all persons. . . . personalism holds that trees and gold and skies are all experience; yet not merely human experience, for they exist when no human being is aware of them. Therefore, they are the experience of the Supreme Person."[8] Where for Berkeley to be is to perceive or to be perceived, for Brightman to be is to experience or to be experienced. Consequently, it becomes possible to say that nothing impersonal exists, for "The 'impersonal' is simply an incomplete or abstract way of viewing what is really personal when fully understood."[9] Of course, this is a glaringly arbitrary way of using words, emptying the "personal" of linguistic sense; but it is indicative of Brightman's doggedly systematizing mind.

One further passage helps to bring out the importance of personal experience as the only possible starting point in philosophy, and as the only possible source of what can be called the "transformation rules" of personalistic logic: "The personalist points out that we derive our conception of unity from the unity of self; our conception of function . . . from the experience of purpose. . . . All science and philosophy, then, are the attempt to apply to the rest of the universe principles which we find in personality. If the attempt is in any degree successful, then there must be something in common between human personality and its cosmic environment. Human spirit thus becomes a clue to cosmic spirit."[10]

We are, in a word, stuck with our experience, but this is no disaster. We can find in our experience, or in what can be reasonably inferred from it, all that we need to know about our self, other selves, the universe, and God. The possibilities of personal experience are rich, extensive, and illuminating. Yet at no time does the possibility of realizing the fruits of experience require us to be anything other than empirical. Brightman's idealism, like Berkeley's, must be understood as an attempt at a radical empiricism—one is not asked to leave the concrete world for the sake of building beautiful speculative castles. On the contrary, one is only being asked to take experience—empirical, easily ascertainable experience—with full seriousness. "Personalism," Brightman contended, "is radically empirical in building (as against sensationalism and behaviorism) on the experienced fact that every item of experience belongs to a self."[11] In the formulation of explanatory hypotheses regarding experience, all such hypotheses must start with personal facts, facts as experienced by personal consciousness. The self, which is the origin of all interpretations of reality, is a unity of empirical experiences: ". . . the whole self consists of all the empirical situations connected with any given empirical situation by valid linkages of memory and anticipation. There is asserted the further knowledge (or belief) that the empirical situation is always an indivisible self-experience . . . and that its identity with past and future situations consists precisely in the experience of such identity in memory and anticipation."[12]

Brightman attempted to give the widest possible meaning to the concept of experience. "Our experience," he writes, "consists of our entire conscious life. . . . It will apply to any and every item of [consciousness], not to a set of privileged items, such as sensations or perceptions."[13] Most importantly for his theism, Brightman grants the existence of "religious experience," which is "any experience of a person taken in its relation to his God. Religious experience is not a unique kind or quality of experience; it is rather a unique way of apprehending experience."[14] As this passage would suggest, however, Brightman displays some ambivalence about singling out any one experience and calling it a uniquely "religious" experience. At times he inclines toward explaining it as the result of adopting a certain perspective on our ordinary experience (and thus involving the conscious choice of a religious vantage point). At other times he seems to accord it a distinct existence alongside other experiences

An important key to understanding this ambivalence is the place Brightman accords the experience of value. He has no doubt that we experience values. There are things we desire and things which attract us: there are bodily goods; aesthetic goods; intellectual, occupational, and social goods. Whether things which seem to us of value are in fact worthy of desire is a function of their coherence with other value claims and the totality of our experiences. But whatever our judgment about the ultimate value of those things which attract us, which become objects of desire, it is evident that some of our experiences can be called "value experiences." It is through our experience of value that we are led directly to the problem of religion. Not only do we experience particular, limited values (physical, mental, cultural), but we are also inclined to assign a general value to the totality of all limited values. To make such an assignment is, in actuality, to posit religious values. These are values "which are experienced when man takes an attitude toward value experience as a whole and toward its dependence on powers beyond man. Insight into this dependence elicits feelings of reverence and acts of worship. . . . religious values are an organization of the total value experience from a special standpoint."[15]

We should be led to see, however, that "a special standpoint" toward value is a necessity. Values do not exist, nor are they experienced, in total isolation; they actually coalesce, supporting and interpenetrating each other. The experience of interpenetration "points toward the conclusion that there is really only one value, namely, the systematic whole of our value experience. No value has sovereignty in its national territory; only the league of values is sovereign."[16] Once this single, overarching, sovereign value is recognized, it elicits the distinctively religious response of worship. "Religion," Brightman remarks, "is not unique in being a social phenomenon or even in being an interest in values; it is the wor-

225

shipful attitude, the attitude of reverent devotion to something divine, that marks it off from other experiences. . . . A religion, then, can be atheistic in the sense of denying some particular idea of God; it cannot be a religion at all if it denies that there is anything in the universe worthy of human reverence and devotion."[17]

God is the Supreme Value and the source of all values. Yet it is important to note that Brightman denied the possibility of a rational "proof" of God's existence. If an analysis of value experience *leads* us in the direction of a God, an ultimate value, it cannot *force* us to go in that direction. That is why, if we are to come to a belief in God, we must adopt (as a deliberate, voluntary act) "a special standpoint." How do we go about choosing a standpoint? That is not difficult at all. The scientific method of forming reasonable hypotheses to explain our empirical experience has proved its worth and is readily adaptable to the problem of religion. Moreover, it has some special advantages for religious thought: it is a method which forces us to stay close to empirical data, to revise our hypotheses when new evidence demands it, and to avoid any kind of religious dogmatism. Religious experience is not self-validating experience. Like any other experience it requires an explanation: "The meaning of any experience lies in the way it is taken; that is, in the hypothesis which explains it, giving it coherence and value. Faith is a name characteristically given by religious believers to their hypothesis. Religious experience is any experience viewed with the eye of faith."[18]

We are led, then, to the "special standpoint" of theistic personalism, first, by the experience of value, second, by recognizing the interconnection between values and their culmination and unity in one Supreme Value and, third, by hypothesizing that this Supreme Value is a personalistic God. The hypothesis of God is indicated in many ways, but in particular because it enables us to escape a troublesome antinomy posed by the experience of value. On the one hand, it is obvious that values cannot exist unless there is personality to experience them; but to concede this is to play into the hands of those who claim that all purported experiences of value are nothing but manifestations of wholly subjective desires, having no roots in any objective order. On the other hand, if the source of values is wholly rooted in aimless subjective desires, then there is no reason why people should seek, or morally be bound by, any values at all. Brightman escapes this dilemma by locating all values in the experience of a suprahuman mind. By this means objective value is separate from human personality but not from all personality. Hence we can see, Brightman argues, "that thought drives us in the direction of the hypothesis of a supreme mind or person as the ultimate reality of the universe and the home of values. The hypothesis, known as personalistic idealism or personalism, is true if it be as it appears to be, the only thoroughly coherent solution of the antinomy."[19]

But to create an explanatory hypothesis is one thing, and to verify it quite another. The one move we cannot make is to step outside of our own experience to verify our hypotheses; we can only know what we personally experience or can reasonably infer from our personal experience. Does this not mean, therefore, that no final religious certainty is possible? That we are left with only a reasonable hypothesis, incapable of any definitive verification? Exactly. But this is no loss, for the impossibility of final verification means that our knowledge is always capable of progress. Brightman quotes approvingly from John Dewey's *The Quest for Certainty,* adding that all we can hope to achieve is an "exploration of the possibilities of experience."[20] At the same time, our lack of ultimate certainty is no reason to feel bereft of any security: "while theoretically all proof is relative and not absolute, practically it is rational to believe that some propositions are really true."[21] That Brightman was influenced by both Dewey and William James in the serenity with which he accepted the impossibility of ultimate certainty seems clear.[22] While one might be tempted to think this an odd quirk in a philosopher so intent on building an all-encompassing religious and metaphysical system, it will seem less so when one recognizes the elements he felt his system had to encompass: personalism, scientific method, empirical experience, and a value-oriented rather than truth-oriented approach to the social community of selves. Brightman's roots may have been in German idealism, but they were watered by the American personalism of Borden Bowne and set in the soil of pragmatic America.

227

II

When Brightman speaks of "verifying" our religious and metaphysical "hypotheses," he has a special sense of verification in mind. Since we cannot get out of the datum-self except by inference, it will naturally follow that any verification will be limited to the range of personal experience. The value of a hypothesis can, then, only be determined by its ability to give a coherent explanation of our experience; to verify a hypothesis is to show its power to give our experience coherence. More explicitly, coherence is present when a hypothesis fulfills the following conditions: "(1) It is self-consistent, (2) it is consistent with all the known facts of experience, (3) it is consistent with all other propositions held as true by the mind that is applying the criterion, (4) it establishes explanatory and interpretative relations between various parts of experience, (5) these relations include all known aspects of experience and all known problems about experience in its details and as a whole."[23] Put briefly, the significance of any one item of experience can be understood only in relationship to all other items of experience, and the totality of experience can be understood only in terms of some hypothesis purporting to explain its significance. The test of a religious belief is the coherence of its account of experience: "One condition, and one only, must be imposed on religious beliefs: that they shall give a coherent account of all the facts of human experience—coherent within itself and coherent with all the experienced facts and also with our interpretation of nonreligious realms of experience. In so far as this ideal is attained, we have religious truth."[24]

Central to Brightman's conception of truth and of religious belief is the need to see wholeness and unity in our experience. Toward this end, experience must be organized and interpreted. "To be conscious," Brightman wrote, "means not merely to be aware of a particular content, but also to be aware of its relations."[25] The reasonableness of theistic belief lies precisely in its ability to give coherence to the totality of our experience—our experience of self, of value, of purpose, of other selves, of matter. Yet theistic belief does not give a completely coherent account of experience; it gives

228

us only a partially coherent account, but one which is, nonetheless, sufficient: "If theistic belief is relatively the most coherent interpretation of experience available, it is reasonable to accept it, unreasonable to reject it. The reasonableness of theistic belief is to be tested, not by its absolute adequacy to solve every problem, but by its relative adequacy as compared with other world views."[26]

In Brightman's eyes, the major problem about God is not whether he exists, but what his nature is. That God exists is "undeniable," but to say this is to talk only of a "barren abstraction."[27] Of interest is not *that* God is but *who* God is. In *The Problem of God* Brightman presents six ways of arriving at the concept of God.[28] (1) *The rationality of the universe:* first, it is necessary that we trust reason for both logical and practical reasons; second, the fact of interaction among things implies a rational ground of interaction; third, the fact that things exist in an orderly relationship points to a rationality, for pure nothingness could not produce rationality. (2) *The emergence of novelties:* the emergence of novelties in the evolution of the world, difficult to explain on a materialistic basis, points to a divine mind controlling this emergence. (3) *The nature of personality:* because of the pervasiveness of personality in the universe and the interaction of mind and things, it is sensible to suppose "that the whole world is one kind, and that the kind we experience directly is consciousness."[29] Since our experience encounters reports of like experience in others, as well as evidence for an infinitely greater experience, there is reason to believe there exists a universal source of experience. "The fact of personality," Brightman explains, "points to a world beyond our personalities, but essentially of the same kind, that is of thought and action and experience, yet on a cosmic scale."[30] (4) *The presence of values:* the otherwise inexplicable presence of values in human experience suggests the need for a cosmic source of values. (5) *Religious experience:* while religious experience is not a self-validating experience, it is nonetheless compelling, requiring an explanation. Taken together, these five considerations point to a God who is rational, evolving, personal, the ultimate source of values and in direct, personal contact with human consciousness.

Of special note is the emphasis Brightman places on human

and divine evolution. The fact of human evolution is scientifically evident; so too, consequently, is the necessity of divine evolution. The only kind of theism which will avoid the dangers of pantheism and deism, atheism and dogmatism is an evolutionary theism. To predicate a concept of God which stresses his absolute transcendence, a God who is "wholly other," is both to cut God off from man and to do violence to our experience of reality. The hypothesis of a God capable of evolving, yet still transcendent to man, does justice equally to God and to human experience. As a general principle, Brightman affirms, "no hypothesis is more plainly consistent with experience than one which supposes the given facts to be a fair sample of all that there is, and hence finds the source of all in an order of being akin to what we immediately experience in our personalities."[31] That such a principle should lead Brightman directly to a God capable of change and development is hardly startling.

Nor is it startling that Brightman would be willing to call this God "finite," or, more specifically, to specify a transcendent God with a finite will. When we consider what we know through our own experience of personality, we find that "personality is a complex whole, in which form, content, and activity are found in indivisible and inseparable unity. By form, I mean the laws of reason; by content, the brute facts of experience (sense data, pleasures, pains, desires and the like); and by activity, the power of will to choose and control the course of consciousness within limits. (If this definition points to a God with a finite will, I lay this to the facts of experience, rather than to theory.)"[32] That God's personality might be radically different from man's is ruled out from the outset. We have, on philosophical grounds, no reason to suppose such a total difference and every pragmatic reason to hypothesize a basic likeness between divine and human personality. God's transcendence is established by the fact that he is the source of all experience, personality and value. His finiteness is established by the fact that what we know of personality points to two important limitations: our will is limited in its power to control events, and our experience shows us that a major limitation to our power is the brute reality of evil in the universe. The main defect in earlier theisms was the inadequacy of their treatment of the problem of

230

evil. They teetered between a total negation of God's transcendence, on the one hand, and an absolutizing of that transcendence, on the other. The special danger of the latter course is the discontinuity it introduces between God and man, thus leaving human suffering and its implications for the God-man relationship wholly obscure.

The main support, then, for the hypothesis of a finite God is the possibility of a coherent explanation of the experience of evil. At the same time, it is a hypothesis consistent with the scientific theory of evolution, with the findings of the physical sciences concerning the nature of the material world, and with religious experience (which, Brightman thought, intimates divine limitation). "A theistic finitist," Brightman explained, "is one who holds that the eternal will of God faces given conditions which that will did not create, whether these conditions are ultimately within the personality of God or external to it. . . . All theistic finitists agree that there is something in the universe not created by God and not a result of voluntary divine self-limitation, which God finds as either obstacle or instrument to his will."[33] Everything we know of human experience (and, therefore—for what else are we free to say?—of experience as such) exhibits opposition and struggle, possibility and limitation. Only by supposing that the source of all experience, God, is himself beset by the same dichotomies and ambiguities can we have a theory of God consonant with our experience. Moreover, the scientific evidence of evolution displays two striking characteristics. Evolution is extremely wasteful insofar as it throws off, with almost reckless abandon, innumerable useless by-products and defective material, but also extremely productive in displaying an apparently perpetual refinement of what remains. This dual result shows forth both good and evil—the end result of evolution if unceasingly productive of value, but the cost of achieving it comes high. Most significantly, there seems to be no way of avoiding this high—and one would have to say "evil"—cost. It appears evident, therefore, that there exists in the universe some kind of irreducible "Given," which limits both God and man; of necessity, both will have to struggle unceasingly to evolve values in the face of this Given.

231

The positing of a Given has a number of obvious advantages. It enables us to envision God and man together struggling to achieve value (and thus, in a real sense, it can be said that God suffers along with man). It allows us to avoid the danger of being forced to attribute the source of evil to God's will. It leads us to discern that God's goodness is a more important attribute than his power (again bringing God closer to man), and that this goodness is the predominant force in the universe.[34] It enables us to maintain an eternal distinction between good and evil. Finally, the positing of a Given is consistent with our empirical experience, which always confronts resistance and difficulties in seeking to realize value.

As might be expected, however, Brightman also realized the problems inherent in trying to introduce an irreducible Given into the universe. He continually stresses that it is a hypothesis, one necessary to explain the coexistence of good and evil without falling into some of the historical traps lying in wait for any theist who tries to do so. Among these are an obscurantist recourse to mystery (which is simply to throw up one's hands in despair) or, equally unattractive, a falling back on a Manichean dualism. Brightman met the latter problem by employing the model of human sense experience. The Given "may be conceived as a conscious datum or perception, analogous to human sense experience, yet not produced by any stimulus or cause external to God. Just as human sense data create for men an *unendliche Aufgabe,* so the Given is the source of an eternal problem and task for God. It is irrational, not in the sense of containing logical contradictions or immoral purposes, but in the sense of being given to reason as a datum and not derived from rational premises or purposes. In itself it cannot be understood; yet an understanding use may be made of it, and through the conquest and shaping of it meaning may be achieved."[35] Brightman does not achieve much greater clarity than this (which is to say, not much). He is still left with the problem of where to locate the Given—internal or external to God. The latter possibility he rejects; that would clearly establish a dualism in the universe, if not necessarily a dualism of good and evil (for the Given, in its entirety, is not necessarily evil; only perhaps some elements).

In some way, therefore, the Given must be part of the nature of God. But how could this be? Brightman seems to have realized that the analogy with human perception is not really very helpful; for it presupposes some kind of external source of experience which Brightman cannot allow in the case of God (without falling into a dualistic universe which contains a source of experience independent of God). In the end, Brightman never does offer a satisfactory description of the relationship of the Given to God's nature, other than to include it as a part of that nature. At most, he is willing to say three things: (1) to have a self (and God has a self) is necessarily to be limited; (2) even an uncreated and eternal self must be limited—it is limited at least to being uncreated and eternal; (3) the will, we know from human experience, is limited; God's will must likewise be limited. None of this is very satisfactory, but Brightman believed that however difficult it is to explain the Given and its relationship to God in any satisfactory detail, it is a far more reasonable hypothesis to work with than any other ever proposed. One asks of hypotheses, not that they be perfect in their explanatory power, but only that they be better than any others available.

Perhaps the consideration most persuasive to Brightman in the hypothesis of a finite God are the new possibilities it opens to men in working out their relationship with God. A finite God, it turns out, will seem far more worthy of human worship than a supremely distant, transcendent God. A God who struggles for us is a God worthy of worship; a God who merely stages a struggle in our behalf is not: "Thus we see life as the drama of a suffering and striving God who never loses courage in his wrestling with The Given, but who always faces in his struggles conditions which he did not create, and for which it would be unreasonable to hold him responsible."[36] Brightman concludes *The Finding of God* by pointing to the hopeful changes an acceptance of a finite God will bring with them.[37] Insofar as we come to see God as coping with The Given we will perceive the value of man's cooperation with God and the infinite possibilities of growth. Rather than a blind faith in an incomprehensible, infinitely remote God we will have an intelligent faith in a God who strives to serve us. Rather than a changeless immortality we can foresee a laboring with God to bring about ever greater values. Rather than fearing God as absolute power we can now envision him as the source of goodness and love. Brightman also indicates that the idea of a finite God will require a revised conception of perfection. Perfection as traditionally understood, Brightman felt, is neither comprehensible nor related to any human experience. Neither does it satisfy any actual human longing. A more profound theory will work with the ideal of inexhaustible perfectibility, which leaves God open to perpetual growth and more fully satisfies our own longings for a developing, unfolding perfection rather than a frozen completeness. The goodness of God is not a static, passive goodness, or a goodness detached from struggle; instead, it is "an active goodness and a suffering goodness,"[38] forever in movement toward greater perfection, forever working to impose goodness and rationality on the Given.

III

I mentioned at the outset that the pitfalls in Brightman's attempt to develop a plausible theism far outnumber the attractions. Let us note some of these pitfalls. The most obvious, common to most idealists, were noted long ago by Ralph Barton Perry: the fallacy of "definition by initial predication"[39] and the "egocentric predicament."[40] The fallacy, Perry noted, lies in "regarding some early, familiar, or otherwise accidental characterization of a thing as definitive." In Brightman's case, this fallacy took the form of predicating of the universe as a whole the most familiar characteristic of the human self: personality. It does not follow that because I experience my own selfhood as personal, as seeking to realize values, as rational, the universe as a whole must necessarily be constituted along the same lines. Brightman of course might respond that he offers only a hypothesis, not a tight deductive argument. But then one would have to say there is no special reason to suppose in the first place that the universe as a whole has any relationship whatever to the structure of our consciousness. Similarly, by asserting that nothing could exist unless experienced by a conscious self (either God or man) Brightman traps himself within the "egocentric predicament." If we are not able to get beyond the "datum-self," then we are in no position to lay down conditions for the

234

existence of objects which do not form part of that self; of necessity, we are totally ignorant of the metaphysical nature of objects beyond our own experience.

Another difficulty with Brightman's theism lies in his attribution of transcendence to God. He supports this belief by following a well-worn path: God is transcendent because, as the source of value, experience, and rationality, he must necessarily possess greater powers than man; hence, he transcends the human condition. But Brightman has a dilemma on his hands at this point. He also wants to say, for the sake of maintaining a close relationship between God and man, that this transcendent God also shares with man one common problem, that of evil with its attendant need for struggle and suffering. But can one have it both ways? It is hard to see how, for the net result is to make of God little more than a superman, surely transcendent to ordinary men, but by no means so transcendent that he escapes the basic condition of human existence: limitation, frustration, opposition. God, in brief, far from transcending the human continuum, is left standing at its farthest reaches. He remains "transcendent," but in a notably pedestrian way. We might well respect such a God, just as we would respect an especially gifted human being who could do far more than we, but would we be willing to worship such a God? Would it not be wiser, actually, to stand in awe of the Given, for that is the one element of existence, human and divine, which neither we nor God can ever hope to conquer. Have we, for that matter, any solid evidence that God has made progress against the Given? Even if we grant he has—by affirming, say, that life today displays greater riches, values, and happiness than life in earlier times—what ground have we for assuming that this progress will go on indefinitely? Even if it does, what possible good will this be for all those millions of people who led wretched lives, and died miserable deaths, before the progress was achieved? Brightman was willing to say that God's goodness implies human immortality. But if God cannot overcome the evil of our mortal life, what guarantee is there that he will fare any better with our immortal life? Infinite perfectibility is an attractive idea, but one could get terribly weary with an infinitely long struggle against the Given.

The possibility that the experience of some people would be

such as to find an infinite, even though progressively successful, struggle as dreary a prospect as others would find the prospect of a static, perfect immortality, points to another problem. Brightman wants to remain true to experience, a laudable enough goal. Yet quite apart from the vagueness with which he defines experience, there remains the further question of establishing some priorities among our experiences. Is the experience of value a more significant experience than, let us say, sense experience? Is the experience of conscious selfhood a more important experience than the experience of behavior motivated by unconscious motives and conflicts? Brightman provides no clue about how we might answer questions of this sort. He does not go beyond emphasizing that our hypotheses must take into account the whole of our experience, making of them a coherently explained unity. Yet surely it is possible that our experience could badly mislead us in many respects, requiring that some experiences be ignored for the sake of the coherence of our other experiences. Brightman might well have covered this difficulty by saying that the search for coherence would imply such a discrimination, but, unfortunately, he left us with no tools to do so. Again, what is to stop us from choosing as a hypothesis whatever most pleases us, selecting just that evidence and just those experiences which suit our pre-established purposes? A man could well say that his most meaningful experience is that of personal autonomy and then set about looking for a hypothesis which will keep this experience intact, even if it means explaining away what appears to be an experience of God.

Experience is not only something we have; it is something whose contents we can alter by the way we choose to position ourselves, intellectually, psychologically, and socially. The experience a person has at one stage of life may radically differ from his experience at another stage. The inmate of a concentration camp will experience the universe and his own personality very differently from the man who runs the concentration camp; the experience of a child will differ from that of his parents. Each, presumably, could achieve a hypothesis which explained the full range of the experiences of himself and others; but each would arrive at quite different hypotheses. Throughout his works Brightman assumed that we all experience more or less the same reality in the same way, but clearly we do not. The point made by many modern theologians, for instance, is that contemporary man experiences the world in a very different way from the man who lived at the time of Christ. Change a man's physical environment, his social setting, his language, and you will change his way of experiencing himself and the world around him.[41]

But let me call a halt to this kind of sniping. One could raise problems indefinitely with Brightman's entire theistic project. It breaks down in a dozen places, even when allowance is made for the tentative nature of his speculations. The measure of a philosopher, however, ought not to be the success of his work in meeting all objections. It is unlikely that any philosopher will ever succeed in doing that, if only because later generations will, as I have suggested, experience the world differently from earlier generations; at the very least, they will choose different starting points, perhaps only out of boredom or a desire for a new kind of speculative play. Brightman himself, though not sensitive to the way culture shapes experience, was acutely sensitive to the need for taking into account fresh scientific data. Such data alone are enough to ensure that any system of totalistic explanation—or, as Brightman called it, "synoptic" explanation—will rapidly become obsolete. Brightman's own notion of an evolving God is heavily dependent on a model of human evolution which assumes unlimited progress and development; but of course it is conceivable that further scientific evidence might require a very different kind of model.

That much said, it nonetheless remains that Brightman saw very vividly some of the major requirements for an acceptable theism. First of all, he did not allow himself to be seduced by any of the traditional attempts to reconcile the presence of evil in the world with the affirmation of a wholly good, totally omnipotent God. He rejected what he called a "theory of multiple meanings" whereby what seemed evil in our eyes might not be accounted evil in God's eyes.[42] Faced with having to choose between a theory of God which left evil unexplained or a theory which built the origin of evil into God's nature, he chose the latter (taking care, naturally, not to make God responsible for the evil). If this choice introduces a whole set of new problems, they are hardly any worse than those imposed by a choice of the former option. Brightman recognized, brilliantly I think, that traditional theism had come to the end of the road in its futile attempts to provide a rationale for the presence of evil. It would not be possible, henceforth, to continue the wild goose chase for an ingenious solution to the problem of evil, one which left wholly intact the traditional perfection, goodness, and omnipotence of God. Put another way, one might well ask with Brightman why the traditional concept of God should be sacrosanct. Why, when it has failed so miserably to deal with evil, should it retain its privileged position? To continue according it a special, untouchable status is to ensure that the concept of God will seem infinitely remote from the world and the self as it is experienced. Brightman did not succeed in showing how evil could be encompassed within God's nature, but he did show that it is time we began looking in that direction. Where else, when all has failed, can we look?

Second, Brightman saw clearly that a significant concept of God—one which had human and not merely theoretical significance—would have to be based on the full range of human experience. I have pointed out that Brightman did not tell us how we should go about evaluating and ordering our experience. That omission should not distract our attention from what he did point out. Our concept of God must take into account the totality of experience and not be limited to one species of experience only. We need this kind of experiential scope not only for the sake of a sufficiently rich concept of God, but also for the sake of a concept of God which holds out the promise of a reality with whom humans can establish a meaningful relationship. Though Brightman at no place attempted to spell out his thoughts in any detail on what such a relationship would presuppose, it is easy to discern his implicit position. Above all, both God and man must retain their individuality and autonomy; neither can lose himself in the other, God by way of pantheism or man by way of a self-consuming absorption in the being of God. At the same time, a viable relationship requires a common ground of existence and purpose. A God-man relationship which is solely one of obedience and worship on man's part, transcendence and self-perfection on God's part, provides no such ground. The gap between man and God will remain infinite, the relationship totally one-sided. Brightman's positing of the Given, with which both God and man must struggle, was meant in part to provide the missing ground. However beset with difficulties, it does what a theory of the God-man relationship should do—provide a point of contact, and a projection of common purposes, needed to sustain a relationship into which humans can enter with individuality and integrity.

A God wholly transcendent to man, a God who shares none of man's problems and grants no common sharing of purpose, is a God begging to be rejected by man. Job, one might say, did the right thing in cursing God for inflicting evil upon him; it was the only thing Job could do and retain his honor. One of the attractions of representative government, which draws its leadership from those who have shown they are finite and who must continually display their capacity for entering into the struggles of all, is precisely the humanizing of the relationship between those who lead and those who are led. Sensitive people do not want leaders who are transcendently superior to them, cut from a wholly different cloth, however much such people may give every promise of solving their problems and meeting their needs. Enlightened dictatorships are rejected because of a realization of what they do to human relationships, especially the relationship between the weak and the powerful. This example is a homely one but it is consonant with what Brightman sought: a God-man relationship which brought God and man together in a mutually productive way. A transcendent, wholly enlightened God may appeal to a culture conditioned to aristocracies, but he will not appeal to a culture whose experience has underscored the importance of mutuality.

Third, Brightman was acutely aware of the way an evolutionary perspective on man and the world was bound to have an impact on our way of conceiving God. In anticipating recent process philosophy, he saw that once we gave up a static conception of material reality and human personhood, we would also be forced to give up earlier static conceptions of God. Brightman was wholly American in his distaste for dualisms of all varieties. To him it was inconceivable that men would for long remain contented with the dualism of a changing universe and an unchanging God. To be sure, the concept of a God in process poses no end of problems, but then so too does a perfect God, complete and final in all respects. It is sufficient, not that Brightman proved the God is in process, but that he pressed philosophers to look in that direction. Taken together, the concept of a God in process, a God who works with and in some sense suffers along with man, a God who can be understood by man through a reflection on his own personality, is a concept with a rich resonance. Though it is unlikely that many will be tempted to follow Brightman any longer in the details of his system, it seems certain that any theism devised in the near future will want to achieve with its concepts the same goals Brightman sought: coherence with the fullness of experience, the possibility of relationship, attentiveness to the centrality of the self, and responsiveness to the data of the physical sciences.

One could, quite justly, say that Brightman's theism is uncompromisingly anthropomorphic. One could also say that it plays right into the reductionist hands of all those—think only of Feuerbach and Freud—who see all notions of God as nothing more, ultimately, than human projections. One could say, finally, that any God presented as no more than a tentatively persuasive hypothesis is not the kind of God humans have historically needed or wanted. But why not turn the tables, admit all these objections, and say that no other viable options remain? What, after all, is so embarrassing about being frankly anthropomorphic? We have to start with what we know or conceivably could know; so too we have to use the language we have (or conceivably could have if we choose to fashion another). The only model we have for God is a model drawn from human exemplars; it cannot be otherwise. The only language we can use is human language; even the word "mystery," often employed when all else fails, is a human word drawn from human experience. If God is wholly other than man, transcending altogether man's language and concepts and experience, then nothing whatever can be said or thought about God; in the end, all theories of analogical language must fail if God is as totally mysterious as the tradition has held him to be. In so hopeless a situation (if we

240

accept a wholly transcendent God), silence is the only intellectually viable course. Silence and its implied behavioral correlate—a life lived as if God did not exist and human destiny lay solely in human hands. An open anthropomorphism (for such I take Brightman's theism to be) has, to be sure, many incipient drawbacks. There is nothing to stop men from fashioning a God who will serve their evils and injustices; it has been done before and it can be done again. Nor is there anything to stop them from fashioning a frivolous concept of God, failing to take seriously the way a concept of God works itself into the tissue of society and thereby influences its life-patterns.

Yet to point out these dangers is not to say they cannot be overcome, or at least minimized. The trouble with most earlier theisms is not that they fell prey to these same threats (which is understandable) but that they were led to pretend to themselves that they had not. For so long as it was thought possible to frame an interest-free concept of God (mainly by the employment of metaphysical concepts thought to be independent of cultural thought-patterns) there were not available the tools for a rigorous self-criticism. There remained always the illusion that something real was being talked about, with the more sophisticated philosophers prattling on at great length about the inadequacies of human language and concepts to plumb the depths of the mystery of God. But is this, in the end, to say anything illuminating whatever? Language is inadequate to say anything definitive about anything, from an experience of God (if such there be) to an experience of a dirty gray pebble lying in the street. The point is that we know nothing at all apart from our way of conceptualizing experience and talking about it. We can never put ourselves in a position to determine whether our concepts are adequate or inadequate to our experience. By the time we even get to our experience it is mediated, conditioned experience, existing not in isolation from our social, psychological, intellectual, and genetic situation and history but as imbedded in that situation and history. Instead of saying our language about God will always be inadequate to its referent, it would be more proper to say it is always inadequate to its referent as we have previously conceptualized that referent. The measure of adequacy, in other words, should not be some hoped-for one-to-one relationship between human word and transcendent referent, but between referent as conceptualized by past generations (or, for the individual, past selves) and referent as conceptualized on the basis of present experience. The common assertion that our language about God does not and cannot suffice to capture the richness and mystery of God can rest only on the assumption that somehow we *already* possess enough knowledge of God to perceive the discrepancy between human word and divine reality. But apart from an acceptance of revelation, we do not possess such knowledge; the only knowledge we possess is our own conceptualized experience. If there is to be any norm by which we measure our language about God, it can only be this conceptualized experience as it interacts with the experience we are at the moment in the process of conceptualizing.

An unashamedly anthropomorphic approach to the concept of God could avoid the inevitable logical and epistemological tangles which arise when there is a pretense of somehow knowing more about God than we are able to say. How could we know we know more? Brightman's mistake in assuming that the datum-self as we experience it is a fair sample of everything which exists would not have been a mistake if he had proposed it as a policy rather than as a metaphysical inference. We have no metaphysical reason whatever for supposing that the whole universe (much less God) is constructed along the same lines as our own psyche. But we do have good pragmatic reasons for adopting such an assumption as a working philosophical policy: treat the world as if it mirrors our own personality, because by doing so we can then project a concept of God which is humanly meaningful. The key here is to accept the necessity of projection. We have no choice anyway but to model God on man, to abstract from what we know of man those qualities and attributes which would seem most useful in forming a coherent concept of God.

How do we determine what is "most useful"? Here again we are forced back to a policy decision. If one central purpose in attempting to form a concept of God is to give value an ultimate ground, then we must set about the task of determining what is valuable in man and what is not, as a preliminary step. That done (and such a task is of necessity endless and the results never final), we will then be in a position to project a God who provides a ground for these values. The final step is to establish a dialectic between the God we project and our unceasing efforts to understand more clearly the nature of value as experienced and formed by man. The same process would apply in attempts to give the universe "meaning." The first step is to discover how we find meaning in ordinary life, the second to project these discoveries on a cosmic scale, and the third to establish a dialectic between the projected meaning and our own further attempts to refine the discerned human meanings.

I have gone far beyond Brightman's goal here. I have also, no doubt, gone further than the sensibilities of most Christian theists would allow. It would take more than one chapter to spell out my proposal in detail and to hope for the possibility of a successful defense. Two points will suffice for the moment. (1) If, as the Jewish and the Christian traditions hold, man is made in the image of God, then we do no disservice to God by fashioning our concept of him from what we know of man. Indeed, we may do a distinct disservice to God if we continue to insist that he is unattainable mystery; for that is to doom God to isolation, making a mockery of the powers God himself supposedly gave man. The problem of God today is not to deepen the mystery of God, but to get to the bottom of it. If God is to remain a mystery, then mankind will be left to its own resources anyway. It is as plausible to adopt as a working hypothesis that man is the mystery as it is to locate the mystery in God. What Brightman has taught us is that it makes as much sense to reshape our concept of God as it does to continue working with a fixed, immutable concept of God. The choice is ours.

(2) If a proposal to embrace unrelieved anthropomorphism as the way to God and to project a God consonant with human experience and human value seems scandalous, a question must then be asked. Can anyone prove that this is not what theists have always done, even if they have been unwilling to admit it to themselves? It appears to me that they have done just what I am proposing, however unconsciously. I am only suggesting that we drop the self-pre-

243

tense and bring to the surface the only (philosophical) way to God open to man—a God fashioned wholly by human tools to serve human needs and conceptualized in a wholly human way. To say that such a humanly created God could bear no relationship to the true God is to beg the question. We do not know the true God.

NOTES

1. W. H. Werkmeister, *A History of Philosophical Ideas in America* (New York: Ronald Press, 1949), pp. 576-77.

2. Edgar S. Brightman, *Person and Reality: An Introduction to Metaphysics,* ed. by Peter A. Bertocci in collaboration with J. E. Newhall and R. S. Brightman (New York: Ronald Press, 1958). (Unless otherwise indicated, all further references will be to the works of Edgar S. Brightman.)

3. "Personalism as a Philosophy of Religion," *The Crozer Quarterly,* V (1928), 382.

4. "Religion as Truth," in *Contemporary American Theology,* ed. by V. Ferm (New York: Round Table Press, 1932), p. 74.

5. *Is God a Person?* (New York: Association Press, 1932), pp. 11-12.

6. "Personalism as a Philosophy of Religion," *op. cit.,* p. 382.

7. *Ibid.*

8. *Ibid.,* p. 394.

9. *Is God a Person? op. cit.,* p. 4.

10. *Ibid.,* p. 13.

11. "Personalism and the Influence of Bowne," *Proceedings of the Sixth International Congress of Philosophy* (New York: Longmans, Green, 1927), p. 162.

12. "What Is Personality?" *The Personalist,* XX (1939), 135.

13. *A Philosophy of Religion* (Englewood Cliffs: Prentice-Hall, 1940), pp. 164, 414.

14. *Ibid.,* p. 415.

244

15. *Ibid.,* p. 99.

16. *Ibid.,* p. 101.

17. *Ibid.,* pp. 133-34.

18. *Ibid.,* p. 416.

19. *An Introduction to Philosophy* (New York: Henry Holt & Co., 1925), p. 164.

20. *A Philosophy of Religion, op. cit.,* p. 130.

21. *Ibid.*

22. It is amusing to note how Brightman's serenity in the face of uncertainty scandalized the author of a 1936 dissertation at the Catholic University of America. The author, James McLarney, could only conclude that whatever Brightman himself might have thought of his own success, "As a logical consequence it may be asserted that a theistic philosophy is impossible to him" ("The Theism of Edgar Sheffield Brightman" [Washington, D.C.: Catholic University, 1936], p. 73). These days, I suspect, doctoral candidates at Catholic University would find Brightman's serenity in uncertainty a most charming quality.

23. *A Philosophy of Religion, op. cit.,* p. 128.

24. *Ibid.,* p. 329.

25. *An Introduction to Philosophy, op. cit.,* p. 59. Cf. *Religious Values* (Nashville: Abingdon Press, 1925), p. 23, for a description by Brightman of the influence of Kant on his thinking about coherence.

26. *Religious Values, op. cit.,* pp. 30-31.

27. *A Philosophy of Religion, op. cit.,* p. 203.

28. *The Problem of God* (Nashville: Abingdon Press, 1930), pp. 148 ff.

29. *Ibid.,* p. 155.

30. *Ibid.,* p. 156.

31. *Personality and Religion* (Nashville: Abingdon Press, 1933), p. 61.

32. "Personality as a Metaphysical Principle," *Personalism in Theology,* ed. by E. S. Brightman (Boston: Boston University Press, 1943), p. 57.

33. *A Philosophy of Religion, op. cit.*, pp. 313-14.

34. The Influence of Plato's *Timaeus* is obvious here and was acknowledged by Brightman (*ibid.*, p. 288).

35. *The Problem of God, op. cit.*, p. 183. Brightman is unclear, perhaps because he was uncertain, about whether the Given contains at least some elements of intrinsic evil. On the whole, he shies away from this conclusion, though admitting the possibility. Cf. *A Philosophy of Religion, op. cit.*, pp. 245-46: "A surd in mathematics is a quantity not expressible in rational numbers; so a surd in the realm of value experience is an evil that is not expressible in terms of good, no matter what operations are performed on it. . . . It is at least debateable whether there are dysteleological surds; it is at least conceivable that such surds may exist."

36. *The Finding of God* (Nashville: Abingdon Press, 1931), p. 174.

37. *Ibid.*, p. 192.

38. *Ibid.*, p. 182.

39. *Present Philosophical Tendencies* (New York: Longmans, Green, 1929), p. 128.

40. *Ibid.*, p. 131.

41. For a good critique of Brightman's restriction of the self to conscious experience, see James E. Will, "The Psychological Method of Personalistic Theology," *Religion in Life* XXXV (Winter, 1966), 732-50.

42. *An Introduction to Philosophy, op. cit.*, p. 338.

9

WILLIAM JAMES AND THE PHENOMENOLOGY OF RELIGIOUS EXPERIENCE

BY JAMES M. EDIE

Paul van Buren suggests in Chapter Three (supra) that William James provides a starting place from which a philosopher's sympathies can move in two directions at once: in that of Continental phenomenology and that of English language analysis. The present chapter argues a similar point at greater length and in a different context. While Royce (Chapter Seven, supra) was giving his Gifford Lectures in 1901—idealist and abstract regarding religion—William James was already collecting the notes and writing the drafts that were to be put in final shape as The Varieties of Religious Experience, *the Gifford Lectures of 1902. James, as we saw, was thenceforward to have a great influence upon Royce before the latter's death in 1916. In this essay, James M. Edie of Northwestern University describes James's "phenomenological method" in studying religion, and locates it among other, Continental conceptions of phenomenology. James had a great relish for human experience in all its complexity and confusion; he responded to sky and sea, to solitude, to intellectual effort and striving, to risk and decision-making. He understood that chemical means (in James's day the common means was alcohol) could expand the mind until, the censors of humdrum and pragmatic experience removed, it could give a great "Yes" to life. James found that "Yes" implicit in all intellectual and pragmatic striving; the man who acts*

247

says it despite himself. James was fascinated by the seemingly infinite variations of this "Yes" in human experience.

The aim of this study is to investigate William James's contributions to the phenomenology of religious experience. To some it may appear strange that James "the pragmatist" should so forthrightly and without apologies be incorporated into the phenomenological viewpoint.[1] But I want to show that James's methodological contributions to the study of religious experience are not only more sound phenomenologically than some of the studies which have, under the influence of Husserl, up to now explicitly invoked the phenomenological method, but that they are also the first to establish any solid basis for a true phenomenology of religious experience.

I

Husserl, himself, was not—at least throughout most of his life—much interested in religious phenomena.[2] His major successors, Heidegger, Sartre and Merleau-Ponty, have likewise taken phenomenology to be a philosophy of the *Diesseitigkeit,* and have thus almost completely neglected religious experience. Heidegger has said that in the present state of philosophical thought it is impossible to pose questions about religious experience.[3] While it is true that Sartre is obsessed with the idea of God, both as it acts in human experience,[4] and as the self-contradictory "limit concept" in terms of which we must understand the eternally futile attempt of consciousness to give itself "substance" or "being," he has certainly not given any sympathetic attention to the phenomena of religious experience as such. Merleau-Ponty alone among the major disciples of Husserl has mentioned the intrinsic interest and value of such an investigation from the phenomenological point of view, and he left a place for such a branch of phenomenology in his own program.[5] However, like Husserl, he did little more than express an interest in the possibility of such an investigation and made no contribution of his own toward fulfilling it. Even Gabriel Marcel (to turn to contemporary representatives of non-Husserlian phenomenology) has left his original doctoral project, an approach to the phenomenology of mystical experience, incomplete and unpublished. Thus, the founders and "fathers" of the phenomenological movement in Europe have given us nothing in the way of a phenomenology of religious experience.

There is, it is true, a more or less unified school of thought in the history and philosophy of religion, represented by such names as G. Van Der Leeuw, Joachim Wach, Mircea Eliade, Rudolph Otto, and others who have practiced the "phenomenology of religion."[6] The work of this "school," which owes much more to Dilthey than to Husserl, needs no apologist. Basing itself on the late nineteenth-century German *Verstehendepsychologie,* and utilizing the classificatory schemas inaugurated by Dilthey, this school has developed a comprehensive (*Verstehende*) hermeneutics of religious symbols, institutions, and the like, and has established a more or less universal sociological and anthropological "morphology" (Eliade) or "typology" (Wach) for the interpretation of historical religions. The concrete details of such typologies differ from author to author, but they are imbued with a common direction and method. Van Der Leeuw says this method can as well be called "The General Science of Religion," or "Transcendental Psychology," or "Eidology," or even *Formenlehre der religiösen Vorstellungen* as "Phenomenology of Religion;" this last denomination is now the most current and widely accepted.[7]

This last approach to the study of religion is, at least in intention, truly phenomenological. In their various methodological reflections these authors show clearly that they adopt a purely descriptive, phenomenological approach; that such an approach cannot be "normative" or serve as the basis for any theology; finally that it is not pure history or sociology but eidetic inquiry into the essential structures of religious institutions and religious symbols.[8] Van Der Leeuw says that the purpose of such an inquiry is to discover "meanings" or "types" and "structural connections" within and among such "types" which are "neither factual relationships nor causal connections," which are "timeless and need not actually occur in history."[9] And Wach writes: "Neither history nor psychology can do the job of phenomenology. Neither deduction nor abstraction secures the 'essence' (*eidos*) vouchsafed by the *Wesen-*

schau."[10] Such a study is clearly not just history, nor is it psychology, textual criticism, metaphysics, or theology.[11] It is a genuine phenomenological attempt to arrive at the ultimate and foundational structures empirically incarnated in the various historical religions. None of these structures is ever exhaustively instantiated in any given historical case. Such a study results in an eidetics (or "typology") of religious expressions (symbols) and institutions common to man as *Homo religiosus.*

Nevertheless, even though none of these authors can be accused of historical relativism or psychologism, their approach to experience is not through direct reflection upon what is immediately given. Instead, it must pass through "the control of philological-archaeological hermeneutics."[12] Van Der Leeuw even seems to identify "phenomenology" in this sense with Dilthey's "hermeneutics." Wach and Eliade also tie their "phenomenology" essentially and necessarily to the history of religions. Thus, rather than being a method (or a "science") in its own right, such phenomenology is the way in which the historian of religions exercises his "understanding" within his own field *qua* historian.[13]

II

But there is another phenomenological approach possible in this area, and one which would appear to be much closer to what Husserl and Merleau-Ponty envisaged as the properly phenomenological elucidation of this domain of experience. It would be a phenomenology precisely, not of *religion*—in some or in all of its manifestations—but of *religious experience as such.* It would be a study not of historical and philological origins of religious meanings and symbols, but of the foundations of such meanings in consciousness itself. The *Ursprung* of such meanings would not be found through historical, sociological, and anthropological investigations but through an analysis of actual, present religious experience. It would be, in short, less a hermeneutics of texts and institutions than a turn to naïve, unreflective experience, as we find it prior to any theory or doctrine about it.

This is the orientation of William James in his *Varieties of Religious Experience,* and this is what radically distinguishes him from other phenomenologists and philosophers of religion. Though he undertook these investigations utterly independently of and without any reference to Husserl, the approach he takes would seem to be more directly Husserlian than that of the "school" which formally claims the name. I am not, of course, claiming that these two approaches are mutually incompatible or irreconcilable; they clearly are not. I am, rather, claiming that William James was the *first* to attempt a phenomenology of religious experience in an experiential sense, and I would point out that he has had almost no successor in this endeavor up to the present time. As is characteristic of James's contributions to philosophy, he but opened up a way which he left incomplete and unfinished at his death, a method which has been unaccountably neglected by his successors and disciples; and I would suggest that by prosecuting this method we would discover another of the remarkable points of convergence between Husserl's philosophy and that of James.[14]

James remarked once, in 1897, that "Religion is the great interest of my life,"[15] and when he was offered the Gifford Lectureship in 1898 (it had been suggested already in 1896), he began the systematic collection and analysis of the great mass of material which went into those lectures (1901-2) and which was published as *The Varieties of Religious Experience, a Study in Human Nature* in New York in 1902. This was not a historical study; James had, indeed, very little interest in the social and institutional aspects of religion and considered them rather unimportant.[16] Though he necessarily uses historical documents and the reports of the experiences of others, he does so only in order to understand "what goes on in the single private man," in order to get at the concrete and individual experience itself insofar as possible, and not its "conventional expression." He believed that there were specifically and uniquely religious data or "facts" and he wanted to get at the meaning of these facts. He is very clear, from the outset, that he is not going to present a philosophy of religion but, rather, what we can now rightly call a "phenomenological" description of the whole complex structure of interlocking needs, motives, ideals, desires, feelings, moods, etc., which, taken together, constitute religious experience in its various modalities.

> Religion [he wrote] is the very inner citadel of human life, and the pretension to translate adequately into spread-out conceptual terms a kind of experience in which intellect, feeling and will, all our consciousness and all our subconsciousness together melt in a kind of chemical fusion, would be particularly abhorrent. Let me say then with frankness at the outset, that I believe that no so-called philosophy of religion can possibly begin to be an adequate translation of what goes on in the single private man, as he livingly expresses himself in religious faith and act.[17]

James *did* hold some elements of a philosophy of religion, at least in the sense of certain conclusions about the nature of consciousness, God, and the universe as a whole, but these are only very sketchily presented in the *Varieties*. James recognizes that they are somewhat gratuitously introduced toward the end of his treatise and does not claim that they are conclusions which strictly or necessarily follow from the descriptive part. He many times expresses his intention to write a sequel to the *Varieties* in which he would expound his religious philosophy in full detail, but he was prevented from undertaking it by his death. In any event James's religious ideas and his positive religious philosophy fall entirely outside the scope of the present investigation. My purpose is not to recapitulate James's conclusions but to study his *method;* not to give an inventory of the results of his work, but to attempt to discern the nature and importance of his methodological contribution.[18] The fact that he himself explicitly distinguishes his purely descriptive approach to the phenomena of religious experience from any metaphysical conclusions or religious philosophy justifies our decision to focus exclusively on his descriptive method.

He states, as the first postulate, that he is not going to investigate, at least for their own sake, questions of the *origins* of religious meanings either historically or psychologically. This would be an interesting approach to religion but it is methodologically distinct from the study of the essential meaning and value of religious experience as it is lived. His approach, he tells us, will not be "dogmatic" (i.e., "rationalistic") but "empiricist." It will not look for conceptual "tests for truth which might dispense us from appealing to the future".[19] Rather than elaborate explanatory hypotheses, he will examine "the immediate content of the religious consciousness" (p. 28). He will adopt "the purely existential point of view" (p. 24), "the experiential point of view" (p. 44) and, "by addressing [himself] directly to the concrete facts" (p. 57), will aim just at "the description of the phenomena" (p. 354).

The first essential distinction to be made is that between the *psychological origin* of certain religious phenomena (such as conversion for instance) and their meaning or "worth." Even should we find evidence of "nervous instability," of "exalted emotional sensibility" in some "religious geniuses" (p. 24), we cannot thereby dismiss them as just so many "hysterics" (p. 205) because, in fact, "the best fruits of religious experience are the best things that history has to show" (p. 207). In other words we cannot either dismiss or exhaustively "explain" the importance and religious genius of Martin Luther because of certain supposed and hypothetical anal-erotic character traits, or account for his doctrine of justification by faith by the fact that he received his inspiration for this interpretation of Paul's Epistle to the Romans while seated on the toilet. James proceeds like Husserl in a methodological attempt to distinguish the "what" (the essence or meaning) of experience from its existential and psychological conditions and origins. Similarly, we could adduce the case of the Russian religious philosopher, Vladimir Solovyov, who was subject to religious hallucinations from early in childhood (the periodic visitations of "Holy Wisdom" in feminine form); Solovyov was fully conscious of the hallucinatory character of his experiences but found no reason, in that, to discount their value or to refuse to learn from them.[20]

> Saint Teresa [writes James] might have had the nervous system of the placidest cow, and it would not now save her theology, if the trial of the theology by these other tests should show it to be contemptible. And conversely if her theology can stand these other tests, it will make no difference how hysterical or nervously off her balance Saint Teresa may have been when she was with us here below (p. 32).

The "medical materialism" which would finish St. Paul by calling his vision on the road to Damascus a "discharging lesion of the occipital cortex," or snuff out St. Francis of Assisi as a "hereditary degenerate," or explain George Fox's pining for spiritual veracity as a "symptom of a disordered colon" requires that we reduce experience to its psycho-physiological *origins* (p. 29). But experience itself knows nothing of such origins; my life has a meaning and value for me even if I understand nothing of nervous or circulatory systems and even if I have never read a word of psychopathology. The consideration of the various possible causal explanatory hypotheses of behavior is indeed a branch of knowledge but it must be methodologically excised from any consideration of experience as such.

We know from James's philosophy as a whole (his pragmatism, his meliorism, his pluralism) that what chiefly interested him in human behavior ("what makes life significant") were the phenomena of courage, struggle, bold and strenuous action, risk, heroism. He believed that exceptional circumstances generate exceptional inner power and thus he liked to examine the limit cases, when men are under the highest pressure. And this is why the phenomena of religious experience so attracted him, because they give the most illustrative examples of the "strenuous life" (p. 207).

Like the existentialists Sartre, Malraux, Camus, and Dostoevski—and unlike traditional British moralists—James turns to the extreme cases for their illustrative value.[21] This turn is essential to his method. In order to see the varieties of mind which religious experience covers, we must place all these experiences "in their series": "Phenomena are best understood when placed within their series, studied in their germ and in their over-ripe decay, and compared with their exaggerated and degenerated kindred" (p. 294).

To study the ordinary or the conventional "would profit us little." "If we are to touch the psychology of religion at all seriously, we must be willing to forget conventionalities, and dive below the smooth and lying official conversational surface" (p. 125). He even called his attempt to get at the "existential study of its conditions" "my pathological programme" (p. 35). ". . . it always leads to a better understanding of a thing's significance to consider its exaggerations and perversions, its equivalents and substitutes and nearest relatives elsewhere" (p. 35).

Thus we can say that James's method is an attempt to arrive at experientially based descriptions of religious phenomena such as conversion, sanctity, mysticism, etc., through an examination of *all* the existential components of such an experience as they are ranged on a continuum from the most ambiguous instances of lowest intensity to the most specific and extreme cases of maximum intensity. It is because the extreme cases allow us to identify the phenomenon most clearly that our knowledge of such cases will enable us to discern the same essential structures more or less partially realized in more amorphous, embryonic, and ambiguous cases. We will, then, come to see that the structures of religious experience which are discernible in the extreme cases are also present in the most ordinary and banal human behaviors and, indeed, that the religious structures of experience are the most basic and deep-seated of all.

III

William James's greatest single contribution to the study of religious experience was to show us how it could be found, delineated, and defined in a manner which would remain faithful to the uniqueness, the primordiality and the intrinsic complexity of the experience itself. He did not try to reduce it to one or another of its constituent infrastructures, but to locate all its various levels and aspects as they are in fact interrelated in actual experience.

It is amazing what simple-minded theories philosophers throughout the history of philosophy have propounded to account for religion. Since the time of the early Greeks, philosophers have attempted to give us essential definitions of things. Perhaps because of the very nature of the Greek language, with its system of articles, Socrates and Plato seemed to believe that such things as "Piety," "Courage," "Knowledge," "Justice" and even "the Good," "the Beautiful," "the Useful," etc. could be defined in some one, comprehensive formula, a *to koinon;* and Aristotle established the method for making such definitions through an analysis of species and specific differences. The Greeks of course recognized dimly that there were certain "transcendental" terms which could not be defined in this way; but these were a very restricted number. In recent philosophy, both analytical and existential, we are becoming laboriously more aware of how many of our words and concepts are "polymorphous" and how difficult it is to define anything at all. With his clearly phenomenological approach to this problem, James was well ahead of his time and his lead must now be followed.

Other philosophers have been content to define religious experience by saying that it is *nothing but* so and so. Lucretius identified the essence of the religious impulse with "fear," fear of death, fear of fate, fear of the gods; and, in the full light of the twentieth century, Bertrand Russell finds this view still an acceptable and exhaustive definition of religion.[22] Hume found the source of religion to lie in such natural emotions as terror of death, thirst for revenge, appetite for food, and other biological necessities. Mill identified the source of religion as "hope" and Spencer found it in the experience of "the Unknowable." Schleiermacher defined religion as "the feeling of absolute dependence" and Rudolph Otto said it was "the experience of the holy (*Numen*)." Some have defined it socially, as the need for companionship, in "the brotherhood of men under the fatherhood of God," while others, like the Yogis, have found it to lie exclusively in man's most private, solitary existence *solus cum solo*. Freud perhaps represents the most magnificent and articulated attempt to reduce religious experience to "one thing," to one unique source in human psychology: religion, he said, is a result of sex repression.

It is interesting to note that, though James had read very little Freud and met him only once at the end of his life (some time after writing the *Varieties*), he was nevertheless aware of the force of this argument and was well aware of the erotogenetic theory of religion and of the large place of sexual symbolism, both normal and abnormal, in religious experience. He cites the coprophilia of Margaret Mary Alacoque, Francis Xavier, St. John of God, and others who cleansed the sores and ulcers of their patients orally, with their tongues (p. 225). The writings of St. Gertrude remind him of "an endless amatory flirtation . . . between the devotee and

256

the deity" (p. 270), and he quotes such passages as the following from Sister Séraphique de la Martinière: "Often the assaults of divine love reduced her almost to the point of death. She used tenderly to complain of this to God. 'I cannot support it,' she used to say. 'Bear gently with my weakness, or I shall expire under the violence of your love' " (pp. 220-21). But, against Freud, he would argue that to reduce religious experience to this one facet of it is a gross oversimplification. "It seems to me that few conceptions are less instructive," he wrote, "than this re-interpretation of religion as perverted sexuality" (p. 27). In fact, he writes, one might just as well interpret religion as a perversion of the respiratory function.

> The Bible is full of the language of respiratory oppression: "Hide not thine ear at my breathing; my groaning is not hid from thee; my heart panteth, my strength faileth me; my bones are hot with my roaring all the night long . . . my soul panteth after thee . . ." (p. 28).

Religious life depends just as much, he said, on the spleen, the pancreas, and the kidneys as on the sexual apparatus. Human needs for food, warmth, shelter have provided a rich symbolism. While it is true that explicit religious interest in the world develops more or less synchronously with the onset of puberty, so too does every other interest, since it is "the entire higher mental life which awakens during adolescence." As always, James is impatient with any attempt to reduce religious experience to its supposed physiological and psychological origins and, instead, demands that it be taken in its total meaning, as a complex skein of interlocking drives, emotions, desires, motives, ideas, and feelings which must be described in their intentional unity.[23] We must adopt not a monistic but a pluralistic method:

> In the psychologies and in the philosophies of religion, we find the authors attempting to specify just what entity it is. One man allies it to the feeling of dependence; one makes it a derivative from fear; others connect it with the sexual life;

257

others still identify it with the feeling of the infinite; and so on. Such different ways of conceiving it ought themselves to arouse doubt as to whether it possibly can be one specific thing. . . . There is religious fear, religious love, religious awe, religious joy, and so forth (p. 40).

Religious experiences, we might say, involve the intentionality of the whole human organism and are specified not by their psychological mechanisms but by their intentional objects.

But religious love is only man's natural emotion of love directed to a religious object; religious fear is only the ordinary fear of commerce, so to speak, the common quaking of the human breast, in so far as the notion of divine retribution may arouse it; religious awe is the same organic thrill which we feel in a forest at twilight, or in a mountain gorge; only this time it comes over us at the thought of our supernatural relations; and similarly of all the various sentiments which may be called into play in the lives of religious persons. As concrete states of mind, made up of a feeling *plus* a specific sort of object, religious emotions of course are psychic entities distinguishable from other concrete emotions; but there is no ground for assuming a simple abstract "religious emotion" to exist as a distinct elementary mental affection by itself, present in every religious experience without exception (p. 40).

One could hardly hope for a more explicit statement of the intentional structure of religious experience. In phenomenological research we are concerned with the "meaning" of the experience. Such meanings are found within the total psycho-biological dynamics of individual human life and must be approached as such. It is because of this primary complexity that "we have really different types of religious experience" (p. 98), and that religious experience does not exhibit any one "essence." If we are to define it, then, we must do so morphologically. We will not get a clear and distinct concept defined through genus and specific difference but a polymorphous (James says "collective") concept, "no one essence, but many characters" (p. 39).

258

Religious experience, according to James, then, is a dimension of human intentional life as a unified whole. It is, we might say, a way in which a man uses his moods, feelings, emotions, aims, all of which are given in biological and psychological nature with their own specific nonreligious teleologies, but which, together and in various mixtures and gradations, can embody religious intentions and attitudes. Religious experience, then, is an expressive use of the human body. In his studies on language Merleau-Ponty points out that when a child begins to speak he does so by beginning to use the organs of his body for a purpose which is not "natural" to them. All of the organs which are used in speech (the tongue, lips, palate, throat) have specific biological functions which do not require that they be used for speaking. Language is thus a "superstructure," he says, a phenomenon of a higher order than the biological, but which employs given biological organs for "another purpose," with another intention, "to sing the world."[24] It is somewhat in the same way, I think, that James means us to understand the emergence of religious experience amid the diverse and disparate functions of our psychic life. Religious experience does not have any particular bodily organ, is not situated in any specific bodily drive or emotion, but uses them all to express an intention of a higher order.

One of the great difficulties in discussing religious experience, then, lies in the fact that the use of the human psycho-biological organism to experience (or "constitute") religious meanings and values is one of the most all-pervasive, most deep-rooted, inescapable, and global of all human behaviors. It can appear in so many guises and so many complex manifestations that the task of laying them all out with exhaustive analytical clarity seems hopeless. There is no man totally devoid of religious feeling in this sense; such feelings are, indeed, "amongst the most important biological functions of mankind" (p. 382). It has even been suggested that the origin of religious experience antedates the appearance of the human race on earth, since some of the higher anthropoids occasionally seem to perform a kind of ritual dance together and deck themselves with leaves and fruit peels as if in an expression of a religious attitude toward the world and one another. Such leaves and fruit peels would then have been the first liturgical vestments. It is not, perhaps, necessary to go so far, but I think James has shown well that religion lies very deep in the structures and substructures of human consciousness. It may be precisely this fact which has prevented philosophers from making much headway up to now in the delineation of religious phenomena.

IV

It is not my intention to recapitulate all the results of James's analyses or repeat all his attempts to give morphological definitions. We must limit ourselves here to one example as an illustration of his method. In modern phenomenological terminology, we could call his study of "mystical experience" an attempt to establish an eidetic definition of such experience. Nobody, least of all James himself, would claim that he has discerned all the elements which go to constitute such an experience, that he has exhaustively grasped the phenomenon and definitively interrelated all its substructures. But he made a start and gave an example of what such an attempt might achieve.

His analysis of mystical experience is made against the background of certain distinctions already established. He had already distinguished religious experience from its psychological origins. He also distinguished religious experience from the merely ethical. No doubt ethical structures are frequently associated with religious experiences, but religion cannot be identified with the ethical; it involves "impulses to sacrifice" (and self-sacrifice), phenomena of resignation, and many others which are nonethical in character. Moreover, religion antedates and is independent of purely moral or ethical impulses and behaviors. Perhaps the distinction of religious from merely ethical phenomena is nowhere better illustrated than in mysticism. Mystical experience is not at all necessary to the ethical life; we can be "good Christians" or "good Jews" without it. It is something superfluous, above and beyond natural expectations or needs, something which may require an ethical preparation but which is certainly not the aim or intention of morality.

Throughout the *Varieties* James reminds us that "my method," as he terms it, is "empirical" and can thus never bring us to a full vision of the truth, established once and for all; its conclusions will never be more than presumptively true and "no empiricist ought to claim exemption from this universal liability" (p. 260). "I may seem to despair of the very notion of truth. . . . I do indeed disbelieve that we or any other mortal men can attain on a given day to absolutely incorrigible and unimprovable truth about such matters of fact as those with which religions deal" (p. 261).

We know that both temperamentally and philosophically James had, as he put it, "to fall back on a certain ultimate hardihood, a certain willingness to live without assurances or guarantees,"[25] and nowhere are his investigations more precarious than in the field of mysticism.

> [Yet] . . . such states of consciousness ought to form the vital chapter from which the other chapters [of the *Varieties*] get their light. Whether my treatment of mystical states will shed more light or darkness, I do not know, for my own constitution shuts me out from their enjoyment almost entirely . . . (p. 292).

Thus he proceeds cautiously, and with the limited aim of discovering the "reality" and the "paramount importance" of such ranges of experience. He attempts to range them "in their series" and to establish their general characteristics as they build up from "phenomena which claim no special religious significance" to "those of which the religious pretensions are extreme." The first levels are "sporadic," i.e., they represent "mystical states" which come upon one without special preparation or cultivation, from sudden insights into the deeper significance of common words or situations, to sudden invasions of a sense of mystery and "of the metaphysical duality of things" (i.e., of the transient, phenomenal, unreal character of this world as opposed to a "deeper" level of consciousness and meaning into which we are sometimes plunged in "dreamy states," at times of stress, and other occasions). James discusses the power of nature to produce sudden transports of at least a quasi-mystical character—which he is willing to call "cosmic consciousness"—a sudden grasping of the whole of reality and the realization of one's total identification with it. Such experiences of

AMERICAN PHILOSOPHY AND THE FUTURE

awe, wonder, or exaltation frequently occur in solitude, when one is walking alone in a forest or along a mountain path, or when gazing at night at the stars. This intuitional grasp of the "oneness" of things is a characteristic note, James believes, of all mystical states from the highest to the lowest, and that is why it is permissible to discover a mystical element in experiences of this kind which almost all men have at some time or other.

Among the lower mystical states James includes the use of alcohol, mescal, chloroform, ether, and other drugs and poisons which are known to bring about temporarily elevated states of consciousness. He writes of them in his inimitable Victorian prose:

> The next step into mystical states carries us into a realm that public opinion and ethical philosophy have long since branded as pathological, though private practice and certain lyric strains of poetry seem still to bear witness to its ideality. I refer to the consciousness produced by intoxicants and anaesthetics, especially by alcohol. The sway of alcohol over mankind is unquestionably due to its power to stimulate the mystical faculties of human nature, usually crushed to earth by the cold facts and dry criticisms of the sober hour. Sobriety diminishes, discriminates, and says no; drunkenness expands, unites, and says yes. It is in fact the great exciter of the *Yes* function in man. It brings its votary from the chill periphery of things to the radiant core. It makes him for the moment one with truth. Not through mere perversity do men run after it. To the poor and the unlettered it stands in the place of symphony concerts and of literature; and it is part of the deeper mystery and tragedy of life that whiffs and gleams of something that we immediately recognize as excellent should be vouchsafed to so many of us only in the fleeting earlier phases of what in its totality is so degrading a poisoning (p. 297).

And, referring to his own experiments with nitrous oxide intoxication, he concludes that our ordinary, waking, "rational" consciousness is but one type of consciousness and that, "parted from it by the filmiest of screens," there are other types and potential forms of consciousness of an entirely different order. This is as far as

262

James is able to go on the basis of his own experience, but he means to show that even those of us who have no access to the higher mystical states are not totally cut off from them or utterly unable to feel what they may mean to those who experience them in a fuller sense. Nearly all men have "such mystical moods" at some time or other, experiences which are their own justification, which need not be proved real to their possessor, which are "ineffable" and cannot be transmitted by talk but which can only be experienced and enjoyed in quietude.

The higher orders of mystical experience are, of course, limited to rather rare individuals and are methodically cultivated as a part of the religious life by certain persons as a means of achieving experimental union with the divine. No major religion has been without mystics in this sense and James tries to draw together sufficient evidence to delineate certain undeniable characteristics of such experience. First of all such experiences, though they involve states of feeling, have a decidedly "noetic" quality and give the experiencer an "insight into depths of truth unplumbed by the discursive intellect" (p. 293). Sensorial images play a very large part in such experiences: "they are absolutely sensational in their epistemological quality . . . that is, they are face to face presentations of what seems immediately to exist" (p. 324). On the other hand, the "knowledge" which is acquired in such states is strictly intuitive and nonconceptualizable. James takes the "consciousness of illumination" to be the most essential mark of mystical states (p. 313), but he notes that this illumination brings with it "no specific intellectual content whatever of its own" (p. 326), that there is no basis in such experience to distinguish the Christian from the Hindu or the Sufi from the Buddhist. When what is experienced is called "God," he is spoken of afterward in negative and often self-contradictory terms: *Deus propter excellentiam non immerito Nihil vocatur* ("God on account of his very excellence is not implausibly called Nothingness") (p. 319).

A final characteristic of mystical experience is that it involves a strong feeling of absorption, unity, and oneness (with God, with the world, with the ocean of consciousness) in which individual identity is lost or at least greatly reduced. This sense of oneness is

263

another universal characteristic of mystical states. Such states seem to come upon the experiencer in attitudes of passivity and cannot be produced or reproduced at will (though certain preparations can be made which would favor their occurrence). Also they are relatively brief and, though never forgotten, cannot be recalled with distinctness. If one were to state, finally, the "pretty distinct theoretic drift" given to such experiences by those who have attested to them, they would tend, James believes, to support an "optimistic" and "monistic" religious philosophy.

I will not follow James into his tentative assessment of the value or the "authority" of such experiences for persons who do not have them (he believes them to be "absolutely authoritative" for the experiencer himself) because this would get us beyond the discriptive method which is our sole concern here. I have, by thus recapitulating and paraphrasing one of James's attempts to delineate a given type of religious experience, tried to show how one would establish its "series," so to speak, by the choice of a number of crucial paradigm cases and then describe, insofar as possible, its structure within the total intentionality of the human organism. James has produced no more than the elements of such an eidetic description and it must be extended and complemented in many directions, particularly in the study of those "subliminal," "marginal," and other "potential" forms of consciousness which James alludes to but which he is unable to confront directly. He showed, in his own masterful way, what an experiential or phenomenological approach to such religious phenomena might involve.

V

In conclusion, we must pose the final methodological question of the value and limits of phenomenology as a philosophical method in the realm of religious experience. If it is to remain true to its claim to study only and exclusively the structures of experience, it cannot, clearly, answer some kinds of philosophical questions, though it may provide valuable evidence for argument. For example, it cannot come to any theological conclusions or make any statement on the ultimate nature of God, or the ultimate purpose and nature of reality. It can approach God and other noumenal realities only to the extent that they are experienced, and its statements must be restricted to what can be said from such a viewpoint. It is not even certain that phenomenology, in the strictest sense, can use the name of God at all, since the "what" of religious experience (and the "what" of mystical experience) is not always designated in this personal manner by the human experiencer. (It can, of course, speak of the concept of "God" as a cultural institution, etc.)

Thus it might seem that the phenomenology of religious experience, though of the highest value for our study of man—since it deals with perhaps the most foundational and inclusive meaning-structures of human life—is of very limited value to metaphysics and of no value at all to theology. This seems to be James's own view of his work and he does not claim to deduce his own religious philosophy—such as it is—from his descriptions of experience. Yet there may be at least a minimal sense in which something can be said about God: "God is real since he produces real effects" (p. 389). But in another place he wrote: "The divine can mean no single quality, it must mean a group of qualities, by being champions of which in alternations, different men may all find worthy missions." It is quite clear, then, that from this perspective the elaboration of an "objective," "necessary," and "universally true" philosophy of religion is beyond the resources of a pure phenomenology. The question of God can only be posed as the question of the way in which divine and religious power acts in the lives of men, of God not as he is in himself but as he operates in human experience. There seems to be no reason, however, to restrict phenomenological investigations merely to the study of those structures of experience which are common to all men. I see no reason why, after a general phenomenology of religious experience (which was what James had primarily in mind), one could not do more specific phenomenologies of Christian or Jewish or Muslim experience and perhaps, eventually, of even more restricted "worlds" and communities within these common traditions.

That phenomenology is not a "total" philosophy or a "totalitarian" method is clear; there are limits to what such an approach can attain. But at this moment when we have just discovered the

265

unexplored thresholds which James opened up for us, we should be more concerned with getting on with the work and with discovering what *can* be done, rather than with lamenting that it will not bring us to the immediate solution of all our theological difficulties.

NOTES

1. I am undertaking this study in the same spirit as one published earlier under the title "Notes on the Philosophical Anthropology of William James," *Invitation to Phenomenology* (Chicago, 1965), pp. 110-32.

2. In some of his later writings, however, Husserl did speculate on whether his teleological conception of (trans-personal) consciousness might not imply an *absolute ideale Polidee* which might be called "God," more in a Whiteheadian sense of a Becoming God than in the Kantian sense. Stephan Strasser has collected most of the material left us by Husserl on this subject and published it in an excellent article, "Das Gottesproblem in der Spätphilosophie Edmund Husserls," in *Philosophisches Jahrbuch,* Vol. 67. On Husserl's own attitude toward religion cf. also Herbert Spiegelberg, *The Phenomenological Movement* (The Hague, 1960), Vol. I, pp. 85-87.

3. Cf. Martin Heidegger, *Letter on Humanism,* tr. Edgar Lohner, in *Philosophy in the Twentieth Century,* ed. by Henry D. Aiken and William Barrett (New York, 1962), Vol. II, pp. 294 ff.

4. Cf. Pierre Thévenaz, *What Is Phenomenology?* (Chicago, 1962), pp. 80 ff.

5. Cf. Maurice Merleau-Ponty, *The Primacy of Perception* (Evanston, 1964), pp. 35 ff., and *In Praise of Philosophy* (Evanston, 1963), pp. 41 ff.

6. Cf. Herbert Spiegelberg, *The Phenomenological Movement, op. cit.,* Vol. I, pp. 10-11, Vol. II, pp. 605-6. As will become clear in the sequel, I agree with Spiegelberg's view that it would be misleading "to confuse a mere typology of religious institutions with a phenomenology in the philosophical sense, which concentrates on the religious acts and contents in religious experience and explores their essential structures and relationships."

7. G. Van Der Leeuw, *Religion in Essence and Manifestation* (*Phä-nomenologie der Religion*) (New York, 1963), p. 674 n.

8. The studies by Joachim Wach are distinguished from those of Mircea Eliade chiefly by the fact that Wach was primarily interested in establishing a "typology" of the sociological institutions of religion whereas Eliade is primarily concerned with elucidating the universal religious symbols, anterior to reflection, through which the world is constituted as "real" and "sacred" to man. Cf. Mircea Eliade, "Methodological Remarks on the Study of Religious Symbolism," in *The History of Religions,* ed. by Mircea Eliade and Joseph M. Kitagawa (Chicago, 1959), pp. 86-107; and *Images and Symbols* (London, 1952). Wach makes his most explicit statements on methodology in *The Comparative Study of Religions* (New York, 1958), though there are some methodological sections in *Types of Religious Experience* (Chicago, 1951), and in earlier works. Van Der Leeuw's discussion of methodology is given in the somewhat unsatisfactory and confusing form of an appendix, "Epilegomena," to the second edition of his *Phänomenologie der Religion.*

9. Van Der Leeuw, *op. cit.,* p. 673.

10. Wach, *The Comparative Study of Religions, op. cit.,* pp. 24-25.

11. Van Der Leeuw takes care to distinguish the "phenomenology of religion" from what it is not: namely, a poetics of religion, the history of religion, the psychology of religion, the philosophy of religion, or, finally, theology (*op. cit.,* pp. 685-88). His more positive statement as to just what it is, is much less satisfactory.

12. *Ibid.,* p. 677; Wach, *Religionswissenschaft* (Leipzig, 1924), p. 117; Eliade, "Methodological Remarks . . . ," *op. cit.,* pp. 88 ff.

13. Henry Duméry criticizes this group of authors in a similar manner: "M. Joachim Wach . . . tout en se réclamant de la typologie, a le souci d'une méthode normative. Sa façon de classer les grandes formes de l'expérience religieuse aboutit en fait à un choix fort raisonnable. Mais elle ne s'appuie guère sur des critères philosophiquement élaborés. On peut en dire autant de Van Der Leeuw et d'Eliade, dont les travaux sont par ailleurs extrêmement précieux" (*Critique et Religion* [Paris, 1957], p. 204).

14. While the great contrast between James's approach to religious experience and that of the school of the "phenomenology of religion" is evident, and while James presents a much more authentically phenomenological approach (taken in the general sense of

267

Husserl and Merleau-Ponty), I do not want to make the absurd claim that James thus becomes *illico presto* a pure Husserlian. He had almost no knowledge of Husserl and, in many ways, was almost an exact opposite in philosophical temperament. In a letter to Stumpf he once wrote: "I . . . have an *a priori* distrust of all attempts at making philosophy systematically exact just now. The frequency with which a man loves to use the words *streng wissenschaftlich* is beginning to be for me a measure of the shallowness of his sense of truth. Altogether, the less we have to say about *Strenge* the better . . ." (Ralph Barton Perry, *The Thought and Character of William James* [Boston, 1935], Vol. II, p. 185). Thus it would be wrong to attempt to force James's own work into the mold of a strictly "scientific" phenomenological investigation as Husserl conceived it. James's phenomenology, if it can be called that (and I am arguing that it can), is of a much more general sort, and would certainly fall within what Alfred Schutz has called "the phenomenology of the natural attitude"—but then so does a very large part of the phenomenology which has been undertaken by the disciples of Husserl themselves. In what follows I limit myself strictly to James, while pointing out what appear to me to be certain undeniable affinities, parallels, similarities, and convergencies with the phenomenological method strictly so called. It remains that James could perhaps have prosecuted the kind of study he had in mind, free both of psychologism and metaphysics, with greater economy and precision if he had been aware of some of the conditions of eidetic analysis as established by Husserl.

15. Ralph Barton Perry, *op. cit.,* Vol. I, p. 165.

16. Of James's personal attitude toward religion Perry writes: "James' religion took the form neither of dogma nor of institutional allegiance. He was essentially a man of faith, though not a man for any one church or creed against the rest. Unlike his father, he was not interested in the elaboration and specific formulation even of his own personal beliefs" (*op. cit.,* Vol. II, p. 358).

17. *Ibid.,* p. 239, from the original opening paragraph of the Gifford Lectures.

18. This study is, then, no attempt whatever to systematize James's religious philosophy; it is, moreover, quite strictly limited to the method established in *The Varieties of Religious Experience,* though I have had in mind as well the few places in his other works where he touches on this problem.

19. *The Varieties of Religious Experience, a Study in Human Nature*

(New York: Mentor Book, 1958), p. 33. Page numbers given in the text hereafter refer to this edition of James's work.

20. James does not, of course, actually mention either Luther or Solovyov in this connection, but I am confident that this would be his attitude, as it is mine, to their post-Freudian debunkers. Cf. *Varieties,* p. 316: "To the medical mind these ecstasies signify nothing but suggested and imitated hypnoid states, on an intellectual basis of superstition, and a corporeal one of degeneration and hysteria. Undoubtedly these pathological conditions have existed in many and possibly in all cases, but that fact tells us nothing about the value for knowledge of the consciousness which they induce. To pass a spiritual judgment upon these states, we must not content ourselves with superficial medical talk, but inquire into their fruits for life."

21. James nevertheless remained a child of his Victorian period in several respects. He shows no knowledge of or sensitivity whatever to the major nineteenth-century critique of Christianity begun by such thinkers as Feuerbach, Nietzsche, Dostoevski and Kierkegaard. One of his few references to Nietzsche links him with Schopenhauer and then James says that at least half their writings seem to him "the sick shriekings of two dying rats" (p. 47). In his writings on religion as elsewhere, for all his use of pathological and neurotic material, James remains an optimist and fails to see the "dark side" of the religious question, the problem of the radical alienation of man in contemporary civilization. In this one respect James is much less of a prophet than Nietzsche, whom he clearly did not understand. He even seems to think that Nietzsche's attack on the Christian notion of sainthood was due to his being a "carnal man" (p. 286).

22. Bertrand Russell, *Why I Am Not a Christian* (New York, 1957), p. 24.

23. Gordon W. Allport in *The Individual and His Religion* (New York, 1950), develops some of these suggestions by James in an extremely interesting and creative way, without, however, undertaking the task of a full-fledged continuation of the project of a phenomenology of religious experience. See especially his discussion "Is There a Single Form of Religious Sentiment?" pp. 3 ff.

24. Maurice Merleau-Ponty, "La conscience et l'acquisition du langage," *Bulletin de psychologie* (November, 1964), p. 229.

25. Ralph Barton Perry, *op. cit.,* Vol. II, p. 354.

10

PRAGMATISM, RELIGION, AND "EXPERIENCEABLE DIFFERENCE"*

BY R. W. SLEEPER

The last two chapters in this volume make contact again with questions raised by the first four chapters. What sorts of evidence count when we go about trying to make a reasonable choice between one way of life and another? In a relativistic, various world, many options lie before each of us. In a mobile, pluralistic society, there is no reason why any of us need to maintain "the faith of our fathers" or the world-view we inherit—even from our college professors. The style of life we shall lead, the types of evidence that we shall deem relevant in such choices, our very construal of what it means to be "reasonable" are left to our own responsibility. We fashion our own identity, consciously or merely by drifting with some in-group or other. There seems to be an urgency among many young people today—not least among the most intelligent and most sensitive—to shoulder this responsibility. Many feel "alienated" from ways of life they see around them (in their families, their fellow students, their professors). They want to make a wise and autonomous and "authentic" choice of their own. How does one go about it? The answer of the American philosophical tradition is always, in one form or another, "attend to your experience." Yet "experience" does not mean for American philosophers what it seems to mean for English philosophers: atomic bits of information registering on our observational screen, sense data, or objects per-

* This essay is an adaptation of a chapter from my forthcoming book, *The Predicament of Belief* (World Publishing Co.), a study of pragmatism, existentialism, and linguistic analysis.

270

ceived as discrete wholes. For American philosophy, experience is always richer than our present perceptions, always complex and confusing and in motion and inexhaustible. Experience is, as it were, a sea in which we swim, slowly appropriating it and making of it with our poor theories what we can. R. W. Sleeper of Queens College tries to get a handle on this American conception under the more precise rubric of "experienceable difference."

> I fully expect to see the pragmatist view of truth run through the classic stages of a theory's career. First, you know, a new theory is attacked as absurd; then it is admitted to be true, but obvious and insignificant; finally it is seen to be so important that its adversaries claim that they themselves discovered it.
>
> William James, *Pragmatism* (1907)

In the half century which has passed since James wrote these words it must often have seemed as though the final stage would never come, that philosophers would never get around to flattering pragmatism by imitating it. First logical positivism and existentialism, then linguistic empiricism and phenomenology, have occupied the center stage in American philosophy, crowding pragmatism further and further into the background of obsolete and old-fashioned ways of thinking. It is the method of "analysis" which occupies the growing edge of philosophy and not the method of "experience" and "practice." The high hopes for pragmatism's ultimate vindication seem now more remote than ever before. Or so, at least, the argument might go: Pragmatism has run its course and failed to place itself among the great philosophies, failed to make a permanent contribution, failed to leave a permanent deposit in man's thinking.

It will not be the purpose of this chapter to contest this judgment on pragmatism either in principle or in detail—although I think that could be done were sufficient space allowed—but to suggest some reasons why a different judgment might be made. I shall not try to defend pragmatism against its critics; above all I shall try to avoid the chauvinistic claim that pragmatism is superior to its successors in philosophy because it "got there fustest with the mostest"—a claim which may seem implicit in James's expression of his expectation. Nor shall I ring the changes on the uniqueness of pragmatism as America's only claim to have produced a native philosophy of world importance. For, if pragmatism has failed to make a dent on the world's line of thought, such a claim to uniqueness—even that special uniqueness which pragmatism is said to owe to its grounding in the "American Experience"—must be woefully and pathetically misguided.

My intention, then, is to call attention to certain neglected features of the pragmatist case, certain of its prime contentions which are usually disregarded when it comes up for appraisal. These features I group together under the title phrase, "Experienceable Difference." By means of this phrase I hope to capture something of the meaning of pragmatism's contention that the best way of testing any claim is to apply it to experience, to measure it against the facts, to bring it to bear upon reality by adopting it in practice. With respect to matters such as the nature of truth, the relation of facts to values, the meaning and grounds of beliefs and ideals, pragmatism speaks from a consistent perspective. It is the view that experienced reality corrects and transforms our claims and assertions—or grounds and confirms them. It is from this perspective, namely, that ideals and beliefs have no intrinsic value apart from their instrumental use as ways of dealing with problems of men, that pragmatism works out its theories of criticism and its metaphysics. Thus, it is in the idea of "experienceable difference" that we can discern most clearly the perspective of pragmatism. For it is through their experienceable differences that we learn to discriminate the good things from the bad, the truths from the falsehoods, and the real from the merely imagined.

One qualification, however, needs stating. This topic is too central in pragmatism to allow a complete elaboration of its implications for all the different fields of its application within the limits here prescribed. Accordingly I have been forced to choose a single field to serve as an illustration of how the idea of experienceable difference can be applied. The idea itself, of course, is a "metaphysical" one. Which is only to say that it is capable of general and wide application to a variety of subject matters. As such it is a "leading" principle; it can be followed in *any* of the special fields of philosophy. The philosophies of religion which I shall discuss are but examples of what results from following this principle in one field. The results in ethics and aesthetics, in logic and scientific method, in political science and the philosophy of education, are similar and related owing to the fact that the same metaphysical perspective pervades them all. It is the metaphysics of the experienceable difference that provides the "glue" which holds our conceptual universe together, makes it a *universe* despite the pluralism of its contents which the different inquiries celebrate. Which is only to put in other words the claim that it is the subject matter which governs the appropriate method of inquiry, that it is the subject matter itself which determines the nature of the truth conditions and criteria of judgment appropriate to itself. The idea of experienceable difference refers to the subject matter which consists of all other subject matters. It is a "metaphysical" subject matter only in the sense that it is also "meta-ethical" and "meta-logical," "meta-aesthetic" and "meta-linguistic." In this sense John Dewey referred to metaphysics as the "ground-map of the province of criticism." Accordingly, the philosophy of religion is no more and no less illustrative of the metaphysical perspective of pragmatism than ethics or logic, aesthetics or philosophy of science.

I. HOW WE THINK

The "official" textbook approach to pragmatism is to begin by explaining its method of inquiry, its theory of knowledge or epistemology, and then to go on to such other matters as its way of conceiving reality, its ethics, aesthetics, philosophy of science, and its philosophy of religion. Sometimes the question of the metaphysics of pragmatism is left out altogether; more often it is assumed that pragmatism is little interested in metaphysics except in a negative sense and that its method, its way of insisting that ideas be judged in terms of their "cash value," is more important than its metaphysics. It is widely thought that pragmatism *imposes* its method on any and every subject matter, molding reality to its own methodological requirements, as it were, and that its metaphysics is just the by-product of its method.

The explanation of why this approach to pragmatism has been taken is as simple as the approach itself is wrong. Since Hume's skeptical attacks on metaphysical concepts and Kant's reconstitution of metaphysics as the critique of reason and knowledge, philosophy has been dominated by the habit of taking epistemology rather than metaphysics as "first philosophy." The "philosophy of knowledge" rather than the "philosophy of being" has provided the groundwork of thought, the foundation on which to build the structures of ethics, aesthetics, philosophy of science, and the rest. Not only does this tradition suggest that the place to begin a study of pragmatism is with its method and its epistemology; the pragmatists themselves suggest it. Thus, the two contributions which are usually said to have initiated the pragmatic movement, C. S. Peirce's article for the *Popular Science Monthly* in 1878, "How to Make Our Ideas Clear," and William James's lecture at the University of California in 1898, "Philosophical Conceptions and Practical Results," both appear to confirm the official view that pragmatism is mostly a method and, if it has a metaphysics at all, that metaphysics must be secondary and derivative. As for Dewey, the official view receives ready confirmation from a reference or two to his book *How We Think* (1910), which seems to set the tone for so much of his emphasis on methodology. Or, perhaps, to his even earlier (though less widely read) *Studies in Logical Theory* (1903).

But there is something wrong about this official approach, I want to argue, that results in some strange misreadings of what pragmatism has to say. Accordingly, I suggest that we try the experiment of approaching pragmatism differently. Reversing the official view, let us see what happens if we begin by supposing that pragmatism is a method born out of a certain metaphysical union between the elements in experience which Dewey was later to call the "stable" and the "hazardous." Let us suppose that the method is a response to the challenge which experience affords and that it is governed by a metaphysical perspective which grows out of direct prephilosophical contact with environment. Here, our experience tells us, is a world which is changing all the time, a world of chance but with elements of order in it. An "open" universe, a world not yet finished. This is the world with which Peirce begins. And James. For it was of James that Dewey wrote:

> And long after "pragmatism" in any sense save as an application of his *Weltanschauung* shall have passed into a not unhappy oblivion, the fundamental idea of an open universe in which uncertainty, choice, hypotheses, novelties and possibilities are naturalized will remain associated with the name of James; the more he is studied in his historical setting the more original and daring will the idea appear.[1]

Now this sort of world, the world which is *given* to experience if we approach it without preconceptions, is the ground of the pragmatic perspective. It is a world which *requires* a method appropriate to it. If pragmatism relies on experimental methods it is not merely that these methods have proved themselves to be successful in other fields, but it is because the subject matter of philosophy itself *requires* the use of such methods. It will yield its secrets to none other. How we think, if we are to think to some purpose, must be appropriate to how things are.

"How things are . . ." What a problem that poses! Are we to try to get at how things are "in themselves"? Are we to seek a "truth" which is independent of our investigations altogether and so is "absolute" and completely "objective"? The thrust of the pragmatist criticism of rationalism is dead against this. Where rationalism seeks the regular and assured, the mathematically demonstrable truth, pragmatism poses a view of the world in which such complete regularity and assurance can have no place. Thus, as Dewey records its challenge:

> As against the common identification of reality with what is sure, regular and finished, experience in unsophisticated forms gives evidence of a different world and points to a different metaphysics. We live in a world which is an impressive and irresistible mixture of sufficiencies, tight completenesses, order, recurrences which make possible prediction

275

and control, singularities, ambiguities, uncertain possibilities, processes going on to consequences as yet indeterminate.[2]

The subject matter of philosophy is this world, this world as we live in it. Not this world as it might be in itself, but just this world as we inhabit it and experience it. As we act upon it and as it acts upon us. In short, what philosophy deals in is human experience. The experienced encounter with reality is at the bottom of every inquiry, and every inquiry begins with an experienced problem. And every solution, every question answered, every need successfully met—all these are made possible by noticing some "experienceable difference."

Of course, the idea of an "experienceable difference" as the key to philosophy, as the mark of its most basic grounding, was not an invention of pragmatism. As the following passage from Dewey shows, the pragmatists were well aware of their borrowings from the tradition of British empiricism:

> Experience thus comes to mean, to use the words of Peirce, "that which is forced upon a man's recognition will-he, nill-he, and shapes his thoughts to something quite different from what they naturally would have taken." The same definition is found in James in his chapter on "Necessary Truths": "Experience means experience of something foreign supposed to impress us whether spontaneously or in consequence of our own exertions and acts." As Peirce points out, this notion of experience as the foreign element that forces the hand of thought and controls its efficacy, goes back to Locke. Experience is "observation employed either about external sensible objects or about the internal operation of our minds" . . . as furnishing in short all the valid data and tests of thinking and knowledge. This meaning, thinks Peirce, should be accepted "as a landmark which it would be a crime to disturb or displace."[3]

But what pragmatism did, as Dewey goes on to demonstrate, was to take the narrow Lockean view of experience here expressed and to expand it. Rejecting the dualism implicit in Locke's formula, a dualism between the "external sensible objects" and "the internal operations of our minds," pragmatism began to think of "internal" and "external" experiences as phases in a continuous process. And not only this. Pragmatism began to think of "feelings" and "emotions" as continuous with "thought" and "ideas." The dualism of Locke's remaining rationalism, which assumed an essential bifurcation between "emotion" and "cognition," was gradually rejected, and in its place was developed the theory that knowledge is not separable from emotive response, that sensing is *feeling* and *valuing* as well as "observing." Experience thus came to include not just that which is "mental"—where "mental" is defined as nonphysical—but that which is made up of "mental" *and* "physical" elements passing into each other by imperceptible degrees. In this view of experience, in fact, there was no room for the supposedly hard distinctions between "mind" and "matter" which continued to be made in British philosophy. And no room, either, for the insuperable gap between "values" and "facts" which that philosophy inevitably leaves. Thus pragmatism came to avoid the temptation to reductionism which is ever present in British philosophy. "Matter" is no more reducible to "mind" (*pace* Berkeley) than "mind" is reducible to "matter" (*pace* Hobbes). Nor are they separate "substances" (*pace* Descartes) or "attributes" of one "infinite" substance (*pace* Spinoza) to which the geometrical method is alone appropriate; the dogmas of rationalism no less than the dogmas of British empiricism were anathema to the spirit of pragmatism. And not the least reason why this was so was because they failed to meet the demand for an *"experienceable difference."*

II. PEIRCE ON "HOW THINGS ARE"

How we think depends upon how things are. This is the conviction of pragmatism. And how things are can be got at only by means of experience, by noticing experienceable differences. There are three metaphysical theses reflecting this basic conviction for which C. S. Peirce is mainly responsible. Together they make up what has been called the "metaphysical perspective" of pragmatism. They govern its method, control its conceptions of meaning and truth, and are the decisive factors in its philosophy of religion. These three theses, which attempt to state the most general "facts" or features of the universe which we actually experience, are as follows: (1) The universe is changing, is not "static" though it contains "laws" of regular development and orderly process, is best characterized by such terms as "growth" and "evolution." (2) There is, in the universe, a natural continuity between "thought" and "feeling," between "values" and "facts"; this continuity is what accounts for the process of growth. (3) There is an element of "chance" in the universe; the process of evolution is open to novelty, involves risk, and makes it impossible to arrive at general truths with absolute certainty.

Peirce's views on these matters were worked out in a series of articles in the *Monist* of 1892 and 1893. Here, in the course of an examination of the traditional doctrines of realism and nominalism, Peirce introduces the basic notions which he calls "tychism," "synechism," and "Agapasm." Tychism is the view that there is an element of absolute chance in the universe. It is worked out in opposition to the view of mechanical determinism, the view of classical physics which held that "every single fact in the universe is precisely determined by law."[4] In accepting part of the realist notion that there are real laws operative in the universe independently of man, Peirce opposes the doctrine that these general laws are absolute. As a consequence, certainty with respect to them is impossible. He bases his argument on the ubiquity of growth and the ever increasing complexity of the forms of life evolved in the universe. Thus:

> Question any science which deals with the course of time. Consider the life of an individual animal or plant, or of a mind. Glance at the history of states, of institutions, of language, of ideas. . . . Everywhere the main fact is growth and increasing complexity. . . . From these broad and ubiquitous facts we may fairly infer, by the most unexceptionable logic, that there is probably in nature some agency by which the

R. W. SLEEPER

complexity and diversity of things can be increased; and that
consequently the rule of mechanical necessity meets in some
way with interference.[5]

Although this argument is so general as to be something less than
convincing (as Peirce himself admits on 6.64), and fails to rule out
the possibility of mechanism entirely, Peirce takes it as "pragmatically" justified. It is especially useful, he says, in accounting for the
emergence of genuine novelty and for the actual absence of certainty from the natural sciences. He rejects the suggestion that
chance may be "mere appearance," owing to the incompleteness of
our present knowledge, and attacks the very *possibility* of complete
knowledge. It is worth noticing, at this point, how Peirce lumps
together evidence from the natural and the social sciences, how he
refuses to admit any basic discontinuity between the "lower" and
the "higher" realms of the evolutionary scale. And it is worth noticing, too, how he thinks of the "community" as having a decisive
role in verification—implying that meaning, at least, if not truth
itself, is a function of *common* experience—as the following passage suggests:

> We cannot be quite sure that the community will ever settle
> down to an unalterable conclusion upon any given question.
> Even if they do for the most part, we have no reason to think
> the unanimity will be quite complete, nor can we rationally
> presume any overwhelming consensus of opinion will be
> reached upon every question. All that we are entitled to as-
> sume is in the form of a hope that such conclusions may be
> substantially reached concerning the particular questions
> with which our inquiries are busied.[6]

But if the price of tychism is uncertainty, its effects are scarcely
damaging to the cognitive enterprise. With certainty, with the belief
that the truth has been achieved, inquiry ceases. The cognitive endeavor is closed out, the spirit and values of the quest are put aside,
the mind atrophies and dies. Uncertainty keeps the adventure alive,
tests the minds of men ever anew, supports the values which accrue
to human life from facing such a continuous challenge. And, in any

case, tychism is met—in part at least—by the principle of "synechism."

Synechism, in Peirce's special jargon, is the doctrine of continuity in the universe. According to it, ideas are as much subject to the laws of growth and complexity as are the forms of organic life. Indeed Peirce seems to regard ideas *as* a variety of organism. Thus:

> There is but one law of mind, namely, that ideas tend to spread continuously and to affect certain others which stand to them in a peculiar relation of affectability. In this spreading they lose intensity, and especially the power of affecting others, but gain generality and become welded with other ideas.[7]

And, suggesting Peirce's antipathy to nominalism and his sympathy with the Scholastic realism of Scotus: "The one primary and fundamental law of mental action consists in a tendency to generalization. Feeling tends to spread; connections between feelings awaken feelings; neighboring feelings become assimilated."[8] Accordingly, the particular and individual tends toward the general and universal; it *becomes* these things. The process is not from the general to the particular but the reverse; evolution points the arrow of time, "habits" are formed in nature from individual instances, "laws" are generated from particulars. Even the history of thought is put in this same perspective; it is a process consisting of a developing continuum of feelings and ideas (with no hard distinction between them) becoming progressively more generalized the more adequate to the process of reality they become. Ideas and feelings that fail, that lose pace with the developing world of nature, drop out and are rejected.

It is in relation to the doctrine of synechism, the notion that institutions and ideas are subject to laws of continuous development and growth, that the first hint of Peirce's philosophy of religion appears. Rejecting, almost out of hand, the theory of religion which holds that it is the purpose of religion to provide man with "truth from beyond," Peirce accepts the ideas and institutions of religion as contributing ways of expressing knowledge gained from other fields and sources. Religion is not a special source of knowledge that could not be got at in any other way; rather, it is the means of dedicating what knowledge we have and can aspire to, a way of consecrating knowledge in practice. Thus, the purpose of religion is to support and further man's vision of the divine, to enhance and expand discovered values, to secure an ever wider distribution of the riches which life affords. The specific agent of religion is "habit." "Habit is that specialization of the law of mind whereby a general idea gains the power of exciting reactions."[9] Religion, for Peirce, is thus to be understood as an elaboration and refinement of the "specialized" habit of seeing the universe as the representation of God's purpose working itself out in time. The cosmogony which this "religious" vision embodies is given philosophical expression in what Peirce calls the doctrine of "Agapasm" or "evolutionary love."

In explaining this doctrine, Peirce distinguishes between three types of evolutionary theory: 1. "Tychasm" [*sic*] is the Darwinian doctrine that evolution is carried forward by fortuitous variation, is a consequence of statistical probabilities. 2. "Anancasm" is the doctrine that holds evolution to be the result of mechanical necessity. 3. "Agapasm" is the belief that evolution is the result of the creative operations of love (Gr. *agape*). Peirce's preference for the latter view, he admits, is largely based on his "passionate predilection for it."[10] And he acknowledges that his willingness to rest his belief on "emotional" grounds "will probably shock my scientific brethren."[11] He argues, however, in ways that suggest those in which James would later, that his right to believe in Agapasm, on whatever grounds, is assured so long as neither "tychasm" nor "anancasm" could be asserted as a matter of scientific certitude. The very lack of certainty in cosmogony, which is admitted by all sides, militates against anyone who would press for either "absolute chance" or "mechanical necessity" as governing all change as against Agapasm. As Peirce was aware, there is something incongruous in a passionate defense of either chance or pure determinism. But there is nothing at all incongruous in a passionate defense of Agapasm.

But Peirce's doctrine of Agapasm is not just the result of a

281

whim on his part; his choice of it, while "passionate," is far from arbitrary. It is the only doctrine of evolution which is adequate to both our experience of the world around us and to our experience of ourselves. Agapasm expresses our experience of an ordered environment without reducing that order to the single factor of mechanical necessity. It accounts for the spontaneity that we experience without reducing that spontaneity to statistical "chance." But, above all, only Agapasm accounts for the fact of "self-control" as a factor in evolutionary development and, argues Peirce, "In its higher stages, evolution takes place more and more largely through self-control. . . ."[12] It is this fact, the fact of self-determination and freedom of action, which Peirce puts forward as carrying the weight of his argument for Agapasm. Thus:

> But no mental action seems to be necessary or invariable in its character. In whatever manner the mind has reacted under a given sensation, in that manner it is more likely to react again; were this, however, an absolute necessity, habits would become wooden and ineradicable and, no room being left for the formation of new habits, intellectual life would come to a speedy close. Thus, the uncertainty of the mental law is no mere defect in it, but is on the contrary of its essence. The truth is, the mind is not subject to law in the same rigid sense that matter is. It only experiences gentle forces which merely render it more likely to act in a given way than it otherwise would be. There always remains a certain amount of arbitrary spontaneity in its action, without which it would be dead.[13]

> The agapastic development of thought is the adoption of certain mental tendencies, not altogether heedlessly, as in tychasm, not quite blindly by the mere force of circumstances or of logic, as in anancasm, but by an immediate attraction for the idea itself, whose nature is divined before the mind possesses it, by the power of sympathy, that is by virtue of the continuity of the mind.[14]

Thus all those later philosophers who were to make much of evolution as a "support" for religion were anticipated not only by Schelling but by Peirce. If, as Peirce argues, self-control lies behind intelligent and reasonable reflection, it most clearly functions at the very center of all moral and judicial decision. Accordingly, Peirce can maintain, evolution tends toward an ethical goal—religion can provide a valuable practical aid to the pursuit of moral ideals. And all this can be maintained without relying on a foreordained or predetermined teleology. Chance is real enough, and so is order. Peirce cuts the Gordian knot between absolute teleology and a "purposeless" world of pure chance.

But why call in *agape?* Why use a word traditionally associated with Christian theism as a label for this evolutionary theory? It seems clear that Peirce always harbored within himself a preference (which, after Hume, he sometimes calls an "instinct") for the Christian "world-view." A "convert" from his eminent father's Harvard Unitarianism to the Episcopal Church, Peirce admits his bias in favor of a personalistic conception of God:

> A pseudo-evolutionism which enthrones mechanical law above the principle of growth is at once scientifically unsatisfactory, as giving no possible hint as to how the universe has come about, and hostile to all hopes of personal relations to God.[15]

One of the decisive influences on Peirce's early life and thought was the person and work of F. E. Abbott. Abbott, along with Peirce, William James, Chauncey Wright, and Oliver Wendell Holmes, Jr., was a member of the "Metaphysical Club." This remarkable group of men were in the habit of gathering regularly in Cambridge, Massachusetts, in the 1870's for the purpose of discussing philosophical ideas. From Abbott, who wrote a book called *Scientific Theism* which has been long since forgotten, Peirce first got the notion of a strong connection between the evolving processes of nature and the age-old Christian notion of a Divine Plan in reality. Abbott strongly opposed the nominalist tendencies of current scientific thought and suggested that realism, particularly that of Scotus, was in better accord with the evidences of science.[16]

From these suggestions much of Peirce's philosophy of religion

283

is developed. We can but guess at the full elaboration of this philosophy, for he produced only an outline of it in published form.[17] Some idea of what he had in mind, however, can be gleaned from fragments such as the following:

> Every reality, then, is a Self, and the selves are intimately connected, as if they formed a continuum. Each one is . . . a quasi-map of the entire field of all the selves, which organic aggregate is itself a Self. . . . So far as a philosophical conception can be identified with God it is God.[18]

> The universe is a vast representamen, a great symbol of God's purpose, working out its conclusions in living realities . . . [which] is that Reasonableness for the sake of which the Heavens and the Earth have been created.[19]

This "cosmic perspective" in which Peirce constantly viewed religion is, of course, an anticipation of the ideas of Teilhard de Chardin. But it bears comparison, as well, to the more orthodox views of F. R. Tennant and to the "personalistic" theism of such theologians in England as John Oman and H. H. Farmer. Closer to home, Tillich's "belief-ful realism," developed in his *The Religious Situation,* espouses much of Peirce's perspective. In not one of these instances is "God" or the "Supernatural" taken to be a *separate* reality; it is that which is manifest as man becomes aware of the "depth" dimension of his one world. In all of these views, as in Peirce, the universe presents itself as containing the possibility of religious interpretation. In all of these views "God" is present to experience, as Peirce puts it, "in the long run": His presence makes an *experienceable difference.*

It deserves considerable emphasis that Peirce took religion for its "long-run" effects rather than for its "short-run" practices. In the short run, religion is all creeds and sects, full of what he calls, in a letter to James, "metaphysical formulae, dead as the dust of the catacombs." Nevertheless Peirce asks James: "Why don't you join the Church?" And, after "converting" to Episcopalianism, Peirce wrote to Lady Welby as follows:

284

> I say the creed in church with the rest. By doing so I only signify, as I presume the majority do—and hope they do— my willingness to put aside, most heartily, anything that tends to separate me from my fellow Christians. For the very ground of my criticism of the creeds is that every one of them was originally designed to produce such a separation, contrary to the notions of Him who said "He that is not against me is for me."[20]

Here is expressed Peirce's "great hope" for unity and the instrumental role which he took religion to play in evolution toward that end. His criticism of the "creeds" of Christendom[21] did not prevent him from seeing the value of "the Christian theory of the way in which the world is to be made better and wiser."[22] In fact he sees Christianity itself as an evolution "out of Buddhism, modified by Jewish belief in a living God," and argues that it is not the uniqueness of Christian belief which is in its favor, but the fact that its gospel of love is widely held by other religions: "The higher a religion, the more catholic."[23] But there is always need, said Peirce, for religion to have some institutional "home": a point not often conceded by either James or Dewey. Thus: "Without a church, the religion of love can have but a rudimentary existence."[24]

What Peirce proposes, of course, is that experience can teach us to discriminate the living and essential elements in a creed from the "earthen vessels" in which it is contained. An example of this ability to discriminate, to make religious judgments in an empirical way by relying on the idea of an experienceable difference, is Peirce's often criticized, often excoriated, treatment of the Christian doctrine of the Eucharist.[25] Peirce applies the "Pragmatic Maxim" to the doctrine of transubstantiation, long the subject of controversy between Roman Catholics and other Christians. Peirce concludes that "It is foolish for Catholics and Protestants to fancy themselves in disagreement about the elements of the sacrament, if they agree in regard to all their sensible effects." And, in this same context, Peirce refers to the "Pragmatic Maxim" as "The sole principle of logic which was recommended by Jesus" (in the teaching

"By their fruits ye shall know them").[26] For Peirce, it should be emphasized, however, that the "Pragmatic Maxim" does not solve any *real* problems; it only removes pseudo-problems.[27] Applied to theology it could "prove" religious claims only in the sense advocated by St. Paul: "Prove all things; hold fast that which is good."[28] *Its function is to test ideas for meaning, not for truth* and, Peirce no doubt thought, since many of the theological ideas which divide men are "meaningless," the application of pragmatism to theology cannot fail to have sanguine results.

III. PEIRCE AND JAMES: FROM "MEANING" TO "TRUTH"

Pragmatism, whether we take it as a metaphysics, a method in logic, or as a philosophy of religion, was an obscure and relatively unknown position when James first began to publicize it in his California Union address of 1898. Not the least of the reasons why this is so rests in the fact that Peirce had failed to provide his doctrine with an easily remembered "catch phrase" or summary statement. Its "maxim" was not even given the label "pragmatism" when it first appeared in 1878 in the essay "How to Make Our Ideas Clear." It there appears as "the rule for attaining the third grade of clearness of apprehension"[29] and is couched, paradoxically, in language so opaque that it is little wonder that even James should have had great difficulty in getting at what Peirce meant:

> Consider what effects, which might conceivably have practical bearings, we conceive the object of our conception to have. Then, our conception of these effects is the whole of our conception of the objects.[30]

As every student of modern philosophy knows, this is the "rule" which James converts into a statement of "truth" conditions and uses as a test of belief—arguing that the "truth" is a matter of "cash value," "what pays" or what "works," and that the results of a belief which are experienced as "good" or "satisfactory" are evidence that the belief may be counted "so far forth" true.

286

James's account of pragmatism is an expression of his own "nominalist" leanings, his interest in psychology and of his own, not Peirce's, conception of the place in reality occupied by the individual. Pragmatism for James was also closely bound up with his doctrine of "radical empiricism" and his contention that most of our intellectual beliefs can be justified only on the grounds of their biological, moral, and social utility. Moreover, James was convinced that, on issues in which purely intellectual considerations give no practical guidance, the claims of our "passional and volitional" nature should be permitted to have the decisive role in determining what we shall believe. Now, quite apart from whether James's contentions are justified or not, it is amply clear that they were not the same as Peirce's. Thus, even before James's immensely popular book, *Pragmatism, a New Name for Old Ways of Thinking,* appeared, Peirce wrote to his friend that he was willing to concede to James the right and title to the name "pragmatism" and chose the new name "pragmaticism" for his own original principle, a word which he thought "ugly enough to be safe from kidnappers."[31] And, after the book appeared, Peirce wrote again to James urging him, even begging him, "to try to learn to think with more exactitude" and concluding with a remark intended to point up the crux of his difference with James: "What is utility, if it is confined to a single person? Truth is public."[32]

Quite simply, the difference between Peirce's and James's doctrines is the difference between a doctrine of meaning and a doctrine of truth. Another way of saying this is that for Peirce "pragmatism solves no real problems. It only shows that supposed problems are not real problems."[33] But for James pragmatism *was* a way of solving problems, it enabled him to *decide* options when the usual modes of knowledge are at an impasse and where the subject-matter is such that usual methods of proof are impossible. In this procedure truth is *made,* as it were, and not discovered. James's doctrine, which was applied to religion in the famous essay on "The Will to Believe," struck Peirce as simply "suicidal." And James's biographer, Ralph Barton Perry, has remarked that "the philosophical movement known as Pragmatism is largely the result of James's misunderstanding of Peirce."[34] In his California Union address

James exhibits his misunderstanding of Peirce's doctrine by his emphasis on the "particular" experience rather than the "generalized habits" that Peirce, in his *Monist* articles, made the test of meaning. Thus James says:

> The effective meaning of any philosophic proposition can always be brought down to some particular consequence, in our future practical experience, whether active or passive; the point lying rather in the fact that it must be *particular,* than in the fact that it must be *active*.[35]

Yet, as Dewey remarks:

> Now the curious fact is that Peirce puts more emphasis upon active practise (or conduct) and less upon the particular; in fact, he transfers the emphasis to the general.[36]

Thus, for Peirce, the meaning of a proposition is itself another proposition. It is the general proposition which "must be simply the general description of all the experimental phenomena which the assertion of the proposition virtually predicts." As such, Peirce's criterion of meaning leads, not to the *particular* at all, but to the "conception" insofar as it may have some practical bearing upon the conduct of life. Thus Peirce continually emphasizes that truth is not a describable or predictable element in any *individual's* experience: "It is not 'my' experience, but 'our' experience that has to be thought of."[37] And, as W. B. Gallie has said, Peirce "finds the clearest proof of this thesis in the way that language guides and controls the greater part of our thinking: for language is essentially a vehicle whereby one expresses those parts of one's experience that *are* general, that must be 'ours' rather than 'mine' if they are to be communicated at all."[38]

For Peirce, then, the sort of investigation conducted by James in his *Varieties of Religious Experience* could have but little relevance to the topic which James sets himself—the "justification of faith." Instead of leading us into greater understanding of accidental, private, and idiosyncratic theology, pragmatism should lead to an ever greater development of public, essential religion. It is no accident that Peirce found his principle of religious "tolerance" in the ground of "fallibilism" rather than, as James, in the sheer "variety" of particular and individual *fruitful* religious experiences. It was religion "on the whole" and "in the main" that commended itself to Peirce, not the particular and unique religious experience. The criterion of an "experienceable difference" remained ineluctably a matter of *public* experience for Peirce, while James went on to investigate its more "private" and "personal" implications.

Thus, in James, the pragmatist philosophy of religion became more a "psychology of religious experience." Perhaps because of his family background, perhaps because his early education was in art and medicine rather than in logic and mathematics, perhaps because of the simple fact of his greater personal warmth of style and his more "humanistic" conviction of the weight and worth of individuals, it was James rather than Peirce who made of religion a matter of intense personal concern both in his own life and in his professional writings. Sharing with Peirce the conviction that the basic issue of his age was the struggle between mechanism and free will, James held this to be but a continuation of the earlier struggle between orthodoxy and unorthodoxy in religion—a struggle which had long dominated the New England conscience and in which his father had been an active participant. But, where Peirce is given to analyzing the issues in the most impersonal terms—even his "conversion" from Unitarianism to Episcopalianism was rather "impersonal" so far as we can gather from his letters—James felt himself to be deeply involved. He plays the existentialist to Peirce's logical analyst.

Describing the feeling of melancholia which descended upon him as the result of seeing a dehumanized epileptic in an insane asylum, James expresses his horror at the prospect of his own potential reduction to this machinelike existence: "He sat there . . . looking absolutely non-human. This image and my fear entered into a species of combination with each other. *That shape am I,* I felt potentially. Nothing that I possess can defend me against that fate, if the hour for it should strike for me as it struck for him."[39] His way out of this horror was his conversion to belief in free will.

He employs a "metaphysical doctrine," characteristically, to resolve a personal problem; it is not that the doctrine solves the problem for him, but his *belief in* the doctrine is what produces the cure. Thus, as he wrote in one of his notebooks:

> I think that yesterday was a crisis in my life. I finished the first part of Renouvier's second "Essais" and see no reason why his definition of Free Will—"the sustaining of a thought *because I choose to* when I might have other thoughts" —need be the definition of an illusion. At any rate, I will assume for the present—until next year—that it is no illusion. My first act of free will shall be to believe in free will.[40]

This is pragmatism given an entirely new use from that suggested by Pierce, a use which was to have a profound effect upon James's philosophy of religion. If he saw the function of religion in such completely individual and psychological terms, the reason may lie here, in his own struggle to believe.

In the earliest of his writings primarily devoted to philosophy, "The Sentiment of Rationality" (1880), we encounter this struggle as James sought to represent it in philosophical terms and it was a struggle which continued to preoccupy him throughout the remainder of his professional work. This is the issue of "The Will to Believe" (1896) and of the California Union lectures. It is a recurrent theme underlying his *Varieties of Religious Experience* (1902), *Pragmatism* (1907) and *A Pluralistic Universe* (1909). And in the volume on which he was at work when he died, James was still arranging and rearranging his ideas on the subject. Little wonder, then, that James should have seized upon the principle of pragmatism—seeing in it something which was expressly denied by Peirce, namely, the solution of his own personal problem.

The possibility that the pragmatic method offers to James is the reconciliation of factors at war within his own soul, and to which he gives objective expression as the "conflict between science and religion." What pragmatism offers to James is no less than a synthesis of the "tough" and "tender-minded" elements in his own character and, by a characteristic extension, of the world's philosophies. Thus:

290

I offer the oddly-named thing pragmatism as a philosophy that can satisfy both kinds of demands. It can remain religious like the rationalisms ["tender-minded"], but at the same time, like the empiricisms ["tough-minded"], it can preserve the richest intimacy with facts.[41]

And again:

The pragmatistic philosophy . . . neither begins nor ends by turning positive religious reconstructions out of doors—it treats them cordially as well. I hope I may lead you to find it just the mediating way of thinking that you require.[42]

James's contention that pragmatism is a way of "mediating" between two ways of thinking rests on the concept that science deals with facts and events existing in a temporal past so that scientific inferences to a temporal future always leave out of account temporally present efforts of consciousness which may have a transforming effect on the future. Religion, on the other hand, is just the place where these efforts are recognized and given support. Thus, in discussing Herbert Spencer's materialistic *Psychology*, James is willing to concede that it makes little difference whether we assign the creation of the world to purely material forces or to God—*so long as we are thinking only of the past*. Whatever we find to be factually true of the past remains factually true; the world is what it is, and was made the way it was made, whatever we may want to say about it and however we may wish to interpret it. Furthermore, there is little or no advantage, even some real *dis*advantage, in introducing the word "God" into such scientific explanations. This is, in fact, why there are so many foolish mistakes in the so-called "scientific" defenses of religion; religion is no more able to provide scientific explanations than science is able to perform the functions of religion.

What James suggests, both in his California address and in *Pragmatism,* is a way of thinking about things in terms of their "futures" that will take into account not only their past but also those present factors which can bring about changes from what we might expect if we were to take into account only past performance. This way of thinking he called "The Will to Believe" although, as he later admitted, a better terminology might have been "the right to believe."[43] What James had in mind was not just that there is no way of settling between conflicting religious claims, but the much stronger doctrine that by willing to believe something we may actually help to bring it about, that religious claims can somehow be "made" true through the conscious efforts of faith. This doctrine, even when it is weakened by calling it the "right" instead of the "will" to believe, goes contrary to what could be claimed on Peirce's grounds, and Peirce was quick to dissociate himself from it. He wrote to James that it is "the kind of expression which hurts a serious philosopher very much."[44]

A simple example may help to show what James was driving at in this controversial doctrine. Suppose that a nearby house is discovered to be on fire and someone says, "That house is on fire!" This is both an exclamation embodying "feeling" and a straightforward scientific assertion. As a statement of fact it can receive the usual sort of empirical verification. If it is verified, then it stands as a claim about what *has been* experienced. This, James would say, is why scientific claims are always about the *past*. Then suppose that someone says, "The fire is spreading rapidly and will soon destroy the house." This is still a "scientific" assertion, even though it has reference to the future, because it relies on past data to make its prediction. As soon as the assertion is verified it will then cease to refer to the future and will have only a past reference. But if someone then says, "Quickly! Help me put out the fire or I'll lose everything!" we pass at once from science to where human effort, i.e., "conscious" effort and "will" enter in. There is no *conflict* between the "scientific" assertion and the "voluntaristic" claim here. Indeed, James held that the intentions of the will could hardly be made with any rationality at all except that "scientific" assertions be taken into account and used correctly. But what he was holding out for was the possibility of human effort changing outcomes, "falsifying" assertions that would otherwise come true. What James wanted to establish in his criticism of Spencer—and in his espousal of pragmatism at large—was that a *complete* analysis of human life and consciousness cannot be achieved by reducing truth to past matters of fact. What he saw was that human effort can make an *experienceable difference*. If the fire is extinguished and the house is saved, certain predictions will have been falsified and others verified by the experienceable difference which is due to human effort. And this James wishes to maintain, even in the weakened form of his doctrine which speaks of the "right" to believe instead of the "will" to believe.

Peirce's disapproval of this doctrine is largely owing to the fact that Peirce was seeking a "general" doctrine of meaning, "laws" that could win the general acceptance of the scientific community and which could be established by repeated experiment. By contrast, James was interested in *particular* events and outcomes. Peirce could hold that the case of the burning house merely exhibits such general "laws" as that "houses burn," "fire is destructive of some forms of property," and "fire extinguishers can put out fires." James puts all these together and comes up with a defense of the *individual* free will and a *justification* of belief. Peirce's doctrine of the "experienceable difference" applied to the clarification of *meanings,* to what he called the "fixation" of belief. James goes beyond this to the *different* problem of "justification."

To make this difference between Peirce and James a bit clearer we might draw up a comparison between "fallibilism" and the "will to believe" as each relates to religion. Peirce deduced his doctrine of fallibilism from three basic assertions: (1) a proposition is verified by its experienceable consequences; (2) these consequences are potentially endless, so that all we can possibly do is to verify any proposition to the probability of 1; but, (3) a probability of 1 is not a "certainty," for if the set of possible verifying data is infinite, then no finite number of exceptions can lower the probability ratio from 1 to a proper fraction. The conclusion is that there is no way of getting empirical certainty. Applying fallibilism to religion, according to Peirce, has the effect of promoting religious humility and understanding tolerance. By putting doubts in a man's mind, by challenging the certainty of his own beliefs, fallibilism serves the cause of religious unity. The separation between individuals is broken down, individual beliefs are made less rigid, and the cause of common purpose and community "welding" is served.[45]

293

What Peirce has in mind is religion in the service of morals; fallibilism serves a moral aim when it brings individuals into a community of being, into continuity with each other. "The principle of continuity is the idea of fallibilism objectified."[46] And: "All communication from mind to mind is through continuity of being."[47]

James agrees with the doctrine of fallibilism only to the extent that it allows him a "gap" in knowledge through which he can work out the *justification* of belief. In the doctrine of the "will to believe" James does *not* argue that *all* kinds of truth depend on our belief, for the consequences of many an idea will follow whether or not we believe the idea to be true. And he does *not* say that you can make *any* idea true simply by believing it hard enough. But James *does* argue that reality is open enough, offers sufficient "options," that efforts of the will may often just make the difference between an idea being true and an idea being false. Thus, in the example given, a man's effort to extinguish the fire may prove successful and so falsify the prediction that the house will be destroyed. What James wanted to show was that we have all sorts of chances to influence the outcomes of future events through our choices and decisions *now*. And he held that our own natures, our own personal characters, will be radically determined by the sort of choices that we make. In this, it scarcely needs to be added, James was advocating a doctrine which anticipates the existentialist emphasis on freedom and "authenticity," that we are in "essence" what we choose in "existence." Freedom of choice, which Peirce's doctrine of fallibilism leaves room for, is taken by both James and the existentialists as warrant for the celebration of the individual as a moral creator. Uncertainty drives men into closer relations, according to Peirce; according to James and the existentialists it warrants an even greater degree of individuality, it is a "threat" that can be met only through radical self-determination.

But James, despite his favorable references to such early "existentialists" as Pascal and Kierkegaard, despite his emphasis on the open texture of the universe, never went so far as to make *freedom* an absolute. More nominalistic than Peirce, James was yet a realist by comparison with the existentialists. This undercurrent of realistic metaphysics in James's perspective can be brought out

294

by showing how "limited" is the range of choice that we have, how "finite" the options are in actual life. There are, says James, three characteristics of all our options which deserve consideration. An option may be either "live" or "dead" depending on whether it strikes some spark of interest in us—and he quickly concedes that religion may indeed be a "dead" option for many. Second, an option may be "forced" or "avoidable"—and here he argues, in somewhat the fashion of Pascal, that while religion may *seem* dead it is nonetheless a forced option for which we *must* decide one way or the other; there is no neutral ground. Finally, an option may be "momentous" or "trivial"—the religious option, unlike the option to extinguish the fire in our example, is "momentous" because it is a "once in a lifetime" case on which our whole future may depend. Thus, James argues, the religious option is live, forced and momentous: our choice will make an experienceable difference, of this there can be little doubt. And yet, James points out, reason is only of partial help in reaching a decision here.

In *Varieties,* for example, James shows the incapacity of reason to arrive at certainty with respect to the existence of God by means of the traditional aguments, each of which contains flaws and none of which reaches to the "heart." But, where there are no rational grounds for decision we are not only *free* to make our decision on emotional grounds, we are *compelled* to do so. James is under no illusion that belief in the existence of God will make God suddenly spring into existence when he had not existed previously. Nor does James doubt that if there is no God, belief is in vain. But what he *does* contend is that whatever decision we *do* make, with respect to the proposals of religious belief, this decision will have a palpable effect on our lives. There are those, of course, who would judge the consequences of any conventional religious belief as damaging in the extreme—the views of Bertrand Russell could be discussed in this regard, as could the more current opinions of Antony Flew. And it is to these that James addresses the major theses of his *Varieties*. These amount to an attempt to "justify" faith by pointing to its consequences in the "case histories" of all sorts of individuals exemplifying a wide range of social and historical circumstances and of psychological temperament. Religious experience is found to be in some cases the "normal" development of the "healthy minded" personality. In others, religion is curative of the "sick soul." In the main, James concludes, his examination shows religious experience to be an effective source of support for moral ideals and a personal source of courage in the face of anxiety and despair. The purely theological content of this goes somewhat beyond the pragmatically justified, however, and James refers to it as his "over-belief," which is summarized as follows:

> The believer finds that the tenderer parts of his personal life are continuous with a *more* of the same quality which is operative in the universe outside of him and which he can keep in working touch with, and in a fashion get on board of and save himself when all his lower being has gone to pieces in the wreck.[48]

But this "wider self" from which saving experiences flow, if it be God, is yet for James a "finite" God. And this despite the evident fact that God is "transcendent." If James is a "supernaturalist" at all it is clear that the usual meaning of that label must be severely limited and qualified.

In his *Pluralistic Universe* James argues for this theology of the finite God (somewhat unconvincingly) as the result of "the drift of all the evidence" found in the "melioristic" universe. His argument is more interesting (and perhaps more convincing) as a piece of metaphysical speculation than as philosophical theology, and I shall take it as such. Thus, whatever we decide about the "finitude" of God, the fact that we decide on the basis of our experience of the universe which surrounds us is the important thing. And that universe, as James sees it, is not necessarily getting better or necessarily worse. But it does present us with at least the possibility of being improved upon. Such improvements, in the absence of a benevolent and all-powerful God, depend largely upon our own efforts. If New England Puritanism tended to make man nothing by making God everything, James was out to push the balance in the opposite direction. In so doing he expressed the broadest-based belief—which is assuredly part of the American tradition although not unique to it—that each individual is a center of intrinsic value and that his efforts *do* count for something in the larger scheme of things. What remains, then, of permanent significance in James's philosophy of religion is his vision of man changing the universe —doing God's work for him. The function of religion is thus the *catalysis of change,* first in the self, then in society and, because in these, in the universe itself. If James, unlike Peirce, prefers to make his case for all this on psychological grounds, it is nevertheless clear that he has a metaphysical application in mind. The "experienceable difference" which is made by the reality of God (and which religion celebrates) is recognized first in terms of psychological change—and only then does it become a factor in social transformation. If Peirce tends to neglect the "solitariness" (as Whitehead calls it) of the religious man, relying almost exclusively on the "public" dimensions of truth, James makes up for this neglect.

In the end James is not far from Peirce despite their different ways of applying pragmatism, their different temperaments and training, even their different religious hopes and expectations. Thus, in his essay "What Pragmatism Means," James acknowledges that the claim of theology for truth is a strictly limited one. Its claim is such that it needs to be continuous with *other* claims for truth or it will count for little: and this is what Peirce maintained in his doctrines of "synechism" and "Agapasm." The experienceable difference which religion attributes to the reality of God must, in the long run, be connected with and continuous with all *other* experienceable differences. Thus, says James of the pragmatic method in theology:

> Interested in no conclusions but those which our minds and our experiences work out together, she has no *a priori* prejudices against theology. *If theological ideas prove to have value for concrete life, they will be true, for pragmatism, in the sense of being good for so much. For how much more they are true, will depend entirely on their relations to the other truths that also have to be acknowledged.*[49]

Though Peirce thought of pragmatism as a method of "fixing beliefs" by making them "clear" and James thought of it as a method

297

of "justification," their common agreement that beliefs are rules for action, "habits" of thought and behavior grounded in what we have called an "experienceable difference," brings them together in the end.

IV. JOHN DEWEY: FROM "RELIGION" TO THE "RELIGIOUS"

Writing of Peirce and James, his teachers in pragmatism, Dewey has this to say:

> The difference between Peirce and James . . . is the greater emphasis placed by the former upon the method of procedure. Everything ultimately turned, for Peirce, upon the trustworthiness of the procedures of inquiry. Hence his high estimate of logic, as compared with James—at least James in his later days. Hence also his definite rejection of the appeal to the Will to Believe—under the form of what he called the method of tenacity. Closely associated with this is the fact that Peirce has a more explicit dependence upon the social factor than has James. The appeal of Peirce is essentially to the consensus of those who have investigated, using methods which are capable of employment by all. It is the need for social agreement, and the fact that in its absence "the method of tenacity" will be exposed to disintegration from without, which finally forces upon mankind the wider and wider utilization of the scientific method.[50]

From this we get some clue as to why, when he finally got around to giving a sketch of his philosophy of religion in his own "later days," Dewey should have called his lectures *A Common Faith*. In his own relations with the established religions, Dewey was, if anything, less at home than either Peirce or James. He lacked Peirce's great hope and confidence in "the Christian theory of the way in which the world is to be made better and wiser."[51] The "Common Faith" which Dewey had in mind was clearly not that of *institutional* Christianity at all. In this he shared James's lifelong distaste for

298

church "affiliation." And yet, as Dewey himself was well aware, the *spirit* of his "Common Faith" is close indeed to the spirit of Peirce's Agapasm.

Although Dewey wrote little directly on religion for many years, there are traces of Peirce in several of his early works—those produced during his "Hegelian" period. Thus in his *Psychology,* which was first published in 1887 and which ran through at least three editions, Dewey wrote:

> The true self-related must be the organic unity of the self and the world, of the ideal and the real, and this is what we know as God. . . . It is the intuition of God as perfectly realized intelligence that forms the cognitive side of the religious consciousness.[52]

And in the same work, he wrote that the religious *feeling* is one which is "universal" in that we recognize the dependence (à la Schleiermacher) of the self, foreswear the private and separate self, and surrender wholly to the perfect personality, God. The religious feeling is that of complete reconciliation and harmony. These are views which he reiterated in *A Common Faith* after a gap of some forty-seven years, though in restating them Dewey gives evidence that he no longer rests them on a "Hegelian" foundation or even on such a cosmic "evolutionism" as Peirce had in mind. His long and studied "neglect" of the problems of philosophy of religion is explained by Dewey as follows:

> While the conflict of traditional religious beliefs with opinions that I could myself honestly entertain was the source of a trying personal crisis, it did not at any time constitute a leading philosophical problem. This might look as if the two things were kept apart; in reality it was due to a feeling that any genuinely sound religious experience could and should adapt itself to whatever beliefs one found oneself intellectually entitled to hold—a half unconscious sense at first, but one which ensuing years have developed into a fundamental conviction. In consequence, while I have, I hope, a due degree of personal sympathy with individuals who are under-

299

going the throes of a personal change of attitude, I have not been able to attach much importance to religion as a philosophic problem; for the effect of that attachment seems to be in the end a subordination of candid philosophic thinking to the alleged but factious needs of some special set of convictions.[53]

And he goes on to remark, in characteristic fashion, how little positive good results from allowing one's religious predelictions to bias one's philosophical views—noting in passing, the almost universal tendency of theologians to allow themselves to be moved "more by partisan interest in a particular religion than by interest in religious experience."

When it comes to democracy, the possibilities of self-realization through interaction with nature, the future application of scientific methods of inquiry to an ever increasing range of human problems—with respect to all these and more—Dewey's optimism is nearly boundless. When it comes to organized religion and its effects on the public future, Dewey's pessimism knows no rival. Not for Dewey does religion, in its institutional garb at least, offer any hope for the future unity of mankind; not for Dewey the great hope that sustained Peirce's membership in the Church despite his reservations about the literal meaning of the creeds, and not for Dewey the view of James that religion can be justified solely as a psychological "cure of souls." Compared with Peirce and James, Dewey appears as the hardbitten naturalist and atheist, what we would call in today's parlance a "dedicated secularist." And yet, it would be wrong to think of Dewey's rejection of institutionalized religion as a rejection of all that religion meant to Peirce and James. In his own way he tries to account for all that is positive and creative in religion, all the "fruits" of religious zeal and practice which commended religion to Peirce and James on pragmatist grounds of meaning and truth. Indeed, in retrospect Dewey seems closer to the Christians who are known today as the "God is dead" theologians than to the religious "liberals" of his own generation. For in rejecting the creeds and churches, in his unremitting criticism of supernaturalism and the authoritarianism and absolutism which accompanies it, Dewey sought to dispose of the "excess baggage" of religious faith. And he did this in order to release the religious spirit from its chains, to permit the *essence* of the religious spirit to gain a new lease on life. In truth, Dewey's attack on "religion" was a *defense of the religious life* and a sustained attempt to free the creative faith of the ordinary believer from the irrelevancies and the outright falsehoods of the traditional creeds and dogmas. That success in this liberation of the "religious" essence from the fetters of "religion" could be achieved, Dewey never doubted. In this sense, *but in this sense only,* Dewey was a religious optimist.

The basic theme of this espousal of the "religious" element and quality of experience is, of course, stated most fully in his Terry Lectures at Yale, but it is a theme which runs throughout his work. Thus, in *Reconstruction in Philosophy* (1920), he wrote:

> When the emotional force, the mystic force one might say, of communication, of the miracle of shared life and shared experience is spontaneously felt, the hardness and crudeness of contemporary life will be bathed in the light that never was on land or sea.[54]

"Communication," "shared experience"—these are the means and the ends of the religious life which may even, Dewey boldly suggests, be served by the gradual decay of the churches and the decline of ecclesiastical influence over the common life of men and women. Thus, in *Characters and Events* we find the following passage, written in 1909:

> We may indeed question whether it is true that in any relative sense this is a peculiarly irreligious age. . . . We are still, even those who have nominally surrendered supernatural dogma, largely under the dominion of the ideas of those who have succeeded in identifying religion with the rites, symbols, and emotions associated with these dogmatic beliefs. As we see the latter disappearing, we think we are growing irreligious. For all we know, the integrity of mind which is loosening the hold of these things is potentially much more religious than

301

all that it is displacing. It is increased knowledge of nature which has made supra-nature incredible, or at least difficult of belief. We measure the change from the standpoint of the supranatural and we call it irreligious. Possibly if we measure it from the standpoint of the natural piety it is fostering, the sense of the permanent and inevitable implication of nature and man in a common career and destiny, it would appear as the growth of religion.[55]

This "optimism," which finds the decay of the traditional ways of organizing and interpreting religious experience a positive gain in fostering the genuine religious life, was still alive after thirty years when Dewey wrote, in retrospect, that all his writings on religion had been "devoted to making explicit the religious values implicit in the spirit of science as undogmatic reverence for truth in whatever form it presents itself, and the religious values implicit in our common life, especially in the moral significance of democracy as a way of living together."[56]

In support of this apparently perverse doctrine—"perverse" because it runs exactly counter to the official view which habitually measures the strength of the "religious" in terms of the power of organized religion—Dewey offers evidence to show that the traditional religious perspective on experience is a distortion of the truth. He argues that the division of religious experience into the "super-natural" and the "natural" sets up a false dichotomy which is damaging in the extreme to both the creative possibilities of religious faith and to the natural possibilities of self-realization. Owing to its fixed commitment to obsolete and irrelevant conceptions of both man and nature, traditional religion supports a morality which no longer meets the actual moral needs of men and, instead, drives between man and man, between man and nature, a wedge of alienation. Dewey's objections concerned not merely the failure of the churches to "keep up with the times," not merely the fact that *fixed* creeds, cults, and moral codes are so inflexible as to remove from everyday life the practical guidance in the conduct of human affairs that it is the sacred obligation of religion to provide, and not merely the almost continuous resistance to change that the established religions are noted for. What Dewey has in mind is all of these things

302

and more. It is, ultimately, the fact of religion's claim to a final and finished *truth* which offends against Dewey's natural piety and does violence to his conception of what the authentic role of religion is.

Religion should promote the unity of men, it should promote communication among them, harmonize diverse interests, bind them in common purpose for common goods. In these endeavors —which have marked religious life at its best—the function of religion has been to support inquiry and to consecrate what knowledge can be had to the furtherance of life on earth. Inquiry, knowledge—these are made both possible and necessary by the conditions in which man finds himself. When he readily acknowledges his natural setting, his continuity with natural forces and the natural powers around him, inquiry and knowledge serve an instrumental role in securing an ever wider distribution of those goods which he universally seeks. Dewey's view of nature is not that of the romantic; nature is sometimes kind but often cruel:

> The union of the hazardous and the stable, of the incomplete and the recurrent, is the condition of all experienced satisfaction as truly as of our predicaments and problems. . . . While the precarious nature of existence is indeed the source of all trouble, it is also the indispensable condition of all ideality, becoming a sufficient condition when conjoined with the regular and the assured.[57]

In such a setting, morals are contingent upon continuous inquiry and investigation. Human goods are grounded in a natural context, but that context is not always secure; support is withdrawn at crucial moments, values collapse. Intelligent inquiry begins at such moments in order that values may be made more secure, to enstate the goods in a more stable, because reconstructed, environment. Knowledge that issues from despair results in controlled and enriched experience:

> Possession and enjoyment of goods passes insensibly and inevitably into appraisal. First an immature experience is content simply to enjoy. But a brief course in experience enforces reflection; it requires but a brief time to teach that

some things sweet in the having are bitter in the after-taste and in what they lead to. Primitive innocence does not last.[58]

If man can pursue ideals, can bring ideals to bear upon his every-day life, it is because he possesses natural powers of intelligence and imagination:

> Nature thus supplies potential material for embodiment of ideals. Nature, if I may use the locution, is idealizable. It lends itself to operations by which it is perfected.[59]

Thus man is bound to nature and to his fellows, the focus and function of religion is the consecration of intelligence to what Dewey here calls nature "perfected" through those ideals which are empirically rooted in "shared experience."

Piety toward nature is deeply seated in Dewey's philosophy of religion, but it would be wrong—embarrassingly and pathetically wrong—to think of Dewey as in any sense a "pantheist." There is much to be endured and undergone, of course, but never with Stoic calm or with the rationalistic conviction that we are somehow al-ready in the "best of all possible worlds." Dewey's faith is in the ideal as possible, not in the ideal which is already actual but some-how hidden from view:

> For all endeavor for the better is moved by faith and what is possible, not by inference to the actual. Nor does this faith depend for its moving power upon intellectual assurance or belief that things worked for must surely prevail and come into embodied existence.[60]

Faith involves, as the existentialists have also taught us (though their reasoning here is quite different), an infinite risk. And yet, there are rational grounds for accepting this risk. The realm of nature may not be finished and perfect, but it does assure that risks intelligently taken are not just leaps into the absurd. Risks taken on behalf of ideals can be well grounded in what does exist. We are given a glimpse of what this grounding means for Dewey, and how it sustains religious dedication:

304

Infinite relationships of man with his fellows and with nature already exist. The ideal means a sense of these encompassing continuities with their infinite reach. This meaning even now attaches to present activities because they are set in a whole to which they belong and which belongs to them. Even in the midst of conflict, struggle and defeat a consciousness is possible of the enduring and comprehending whole. . . . Religion has lost itself in cults, dogmas and myths. Consequently the office of religion as sense of community and one's place in it has been lost. In effect religion has been distorted into a possession—or burden—of a limited part of human nature, of a limited portion of humanity which finds no way to universalize religion except by imposing its own dogmas and ceremonies on others; of a limited class within a partial group; priests, saints, a church. Thus other gods have been set up before the one God. Religion as a sense of the whole is the most individualized of all things, the most spontaneous, undefinable and varied. For individuality signifies unique connections in the whole. . . . Every act may carry within itself a consoling and supporting consciousness of the whole to which it belongs and which in some sense belongs to it.[61]

And again, the "one God" to whom Dewey refers in the passage above must not be confused with the God referred to so scornfully by Pascal as *"Le dieu des philosophes et savants."* If it is not *exactly* *"Dieu d'Abraham, Dieu d'Isaac, Dieu de Jacob";* it is not the God of Spinoza and Einstein either:

Religious faith which attaches itself to the possibilities of nature and associated living would, with its devotion to the ideal, manifest piety toward the actual. . . . Nature and society include within themselves projection of ideal possibilities, and contain the operations by which they are actualized. Nature may not be worshipped as divine even in the sense of the intellectual love of Spinoza. But nature, including humanity, with all its defects and imperfections, may evoke heartfelt piety as the source of ideals, of possibilities, of aspiration in their behalf, and as the eventual abode of all attained goods and excellencies.[62]

In the end Dewey was satisfied as little by institutionalized religious humanism as he was by other settled forms of churchly piety. As Randall has succinctly remarked of his elder colleague's relationship with the religion of humanism: "Mr. Dewey's willingness to sign the *Humanist Manifesto* in 1933 was thus a matter of basic conviction as well as of good nature; it characteristically led to no association with *the* Humanist religion."[63] Dewey's religious naturalism and humanistic piety was closer to the Christian humanism of Erasmus and More than to the pessimistic "naturaliam" of Hobbes and de la Mettrie—or, in our own time, closer to the religious "atheism" of Paul Tillich than to the humanism of Corliss Lamont or the naturalism of Julian Huxley.

God is real, William James could argue, because he produces real effects. And in this sense, at least, God is real for Dewey. God's *presence* is felt and makes an "experienceable difference":

> We are in the presence neither of ideals completely embodied in existence nor yet of ideals that are mere rootless ideals, fantasies, utopias. For there are forces in nature and society that generate and support the ideals. They are further unified by the action that gives them coherence and solidity. It is this *active* relation between ideal and actual to which I give the name "God." I would not insist that the name must be given.[64]

If theism be identified with the belief that there is a God "out there" or "up there"—to use the phrases so trenchantly criticized in the Bishop of Woolwich's book, *Honest to God*—then Dewey is certainly no theist. But, and the point is equally important, *if atheism is identified with the doctrine that there is no God at all, then Dewey is certainly no atheist.* But it matters little, when it comes to the crunch, what label is attached. What *does* matter is that Dewey's faith was in the possibilities which are given to each and every one of us, possibilities which stretch before us as an infinite challenge to self-transcendence, and in the methods of intelligence by means of which those possibilities of reunion with each other and with the best that is in us may alone be realized. In this faith

Dewey embodies both Peirce's conviction that it is the community of belief which can alone settle the issue of the truth and James's high hope for religion as the cure of souls.

V. THE PROBLEM OF RELIGIOUS KNOWLEDGE OF GOD

It is sometimes said by English historians of philosophy that the mistakes made by British philosophers are easily exported to America where they enjoy a long and well-respected afterlife. The pragmatist defense of religious faith is offered as a case in point. Thus Bertrand Russell has remarked:

> I can respect men who argue that religion is true and therefore ought to be believed, but I can feel only profound reprobation for those who say that religion ought to be believed because it is useful, and that to ask whether it is true is a waste of time.[65]

And A. C. Ewing, writing on the "Autonomy of Ethics," has said:

> If it could be shown that the belief in God is presupposed in the very possibility of any ethics at all, this would seem to me a quite conclusive argument for God, since we certainly know some ethical propositions to be valid. But if it can be shown only that the belief is a great help in the ethical life, this weakens the argument immeasurably. I do not myself see any legitimate way of passing from the premise that a belief is useful to the conclusion that it is true unless some specific reason be produced for thinking that the belief would not have been useful if it had been false.[66]

But before we hastily admit the vulnerability of the pragmatist case for religion it would be well to recall what John Stuart Mill, himself no enemy of the "principle of utility" in morals, has said in his essay on "The Utility of Religion":

307

> If religion, or any particular form of it, is true, its usefulness follows without any other proof. . . . The utility of religion did not need to be asserted until the arguments for its truth had in great measure ceased to convince. People must either have ceased to believe, or have ceased to rely on the belief of others, before they could take that inferior ground of defense without a consciousness of lowering what they were endeavouring to raise.[67]

The presupposition which Mill makes, and which seems to be shared by Russell and Ewing, is that the "truth" of religion is one thing and its "usefulness" quite another, that we can separate these two things and explore each independently, that we can develop quite independent criteria for judging them as separate issues.

According to this view the pragmatic criterion is acceptable only as a secondary and inferior line of defense (if at all), there being a primary and superior criterion of truth. What this "superior" criterion consists of is not always clearly stated; it may be the "correspondence" between thought and thing, or even the "coherence" of any truth with the whole body of accepted truths. A clearer statement than most of what this primary criterion might be is given by F. R. Tennant, himself an astute philosopher of both science and religion. Of the process of verification in science, Tennant says that it ". . . consists in finding that the postulate or theory is borne out by appeal to external facts and tallies with them." But he goes on to say that such "objective" verification cannot be found in matters of religious belief:

> Successful faith . . . is illustrated by numerous examples of the gaining of material and moral advantages, the surmounting of trials and afflictions, and the attainment of heroic life, by men of old who were inspired by faith. It is thus that faith is pragmatically "verified" and that certitude as to the unseen is established. . . . such verification is only for [subjective] certitude, not a proving of [objective] certainty as to external reality. The fruitfulness of a belief is one thing, and the reality of existence of what is ideated is another. There are instances in which a belief that is not true, in the sense of

308

> corresponding with fact, may inspire one with lofty ideals
> and stimulate one to strive to be a more worthy person.[68]

Thus the "truth of faith" is compared unfavorably with the "truth of science" even by one who, as Tennant himself professed, believed the "truth of religion" implicitly.

One response to this dilemma has been the denial of "truth" to the judgments of religion entirely. Perhaps the most persuasive of such arguments—and one which is deeply influenced by pragmatism—is that advanced by J. H. Randall, Jr., who compares religion to the arts. Without in any way denying that religion, like the arts, "reveals" and "teaches" us how to live, Randall nevertheless denies that it is the function of religion to provide "knowledge" in any conventional sense. Thus, although the religious prophet and the saint fulfill the useful, even the *imperative,* function of teaching us "how to see what man's life in the world is, and what it might be, it offers no descriptions and no explanations." Thus: "It is well to keep 'truth' for the knowledge that is science, with all its complex procedures and criteria for verifying propositions that can be stated in words."[69]

There is, assuredly, much to be said for this "non-cognitive" response to the verificationist challenge. One finds, in recent English philosophy of religion, a similar response to the challenge of the positivists' "verification principle" of meaning. Here, quite independently of any direct influence from pragmatism, the acute and sensitive analysis of religious language has again and again left defenders of the faith with little alternative but to fall back upon an essentially pragmatic defense. Thus, in John Wisdom's widely reprinted essay "Gods," linguistic analysis quickly shows that assertions about God are not just like ordinary statements of fact, that the issue of "the existence of God" is not an "experimental" issue, as it was once thought to be. Thus, if we confine the use of the word "true" to denote those descriptions which *are* subject to experimental verification, religious claims are neither true nor false. They are, instead, as A. J. Ayer argued in *Language, Truth and Logic,* cognitively meaningless.

But Wisdom also argues that there is something wrong with

the suggestion that claims about God are *mere* expressions of subjective attitudes. In a vein which is similar to Randall's but goes beyond, Wisdom suggests that religious discourse is not just "emotive" discourse but tells us something about how things are. Religious language may not be simply descriptive in just the way that scientific language is, but it nevertheless has a *use* and a *meaning* which is at *least* comparable to that of great works of art and perhaps even more. Thus he says, "Things are revealed to us not only by the scientists with microscopes, but also by the poets, the prophets, and the painters." And, pushing this comparison further, Wisdom brings out the relevance of facts to religious claims, a relevance which somehow goes beyond the similar relevance of facts to works of art. This is brought out by analysis of a crucial question for religion:

> Was there someone, Jesus, who was God incarnate? The question calls for investigation but it also calls like every other question for thought, reflection, reason. He made himself the Son of God. "Preposterous presumption" the priests said, but was it the truth? The facts agreed upon, still a question is before the bar of reason as when, the facts agreed upon, still a question comes before the court, "was there negligence or not?" . . . Was Jesus God incarnate? The law in this matter is not as simple nor as definite nor as fully written out in statutes as we might wish it could be. The question is large, slippery, subtle. But it is not true that nothing is more relevant to it than another, so that nothing supports one answer more than it supports another. On the contrary every incident in the life of Christ is relevant to this question as every incident in the life of Nero is relevant to the same question about him. To both much more is relevant. For an affirmative answer to either implies the existence of God. And to this question every incident in the history of the world is relevant—whether it is the fall of a sparrow or the coming of harvest, the passing of an empire or the fading of a smile.[70]

Accordingly, though there are no simple answers, the old question "Does God exist?" is not senseless, is not beyond the scope of

310

thought and reason. But it does call for a new awareness of what has been so long about us, "in case knowing nature so well we never know her."

What Wisdom here is hinting at is not far from what Peirce suggested as the way of approaching "the reality of God" through the relaxed contemplation of one's *total* environment which he called "musement," a way in which religion is seen as a rational and thoughtful response to the "signs" around us—a response which is no more *reducible* to other things or to the "signs" or facts themselves than is any other general truth about the world.[71] But Peirce notes, as Wisdom does not, the extreme difficulty in making any such "general truth" stick, of "justifying" it in any way short of an appeal to consequences. For Peirce "the reality of God" is *independent* of whatever we may believe about him; assertions about God are clearly *true* or *false* independently of what their consequences are when believed by us. The consequences of taking God as real are justified because God *is* real—the "logic of God" does not pass from the usefulness of the idea to its truth but from its truth to its usefulness. But if we try to *justify* the idea to *others,* to clarify its meaning and to "fix the belief" itself, we have no recourse but to point to its consequences. For the religious man, belief is a living thing, ". . . a deep recognition of something in the circumambient All" which is "a thing to be lived rather than said or thought."[72] Thus, religious perceptions, ideas, and activities are *generated* by the "religious sensibility" and are seen to be *true* in the "lively exercise of . . . religious meditation. . . ."[73] The pragmatic note comes into Peirce's philosophy of religion only when it comes to his consideration of what the religious ideas and conceptions mean in terms of their consequences in the lives of men and women. Thus, if we *were* to take God's reality as a *hypothesis* it would differ in a radical way from ordinary experimental issues:

> Any normal man who considers the three Universes [of internal, external, and logical facts] in the light of the hypothesis of God's reality . . . will come to be stirred to the depths of his nature by the beauty of the idea and by its august practicality, even to the point of earnestly loving and adoring

311

his strictly hypothetical God, and to that of desiring above all
else to shape the conduct of his life and all the springs of
action into conformity with that hypothesis.[74]

Far from being an ordinary hypothesis, then, the religious claim is
the expression of an "experienceable difference" which touches
every aspect of life; it is a difference experienced in such a personal
way that Peirce even questions the appropriateness of the word
"belief" to designate its expression. Religious experience, he says,
provides a man with "as good reason—putting aside metaphysical
subtilties—to believe in the living personality of God as he has to
believe in his own. Indeed *belief* is a word inappropriate to such
direct perception."[75]

The issue and problem of religious knowledge is thus clearly
drawn. On the assumption that the paradigm cases of knowledge
are those of science, the reality of God is indeed unknowable. But
if, as Peirce maintains and as Wisdom suggests, the "logic of God"
is somehow different from the logic of experiment and direct sen-
sory perception, it may be that religious discourse is meaningful
and religious knowledge possible. Pragmatism cannot show *how*
religious knowledge is possible if it insists that the sole criterion of
the *truth* of such knowledge is its application to life, its use in
practice, its "satisfactory" consequences. *But this was never pragmatism's intention.* Rather, despite James's apparent lapse in "The
Will to Believe," it was the purpose of pragmatism to offer a way of
clarifying the *meaning* of religious ideas. The truth of an idea,
according to an ancient tradition descended to Aquinas through St.
Augustine from Plato, is found in the *adequatio rei et intellectus.* If
adequatio is taken as closer to "adequacy" than to "correspondence," then this is a doctrine to which pragmatism subscribes. For it
is basic to the pragmatist conception of truth that ideas and concepts are never just "copies" or pictures of realities, that our descriptions always fall short of their empirical objects, that they can
never express all that is. But that they can nevertheless be more or
less adequate to the uses we put them to, and that this "adequacy"
can be empirically judged. Truth is not a static, closed correspondence of idea to thing but a greater or less approximation to the

empirically given, to the "experienceable difference," of the idea, the concept, the empirically grounded assertion.

It is, accordingly, simply wrong to attribute to pragmatism the error of justifying "wishful thinking in religion." Faced with Santayana's charge ". . . there is no sense of security, no joy, in James's apology for personal religion. He did not really believe; he merely believed in the right of believing that you might be right if you believed . . . ," James could reply:

> The Pragmatist calls satisfactions indispensable for truth-building, but I have everywhere called them insufficient unless reality be also incidentally led to. . . . For him, as for his critic, there can be no truth if there is nothing to be true about. Ideas are so much flat psychological surface unless some mirrored matter gives them cognitive lustre. This is why as a Pragmatist I have so carefully posited 'reality' *ab initio,* and why, throughout my whole discussion I remain an epistemological realist.[76]

And Dewey could insist that:

> I have never identified any satisfaction with the truth of an idea, save *that* satisfaction which arises when the idea as working hypothesis or tentative method is applied to prior existences in such a way as to fulfill what it intends.[77]

The pragmatist's *full* defense of religious knowledge, then, rests on grounds which are *prior* to knowledge, on there being something *there* to be experienced. It does not depend solely upon the experience itself or the consequences and the satisfaction to be derived from it. In religious experience as in any other form of experience, there can be no substitute for the reality of what Dewey calls "prior existences."

The problem of religious knowledge is thus the problem of showing how religious assertions can be true, not *apart* from their meanings as applied to behavior and the conduct of life, but *in addition to these.* There is certainly nothing wrong in Randall's contention that religion does not function, as science does, to provide descriptions of the empirical world. It may readily be admitted that "religious knowledge" is not of the scientific sort. And it may also be admitted that the function of religious knowledge is more like that of the arts than like that of deductive logic or mathematics. Surely Randall is right in arguing that the role of the prophet and the saint is to show us how to live better, to show us possibilities that we might have overlooked. But to say this is to omit mention of the further role that religious language plays in life. For why should we trust in the vision of prophet and saint unless we have reason to believe that they see things as they *really* are? In the end, even Dewey's defense of the valuable religious qualities of experience, of the qualities of dedication and persistence in the pursuit of "ideal ends" depends on there *being* some reality which these qualities reflect. How can we believe in "ideal ends" at all unless we also believe that these are in some sense *real* possibilities and not just hopeful illusions? Isn't it, in fact, *reality itself* that decides which "options" are *alive* for us and which are dead?

In dealing with the question of the *truth* of religious claims, then, we pass beyond their moral meaning and consequences. We can agree with Richard Braithwaite that:

> Just as the meaning of a moral assertion is given by its use in expressing the asserter's intention to act, so far as in him lies, in accordance with the moral principles involved, so the meaning of a religious assertion is given by its use in expressing the asserter's intention to follow a specified policy of behavior.[78]

But we must go further than this and ask whether the religious meaning intended is appropriate to the reality of the world, is adequate to the totality of empirical things. We can ask, in short, if religious assertions are not only "justifiable" but *true*. We can agree with R. M. Hare that a decision to adopt a particular way of life, "far from being arbitrary . . . would be the most well-founded of decisions, because it would be based upon a consideration of everything upon which it could possibly be founded."[79] In reaching a decision to "believe in God," we shall want to know not merely

314

what the moral consequences of this belief are likely to be, but also that "there is a God." And yet, if such knowledge is possible, it is clear that it cannot be just like other knowledge. So we are tempted to say that it is not "knowledge" at all. Or if we admit that it *is* knowledge we qualify it by calling it "knowing how" rather than "knowing that" and we speak of "believing in" instead of "believing that."

What I want to suggest, in bringing this essay to a conclusion, is that the dichotomy between those who take the "cognitivist" view in philosophy of religion and those who uphold the "noncognitivist" position (like Randall and Braithwaite) is not as conclusive a dichotomy as it may seem. The noncognitivists rightly insist that religious knowledge is not on just the same sort of footing as the knowledge of science and mathematics. But the cognitivists are certainly not happy with the line of thought that then develops—the line that religious assertions are not properly assertions at all, that they are expressions of moral intention, or that they express "visions" or "attitudes" toward the world which are neither verifiable or falsifiable. The cognitivists may well acknowledge, with D. M. Mackinnon, that:

> Of course what we are really looking for is a means of understanding what is beyond understanding, of coming at least to the outskirts of the incomprehensible; it was something which schoolmen like Cajetan believed they possessed in their method of analogy. But because we do not share their "intuition of being," we cannot avail ourselves of that particular instrument; yet it may be that by remembering what they did, or tried to do, we can see something at least of what has to be done.[80]

In this task the religious pragmatists have contributed something that it is well to remember. For throughout their inquiry into the nature and function of religion is the constant thread of realism. For Peirce, this realism was tempered with an appeal to what has since been called a strain of "personalism." Witness his emphasis on the "personal" mode of encounter with God which is, to be sure, "generalized" into a doctrine of "evolutionary love." In James and

315

the early Dewey, personalistic language is used almost exclusively in rendering expression to the reality encountered in religious experience. Finally, in Dewey's later writings, where the metaphors of "person" are given up almost entirely, there is the exception that the religious "qualities" are all qualities of persons and not of things. There is, then, a fairly consistent strain of what might be called "personalistic realism" which characterizes the pragmatic treatment of the problem of religious knowledge.

What this suggests, of course, is that religious knowledge is like the knowledge of another *person* and not like that of things or *objects*. In this, it must be admitted, pragmatism runs the risk of being accused of "projecting" man's own image upon an impersonal and objective reality. But the risk of "anthropomorphism" is not blindly taken. If the commitment of Peirce, for example, to an anthropomorphic conception of evolution in his doctrine of Agapasm is examined it will be found to be an *open* commitment— it is open to correction and amendment by experienceable evidence. If the "truth" of Agapasm is intensely and personally held, because intensely and personally perceived and experienced, it is not merely a subjective bias. It is open to correction by the public experience of the religious (or, if it comes to that, the nonreligious) community. In this respect, Peirce's concern for "objectivity" parallels and anticipates the concern of the linguistic philosophers for the avoidance of the defense of religion by claiming that its "truth" is of a "higher order," that it is invulnerable to the run of objective evidence. If religious discourse claims that *agape* is an *adequate* word for talking about the character of reality, for referring to the "theistic" character of the world evolving around us and within us, it must be because we can supply criteria for showing its adequacy. And, by the same token, we must be ready to admit evidence which, if it exists, would count against its adequacy. I. T. Ramsey, whose discussion of theological "models" is at places reminiscent of Peirce's analysis of "signs," puts the matter as follows:

> The model of "love" will certainly have to meet the challenge of evil and suffering in the Universe and in this way to grapple with the "problem of evil"; but even more importantly

316

> there will have to be specific situations which can legitimately
> be "interpreted by love" if the model of love has any justifi-
> cation at all. There must be a pattern of empirical circum-
> stances which fit "loving" discourse when used of God. Such
> a fit is pragmatic in the widest sense; but it is not given by
> experimental verification in a strict scientific sense.[81]

Ramsey, like Tillich and Buber and for the same reasons, is chary of speaking of God as an "object," as just another "fact" in the world, as a "being" among other beings. And yet, like Peirce and James, he is intensely concerned to defend the objectivity of what is disclosed to the "eye of faith." In the end Ramsey appeals to the experience, not of "encountering God," but of "being encountered" by what is disclosed, the experience of being acted upon by some-thing or someone other than oneself. The closest analogue model that we have for this experience, in which we speak of being "sin-gled out" by God, is the experience of being "met" by another, of being "chosen" by another as the subject of some act of self-disclosure on their part. Thus, Ramsey argues, it is to such "per-sonal" models and metaphors that religious language must *neces-sarily* have recourse if it is to express adequately the *reality* of what is religiously experienced:

> It is in this sense that disclosures reveal objectivity. It is
> certainly not the "objectivity" which belongs to dream
> images, though we need not deny that dream images have
> some sort of objectivity; It is not even the "objectivity" of the
> Atonement in that mistaken (mechanical) sense. Nor is it the
> "objectivity" which belongs to other "people" as the topics
> of social statistics. *It is the objectivity of what declares itself*
> to us—challenges us in the way that *persons may do*. It is in
> this sense that God declares his objectivity, and some would
> say that in a similar sense Duty also declares its objectivity.
> It is to talk of God's objectivity in this sense that personal
> and impersonal models are used.[82]

The important thing to notice here is that one model corrects an-other, that "personal" models correct "impersonal" ones and vice versa. The words that we use in talking about God, in talking about the "experienceable difference" that God makes, are thus self-correcting. If we are tempted to think of God exclusively in terms of one concept, to stress one characteristic of what we feel about God's relation to us, this may be countered by another concept and another stress.[83]

Critics of religion have sometimes suggested that this use of "multi-modelled" discourse in talking about God reveals a weakness, shows that the believer is *determined* to believe regardless of the consequences, that his many models enable him to avoid being "pinned down" as to just what it is that he believes. And those who would defend orthodoxy in religion stress the need to narrow the range of choice, to sanctify as dogma only a selected few of the many possible models, to isolate the "truth" of theology from the criticism of philosophy and the tests of worldly consequences. Against both of these views may be cited the observation of Whitehead to the effect that religion *needs* dogmas, but that it doesn't need *fixed* ones. Against the skeptic it must be pointed out that the use of many models is essential if belief is to be corrigible, if it is to remain open to the pragmatist's "experienceable difference." Against the dogmatist it must be pointed out that limiting the range of models endangers the "truth" of theology by isolating it, by restricting arbitrarily its relevance to the problems of men and realities of experience, by cutting it off from open confrontation with the way things are.

Theological judgments are not just simple judgments of fact, corrigible by immediate reference or by controlled experimentation. Yet, as pragmatism teaches, theology *is* corrigible. In religion as in morals, reality continually "breaks through" to our consciousness and forces corrections to our bad judgments. In religion as in science, the facts are what ultimately make our claims come true or not. Religious believing, to be sure, involves emotion and feeling, passion and commitment, to a degree forbidden to the knowledge of simpler things. But that is no reason to think of it as *above* the demands of empirical criteria, as a "law unto itself."

In matters of faith we start out on any inquiry as we do in every branch of knowledge, as we do in common life. We have beliefs and attitudes that we initially trust and we express them by acting on them. Experience does not generate our beliefs out of nothing, but having them, experience serves to modify them, to redirect our attitudes and correct our judgments. The critical search for reasons for believing in religion, as elsewhere, is the search for information that will either confirm our judgments or force a change upon them. The facts do not present themselves in naked isolation from all values, in complete disjunction from all meaning. Pragmatism has shown us how to begin the task of correlating our valuations with the raw materials of experience, how to begin healing the too often assumed divorce between facts and values.

It was St. Paul who suggested that we "prove" our beliefs in practice by acting upon them, by seeing how they fit the world of our experience. Pragmatism shows us that if we cannot "see" God as we see the objects around us, our "visions" of him may nevertheless be corrected and amended by them. Reality, pragmatism says, is not kind to error. But, if we are not to remain "safe" in our illusions, if we are to claim truth for our religious perceptions at all, we must remain open to the "experienceable difference" which the prior reality of God, if there be a God, *must* make. It would be odd indeed if God were to have supplied ready to hand all the evidence which would justify faith in him with little or no effort on our part. It is to the credit of pragmatism that it has never ceased to hold open this possibility, that it has always been open to the invaluable pedagogy of the "experienceable difference." It has done so in aesthetics as in theology, in science as in politics—in the whole range of our experience as men.

NOTES

1. John Dewey, *Characters and Events: Popular Essays in Social and Political Philosophy,* ed. by Joseph Ratner (2 Vols.; New York, 1929), Vol. II, p. 440.

2. John Dewey, *Experience and Nature* (rev. ed.; Chicago, 1929), p. 47.

319

3. John Dewey, *The Influence of Darwin on Philosophy and Other Essays in Contemporary Thought* (New York, 1910), pp. 202-3.

4. Charles S. Peirce, *Collected Papers of Charles Sanders Peirce*, Vols. I-VI, ed. by C. Hartshorne and P. Weiss; Vols. VII-VIII, ed. by A. W. Burks (Cambridge, 1931-58), Vol. VI, paragraph 36. All subsequent references to these *Collected Papers* follow the standard notation of volume and paragraph; e.g., "6.36" refers to Vol. VI, paragraph 36.

5. *Ibid.,* 6.58.

6. *Ibid.,* 6.610.

7. *Ibid.,* 6.104.

8. *Ibid.,* 6.21.

9. *Ibid.,* 6.145.

10. *Ibid.,* 6.295.

11. *Ibid.*

12. *Ibid.,* 5.433.

13. *Ibid.,* 6.148.

14. *Ibid.,* 6.307.

15. *Ibid.,* 6.157.

16. See Herbert W. Schneider's brief but excellent account of Abbott's influence on Peirce and James in *A History of American Philosophy* (New York, 1946), pp. 515-23.

17. *Collected Papers,* 1.354 ff. This is the essay which Peirce characteristically calls a "Guess at the Riddle."

18. *Nation* LXXV, (1902), 95.

19. *Collected Papers,* 5.119; 2.112.

20. *C. S. Peirce's Letters to Lady Welby,* ed. by I. C. Lieb (New Haven, 1953), p. 28.

21. *Collected Papers,* 7.97 ff.

22. *Ibid.,* 7.274.

23. *Ibid.,* 6.441; 6.442.

24. *Ibid.,* 6.443.

25. *Ibid.*, 5.401. But see also the retraction of 5.541.

26. *Ibid.*, 5.402 n. 2.

27. *Ibid.*, 8.259.

28. I Thessalonians 5:21.

29. *Collected Papers,* 5.402.

30. *Ibid.*

31. *Ibid.*, 5.414.

32. Ralph Barton Perry, *Thought and Character of William James* (2 vols.; Boston, 1935), Vol. II, p. 437.

33. *Collected Papers,* 8.259.

34. *Thought and Character of William James,* Vol. II, p. 438.

35. James's California lecture, delivered before the Philosophical Union of the University of California in 1897, was published as "Philosophical Conceptions and Practical Results" in the *University of California Chronical* (1898), pp. 24 ff. It was reprinted, with minor changes, as "The Pragmatic Method," *Journal of Philosophy,* I (1904), 673-87.

36. John Dewey, "The Pragmatism of Peirce," in *Chance, Love and Logic,* ed. by M. R. Cohen (New York, 1923), p. 303.

37. *Collected Papers,* 5.402 n.

38. W. B. Gallie, *Peirce and Pragmatism* (Hammondsworth, 1952), pp. 28-29.

39. William James, *The Varieties of Religious Experience* (New York, 1903), pp. 160-61.

40. William James, *The Letters of William James,* ed. by Henry James (2 vols.; New York, 1920), Vol. 1, p. 47.

41. William James, *Pragmatism* (New York, 1907), pp. 32-33.

42. *Ibid.*, p. 40.

43. *Thought and Character of William James,* Vol. II, p. 245 and p. 488.

44. *Ibid.*

45. *Collected Papers,* 5.24; 7.52.

46. *Ibid.,* 1.171.

47. *Ibid.,* 7.572.

48. *The Varieties of Religious Experience,* p. 384.

49. William James, *Essays in Pragmatism* (New York, 1948), p. 154. (First published as the second lecture in *Pragmatism* [1907]).

50. John Dewey, "The Pragmatism of Peirce" in *Chance, Love and Logic,* pp. 307-8.

51. *Collected Papers,* 7.274.

52. John Dewey, *Psychology* (New York, 1893), p. 244. (Note: This is from the 3rd edition published by Harper & Brothers).

53. John Dewey, "From Absolutism to Experimentalism," in *Contemporary American Philosophy,* ed. by G. P. Adams and W. P. Montague (2 vols.; New York, 1930), Vol. II, p. 19.

54. John Dewey, *Reconstruction in Philosophy* (New York, 1920), p. 211.

55. *Characters and Events,* Vol. II, p. 515.

56. John Dewey, "Experience, Knowledge, and Value: A Rejoinder," in *The Philosophy of John Dewey,* ed. by P. A. Schilpp (Evanston, 1939), p. 597.

57. *Experience and Nature,* p. 54. (Note: The paperback edition of 1958, based on the revised edition of 1929, carries a different pagination. The quotation appears there on p. 62.)

58. *Ibid.,* p. 398 (paperback edition).

59. John Dewey, *The Quest for Certainty* (New York, 1929), p. 302.

60. John Dewey, *A Common Faith* (New Haven, 1934), p. 25. (Note: In the paperback edition of 1960, p. 23.)

61. John Dewey, *Human Nature and Conduct* (New York, 1922), p. 330.

62. *The Quest for Certainty,* p. 306.

63. John Herman Randall, Jr., "The Religion of Shared Experience," in *The Philosopher of the Common Man: Essays in Honor of John Dewey to Celebrate His Eightieth Birthday,* ed. by S. Ratner (New York, 1940), p. 118.

322

64. John Dewey, *A Common Faith* (paperback edition), pp. 50-51.

65. Bertrand Russell, *Why I Am Not a Christian* (London, 1957), p. 172. (Note: In the New York edition of 1957, p. 197.)

66. A. C. Ewing, "Autonomy of Ethics," in *Prospect for Metaphysics* ed. by Ian T. Ramsey (New York, 1961), p. 46.

67. John Stuart Mill, *Three Essays on Religion* (London, 1875), p. 69.

68. F. R. Tennant, *The Nature of Belief* (London, 1943), p. 70.

69. John Herman Randall, Jr., *The Role of Knowledge in Western Religion* (Boston, 1958), p. 133.

70. John Wisdom, "The Logic of God," in *Paradox and Discovery* (Oxford, 1965), p. 21.

71. *Collected Papers,* 6.465 f.

72. *Ibid.,* 6.429; 6.439.

73. *Ibid.,* 6.433; 6.458.

74. *Ibid.,* 6.467.

75. *Ibid.,* 6.436.

76. William James, *The Meaning of Truth: A Sequel to "Pragmatism"* (New York, 1909), p. 195.

77. John Dewey, *Essays in Experimental Logic* (Chicago, 1916), p. 230.

78. Richard B. Braithwaite, *An Empiricist's View of the Nature of Religious Belief* (Cambridge, 1955), p. 15.

79. Richard M. Hare, *The Language of Morals* (Oxford, 1952), p. 69.

80. Donald M. Mackinnon, "Morality and Religion," in *Christian Ethics and Contemporary Philosophy,* ed. by Ian T. Ramsey (London, 1966), pp. 81-82.

81. Ian T. Ramsey "Talking about God," in *Myth and Symbol,* ed. by F. W. Dillistone (London, 1966), p. 90.

82. Ian T. Ramsey *Christian Discourse* (London, 1965), p. 88.

83. See my article on this subject: "On Believing," *Religious Studies,* II, 75-93.

11

HOW IS RELIGIOUS TALK
JUSTIFIABLE?

BY JAMES WM. MCCLENDON JR.

Most students of philosophy in America, it appears, do not learn much in the classroom about the American tradition. The problems of linguistic philosophy since 1935 dominate the discussion. Consequently, many students come to the questions opened up by the American tradition by a circuitous route: the issues arise just at the end of essays and books in the analytic tradition. Even among theologians, the discovery of philosophy which has taken place in the last decade—as the dominance of Barth over Christian thinking recedes—seems to move first to English philosophy; only slowly (except for those who early discovered "process philosophy") do theologians awaken to a tradition nearer at hand. To be sure, analytic philosophy has a hardness and clarity that attracts, like a stretch of ice up ahead in the sun; one anticipates joyous gliding on it with deftness, swiftness, and precision. Because the route to American philosophy—so much less precise, messier, less static, more luxuriant and confusing—is usually roundabout, it seemed like a good idea to close this book with a chapter that manifests some of the beauty and aesthetic pleasure of the analytic tradition, and yet ends with a question typical of the American tradition. Prof. James Wm. McClendon, Jr. of the University of San Francisco returns us to the problems with which this book began. These problems include justifying a way of life, discerning the dialectical roles of personal experience and community life, and learning to make those basic "moral or aesthetic judgments" which appear to be our

324

*only launching pad to what we call reality: the reality of ourselves
and of our world, the reality which we, each singly and in our
multiple communities, are constantly fashioning as we go.*

I

1. It is still widely assumed in theological circles that religious
belief and philosophical analysis are natural enemies. There was
certainly some justification for that assumption in the work of the
logical positivists, a school of philosophers who flourished in the
1930's in Austria, and whose metaphysical beliefs were scattered as
far as Minnesota and California by the Nazi tempest. However
there were important exceptions: the profound mystical note of
Ludwig Wittgenstein's *Tractatus* was heard already in 1922.[1] And
logical positivism (or atomism) in England yielded in the mid-
century to other methods of analysis, methods which were employed by both unbelievers and believers in order to understand
religious discourse, not dismiss it.

2. We may better apprehend the progress so far made, then, if
we consider, not the real or alleged threat to theology posed by
analysis but, rather, the *substantial problem posed to analysis* by
the existence of religious language. Philosophers had found that
certain philosophical muddles of long standing (e.g., the problem
about subsistent entities) could be evaporated by the analysis of the
language used to express the problems. It was reasonable to hope
that similar relief might be afforded outstanding theological problems—viz. the existence of a god or gods, the relations between
God and the world, the problem of evil, the relation between religion and morals.

3. Now the solution of such particular problems seemed to
depend upon what, in general, religious utterances were—what
they purported to do. Early or positivist theories, as has been hinted,
put forward a simplistic answer to this question: religious discourse
(along with traditional metaphysics and the language of morals)
was catalogued and dismissed as "emotive."[2] Religious discourse
was not false for the very good reason that it could not be true—
that is, it did not describe anything at all. If I say, "Wow!" no one
can accuse me of falsehood or congratulate me on my veracity;

"Wow!" is neither true nor false, it does not report any state of affairs correctly or incorrectly; it merely expresses feeling. But, said the emotivists, the same holds true of "Hallelujah!" It, too, expresses feeling; nor can it be either true or false. It does not *describe,* it merely gives vent to the emotion of the speaker. But the same is true of all purported talk about God; it may *seem* to describe, just as moral language *seems* to describe moral entities ("the good"). But "God is Lord of all" in fact describes nothing; nothing is different in the world whether God is or is not Lord of all; thus "God is Lord of all" is disguised exclamation, roughly equivalent to "Three cheers for God!" Sometimes the emotive theory was demarcated by use of the expression "literally meaningful." Literally meaningful utterances are those which describe some state of affairs (synthetic statements), or which express the necessary relation between concepts (analytic statements). Since emotive utterances do neither, they are not (literally) meaningful.

4. At this point appears the function of what was called the *verifiability principle,* as important in the history of analysis as any single principle: "the meaning of a sentence lies in the means of its verification." That is, sentences which describe some states of affairs can (conceivably) be checked by investigating that state of affairs; if no state of affairs is referred to, so that there can in principle be no such checking, the sentence lacks literal meaning. It should be noted that this was not a demand for *proof,* for very many states of affairs cannot be proved to be as they are. It is, rather, the demand for descriptive *meaning*—meaning such that some evidence might conceivably count toward the truth or falsehood of the purported statement. To say that many of the typical utterances of religious discourse, e.g., "God's in his heaven," did not pass this test was another way of saying what has already been said—that though they *appeared* descriptive, they were in fact emotive utterances, in a class with "Wow!" and "Bravo!"

5. The crux case for the emotive theory was to be found neither in such strictly theological propositions as "Allah is God" (which might be understood as analytic), nor in talk about personal religious experience, "I heard a voice speaking to me . . . and was not disobedient to the heavenly vision" (which might be taken

326

in merely psychological terms). It was found in God-in-the-world claims, which employ "God" as a subject, and predicate of him acts upon or in the world: "God created the world," "God led Israel across the Red Sea," "God was in Christ, reconciling. . . ." Such God-in-the-world talk is clearly not analytic; yet it is in a certain important way unfalsifiable, cannot be checked. On the one hand, these propositions were not straightforward descriptions. On the other, the emotive account of their meaning seemed inadequate. Either they were actually empty utterances, without any possibility of meaningfulness (Flew[3]), or their meaning-status remained to be explored.

6. Several important but incomplete attempts were made, between 1950 and 1960, to overcome this sensed inadequacy. Noteworthy is the work of R. B. Braithwaite, of Richard M. Hare, and of Ian T. Ramsey. Braithwaite[4] proposed that such propositions as those last mentioned, and religious language generally, could be understood as doing work closely akin to that of moral language— that is, declaring the *intention* of the user, in view of such and such a religious vision, to pursue "an agapeistic way of life." The cognitive meaning of the language, then, was not to be found in its purported description of the action of gods, but in the intended conduct of the speaker, and its verification would consist in the speaker's actually so conducting himself. Hare[5] proposed that characteristic religious claims be seen as *bliks*—where "blik" is a coined word referring to certain general beliefs. These beliefs cannot be falsified by empirical tests; nevertheless they affect our behavior. Insane men have bliks, whereas sane men have, not a lack of bliks, but sane bliks; sane and insane differ not on any datum but on the way all the data are construed. To apply the concept to religion, a man with a certain blik about life after death might approach life here and now differently than would a man whose blik rejected life after death. Ramsey[6] gave more careful attention to the actual structure of religious language. He pointed out that religious utterances both express a commitment and witness to a related discernment. The discernment, however, is of a situation which cannot be described in any straightforward way: "Christ is my leader" is *not* logically parallel to "Bill Robinson is my leader."

327

Thus religious language uses ordinary terms in extraordinary ways (Ramsey speaks of "models" and "qualifiers") in order to evoke and evince discernments which cannot in the nature of the case be merely described. Characteristically Ramseyan is the insistence that religious talk must be empirically grounded—such talk always speaks of the empirical situation, and more.

7. These approaches each leave something to be desired as accounts of religious discourse. While Braithwaite has called attention to the element of *intention* in religious discourse, one doubts that he has done justice to religious language's function of referring —e.g., to God. One also wonders whether, if alternative religious (or unreligious) utterances expressed the same intention, their *meaning* would, on Braithwaite's view, be the same. That would certainly be quite contrary to our normal understanding of such language. Similar strictures apply to Hare's bliks. As for Ramsey's account, while it allows for a descriptive role in religious discourse, it never seems to provide for the possibility that this discourse could be true or false. This characteristic, to be sure, might be urged as one of the virtues of Ramsey's account, simply reflecting its fidelity to religious talk as it actually occurs. Does a Christian ever by argument persuade a Muslim, or an atheist a Christian, on points of basic disagreement? Is their talk, then, not devoid of truth-claims? On the other hand, we feel the need for *some* sort of justification of religious talk with which none of these analysts provide us. Particularly we need a justification for the apparent descriptive force of such talk as "God led the Israelites across the Red Sea." It is not enough to say that this is "not literal." The question is, if it is not, how can it be shown to mean anything at all, anything different, e.g., from "God did *not* lead the Israelites across the Red Sea"? And by what decision-procedures could we decide which we ought to say?

II

8. What we need, and seem to have lacked, is any general account of meaning which takes note of the many sorts of things which language can do, and represents the structural relationship between these elements. William Alston[7] has shown how little rea-

son there was, as recently as 1962, to believe that any general theory of meaning was available—any theory which would relate the emotive force of discourse to its descriptive force and to that force which Braithwaite alluded to in his talk about "intention." In 1962, however, there appeared J. L. Austin's 1955 William James Lectures at Harvard, published as *How to Do Things with Words*.[8]

9. Austin came to his more general discovery through the failure of a less ambitious attempt at analysis. He had noted that certain sentences, when spoken in certain conventional human situations, have the effect of *doing* what they say. If in a game of bridge, it being my turn to bid, I say, "I bid one heart," then I *have* bid one heart. Saying it was doing it. Austin called such utterances performatives, and contrasted them with constatives, whose function was to describe (e.g., "The cat is on the mat"). To those uncertain about the usefulness of such a distinction, it might be pointed out that the latter (constative) category is used for setting out the facts, while the former (performative) is characteristic of certain speech-acts of great importance to religion. For example, praying, confessing, committing, blessing, baptizing, confirming, marrying, characteristic religious speech-acts, are performatives, and so too are many of the typical speech-acts of the moral life: advising, reprimanding, evaluating, resolving, blaming, and others.[9]

10. Here however a great difficulty appeared—Austin found the performative-constative distinction broke down upon examination. For he could find no grammatical, no verbal distinction which would infallibly distinguish the two classes. Both classes, further, were subject to the same kinds of misuse (infelicities, or "unhappiness," as Austin called them). And both classes, not merely constatives, seemed to have to bear a certain relation to the facts if they were to come off successfully.[10] (For example, "I thank you" is performative, not constative; but I can't meaningfully thank you— my thanking fails to "come off"—if you have not *in fact* done something for me.)

11. Austin therefore set out on a fresh track (and in this he has been followed in the useful summary by Alston mentioned above). In summarizing Austin's achievement, let us note first a

329

distinction between two among many senses of "saying the same thing." Suppose a baseball umpire, during a game, looks at a sliding baserunner, jerks his thumb, and shouts, "Out!" And that a boy in the bleachers, imitating him, jerks *his* thumb and shouts, "Out!" In one sense, umpire and boy have done the same thing with a word. Call that doing a *locutionary act*. In another sense, the umpire has done what the boy has not done—by shouting, "Out!" he has called a player out. Call this the *illocutionary act,* which is performed in performing the locutionary act. (Note that we *might* have called it the *performative act* in honor of our earlier distinction.) Then we can distinguish a third kind of act—both the umpire and the boy, or either of them, may have irritated (or enraged, or delighted, or satisfied) a spectator in a nearby box seat. Call the irritating, etc., a *perlocutionary act*. Now we can say that *the effective meaning of a sentence is that illocutionary act which is performed by means of that sentence.* And to say that one sentence "means the same thing" as another is to say that it performs the *same* illocutionary act. (Cf. "Out!" and "You are out!") Thus we have not only made a classification of the kinds of acts we perform when speaking; we have located one of these, the illocutionary act, as the likeliest candidate for the act whereby in speaking we *act meaningfully*. (In effect we have very nearly said that all speech-acts are, among other things, kinds of performatives.) If now we can relate the descriptive and emotive force of utterances to this (central) performative or *illocutionary* force, we will be in a position to give a general accounting of meaning.

12. To see this relationship, we may follow the Austinian route of noticing the ways in which an illocutionary act can go wrong, or fail to come off. Suppose, sitting at table, I say to you, "Please pass the bowl." Now for this to *work,* i.e., for it to count as a bona fide request for the bowl, note what must hold:

A.1 There must be a "language-rule" to the effect that bowl-passing is a possible move. Bowl-passing must be a conventional human act in our culture. Thus if in *those* circumstances I had said, "Please contest the bowl," you wouldn't know *what* to do. For we have no bowl-contesting convention, though we might, or some culture might.

330

A.2 There must be a bowl, and a "you" who is capable of passing it.

B. My request must be reasonably clear and exact. For example, if there is a bowl of lettuce and one of potatoes, I must indicate which I am requesting if I say, "Please pass *the* bowl."

C. The speaker must really *want* the bowl passed (and not, e.g., be rehearsing his lines in a play, or trying *merely* to parrot his wife, or practice his long o's).

That these are indeed requirements can be seen by noting that a speaker who said "Please pass the bowl" would be obliged to consider pertinent the replies: "But there is no bowl," or alternatively "I'm sorry, but I can't reach it," or "Which bowl?" or (if he had lately been saying lines), "Are you still rehearsing that play?" In other words the speaker has, by his speech-act, *assumed responsibility* for there *being* a certain bowl and a prospective bowl-passer, for making a certain *request,* and for letting it be understood that he does indeed *want* the bowl. Thus it should be possible, in connection with a given illocution, to determine what descriptive force (in this case the presence of a bowl and a suitable passer), what emotive force (wanting the bowl), and what performative force (requesting the bowl) is implicit in the speech-act.

13. The first thing which becomes evident, on this account of the meaning of an utterance, is that description proper, while not eliminated, has lost its favored status. We can say that earlier theories of meaning were mired in the "descriptive fallacy"—the view that the proper business of words was to make (verifiable) statements, whose virtue was to be true, and vice to be false. "Statements" are not eliminated on the present view, but are just one subclass of performative acts.[11] Nevertheless the descriptive fallacy dies hard, as we shall soon see.

III

14. For now we must ask how the illocutionary theory will serve when it is employed as a tool for inquiring about the justification of specific religious utterances. Consider the utterance:

A. "God led the Israelites across the Red Sea."

Note first that these words may be used by different speakers (or writers) on differing occasions, with consequent differences in meaning. A historian of religion may properly use these words to *relate* the *traditional belief* of biblical men, just as I might say, "Ceres blessed the crops of the ancients" to report *that* tradition, without myself being a believer in Ceres' bounty. Or again these words or, rather, their linguistic equivalent in an ancient language might have been used by a Hebrew of the Exodus, say Moses. Or, with a difference, by a superstitious Egyptian pursuer of the fleeing Hebrews. Or still differently, by a chronicler or psalmist of the fifth century. Let us suppose they are used by a Christian teacher today confessing his own faith in the past providence of God. How in this particular case can their "felicity" be tested? In reply we begin by inquiring, "What objections would the speaker be obliged to admit were (not necessarily valid, but) logically pertinent?" These objections will serve as clues to the responsibility which the speaker assumed in saying what he did. I suggest that the following (descriptive) implications of A will thus appear:

1.1   There is (was) a people, the Israelites, namely those referred to as such in Hebrew Scripture.

1.11 Each of the facts, even the most empirical of facts, in human history is subject to the judgment of the speaker or those on whom he depends (cf. Collingwood). Are "England," "France," "Israel" therefore to be seen as "logical constructs," as some philosophers have held, rather than "real entities"? If we say not, we must acknowledge that 1.1 is an empirical claim in a broader-than-minimal sense of empirical, but nonetheless an empirical claim.

1.2   They did, more or less as related in that Scripture, in fact cross the Red Sea on a historic occasion.

1.21 On the one hand, this implicate is open to falsification by scientific historiography. If, for example, it appears that the Israelites were never in Egypt, the utterance is in a particular way infelicitous. Or if it appears that it was not what we today call the Red Sea that they crossed but, rather, what we today call the Sea of Reeds, the utterance is in another (less damaging) way infelicitous. Thus we might have to substitute for A:

      A' "God led Israel across the Sea of Reeds."

1.22 On the other hand, reference to "Hebrew Scripture" in 1.1

and 1.2 reminds us that the utterance is part of a "universe of discourse," a "language-frame."[12] Whatever it purports to mean, it purports to mean *within the linguistic context* of (let us call it) *biblical* religious talk.

1.3 There is a God, to whom the speaker referred when he said, "God."

1.31 Thus "God" as here referred to cannot be any god, any exalted or numinous worship-object, but must be "God" as understood in the particular language-frame implied.

15. It might now appear that we see at once how to proceed with justification. "Let's just settle the questions of fact raised by 1.1, 1.2, and 1.3 by appeal to scientific history, and appeal to philosophical theologians for proofs or disproofs of the existence of the biblical God, and we will know whether the rest of the task is worth doing—whether illocutionary force here even *matters,* or whether we are talking only falsehoods." But the urge thus expressed is the urge to commit the descriptive fallacy, the fallacy of supposing that everything sayable can be *stated.* Consider a passage from Austin:

> Suppose for example you say to me "I'm feeling pretty mouldy this morning." Well, I say to you "You're not"; and you say "What the devil do you mean, I'm not?" I say "Oh nothing—I'm just stating you're not, is it true or false?" And you say "Wait a bit about whether it's true or false, the question is what did you mean by making statements about somebody else's feelings? I told you I'm feeling pretty mouldy. You're just not in a position to say, to state that I'm not." This brings out that you can't just make statements about other people's feelings (though you can make guesses if you like); and there are many things which, having no knowledge of, not being in a position to pronounce about, you just can't state. What we need to do for the case of stating, and by the same token describing and reporting, is to take them a bit off their pedestal, to realize that they are speech-acts no less than all these other speech-acts that we have been mentioning and talking about as performative.[13]

The difficulty with Austin's "statement" was that we are not in a position, having just encountered a friend, to state his feelings. We might never be in a position to do so. But what if we are also not in a position (in a different sense, now, of "position") to make "statements" about the presence (*or absence*) of God, or about his "existence" (unlovely phrase). Perhaps we are not, say, because as component parts of the world to which God is allegedly "present," or upon or in which God has allegedly "acted," we have no warrant to "state" as if we were sideline observers with a neutral umpire's chair, an Archimedean platform, on which to sit and judge and issue statements! Note that the difficulty is a contrary one in the two cases. We can't state someone else's feelings because those feelings, if they occur, are not occurring to us, and are too remote from us to be accessible. But perhaps we can't state God's "presence" or "action" because it *is* too immediately happening to us, if it happens at all, that God is "present," that God "acts." (It is *something* like the difficulty in "she stated that she was at that very moment gargling": if she did, she wasn't, and if she was, she didn't.[14] What arises here, then, is that the facts are not less important than the descriptive fallacy took them to be. But they *may not be accessible* in as direct a fashion as that fallacy presupposed—a logical difficulty accurately reflected in the complex structure of our actual speech, as Austin's illustration shows.

16. What does count as "getting into position" (not to state, for on our view A′ is not a statement, but to perform the indicated speech-act A′) may be discovered by asking for further implicates of

> A′   "God led Israel across the Sea of Reeds."

> 2.1   The speaker either now assumes or takes up afresh a confessional stance, faith or its logical homogene, with respect to the God who is said to have so acted. I.e., in Austinian terms, the illocutionary force of the utterance is commissive.[15]

> 2.11 To see that this is so, note that it would be pertinent (though of course not necessarily correct) to counter A′ with, "But you're not a Christian" ("Jew," "Muslim"—we shall say

simply "believer"). And to this the speaker may logically reply by saying, "I am indeed," which is a sufficient though not necessarily terminal counter, or (alternatively), "I know I'm not what you *call* a believer—still I have my view of these things" (persuasive-definition counter). Or (again alternatively) "No, I defy the Christian God—but I give him his due" (Promethean counter). What the speaker can*not* say (*logically* cannot) is, "I am [or "I am not"] a believer —what's that got to do with it?" Cannot, because he shows thereby that he does not understand how in our language such utterances are used. For suppose in self-defense the speaker said, "I'm just relating a known fact. Where *I* stand has nothing to do with it." Then we want to reply that the speaker may have *supposed* he was relating a fact, but that he is mistaken—he hasn't yet learned what counts as "relating a fact," what a fact *is,* and A (or A') is not the sort of thing which in our language counts as "just a fact."

17. More might be said, but this may be enough to indicate roughly what is meant by illocutionary force. Can we also claim that a certain feeling-tone, or emotive force, is expressed by the utterance? I think we can, but the present chapter is already too long for convenience. Suffice it to say that the way in which we speak (i.e., cadence, intonation, pattern, stress, transition) or write (context, punctuation) conveys, for a given dialect, both a type and degree of feeling, *and* that *certain* feelings are appropriate to certain locutions[16] and illocutions. Thus if I say, "I love you" (sneering tone), the effect is similar to saying, "I promise to be there, but don't count on me" (self-defeating utterance). Hence:

3.1   The speaker expresses and perhaps seeks to evoke a certain attitude or feeling.
3.11 Thus an appropriate counter to A', "God led Israel across the Sea of Reeds" (*gratefully* spoken) is, "You don't act (or don't seem to feel) as if He'd ever done a thing for you." And indeed this was a frequent prophetic counter to Israel's recital-liturgy.[17] To this counter the speaker can (logically) reply, "I'm very weak-willed," or "I was only

335

imitating gratitude—I don't really believe that old story." What the speaker (logically) cannot say is, "So what?" If he nevertheless does say it, he shows that he does not understand the emotive force, and therefore does not understand the effective meaning, of his speech-act, or the mode of expressing gratitude in his speech dialect, or neither.

18. If this account of the way language, including religious language, works is correct, the following general observations may be made: First, many of the accounts of religious language offered in the last twenty years can be subsumed under or assimilated to the theory here put forward. Those accounts which offered sweeping prescriptions of religious language (e.g., Flew) are seen to fail because inadequate to the complexity of religious (and all) language. But to the extent that accounts call attention to particular features of the language under analysis, they can be adapted and subsumed: Braithwaite's intentionality to our illocutionary force, Hare's bliks to our illocutionary and/or emotive force, Ramsey's models and qualifiers to these and to the (peculiar) descriptive force of talk about God, etc.

19. Second, before any further progress can be made toward the verification (or justification, as we should prefer to say) of religious language, further work must be done. For while we have now a general apparatus for understanding what (religious) utterances do, we have not here examined the variety of illocutionary acts which make up religious discourse. Thus as homogeneous a segment of religious discourse as a recitation of the Apostles' Creed will turn out to be composed of a number of kinds of speech-acts, related to one another in a variety of ways, and if to creeds we add prayers, exhortations, theological reflections, straightforward descriptions, rebukes, requests, questions, answers, complaints, laments, shouts of joy, challenges, warnings, promises, parabolic tales, and many others, we will see how puzzling the task before us is. What are the circumstances which justify us in saying, which make it appropriate to say, "Tithing is a Christian duty," or "Mohammed was the prophet of Allah," or "Nirvana is the fulfillment of life," or even "Hallelujah!"? None of these utterances can

336

be understood apart from the context, the language-frame, in connection with which it is actually used. To ask for their justification is finally, among other things, to ask for the justification of the language-frame in which they are used—indeed for the justification of the way of life in which that language-frame is involved. And it can perhaps be said that finally a way of life is justified only in living it. Such "pragmatic justification" has its place; regrettably that activity is beyond philosophy, which can at best be rational reflection upon, not the actual living of, life itself.

IV

20. How, then, can philosophy or, rather, the mode of philosophy being done here, help? Consider what sort of situation we would like to have. If within the complexity of utterances actually possible in a given language-frame there were a sort, discriminable by certain tests, which turned out as well to be of fundamental importance within the language-frame; if these were actually employed, or likely to be employed, by users of the language-frame in their religious expression; and if further these utterances were found to be intimately related to one another and to the life and behavior of their users; then the justification of these *convictions,* as we might call them, would go far toward the justification of an entire language-frame (e.g., the Christian one) and the life style associated therewith. I believe that a definition of convictions can be offered which does make possible certain sorts of testing, and I propose to devote the remaining paragraphs to an indication of the sort of justification of such convictions which does and the sort which does not seem feasible. Rather than here offer an exact definition,[18] let me point out that we have instances of clusters of such convictions in the leading propositions of certain theologies. (We will call these clusters of convictions, when embraced by an individual or community, a *conviction set.*) Indeed the discerning, collating, and manipulating of a conviction set is the task of a systematic theology. Thus systematic Muslim theology is the task of discerning Muslim convictions, arranging and adjusting them according to some intrinsic (or extrinsic) principle, and interpreting them in relation to one another and in relation to the facts, with a

337

view to their being thus believed. And so Christian theology, Buddhist theology, etc. And very many *philosophical systems* likewise consist in the discernment, the proclamation, and the manipulation of sets of convictions. Such philosophical systems are logically homogeneous with theologies; they are capable of agreeing with or contradicting theological convictions, which discloses their identity as convictional systems. And further it is the case that very many men who espouse no formal theology and who embrace no systematic philosophy will nevertheless be found to have and to employ convictions which *could* be discerned, collated, critically compared and related to one another and to the facts, so that these too are subject to identification and analysis as the conviction sets of their holders.

21. If this is true, then it may be possible for me here to indicate in principle the degree to which such conviction sets, and the individual convictions of which they are composed, may be tested and justified, and the lines along which such justification may proceed. And here we may remind ourselves at once of one sort of testing procedure which has long been familiar to religious theoreticians, i.e., to theologians. That is, a particular conviction set may be tested for *internal or logical self-consistency*. Particular theological doctrines logically contravene other doctrines. To discover and eliminate such inconsistency is one significant step toward justification. The logical complexity of religious discourse, as exposed in work similar to that of the present chapter, may teach us that the work of the theological logician, far from having ended, is just on the threshold of usefulness at present. And further, if such a discriminable strand of religious utterances, namely convictions, which are at the same time of crucial importance to a particular language-frame (the characteristic talk, e.g., of a given religious community) is discerned, it may be possible to say some things which bear not only on the justification of that strand, but of the whole frame, from the vantage point of the linguistic theory already proposed (Section II, above).

22. Here also we must beware of the fallacy called, above, "descriptive" (see #15). We must not suppose that we have access to an Archimedean umpire's chair from which we can look down to

assess the truth of convictions, our own or others. For such assessments must either be or be themselves founded upon convictions (by the definition of conviction given above, #20), and must therefore be subject to the same sort of judgment with which they are judged. For example, if I judge that the conviction designated A' ("God led Israel across the Sea of Reeds") is appropriate or inappropriate, I am thereby giving voice either to my own conviction or to a judgment which is dependent upon my own convictions, about the God of Israel and/or any other gods. Now it appears that everyone does have some convictions. For if convictions are such that to change them would be to change their holder (definition), then consistency of character and of action in any person implies the existence of such convictions. This might leave us with a queer possibility: that those of very erratic and inconstant behavior could alone be considered as candidates for the higher neutrality which could pass appropriate judgment upon the convictions of the rest of us! Alternatively, however, it might be argued that such persons are best regarded, not as lacking in convictions, but as being victims of the strife of two or more conviction sets, or as being constantly converted and reconverted from one to another.

23. Lacking the Archimedean presuppositionless platform, what other possibility appears? One bit of help is that the natural sciences, while not presuppositionless enterprises (the natural scientist, in order to do his work, must as a minimum hold to some conviction such as, "There are facts to be gotten and understood, and it is important, to me at least, to get them and understand them," and perhaps others), yet may require only convictions which are common ground to men who otherwise embrace differing conviction sets. Insofar as such men can agree on the relative independence of scientific investigations, the latter offer a means of getting some facts, and thus providing reference points for the possible falsification of at least some convictions. Some religious beliefs, e.g., do offer what seem to be accounts competitive with geological or astronomical ones about the origin and nature of the earth (Does the earth in fact rest on the back of a great turtle?), the origin and the nature of the human species, etc.

24. Can the same assertion be made with respect to the work

of social scientists and historians? It seems clear that it can only to the extent that these enterprises do not employ as presuppositions convictions which have the logical possibility of agreeing with or clashing with the convictions whose judgment and justification is being sought. To the chagrin of those who seek for objective decision-procedures, this extent is a limited one. Perhaps the nature of the limitation can be most economically represented by noting a distinction between two aspects of coming to understand what one's fellow physicist, say, is doing.[19] On the one hand, one may understand the relationship between the individual physicist and his meters, electrodes, lasers, magnets, vacuum tubes, and the like—between the physicist and his objects. On the other hand, this former understanding is not practicable without also understanding the relationship existing between the physicist and his fellow physicists—the shared vocabulary and concepts, knowledge of the history and developed theory of his science, the way in which physicists in general make judgments, what they count as relevant evidence, etc. Now what happens in the social sciences is that the second kind of understanding and the first kind are not so neatly separable. The sociologist's understanding of his data is not categorically distinguishable from his understanding of his relation to his fellow sociologists. Suppose, for example, that he wants to know to what extent anti-Semitism can be correlated with religious belief. To answer this question in a useful way he must decide what is, what is to count as, a religious belief. But this decision involves the employment of the concept "religious"—a concept which is for many men the subject of convictions. The appropriate use of the concept, that is, is a convictional question. To make a choice of uses is willy-nilly to make what is logically parallel with or counter to some conviction. And it is just these convictions which we had hoped might be justified or falsified by the scientific enterprise! An inevitable circularity thus appears.

25. It is another form of the conclusion reached above which leads R. G. Collingwood to remark that the accounts of "magical" practices offered by "scientific" anthropologists may be masking "a half-conscious conspiracy to bring into ridicule and contempt civilizations different from our own. . . ."[20] (And the same considera-

tions might be shown to apply to the writing of history as well as to anthropology.) The moral, I would suppose, is not that science is of no importance in the evaluation of convictions. It is, rather, the more exacting conclusion that our attention to scientific investigation can at best be a part of the wider enterprise of the assessment and adjustment of our convictions—it can neither proceed in independence of them, nor be used quite independently to adjudicate between them; it can be employed as one of the rational means whereby the interconnections between convictions and whatever else there is in the world can be explored. The more fully the object of scientific investigation is the forms of human life themselves (e.g., as in the study of history), the more fully does this stricture apply.

26. At this point someone may with reason object that the quest for justification of religious talk via scientific investigation is altogether ill-founded. Have not the religious always known another way? "O taste and see that the Lord is good" (Psalm 34:8). If the language-frame permits us to speak of a new vision, a new insight into the ways things are, a new awareness of the Other with whom we are confronted, or if it permits us to predict a new sense of wholeness or integrity, of unity between self and Other, or if it allows us to speak of a "peace that passeth understanding"—and if we then experience such a peace, find such wholeness, envision such an Other—then on its capacity for prediction and interpretation of experience, though viewed merely in its own terms, our theology finds a partial justification, a reason for existing. Even here, however, in the realm of experience most confirmed and judged most authentic, we remain "under the sun" (cf. Ecclesiastes 1:9 *et passim*); our judgments of experience are still in part dependent upon the very convictions we had sought by them to confirm; we have found no bedrock.

27. Again, what if we seek to ground our religious convictions upon moral or aesthetic judgments? What if we test our religious language-frame, and the way of life to which it gives voice, by asking about the moral conduct which it commands, or the moral vigor which it begets? This, too, is no new test. In many strands of religion, not least the Hebraic, the prophet searches the ethical fiber

341

of the religious community. Insofar as conscience and received orthodoxy are independent, conscience can test religious claims, and moral claims put forward in the name of religion. Is there in the religious ethic an augustness, so that we know that here we confront obligation as ultimate demand? Is there an omnicompetence —is the ethic capable of development, of progress, of greater sensitizing so that it becomes suitable to the changing future? In all these ways justification can be sought. But the search leads us back, if our analysis is correct, once again to moral or aesthetic judgments which are held by the individual in a cluster or set of convictions which to change would be to change himself—that is, to convictions which are logical homogenes of the very set which was to have been tested or justified. No escape from circularity lies along this route. The assessment of these moral (or aesthetic) convictions must proceed in interdependence with the assessment of the others in the set.

28. Perhaps it is in order to say a word about the role of reason, which is proposed by some philosophers as a sovereign judge of religious convictions. Can we justify or discredit our convictions by bringing them to reason's bar? Regrettably it is not at all clear what "reason" here could mean. "Reasonableness" may serve as a house flag for conviction sets as diverse as atheistic existentialism, militant humanism, or lukewarm Christianity stirred with sentimental natural theology. Obviously such "reason" is no test, but stands itself in need of testing. If, on the other hand, "be reasonable" is used as a plea for *internal self-consistency among convictions,* together with *attentiveness to all available facts,* together with the mental habit of *critical reassessment of results already reached,* it can certainly commend itself to many of us. But the diverse conviction sets of (in this sense) reasonable and sincere men suggest the insufficiency of the test as proposed. We may "be reasonable," and still disagree while the ages roll. This difficulty is the well-known bane of traditional metaphysics from Thales to Whitehead, as well as of ecumenical theology whether polemic or irenic. (We may seek an intellectually satisfying *Weltanschauung,* denoting it "reasonable," but it is not clear how such satisfaction differs from the sort of aesthetic conviction mentioned in #27 above.)

342

29. In the absence of these Gordian solutions to our problem, let us review again the ground actually gained, and the theory of meaning already proposed. What does appear is that the positivists correctly complained of the nonverifiability of what we are calling convictions, but badly misplaced the source of that nonverifiability. The source, according to them, was the meaninglessness of the religious propositions. But on our view of meaning, such propositions are not meaningless: indeed out difficulty with them lies in the exceeding richness of meaning which they bear. For we have maintained that convictions (and all utterances) possess a three-dimensioned web of meaning: illocutionary, descriptive, emotive. What we find ourselves unable to do in the case of those convictions in which we are interested (e.g., A') is to settle the felicity of their descriptive force in every respect *apart from* the felicity of their illocutionary and emotive force.

30. Is not the result, then, that we must in our quest for justification make a three-pronged attack? The *illocutionary* (or performative) force of A' (uttered as proposed in #14) is that in uttering it the speaker assumes (or resumes) a certain *stance* in the world. He assumes the stance of one who *remembers* (what he calls) Israel and its (alleged) journey—remembers in the sense of reclaiming, of embracing this past as *his* past, the past which is the heritage God has given him. And he assumes or resumes at the same time a stance toward God—as being the sort of God who does lead, who does give us our past to be ours. In brief, the performative force of this utterance is that of *confessing* or its logical homogene (see #16). Is it not clear, then, that the justification of such an utterance lies in the actual taking up, by this illocutionary act, of the stance which with these words we normally take up—the stance toward Israel, the stance toward God? In short, the justification of the performative force of A' is the act of faith which A' performs. We are not playing with words, then, or lapsing into Lutheran or Pauline dogma, if we say that the justification of A' is justification by faith. Do not be misled. We are still talking about what convictions are, about what kind of thing *in general* a conviction can be, how *in general* convictions (not persons) can be justified. In general they are justified by the felicity of their utterance in particular speech-acts by particular persons—and the case of A' was of a

343

speech-act uttered by a man taking his stand in the biblical tradition, a man whose stance was the appropriate faith vis-à-vis that tradition.

31. But we have noted that the felicity of the speaker's utterance, though it depends upon the illocutionary (or performative) force, depends indirectly upon the success of the descriptive and emotive force which that particular performative force requires for its success. That is, our speaker must have the requisite appropriate feelings (wants, attractions, repulsions, etc., in varying intensities and tones); and the state of whatever there is (external reality?) must be such as to justify the implicated descriptions (the sea must have been the Sea of Reeds; God must be God). This last is just the sort of point, however, for which there are no external, open-and-shut tests (theistic proofs or disproofs, e.g.). Biblical language-frames do their work in terms of the biblical God; they cannot *produce* that which they presuppose. And other sorts of frames (science, morality, reason) are not in general capable of *supervening* to confirm or overturn the religious frame (#22-#28).

32. What follows is that *there is no absolute foolproof justification* of those central clusters of convictions by which we live, by which we are what we are. A particular theology may, to be sure, be tested (*a*) for internal consistency, (*b*) for its capacity to predict and interpret experience, including religious experience (does our theology, e.g., promise a peace that passeth understanding, and is such peace with reasonable regularity forthcoming?), (*c*) for the augustness and omnicompetence of the moral conduct it enjoins and the degree to which such conduct is by these convictions engendered, (*d*) for its ability to provide an adequate interpretation of our total apprehension of the world, i.e., an intellectually and aesthetically satisfying *Weltanschauung*. But none of these tests is independent, none is logically superior to the conviction set itself, none is free from the demand that *it* similarly be tested.

THEOLOGICAL POSTSCRIPT

33. The preceding conclusion seems melancholy if we believe, as well we may, that the choice between convictions is an

exceedingly important one. Indeed life itself—the quality of our life, the very possibility of enduring life, maybe—hangs upon such choice. We can only make the best choice we can in the light of what we are as human beings. And that is discouraging for those of us who discern that what we are is far indeed from what we ought to be. To offset this melancholy outlook, however, two words of cheer may be spoken. The first is: *We are not alone. We have our neighbors.* And we are privileged, under the form of life which is given us, both to witness to our neighbors by word and deed, and to be witnessed to, even across the convictional lines which separate us. (Christians in particular have usually been careless about the former and have totally neglected the latter.) Thus it would seem appropriate for all not wishing to remain in the grip of fanatical infelicity in their own confessions to include among their primary convictions the conviction that they ought to expose themselves to whatever gives any promise of correcting—or converting—their own central convictions to more adequate ones. The second word of cheer is this: *If Christian conviction sets are trustworthy, there is another Power* to lead men beyond themselves into the forming of convictions which they have not fabricated, and for which they can truly claim no credit of their own. To that Power the writer of the present chapter does hereby cheerfully commit himself.

NOTES

1. Ludwig Wittgenstein, *Tractatus Logico-Philosophicus* (London: Routledge & Kegan Paul, 1922).

2. The most available form of the emotive theory is A. J. Ayer, *Language, Truth and Logic* (1st ed., 1935; New York: Dover Books, n.d.).

3. See, e.g., A. Flew, "Theology and Falsification" reprinted in *New Essays in Philosophical Theology,* ed. by A. Flew and A. MacIntyre (London: SCM Press, 1955).

4. R. B. Braithwaite, *An Empiricist's View of Religious Belief* (Cambridge: Cambridge University Press, 1955), reprinted in *Christian Ethics and Contemporary Philosophy,* ed. by Ian T. Ramsey (London: Macmillan and Co., 1966).

5. Richard M. Hare, "Theology and Falsification," in Flew and Mac-Intyre, *op. cit.*

6. See Ian T. Ramsey, *Religious Language* (London: SCM Press, 1957).

7. William Alston, *Philosophy of Language* (Englewood Cliffs: Prentice-Hall, 1964), ch. 1.

8. J. L. Austin, *How to Do Things with Words* (New York: Oxford University Press, 1962).

9. Indeed we may here recognize a near parallel to a distinction familiar also to theology since Ritschl: talk about facts (cf. constatives) is to be distinguished from talk involving values (cf. performatives).

10. Austin, *op. cit.*, pp. 90 ff.

11. *Ibid.*, Lecture XI.

12. I owe the term "language-frame" to Ninian Smart, *Reasons and Faiths* (New York: Humanities Press, 1959).

13. J. L. Austin, *Philosophical Papers* (New York: Oxford University Press, 1961), pp. 236 f.

14. Of course she can stop, and can then state that she *was* gargling. But how do we stop the "presence" of God (cf. Psalm 139)?

15. Cf. Austin, *How to Do Things with Words, op. cit.*, Lecture XII.

16. For a brief account of speech as accurate conveyor of feeling within a given dialect, see James Sledd, *A Short Introduction to English Grammar* (Glenview: Scott, Foresman, 1959).

17. Cf., e.g., Jeremiah 23:33-40; Psalm 78; Joshua 24:16-23; and the thrust of Deuteronomy.

18. For the exact definition, we may first in Austinian terms define a *belief:* An expositive, verdictive, or commissive which X is disposed to utter (or to write) as his own is X's belief. A *conviction,* then, is a *persistent* belief, from which X cannot readily be parted, and which he could not relinquish without himself becoming a substantially different person. Note that one man's conviction may be another man's mere belief. Convictions are cognitively richer than psychologist's *attitudes,* and differ from the "beliefs" of rationalists in possessing illocutionary force: they are speech-acts.

JAMES Wm. McCLENDON, Jr.

19. The following highly compressed argument depends upon Peter Winch, *The Idea of a Social Science* (London: Routledge & Kegan Paul, 1958).

20. R. G. Collingwood, *The Idea of History* (London: Oxford University Press, 1946), cited in Winch, *op. cit.,* p. 103.

Index

INDEX

practical reason, 138, 140-147
Pragmatic Maxim, Peirce's use of, 285-286
pragmatism, 107-134 *passim*, 194-195; Dewey on, 71; and inquiry, 147; James on, 290ff.; metaphysics of, 272ff.; as method, 274; methodology of, 274; the move away from, 60; and religion, 271-319 *passim*
Pragmatism (James), 42, 43, 287, 290, 291
Predicament of Belief, The (Sleeper), 270n
prehension, Whitehead's concept of, 152ff., 161
Price, Lucien, 158
Principia Mathematica (Whitebread), 158
Principles of Psychology (James), 29, 41
Problem of Christianity, The (Royce), 196-211 *passim*
Problem of God, The (Brightman), 229
process, definitions of, 149; experience as, 69, 71, 72; God in, 240; Hartshorne's idea of, 161; Whitehead and, 149-150
process philosophy, 149
Process and Reality (Whitehead), 141, 149, 150, 152, 155, 156, 157, 162
process theology, 162
psychology, role of, 16
Psychology (Dewey), 299
Psychology (Spencer), 291
Psychology—Briefer Course (James), 30
Puritan Covenant, 187

Puritanism, 296
Puritans, 64-65, 66
purpose, and inquiry, 114, 121-124, 126; sense of, in religion, 198ff.

Quakers, 64-65
quest, knowing as, 107-134
Quest for Certainity, The (Dewey), 227
questions, philosophical, 1-19 *passim*
Quine, Willard Van Orman, 158

radical empiricism, 88, 94; Brightman's, 224; Dewey's, 44-49; James's, 34-35, 287; significance of, for art, 22-51 *passim*
Ramsey, Ian T., 316-317, 327f., 336
Randall, John Herman, Jr., 306, 309, 310, 313-314
rationalism, 275, 277; and Whitehead, 142-144
rationality, 10; of universe, 229
Ratté, John, 203n
Rauschenberg, Robert, 51n
Rauschenbusch, Stephen, 187
Read, Herbert, 25, 39
realism, 29-30, 283, 315-316; "belief-ful," 284
reality, Brightman's concept of, 221ff.; Emerson on, 70; experience as, 68ff.; feelings and, 161; of God, 306, 311ff.; James's idea of, 97-99; and knowing, 109-113; and language, 99-103; man as constitutor of, 23; man as creator